The American Woman

WILLIAM HENRY CHAFE

# The American Woman

HER CHANGING SOCIAL, ECONOMIC, AND
POLITICAL ROLES, 1920-1970

OXFORD UNIVERSITY PRESS
London   Oxford   New York

OXFORD UNIVERSITY PRESS
Oxford    London    Glasgow
New York    Toronto    Melbourne    Wellington
Nairobi    Dar es Salaam    Cape Town
Kuala Lumpur    Singapore    Jakarta    Hong Kong    Tokyo
Delhi    Bombay    Calcutta    Madras    Karachi

printing, last digit: 20 19 18 17 16
Printed in the United States of America

*for* L. J. W.

# Preface

Just a little more than half a century ago, the women of America gained the vote. At the time, many women's rights advocates believed that enactment of the Nineteenth Amendment signaled a triumphant turning point in the struggle for sexual equality. Suffragists predicted that acquisition of the vote would not only give women new leverage in politics but would also help them achieve a greater measure of freedom and independence in the home and economy. "The whole aim of the woman's movement," Carrie Chapman Catt wrote, "has been to destroy the idea that obedience is necessary to women; to train women to such self-respect that they would not grant obedience; and to train men to such comprehension of equity that they would not exact it."[1] For many women who had devoted their lives to the struggle for equal rights, victory in the suffrage fight represented a major stride toward those goals.

With the benefit of hindsight, it seems clear that much of the suffragists' optimism was misplaced. The revival of feminism in recent years has demonstrated that many women remain profoundly disturbed by the nature of relationships between the sexes. In tones reminiscent of nineteenth-century feminists, Kate Millett and others have denounced America as a patriarchy based on male supremacy and have demanded the overthrow of those institutions which perpetuate female inferiority. By the standards of contemporary women's rights advocates, it would appear that the status of women has not changed at all in the fifty years since adoption of the suffrage amendment.[2]

And yet we know very little about the experience of women in the intervening years. As Aileen Kraditor and Eleanor Flexner have pointed out, historians have generally neglected the role of women in America. Textbooks have dismissed women in a few lines or pages, and monographs have concentrated almost exclusively on the woman's movement itself. The period after 1920, in particular, has largely been ignored by historians.[3] With one or two exceptions, most of the writing on women in modern America has been limited to popular articles or books, and surveys by sociologists, psychologists, and anthropologists. Although speculation has been abundant, accurate historical information has been in short supply. As a result, a gap in our knowledge exists. If the status of women has not altered, it is important to know why. And if change has occurred, it is equally important to know how the shift came about.

The present study is an effort to answer those questions, at least partially, by examining the social, economic, and political roles of women from 1920 to the present. Its principal assumption is that sexual inequality is rooted within the social structure itself, through the allocation of different spheres of responsibility to men and women. In tradition and practice, most societies have developed an elaborate and segregated network of roles for each sex, with little interaction or exchange between the two. The division of labor, in most cases, has led to a division of authority as well. The expectation that males will make "major" decisions is related directly to the activities carried out by men and women and the connotations attached to those activities. There may be no inherent difference between the value of holding a job and the value of keeping a house, but one has clearly been accorded greater weight and prestige than the other. Thus the very existence of different sets of activities for men and women has been a means of maintaining and reinforcing an imbalance of power between the sexes. In practice, if not in principle, separate has meant unequal.

Within such a framework, the most reliable barometer of change is whether the distribution of roles between the sexes has altered over time. It is not enough to concentrate on the woman's movement itself, because the success of feminist organizations depended ultimately on the response of the mass of women, and the willingness of the society-at-large to tolerate a change in relationships between the sexes. The primary focus of the following pages, therefore, is on public perceptions of woman's "place," and the impact of events such as war and depression on the nature of women's sphere. Particular attention has been devoted to the economic role of women, because, more than any other variable, the issue of earning a living has been central to the definition of masculine and feminine responsibilities. Public opinion surveys have demonstrated repeatedly that breadwinning and homemaking are the activities most closely identified with popular images of male and female and most essential to differentiating between the two. Women's economic role has thus seemed deserving of special investigation since any significant change in it held the potential of substantially modifying the polarity of male and female spheres, and shifting the allocation of roles between men and women.

There is no single, effective approach to the study of women's history, of course. The subject is as elusive as it is large, and it is fraught with methodological and conceptual difficulties. From one point of view, females clearly fit Louis Wirth's definition of a minority group. They have been "singled out for differential or unequal treatment . . . because of their physical and cultural characteristics," and they have been excluded from "full participation in society" on the basis of their sex. On the other hand, females cannot be studied in the same way as blacks or chicanos, because, despite their common traits, they do not cluster in residential groups and they have a variety of racial, religious, and economic affiliations which tend to divide rather than unite them. As Alice Rossi has pointed out, inequality based on sex "is the only instance in which representatives of unequal groups live in more intimate association with each other than with members of their own group."[4] Thus there is no sure way of grasping the complex web of inter-relation-ships which determine women's position in society, and any gen-eralization about women as a whole must be tempered with the realization that females are as different as they are alike.

Nevertheless, the division of roles between men and women of-fers one promising point of reference which can be used as a start-ing place for examining the history of the past fifty years. There is need for other perspectives as well, many of which will undoubtedly arrive at different conclusions than those expressed here. But the present approach may represent a beginning, and if it helps to clarify some of the forces contributing to the position of women in the modern world, it will have accomplished its purpose.

W.H.C.

*Chapel Hill, N.C.*
*May 1972*

# Acknowledgments

Although the conclusions expressed here are my own, this book would not have been possible without the assistance of others. For most of the period while this study was in preparation, I received financial support from an NIMH fellowship administered through Columbia University's Social History program. A Woodrow Wilson Dissertation Fellowship supplied additional funds for travel and typing. My research was facilitated at every turn by the kindness of library staffs across the country, and I am especially grateful to the staff of the Schlesinger Library at Radcliffe. It is hard to imagine a more enjoyable place to do research.

The manuscript itself has benefited greatly from the contributions of friends and colleagues. William L. O'Neill generously gave me a typescript draft of his book *Everyone Was Brave* a full year before its publication and discussed my own project with me. Various chapters of the book have been improved by the comments of Dennis Van Essendelft, Regina Morantz, Lorna Chafe, Charles Trout, Robert Twombly, Sheila Tobias, and John Chambers. Lois Banner, Sigmund Diamond, William J. Goode, and Anne F. Scott have read the entire manuscript and I have profited substantially from their helpful suggestions. I am particularly grateful to David Rothman of Columbia University whose perceptive criticisms of the manuscript in dissertation form caused me to revise some ideas and to develop many others. I would also like to express my appreciation to Sheldon Meyer and Vivian Marsalisi of Oxford University Press for their support and wise counsel during the entire publication process.

My greatest debt is to William E. Leuchtenberg. Perhaps only those who have had the privilege of working with him can appreciate the full value of his contribution. His searching questions, personal interest, and constant encouragement have helped to make this work far better than it otherwise might have been.

Needless to say, none of those I have thanked will agree with everything that is said here, but without their candor and criticism this book could not have been written.

# Contents

The American Woman

# INTRODUCTION

# A Narrowing of Vision

In the fall of 1918 Woodrow Wilson journeyed to Capitol Hill to address the Senate of the United States. The nation was engaged in a crusade "to make the world safe for democracy," and he had come to seek help. "The executive tasks of this war rest upon me," he told the lawmakers. "I ask that you lighten them and place in my hands instruments . . . which I do not now have, which I sorely need, and which I have daily to apologize for not being able to employ." The subject of Wilson's appeal was not guns or airplanes but woman suffrage. Its enactment, the Commander in Chief declared, "was vital to the winning of the war" and essential to implementing democracy. The President's plea added one more voice to the rising chorus of support for the suffrage, and within a year, Congress voted overwhelmingly to send the Nineteenth Amendment to the states for ratification.[1]

The woman's movement had not always enjoyed such legitimacy or support. The feminists who gathered at Seneca Falls, New York, in 1848 were far removed from the mainstream of American life. Many had participated in the abolitionist struggle, demonstrating by their actions there the extent to which they deviated from prevailing norms of female behavior. When women abolitionists sought to speak in public or circulate petitions, they were castigated for departing from their proper place. Even male abolitionists were critical of their activities, and in 1840 women were excluded from a world anti-slavery conference in London. In response to such treatment, many of the women determined to seek freedom for themselves as well as for the slave. Bridling at the tradition that men and women should occupy totally separate spheres of activity, they demanded a drastic revision of the values and laws governing relationships between the sexes, and forthrightly attacked all forms of discrimination. Their efforts were greeted with derision and contempt. The Worcester *Telegram* denounced the Seneca Falls convention as an attempt at "insurrection," and a Buffalo paper referred to it as "revolutionary." Women's rights advocates were generally dismissed as a "class of wild enthusiasts and visionaries" and received little popular backing.[2]

The contrast between 1848 and 1918 dramatized, albeit in exaggerated form, the changes which had occurred within feminism during the intervening years. In effect, the woman's movement developed from an isolated fringe group into a moderate reform coalition. Although the change could be traced in part to external forces, it also reflected shifts within the movement itself. The early feminists took an uncompromising stand on almost all issues and set out to eliminate the rigid division of labor between men and women. Suffrage constituted only one of a long series of demands. By the first decade of the twentieth century, on the other hand, the franchise had been elevated to a position of primary importance, and other more far-reaching ideas were de-emphasized. Unfortunately, most historians have defined the feminist struggle primarily as a quest for the vote and, with the Nineteenth Amendment as a reference point, have concentrated on those events and personalities most directly associated with the suffrage. But if we are to understand the suffragists themselves and the fate of the woman's movement, it is imperative that we start with the broad vision of equality which inspired the founders of feminism in the nineteenth century.[3]*

* It should be noted that the purpose of this introduction is not to provide new information on the woman's movement before 1920, but rather to present an

The radical nature of the early feminist movement was revealed in the Declaration of Sentiments and Resolutions passed by the women at Seneca Falls. In the nineteenth century, females were not allowed to testify in court, hold title to property, establish businesses, or sign papers as witnesses. The feminists addressed themselves both to the specifics of such discrimination and the assumptions underlying it. Beginning with the assertion that "all men and women are created equal," the Declaration proceeded to indict mankind for its "history of repeated injuries and usurpations" toward women. The delegates charged that men had denied them political representation, made them "civilly dead," refused them the right to own their own property, and "oppressed them on all sides." In marriage, a wife was compelled to pledge obedience and to give her husband "power to deprive her of her liberty." In business, man "monopolized nearly all the profitable employments." And in morals, woman suffered from an iniquitous double standard dictated by men who claimed it as their right to "assign for her a sphere of action, when that belongs to her conscience and to her God." Hardly an area existed, the feminists concluded, where man had not consciously endeavored to "destroy woman's confidence in her own powers, to lessen her self-respect, and to make her willing to lead a dependent and abject life."

To counter the oppression which they perceived, women's rights leaders proposed the elimination of all barriers separating the activities of the two sexes. Henceforth, they declared, any law which restricted woman's freedom or placed her in a position inferior to men had "no force or authority." Proclaiming the "identity of the race in capabilities and responsibilities," they demanded the "overthrow of the monopoly of the pulpit," equal access to education,

---

interpretive overview of the period by drawing on existing knowledge. Although some new sources are used here, most of the chapter is based on material contained in the secondary works cited in the footnotes. In general, the monographs on the suffrage aspects of the woman's movement are good, but there is a particular need for more intensive investigation of feminism during the years between the Civil War and the turn of the century.

the trades, and professions, an end to the double standard, and the right to move in "the enlarged sphere" which their Creator had assigned them. God had made men and women equal, the feminists asserted, and the treatment of one sex as different from and less equal than the other ran "contrary to the great precept of nature."[4]

The Declaration boldly challenged every social convention concerning woman's proper "place." Although the feminists sought redress of a whole series of specific grievances, the most impressive part of their document was its assault on the framework of assumptions responsible for woman's position. Implicit throughout the Declaration was the view that, as long as society prescribed separate areas of responsibility for each sex, women could never be free. By insisting that men and women were identical in "capacities and responsibilities," the feminists attacked the fundamental premise underlying relations between the sexes—the notion of distinct male and female spheres. Once it was established that the two sexes were alike in the eyes of God, there was no longer any basis for treating women as separate and inferior and the demands for equality in the church, state, and family logically followed. Instead of concentrating just on the suffrage, then, the early feminists advocated a complete transformation in society's thinking about women.

For much of the remainder of the nineteenth century, women's rights leaders continued to press for sweeping social change. The suffrage became a more prominent issue after Congress failed to recognize women's right to vote in the Fourteenth and Fifteenth amendments, but many feminists persisted in tracing female inequality to the sexual division of labor in society and warned against thinking of the franchise as a panacea. Speaking through a journal entitled *The Revolution,* Elizabeth Cady Stanton, a founder of the women's rights movement, dismissed the suffrage as a "superficial and fragmentary" question. "The ballot touches only those interests, either of men or women, which take their roots in political questions," Stanton and her followers declared in 1869. "But woman's chief discontent is not with her political, but with her social, and particularly her marital bondage." Stanton and her allies attacked economic discrimination, urged reform of the divorce laws, and in the 1890's organized a monumental effort to write a *Woman's Bible* to counteract the widespread theological assumption that females were the weak and inferior sex. Perhaps the most significant figure in the woman's movement during the nineteenth century, Stanton supported acquisition of the vote as a partial step toward achieving freedom, but her broader aim remained "to make woman a self-supporting equal partner with man in the state, the church and the home."[5]

The radical persuasion received its most thorough exposition at the turn of the century in the works of Charlotte Perkins Gilman. Although Gilman wrote primarily for a twentieth-century audience, she articulated more brilliantly than anyone else the point of view held by many of the founders of feminism. A writer and lecturer who had been through an unhappy early marriage, Gilman approached her subject with the same disaffection from traditional mores which characterized the women at Seneca Falls and elaborated the sentiments expressed there into a cogent social and economic analysis. Her treatise on *Women and Economics* (1898) was hailed by the *Nation* as "the most significant utterance on the subject since Mills' *The Subjection of Women*," and her writings to this day constitute the most important feminist assessment of women's position in America.[6]

At the heart of Gilman's analysis was her contention that all the roles a female was permitted to play derived from her sexual functions. A man might pursue a variety of activities—build a career, enter politics, join a fraternal organization. But a woman could only marry and have children. The cause of this sexual differentiation, Gilman believed, could be traced to prehistoric times when females first became dependent on males for food and shelter. Thereafter, a woman's survival rested on her ability to seduce and hold a husband. In effect, sex became a female's economic way of life; while "men worked to live . . . women mated to live. . . ." A man might conquer the world in a hundred ways, but for a woman there was only "a single channel, a single choice. Wealth, power, social distinction, fame . . . all, must come to her through a small gold ring."[7]

The pernicious consequences of sexual dependence afflicted everyone. Woman's human impulses to grow and to create were stifled. Men were denied true companions because their wives shared nothing in common with them. And children were psychologically deprived as a result of being dominated by mothers who had never been allowed to grow to mental maturity. A nation which expected to maximize the potential of all its citizens depended upon each individual pursuing his or her unique talents. Yet social convention dictated that half the race perform nothing but menial household tasks. The sexual division of labor thus not only dulled women's minds and limited their horizons; it also robbed the country of the full utilization of its human resources.[8]

Pursuing the logic of her analysis, Gilman concluded that women could achieve freedom only when they gained economic equality with men. The suffrage represented one step in the right direction and received Gilman's endorsement. But gaining the vote was incidental in her mind to the primary goal of providing women with the opportunity to leave the home if they wished. The household in her view constituted a prison which confined women and forced upon them the role of servant. Since it was woman's economic dependence on man which created the chains of her servitude, freedom could come only if wives and daughters went out into the world to earn their own support, thereby neutralizing the chief force which kept them in an abject state. Work, Gilman believed, was "the essential process of human life," and until women shared in that process on an equal basis with men, they would remain "near-sighted," "near-minded," and inferior.[9]

To achieve her goal, Gilman relied primarily on the power of reason and the forces of specialization which were transforming the national economy. The home, she argued, was appallingly inefficient. Women were no more suited or contented to be "house

servants and house keepers than all men would be." The talents
of some women qualified them to be specialists in cooking, cleaning, or child care. But the talents of others could be best utilized
outside the home in business and the professions. The task of society, Gilman reasoned, was to evolve mechanisms which would
allow each individual to cultivate his or her own potential. To
that end she suggested the establishment of central kitchens to
prepare the community's food, the development of public nurseries
to assume responsibility for child care, and the creation of a corps
of expert housekeepers to maintain the cleanliness of the home.
With most women liberated from domestic chores, marriage would
evolve into a partnership of equals; individual human beings would
maximize their diverse abilities; and society would be free of the
crippling effects of a dual system of labor. The result "would be a
world of men and women humanly related, as well as sexually related, working together as they were meant to do, for the common
good of all."[10]

Despite its brilliance, Gilman's analysis was flawed in several
ways. She glossed over the depersonalization which might accom-
pany institutionalized child care and food preparation, and she
failed to see that the nuclear family might have positive as well as
negative attributes. More important, she assumed that even after
women had adopted a life style closer to that of men and had become equal partners in the quest for jobs and status, they would
continue to exhibit primarily the domestic virtues of warmth and
nurture—a desirable goal, perhaps, but a logical inconsistency
given her previous contention that male and female differences
were basically a product of contrasting environmental conditioning. Nevertheless, Gilman's arguments represented the full elabo-
ration of the feminist impulse. More than anyone else, she understood the social implications of the doctrines articulated at Seneca
Falls. If women were to achieve equality, they had to be able to
pursue their individual desires and participate in all areas of life
on the same basis as men. But that required a social transformation
of major proportions, including the establishment of surrogate in-

stitutions to assume responsibility for activities formerly associated with woman's "sphere." To Gilman's credit, she understood that necessity. In effect, she took the broad goals enunciated at Seneca Falls and drew up a careful blueprint to carry them out.

Long before Gilman's views drew public attention, however, it was clear that the changes which she and Stanton advocated had little chance of being accepted. In criticizing the nuclear family, marriage, and the church, feminists like Gilman were attacking institutions to which most people were deeply devoted. Woman's place could not be changed without altering the family and forcing a radical revision of a whole set of social relationships. Yet most Americans reacted to such a prospect with understandable hostility. The idea of woman's "sphere" was one of the cornerstones of society. Even friends of the movement endorsed the concept. Emerson, for example, asserted that woman should look to man for protection. "When he is her guardian, all goes well for both." If a sympathizer of such pre-eminent intellectual independence rejected the feminists' more radical ideas, it was hardly likely that leaders of the church and community could be persuaded to accept them.[11]

The depth of antagonism which the feminists provoked was disclosed in an 1866 Congressional debate on extending the franchise to the women of Washington, D.C. Women's rights advocates demanded the vote on the basis that women were individuals who had the same inalienable right as male human beings to determine their own destinies. As the historian Aileen Kraditor has pointed out, however, most Americans believed that the family, not the individual, constituted the basic unit of society. Each home existed as a "state in miniature." It had only one head—the husband—and he alone represented it in the world outside. Anyone who challenged that structure could logically be charged with attempting to subvert the family and destroy the state. "When God married our first parents in the garden," one senator declared, "they were made 'bone of one bone and flesh of one flesh'; and the whole theory of government and society proceeds upon the assumption that their interests are one . . . that whatever is for the benefit of one is for the benefit of the other." Those who urged freedom for women, he asserted, would "put her . . . in an adversary position to man and convert all the now harmonious elements of society into a state of war, and make every home a hell on earth." Pursuing the same line of argument, Senator Peter Frelinghuysen of New Jersey insisted that women had a "higher and holier" function than to engage in the turmoil of public life. "Their mission is at home," he said, "by their blandishments and their love to assuage the passions of men."[12]

The feminists did not help their cause when they allowed themselves to be identified with proposals to liberalize sexual morality. In the 1870's Victoria Woodhull, a friend of Susan B. Anthony and Elizabeth Cady Stanton, endorsed free love and licensed prostitution in her weekly newspaper. Advocacy of sexual freedom was bad enough, but Woodhull then went on to create a public furor by charging that the respectable reformer Henry Ward Beecher was having a love affair with Elizabeth Tilton. Beecher instituted a libel suit, prolonging the public uproar, and prominent feminists rushed to Woodhull's defense. Horace Greeley, among others, had previously stated that he could not support the feminists because they were too closely tied to the cause of free love. Now, Woodhull's pronouncements, and her widely publicized association with feminists, appeared to confirm Greeley's allegations, and added one more weapon to the anti-feminist arsenal.[13]

Such episodes inevitably took their toll. As the century wore on, it became increasingly obvious that if the woman's movement continued to advocate serious change in marriage and the family, it would be dismissed as a radical fringe and charged with trying to destroy the moral fiber of the nation. Every social movement contains some people who insist on the need for total change and others who are willing to compromise in order to achieve tangible gains. Ordinarily, the two exist side by side—often in the same person—but usually one or the other approach is dominant. In the woman's movement, the forces of compromise gradually gained increased strength. In the years after the Civil War, feminism divided into different camps—the "conservative" American Woman's Suffrage Association, which was concerned almost exclusively with winning the ballot, and the "liberal" National Woman's Suffrage Association, which was committed to more far-reaching institutional change. By the end of the century, the degree of opposition to more radical feminist demands had made the liberal position untenable, and in 1890 the two wings of the movement reunited as the National American Woman's Suffrage Association (NAWSA) concerned primarily with the goal of winning the suffrage—the most respectable and limited feminist demand.

At the same time, women's rights leaders shifted from what Aileen Kraditor has called an "argument from justice" to an "argument from expediency." Again, there was no clear-cut gap between those espousing the different strategies. At various times, Elizabeth Cady Stanton had used the expediency argument, and later women's rights advocates never abandoned the argument from justice. But by the turn of the century there was a shift in the balance between the two positions. Instead of emphasizing the inalienable rights of females as individuals, the feminists tended to emphasize the utility of the ballot as an agent for reforming society. And rather than base their appeal on the similarity of men and women as human beings, they underlined the immutable differences which distinguished the sexes and gave to each a unique role to play in politics.[14]

In large part, the shift developed as a natural response to a hostile political climate. As long as feminists focused on women's right to be free of social constraints, they invited association of their own movement with such issues as divorce and free love. In an age scarred by fear of anarchism and social disorder, it made sense for women leaders to de-emphasize those positions which were most likely to incur public disapproval. At the same time a different generation of leaders took over direction of the woman's movement. By the turn of the century, most of the early feminists had either died or retired from active participation in the movement. Their places were taken by people like Carrie Chapman Catt and Jane Addams—women who shared many of the same ideals as the first generation but who inevitably operated within a different frame of reference. The new leaders evolved a set of tactics designed to minimize controversy, and in the tradition of the American Suffrage Association they maintained a low level of rhetoric. As a result, the woman's movement more and more frequently accepted the opposition's premise on the sanctity of the home and pursued the fight for the vote within the context of conventional ideas on woman's place. The new direction of the movement emerged gradually. It was not marked by any special event, nor did it reflect a Machiavellian plot by any faction or group of leaders. But with the passage of time, the feminist appeal clearly took on a different tone.

The suffragists' acceptance of female distinctiveness represented the departure point for the new strategy. In the past feminist leaders had championed the principle that the two sexes had exactly identical rights to engage in worldly activity. Now, they frequently argued that women deserved the vote precisely because they were different. The suffragists brilliantly exploited traditional assumptions about woman's unique place. Females were primarily spiritual creatures, they claimed. Hence their participation in politics would elevate the moral level of government. Men possessed special talents to cope with material problems based on their experience in the business world. But women had special abilities to cope with human problems based on their experience in the home. Each sex occupied its own particular sphere, but the two were complementary rather than incompatible. Just as the creation of a good family required the contribution of both husband and wife, so the establishment of effective government depended upon the equal participation of male and female citizens. Politics dominated by men alone constituted a half-finished social instrument. Involvement by women was essential to complete it.[15]

The new line of argument was epitomized by the suffragists' claim that the nation was simply a macrocosm of the home. Frances Willard of the Women's Christian Temperance Union had first described politics as "enlarged housekeeping," and suffragists like Jane Addams adopted the phrase to package their appeal to the public. Woman's primary duty, Addams argued in a widely circulated magazine article, was to preserve the health of her children and the cleanliness of her home. In an urban, industrial environment, the fulfillment of her responsibilities depended on the sanitation policies, fire regulations, and housing standards of municipal government. If dirt were to be controlled, garbage collection had to be prompt. If the meat a mother bought for her family was to be free of germs, stringent government inspection was required. And if the clothes her children wore were not to be carriers of disease, government regulation of sweatshops was essential. In short, Addams declared, "if woman would keep on with her old business of caring for her house and rearing her children, she will have to have some conscience in regard to public affairs lying outside her immediate household." Women could preserve the home and remain good mothers only if they acquired the vote and through political involvement protected the family.[16]

By such reasoning the woman's movement broadened its appeal and neutralized the opposition's charge that it sought to destroy the home. The allegation was still made. In the 1917 suffrage debate a Southern congressman declared that giving the vote to women would "disrupt the family, which is the unit of society; and when you disrupt the family, you destroy the home, which is the foundation stone of the Republic."[17] But such arguments no longer contained the power they once had. By avoiding issues which might alienate potential supporters while emphasizing traditional conceptions of women's proper role, the suffragists acquired growing respectability. More and more, they occupied the moderate center of the political spectrum and mirrored the views of the society around them.

The positions the suffragists took on such issues as immigration, race, and religion reflected the extent to which they shared prevailing public opinion. In 1894 Carrie Chapman Catt joined those protesting the influx of foreigners and warned against the effort of undesirables to despoil the nation's wealth. "There is but one way to avert the danger," Mrs. Catt declared: "Cut off the vote of the slums and give it to women. . . ."[18] A year earlier the suffrage convention had blatantly appealed to nativist fears by calling attention to the fact that "there are more white women who can read and write than all negro voters; more American women who can read and write than all foreign voters." Woman suffrage, the convention suggested, "would settle the vexed question of rule by illiteracy" and ensure the perpetuation of the American way of life. Even former leaders could not escape the movement's quest for respectability. In 1895 Elizabeth Cady Stanton published the first volume of the *Woman's Bible,* an attack on established religion's responsibility for woman's subject status. The suffrage convention explicitly disassociated itself from the publication, and, in effect, disavowed Stanton's leadership.[19]

With the advent of Progressivism, the strategy of consensus bore fruit. The suffragists had already defined the vote for women as a means of humanizing government, and in a period of generalized commitment to "reform," they were able to identify their own cause with the larger effort to extend democracy and eliminate social injustice. Progressivism meant a great many things to different people, but in large part it represented an effort to clean up the most obvious causes of corruption, disease, and poverty. Within such a context, the suffragists argued convincingly that extension of the franchise to females would help in the task of improving society. Both the rhetoric and substance of the suffrage program meshed with the ethos of reform. Women, one suffragist declared, were engaged in "a fight of the home against the saloon; . . . a struggle of justice with greed and prejudice; . . . a long strong battle between the selfish citizens and the patriotic ones."[20] To a remarkable extent, the society at large defined the goals of Progressivism in the same way, and as a result, the suffragists succeeded in making the vote for women a prominent item on the agenda of reform.

Female reformers, of course, played a decisive part in shaping Progressivism through their involvement in the social welfare movement. Women like Jane Addams, Lillian Wald, and Florence Kelley started the settlement houses which sprouted up in urban America during the 1890's, and then carried their ideas and experience into national organizations dedicated to securing legislative change. For such women, suffrage and the cause of social welfare were inextricably tied together. Committed to building better neighborhoods and improving the conditions of workers in sweatshops and factories, they realized that they could accomplish little without political power. The construction of new parks and sewers required the approval of city officials, and wages and hours could not be regulated without state legislation. Woman suffrage thus became a natural concern of reformers who hoped to mobilize an independent political constituency which would force party bosses into action. The vote for females, the reformers believed, would add a sympathetic bloc to the electorate and provide the leverage necessary to secure social-welfare legislation. The men and women who founded Hull House and the National Consumers League were powerful figures, and their support substantially strengthened the "reform" appeal of the woman's movement.[21]

Progressivism also provided a vehicle by which millions of hitherto-uninvolved middle-class women became politicized. During the years between 1895 and 1915, Robert Wiebe has written, almost every established group within the new middle class "experienced its formative growth toward self-consciousness." The history of the woman's clubs during the Progressive period testifies to the accuracy of Wiebe's perception. Founded in 1890 with some 500,000 members, the General Federation of Women's Clubs (GFWC) grew to over 2 million members twenty years later. In the tradition of earlier reading and literary societies, the GFWC's original purpose was to encourage women's intellectual development and provide an opportunity for recreation. By the turn of the century, however, the club movement had caught the contagious spirit of reform. "Dante is dead," the federation's new president declared in 1904, "and I think it is time that we dropped the study of his *Inferno* and turned our attention to our own social order."[22] State clubs started nursery schools, lobbied for conservation, initiated experiments in juvenile clinics, and provided a constant stream of support for Progressive legislation, including over one million letters on behalf of the Pure Food and Drug bill of 1906. "Scarcely without exception," Judge Ben Lindsey wrote, "it has been the members of the women's clubs . . . who have secured the passage of nearly all the advanced legislation on the statute books for the protection of the home and the child." Once involved in political affairs the women's clubs recognized the necessity for extending the franchise to women, both as a matter of justice, and as an aid to securing further reform. In 1914 the GFWC formally endorsed the suffrage campaign, and for the first time in its history, the woman's movement had a strong base of support among women themselves.[23]

The close ties between suffragists and reformers became increasingly obvious as the Progressive period moved on. At an early stage, the women's rights movement joined in the cry for social welfare improvements. The number of articles in the *Woman's Journal* advocating reform legislation doubled between 1895 and 1915. More important, an interlocking directorate linked the woman's movement to other groups in the Progressive coalition. Florence Kelley was vice-president of the National Consumers League, a resident of the Henry Street Settlement and chairman of the child labor committee of the General Federation of Women's Clubs. Jane Addams served as a national officer of NAWSA, a board member of the Women's Trade Union League, and an adviser to Theodore Roosevelt. Male reformers like Raymond Robins, Harry Hopkins, Harold Ickes, and Newton Baker worked together with suffragists in many Progressive organizations and sought to achieve the same goals.[24]

The common denominator which united most of these groups was the belief that the vote for women represented an essential step toward a better society. In the tradition of Progressivism, each interpreted the value of the suffrage differently. Civic reformers believed that female voters would help oust corrupt political bosses. Devotees of democratization viewed woman suffrage as a logical extension of the initiative, referendum, and recall. And social-welfare organizations considered it a powerful new weapon in the fight for minimum-wage and child-labor legislation. All agreed, however, that, whatever one's particular definition of "reform," extending the franchise to women would enhance the possibility of achieving it.[25]

By the second decade of the twentieth century, the suffrage movement had succeeded in establishing itself as an important part of the Progressive coalition. Significantly, nine of the eleven states which enacted woman suffrage by 1914 also had adopted the initiative and referendum. Suffrage supporters actively supported most pieces of reform legislation, and reformers reciprocated by pressuring political leaders to join the struggle for the franchise. Both major parties responded by moving closer to endorsement of the suffrage, and when the insurgent "Bull Moose" party headed by Theodore Roosevelt met in convention in 1912, it issued an unequivocal call for a constitutional amendment granting women the right to vote. In the past, the woman's movement had suffered from a lack of allies and a dearth of popular support. Now, after repeated rebuffs, it had achieved legitimacy as an entrenched part of a broad-based reform movement. No longer a deviant fringe, it had become, in the words of the *Woman's Journal,* "bourgeois," "middle class," and "middle-of-the-road."[26]

With the support of leading reformers as an impetus, women activists revived flagging suffrage campaigns in states across the country. In 1910, the state of Washington broke a fourteen-year streak of defeats when its voters approved a suffrage amendment in a popular referendum. Victories followed in Illinois and California, proving for the first time that the vote for women had appeal in areas with large industrial and urban concentrations. In the nation's capital, meanwhile, the militant Congressional Union injected new life into the struggle for a federal amendment. Headed by Alice Paul, a Quaker and veteran of the English suffrage campaign, the Union was formed in 1913 as the Congressional Committee of NAWSA and within two months organized a tumultuous parade of 5,000 women to mark the arrival of Woodrow Wilson for the presidential inauguration ceremonies. The Congressional Union insisted that the party in power be made to answer for the failure to approve the suffrage amendment and in 1914 and 1916 mounted a national campaign to defeat Democratic candidates. Both in spirit and tactics, Alice Paul's organization offended the more conservative bent of NAWSA, and in 1915 the two groups split, but the energy, excitement, and publicity which the Congressional Union generated played a key role in focusing renewed suffragist attention on the necessity for a national constitutional amendment.[27]

Responding to the challenge posed by the Congressional Union, NAWSA reorganized its national office in 1915 and placed Carrie Chapman Catt in charge of the over-all suffrage campaign. Catt immediately formulated a "Winning Plan" based on the concept that state and federal efforts should reinforce each other. For every victory won on a local level, she reasoned, additional congressmen and senators could be persuaded to vote for a suffrage amendment. It was especially important, she felt, for suffrage forces to break the solid front of opposition in the Northeast and South. "If New York wins in 1917," she declared, "the backbone of the opposition will be largely bent if not broken." Catt viewed herself as a field commander and brought to the suffrage movement an unprecedented amount of discipline and efficiency. While crucial local affiliates mobilized their energies to achieve state victories, a carefully selected staff of lobbyists cultivated support on Capitol Hill. Catt herself concentrated on President Wilson. Instead of denouncing him as the Congressional Union had done, she solicited his advice, invited him to address suffrage conventions, and in every way possible associated him with the suffrage cause.[28]

Piece by piece the elements of Catt's "Winning Plan" fell into place. In 1917 the voters of New York passed a suffrage referendum, reversing their decision of two years earlier. A year later Michigan, South Dakota, and Oklahoma joined the suffrage ranks. Fourteen state legislatures in 1917 and twenty-six in 1919 petitioned Congress to enact a federal amendment. The President himself entered the fray after women had rallied to the support of his war policies. "The services of women during the supreme crisis have been of the most signal usefulness and distinction," he wrote Mrs. Catt. "It is high time that part of our debt should be acknowledged and paid."[29] When a new Congress convened in 1919, it was as if no controversy had ever existed. The suffrage amendment passed the House by a vote of 304 to 90, the Senate by a vote of 56 to 25. Fourteen months later, Tennessee became the thirty-sixth state to ratify. Nearly three-quarters of a century after Seneca Falls, the women's rights movement had reached a benchmark. "How much time and patience . . . how much hope, how much despair went into the battle," Carrie Chapman Catt reflected. "It leaves its mark on one, such a struggle. It fills the days and it rides the nights." And now the fight was over. Women had won the vote.[30]

To a large extent, the suffrage victory represented a triumph for the strategy of compromise. By tempering those ideas most likely to offend public sensibilities and playing up the social utility of the ballot, leaders like Carrie Chapman Catt made substantial inroads into the opposition's strength and succeeded in building a political consensus on behalf of the Nineteenth Amendment. The suffragists themselves, on the other hand, were not necessarily aware of the changes which had taken place. When the Nineteenth Amendment was enacted, female leaders believed that they had carried out the mission begun at Seneca Falls and did not perceive the extent to which the vision of the earlier feminists had been narrowed. The woman's movement, Carrie Chapman Catt wrote in 1917, was engaged in a "world-wide revolt against all artificial barriers which laws and customs interpose between women and human freedom."[31] The same purpose had inspired the founders of the women's rights movement. Thus if the nature of feminism had altered, the suffragists did not consciously recognize or acknowledge the change.

At least in part, the contradiction reflected the perspective from which the suffragists viewed the past. "The participants in a historical situation," David Potter has observed, "tend to see the alternatives in that situation as less clear cut, less sharply focused" than historians do.[32] Potter's comments were made in a different context, but they speak directly to the suffragists' perception of their own accomplishments. Although a change in style and tone had certainly taken place within the woman's movement, it occurred over such a long period of time that it was not immediately visible to contemporary observers. There were "conservatives" in the movement in 1848 and "radicals" in 1918, and while the balance between the different points of view altered, there was no overt reversal of direction. The vote had always constituted an important plank in the feminist platform, and simply grew in prominence with the passage of time. Even the "argument from expediency" evolved gradually, never totally dominating the "argument from justice." Since the woman's movement did not split over either issue, there was no reason for suffrage leaders to perceive a discontinuity between the past and present. Indeed, if they had envisioned their goal as anything less than that of the early feminists, they would have found it difficult to justify the dedication and energy they expended in the struggle.[33]

At the same time, the value ascribed to the vote by contemporaries reinforced women's rights leaders in their belief that they were involved in a battle of revolutionary significance. In the Progressive era, it was not unusual for different groups to define reform measures as panaceas. Prohibitionists asserted that the Eighteenth Amendment would purify the nation's morals. Trustbusters pledged that dismantling large corporations would guarantee economic freedom. And social welfare reformers contended that woman suffrage would usher in a new age of protection for workers and customers, while putting an end to graft and indifference in government. The fact that financiers, railroads, and liquor interests went to such great lengths to bankroll the fight against the Nineteenth Amendment encouraged women leaders in their belief that the suffrage would transform society.

Finally, the progress which had taken place from 1848 to 1920 provided some justification for the conviction that extending the franchise would demolish one of the last barriers to equality. Common law restrictions had largely been removed. Educational opportunity was available in a variety of private colleges and public universities. And during World War I, thousands of women had moved into jobs formerly held by men, causing many observers to assert that a revolution in the economic role of women had occurred. If not all the demands of 1848 had been met, enough had received some attention to create a basis in reality for the suffragists' hope that acquisition of the vote would place women on a par with men in society.

Thus when the last state ratified the Nineteenth Amendment, the suffragists had good reason to believe that they had scored a decisive victory in the battle for women's rights. In effect, the ballot had come to symbolize the entire struggle for equality and to embody all the demands of the woman's movement. The question was whether the suffrage could carry the heavy burden assigned to it, whether the right to vote also meant progress toward eliminating the deeper causes of inequality which had concerned the feminists at Seneca Falls. Carrie Chapman Catt told a victory celebration in New York in 1920 that she had lived to realize the greatest dream of her life. "We are no longer petitioners," she said, "we are not wards of the nation, but free and equal citizens."[34] Only the experience of the next generation could prove whether such optimism represented wishful thinking or hard reality.

# PART ONE

## 1920-1940

# 1

# Women and Politics

Politics, understandably, provided the first test of what the suffragists had won with the enactment of the Nineteenth Amendment. A half-century earlier, Elizabeth Cady Stanton and her followers had dismissed the vote as "not even half a loaf; . . . only a crust, a crumb." By 1920, however, such skepticism had been set aside, and the ballot was invested with the power to end sex prejudice and elevate the nation's morals. The change indicated the degree to which the woman's movement had come to view politics as the key to a just society. Female leaders claimed that extending the franchise would speed the passage of social welfare legislation, enhance consumer protection, and reinforce the drive against bossism in America's cities. The nation, led by women, could proceed to solve its problems—peaceably and through the electoral process.[1]

The suffragists' hopes hinged on the assumption that female citizens—by virtue of their sex—would act as a cohesive force to bring about social change. Women were so different from men, the reformers believed, that once they had the vote, the entire political system would be transformed. Pure in spirit, selfless in motivation, and dedicated to the preservation of human life, female voters would remake society and turn government away from war and corruption. The deed was more difficult than the promise, however, for if women were to fulfill the expectations of female leaders, they had to vote together, organize on the basis of sex, and demonstrate a collective allegiance to common ideals and programs. The validity of suffragist claims thus turned ultimately on the question of whether women could create a separate "bloc" in the electorate, committed to a distinctive set of interests and values.

The few instances in which women had played an active role in politics provided some basis for speculation about the development of an independent female constituency. In Illinois, where the votes of the two sexes were counted separately, women gave the reform candidate for mayor of Chicago in 1915 almost as large a plurality as men gave the machine candidate. Massachusetts suffragists successfully mobilized a non-partisan coalition to defeat the anti-suffragist senator John Weeks in 1918. And in Columbus, Ohio, the Franklin County Suffrage Association helped upset the mayor of sixteen years by concentrating five hundred female volunteers in eleven key wards. The women campaigners registered 21,000 new voters, and their candidate won by 19,000.[2]

In addition, many women leaders rejected the regular party apparatus as a vehicle for expressing their ideals. The head of the Illinois Republican Women's Committee bolted her party in 1920 and led a campaign to unseat the Republican mayor of Chicago, William Thompson. Many of the most prominent spokesmen of the newly formed League of Women Voters urged women to avoid joining established political organizations. And Alice Paul of the National Women's Party threatened repeatedly to form an independent political force composed of females alone. The worst fears of party leaders seemed confirmed when Mary Garrett Hay, national vice-chairman of Republican women, strongly opposed the re-election of New York's senator James Wadsworth in 1920 because he had been a leader of the anti-suffrage forces in Congress. Hay's action, one reporter wrote, "exemplifies to the doubting element of both parties the dreaded third party, a petticoat hierarchy which may at will upset all orderly slates and commit undreamed of executions at the polls."[3]

Faced with such a spectre, politicians moved quickly to win the support of the new voters. The Democratic convention of 1920 incorporated twelve of fifteen League of Women Voters proposals in its national party platform, and the Republic convention endorsed five. The Republican presidential nominee, Warren Harding, invited prominent women leaders to his home and called for equal pay for women, an eight-hour day, passage of maternity and infancy legislation, and creation of a federal department of social welfare. Both parties appointed women as equal members of their respective national committees, and each named female aspirants to governmental positions.[4]

State politicians reacted with equal warmth to the potentially powerful new voters. By the end of 1921 twenty state legislatures had granted women the right to serve on juries. Other states passed night work laws and wage and hour legislation specifically designed to accommodate the wishes of female reformers. Michigan and Montana enacted equal-pay laws, Wisconsin approved a far-reaching equal rights bill, and lawmakers throughout the South showed a new flexibility toward social legislation. The Georgia assembly treated women lobbyists with unprecedented respect, and the Virginia legislature granted reform leaders eighteen of twenty-four requests, including a children's code, a child placement bill and a vocational education law.[5]

Congress, meanwhile, demonstrated its concern for women by acting expeditiously on maternity and infancy legislation, the primary demand of female reform organizations. The Sheppard-Towner bill, calling for an annual appropriation of $1,250,000 for educational instruction in the health care of mothers and babies, stirred immediate controversy when it was first introduced in May 1921. Opponents tried to kill the measure by calling it "federal mid-wifery" and "official meddling between mother and baby which would mean the abolition of the family." Supporters of the bill, however, responded with an impressive display of power. Under the banner "Herod Is Not Dead," *Good Housekeeping* documented the tragic toll in human life caused by maternal and infant illness and secured the endorsements of thirty-four governors. Harriet Taylor Upton, national vice-chairman of the Republican party, enlisted Harding's support by repeatedly holding out the threat of feminine retaliation at the polls. Representatives of women's reform groups lobbied intensively for the measure and offered dramatic testimony before legislative hearings. No one spoke with more fervor or greater authority than Florence Kelley, executive secretary of the National Consumers League. Citing the fact that a quarter of a million infants died each year in America, she inquired: "What answer can be given to the women who are marveling and asking, 'why does Congress wish women and children to die?' " The *Journal of the American Medical Association* declared that the women had created "one of the strongest lobbies that has ever been seen in Washington."[6]

Faced with the unremitting pressure of female reform groups, Congress passed the bill. "If the members could have voted in the cloak room," one backer of the measure asserted later, "it would have been killed." As it was, the act passed with only seven dissenting votes in the Senate and thirty-nine in the House. "The Senators did not quite dare to turn it down," a former suffragist wrote. No other event demonstrated so dramatically the eagerness of politicians to win over the unknown quantity introduced into the electorate by the enactment of the Nineteenth Amendment. The statute represented precisely the kind of protection of human life which the suffragists had talked about as women's special concern. And it indicated the influence which women might exert on a continuing basis if they acted in a concerted way to express their wishes on issues and candidates.[7]

In subsequent years, female reformers enjoyed additional successes. Congress passed the Packers and Stockyards bill in 1921 designed to increase consumer protection; the Cable Act in 1922 reforming citizenship requirements for married women; the Lehlbach Act of 1923 upgrading the merit system in the civil service; and the Child Labor Amendment to the Constitution in 1924. Each bill was strongly supported by the Women's Joint Congressional Committee, an umbrella organization established by various female groups to coordinate legislative activity. If not every item desired by women activists was enacted, enough received some attention to sustain the hopes of female leaders.[8]

Beginning in mid-decade, however, women's standing in the eyes of politicians dropped precipitously. A Congressional supporter urged the Women's Joint Congressional Committee to reduce its pressure for a home economics measure because Congress was tired of being asked to pass women's legislation. The Child Labor Amendment, which had engaged the energies of so many reform groups, failed ratification in the key states of Massachusetts and New York as Catholic bishops joined the opposition with claims that the amendment would destroy the sanctity of the home. Appropriations for the Women's Bureau and Children's Bureau were cut, and a two-year extension of the Sheppard-Towner Act was secured only by inserting into the new measure a written statement that the act would permanently expire on June 30, 1929. Congressmen seemed as intent on rebuffing the requests of female reformers in the second half of the decade as they had been in granting them during the first half.[9]

The abrupt reversal of fortune bewildered and demoralized women leaders. Just a few years before, their reform coalition had wielded considerable influence over Congress and state politicians. Now they were an embattled minority fighting a rearguard action against the destruction of programs already established. To some extent, the decline could be attributed to a conservative shift in national affairs. In the 1924 elections, the voters had flocked to the candidacy of Calvin Coolidge and rejected the Progressive challenge of Robert La Follette. The Supreme Court cut the ground from beneath many reform proposals by ruling against a federal child-labor law and minimum-wage legislation for women. And a rash of redbaiting attacks had smeared women's organizations as Communist front groups.[10] Insofar as women's groups were part of a broader Progressive alliance, they were bound to suffer when reform became less popular than it once had been.

Fundamentally, however, women's political standing plum-

meted because the mass of female citizens failed to act in the cohesive and committed manner which the suffragists had predicted.
The recognition which women had received in the years immediately after 1919 was based in large part on the claim that females
would vote at the polls as a monolithic "bloc." With the passage
of time, however, it became increasingly clear that no female bloc
existed, that women in general voted like their husbands if they
voted at all, and that enthusiasm among females for reform was
limited at best. "Not one of the disasters has come to pass that
four years ago glowered so fearsomely upon the politicians' trade,"
a reporter wrote in 1924. "Not a boss has been unseated, not a
reactionary committee wrested from the old-time control. . . .
Nothing has been changed." Other observers agreed. "I know of
no woman today who has any influence or political power because
she is a woman," Democratic Committeewoman Emily Newell
Blair declared. "I know of no woman who has a following of other
women. I know of no politician who is afraid of the woman vote
on any question under the sun."[11]

The poor performance of women voters at the polls constituted
the most crushing blow to suffragist hopes. Despite extensive efforts by the League of Women Voters to educate the new members
of the electorate, women failed to exercise the franchise in substantial proportions. A low turnout in some states in the 1920
elections could be explained by the fact that the suffrage amendment was not ratified until August 1920. But in New York, where
women had been given the franchise in 1917, females cast only 35
per cent of the total vote in 1920. In Illinois, where the suffrage
had been granted in 1913, the figure was slightly higher, but only
46.5 per cent of the women eligible to vote went to the polls in
contrast to 74.1 per cent of the men. Three years later, in the Chicago mayoralty election, women cast only 36 per cent of the vote,
and they comprised 75 per cent of the eligible adults who were
not registered. "Unless they have some personal or family contact
with the political questions at issue," the Illinois *State Journal* concluded, "women do not vote."[12]

Equally devastating to suffragist predictions was the lack of evidence that women voted differently from men. Instead of becoming more and more solidified, a journalist commented in 1923, "the women's bloc . . . tends to become more and more disintegrated."[13] Occasionally, on issues like Prohibition or corruption in government, females voted in slightly larger proportions than men for the "moral" candidate; but in general, women voted according to their social and economic backgrounds and the political preference of their husbands rather than according to their sex.[14] Almost all the newspaper editors polled by the *Literary Digest* in 1924 reported that there was no distinction between the political behavior of men and women. Reform leaders had argued "passionately, if ignorantly" that females would use their ballot unselfishly for all mankind, Democratic national committeewoman Emma Guffey Miller noted, "but our first campaign taught us . . . that women were no more motivated by altruism or sense of historical perspective than men."[15]

In the aftermath of the Chicago mayoral election of 1923, Charles Merriam and Herbert Gosnell attempted to isolate the causes of female non-voting through interviews with those who had failed to go to the polls. Almost a third of the women surveyed pleaded general lack of interest in politics. Immigrant women, in particular, blamed ignorance of the balloting process and fear of embarrassment over language difficulties. The largest specific cause cited, however, was "disbelief in woman's voting." Over 11 per cent of those interviewed stated that females should stay at home and leave politics to men. In addition, many of those who had intended to vote explained that they neglected to go to the polls at the last moment because their husbands had failed to remind them.[16]

Other observers noted the same tendency of women to defer to men when it came to politics. A *New York Times* reporter covering registration activities on the Lower East Side in 1920 commented that females comprised only one out of four new voters and that those women who did register were brought by their husbands. Sue

White, a leading suffragist and Southern Democrat, explained that in her region women stayed away from politics because male party members insisted that government was a man's game. And the Minnesota League of Women Voters reported that female citizens in that state "were too timid to participate in an election where men folks made it plain that they were not wanted." The fact that most women were expected to concentrate on caring for the home further impeded their involvement in politics. Although the suffragists had argued that political activity was simply an extension of women's housekeeping role, a League of Women Voters official in New York noted that many women failed to vote owing to their absorption in homemaking. Women saw little relationship between their votes and the conduct of public policy, the *New York Times* observed, and hence felt no great urgency to go to the polls.[17]

Although much of the discussion of female voting behavior during the 1920's was impressionistic, subsequent research has confirmed the accuracy of earlier commentators on almost every point. A high degree of political participation, political scientists have concluded, depends at least in part on the presence of group pressures emphasizing the importance of the ballot, and the absence of cross-pressures discouraging political independence.[18] In the case of women, each variable worked against their voting in the same proportion as men. Despite the existence of organizations like the League of Women Voters, most women received little encouragement to vote. Unless they had supportive husbands, it was often just as easy not to go to the polls. More important, the whole notion of woman's place contradicted the idea of female political independence. The value of the vote, Angus Campbell has written, "is relevant to role beliefs that presume woman to be a submissive partner. Man is expected to be dominant in action toward the world outside the family; the woman is to accept his leadership passively." Studies of political behavior in the post-World War II period have shown that persons casting a vote for the first time generally follow the example of an authority figure in the family. Where disagreement exists, the new voter usually decides to abstain from political participation altogether.[19]

Projected backward in time, such observations help to explain why women during the 1920's either voted like their husbands or joined the ranks of those who with complete respectability ignored politics entirely. For females to vote at all required a substantial break from their conventional role. To ask that they oppose their husbands or fathers in the process entailed a commitment which only the most dedicated could sustain. As Emily Newell Blair observed in 1925, the very idea of a woman's bloc presumed the existence of a man's bloc as well; yet neither society nor the family could withstand the divisiveness of females fighting for one set of principles and males for another. The suffragists had anticipated that "women would organize along sex lines, nominate women, urge special legislation, and vote en masse." But such an expectation represented a "hallucination."[20] Women differed in emotions, ideals, and prejudices just as men did. They belonged to a variety of groups which held different political opinions. And their outlook was determined primarily by the social and economic backgrounds of their husbands. Ironically, the "special sex-cohesion" which women did manifest was negative rather than positive. Precisely because of the nature of sex roles, it was almost mandatory for wives and daughters to follow the lead of a male "authority figure" when they went to the polls.

The absence of a dramatic "woman's" issue of overriding proportions constituted a final obstacle to the realization of suffragist hopes. In the years before 1920, the vote had been equated with freedom and a substantial number of females had rallied to the suffrage banner. After the enactment of the Nineteenth Amendment, however, no issue of comparable dimension arose. Veterans of the suffrage fight found politics pale and uninspiring, Carrie Chapman Catt wrote, and missed the "exaltation, the thrill of expectancy, the vision which stimulated them in the suffrage campaign." The ballot had provided a "symbol" which united women, Anna Howard Shaw observed, but after the franchise was acquired, the symbol was lost.[21] Even if there had been a cause around which to mobilize female voters, it is unlikely that women would have responded with the same amount of commitment achieved in the suffrage fight. But without such an issue, there was almost no possibility of generating a sense of sex solidarity, or building an independent female constituency.

The problem of defining a separate "female" interest dominated the discussion of the League of Women Voters when it was formed in 1919 to provide organizational leadership for the newly enfranchised citizens. In the tradition of suffragist rhetoric, Carrie Chapman Catt exhorted the delegates to lead a "crusade that shall not end until the electorate is intelligent, clean and American."[22] When it came to specifics, however, the League faced a more difficult task. The central issue confronting the new group was whether it wished to integrate women within the existing political system or segregate them as an independent political force. Both alternatives had support. The whole goal of the suffrage campaign had been to liberate women so that they could join men as equals in the political and social institutions of the country. On the other hand, the fight had been waged on the premise that females had a special set of interests which distinguished them from men and made it necessary for them to have a separate voice. Each position thus represented a powerful segment of the woman's movement. Yet the two were mutually contradictory.

The debate over League policy toward partisan politics polarized the organization's leadership. Carrie Chapman Catt insisted that "the only way to get things done is to get them done on the inside of a political party." She urged women to participate directly in the political process and master party techniques. They would not be welcome, she predicted, but they had to try. "You will see the real thing in the center with the door locked tight. You will have a long hard fight before you get inside . . . but you must move right up to the center." Catt denounced the idea of sex segregation and even suggested that the word "women" be dropped from the League's title.[23] On the other side, however, equally powerful voices eschewed the policy of integration and condemned party politics as the tool of autocrats concerned only with self-aggrandizement. Prominent leaders like Jane Addams believed that unless women retained their identity as a separate interest group they would destroy the very principles which made them unique. Females were concerned with public service and high ideals, males with private profit and personal power. Consequently, if women accepted the discipline of regular party membership, they would violate their conscience and compromise their effectiveness.[24]

Anxious politicians interpreted the debate as a signal that the League intended to start a third party. President Harding warned against "organizing our citizenship into groups according to sex"; Mrs. Medill McCormick, an Illinois Republican leader, charged that the League was obstructing the enrollment of women into regular party groups; and the governor of New York denounced the organization as a "menace" to national life, a threat to traditional political allegiances.[25] In fact, however, there was little chance that women could be united under a single political banner. Females held too many diverse points of view and were too dependent on male leadership, to forge an alliance along sex lines. Moreover, League leaders themselves had neither the will nor the issues to create a third-party movement. Even those members who believed most vehemently in the existence of a separate woman's point of view rejected the idea of establishing an independent political organization. From their point of view, party politics by definition were unsavory.

In the end, the League resolved the conflict over its political role by compromise. Rather than create a new party, it determined to mobilize public opinion behind reform programs and to instruct women in the tasks of citizenship so that they could work more effectively within existing political organizations. "We have got to be non-partisan and all-partisan," Catt said. Democratic and Republican women would work together for common ends, even while moving to the centers of their respective parties.[26] The League still failed to define the "common ends" which united women, however. It retained a diffuse belief that females, by virtue of their sex, had a special concern with issues like social welfare and education, but it was unable to give that concern a convincing focus, or to provide an institutional means by which women could express their interests in a cohesive way. The suffragists had assumed that women would automatically act together for a common set of principles, but their successors found it almost impossible to carry that assumption into practice.

Without a solid "woman's" issue around which to rally female citizens, the League and other reform organizations lost much of the popular appeal which the suffragists had enjoyed. In Dade County, Wisconsin, a thousand women attended a meeting to learn about the ballot but only eleven joined the League of Women Voters. A local officer wrote that the League had not yet demonstrated its value or relevance. "Its reason for existence," she noted, "is far less compelling to the average woman than that of the suffrage organization." The Minnesota League complained that few women were willing to accept responsibility as county leaders, and by mid-1921 the organization in South Dakota was almost moribund. Other reform groups experienced similar problems. The Women's Trade Union League was torn by internal dissension over its future course of action, and the Federation of Women's Clubs—once a decisive voice in the Progressive coalition—abandoned politics entirely, choosing to emphasize home economics and the distribution of electrical appliances rather than political action.[27]

Individual female leaders, of course, continued to make distinguished contributions to a variety of causes. The peace movement proved especially compelling to suffragists like Carrie Chapman Catt and Jane Addams. Catt announced in 1925 that women could never be liberated until war was abolished, and thereafter devoted almost all of her energies to the Committee on the Cause and Cure of War, an organization which she founded. Jane Addams had been a leader of the Women's International League for Peace and Freedom since its beginning in 1915, and toward the last part of her life, spent an increasing amount of time in the effort to mobilize public sentiment on behalf of disarmament. Women peace advocates established an effective lobby in Washington and were directly responsible for the Nye investigation of the munitions industry in the early 1930's. Other women performed invaluable service in the cause of social-welfare legislation and more efficient government. Almost singlehandedly, Florence Kelley kept the fight for a Child Labor Amendment alive, and female reformers in the League of Women Voters and other organizations campaigned across the country for the establishment of the city manager form of municipal government.[28]

Despite such accomplishments, however, no group succeeded in galvanizing the mass of women—as women—into the effective force for change which female reformers had predicted. Five years after the passage of the Nineteenth Amendment, the highly cohesive popular constituency of the suffragists had disintegrated. At the height of its success, NAWSA boasted a membership of 2 million women. By mid-decade, however, the woman's movement had regressed to its earlier status as a small cadre of activists. The League of Women Voters claimed to represent all the former members of NAWSA, but in fact it kept only a fraction. Cleveland contributed 80,000 women to the suffrage fight, only 8,000 to the League.[29] Notwithstanding the claims of some leaders, most women showed no evidence of collective self-consciousness. They responded to public affairs as individuals rather than as members of a special group with a distinctive set of interests.

Without an independent power base of their own, female reformers became dependent on the favor of party officials for whatever influence they might exert. As long as politicians believed that women might constitute a cohesive bloc of voters, they were willing to make at least some positive response to the demands of female organizations. Once it became clear that the reformers had overstated their case, however, the concessions stopped. Male leaders appointed individual women who shared their point of view to party posts, but reformers were either excluded or kept in minor positions. The men retained control, and they preferred women who got down to the "practical things of politics," as Harry Hawes wrote Emma Guffey Miller, over the "visionary theorists" who headed the reform movement.[30]

The women chosen for elective position reflected party policy. Officeholding for females, the reporter Emma Bugbee observed in 1930, was primarily a "widow's game." Two-thirds of those who served in Congress from 1920 to 1930 succeeded their dead husbands, most for only a single term. Of the two woman governors, one—Nellie Ross—took over from her deceased spouse, and the other—"Ma" Ferguson—stood in for her husband in a successful attempt to circumvent a Texas constitutional provision prohibiting the state's chief executive from serving consecutive terms of office. No female officeholder during the 1920's served with special distinction. Most either accommodated male leaders, or remained in office for so brief a time that there was little opportunity to build influence.[31]

The career of Mary Norton exemplified the experience of most female politicians during the 1920's. Norton first came to the attention of local Democrats when she approached Frank Hague, mayor of Jersey City, for help in securing public funds for nursery school education. Two years later, after woman suffrage had passed, the mayor requested her to go on the Democratic state committee to assist in mobilizing the female vote. Norton told Hague that she had no interest in either politics or the suffrage, but her protestations were dismissed as irrelevant. No woman knew anything about politics, Hague said, and in any event the position of state committeewoman was an empty honor which required no work. Four years later, Norton was handpicked to represent Jersey City in Congress, a position which she held for twenty-six years. She later concluded that the leaders of her party wanted "the honor of sending the first woman of the Democratic party to Congress." More to the point was Mary Dewson's comment to party boss Jim Farley that "Mayor Hague did not want any rival in his field and felt safer with the Congressman from Jersey City a woman."[32] Although Norton performed with notable distinction in Congress during the 1930's and '40's, the manner of her selection demonstrated the desire of political leaders to choose female officeholders who were amenable to control by party bosses.

The appointment of Rebecca Felton as the first woman senator highlighted the disparity between the shadow and substance of female power. Mrs. Felton, an octogenarian from Georgia, was named in 1922 to fill a temporary vacancy caused by death. Her tenure lasted for approximately an hour and resulted from a temporary suspension of the rules permitting a postponement of the swearing in of Walter George, the regularly elected senator. For a few short minutes, one commentator wrote, "the woman senator held court . . . on the Senate floor in the midst of flowers and congratulations while national affairs awaited her exit." Once the honorary ritual was concluded, however, the male legislators returned to their seats and Mrs. Felton returned to Georgia. Womanhood had been acknowledged. In contrast, when Eleanor Roosevelt and other female liberals arrived at the 1924 Democratic convention with a series of proposals on the child labor amendment and other social welfare measures, they were virtually ignored. Hour after hour, the women sat outside the Platform Committee hearings, hoping in vain that the Committee would listen to their plea and reconsider its rejection of a favorable resolution on the child labor amendment. The party leadership was ever ready with flowery honors. But when it came to the formation of party policy, woman's place remained that of an outsider.[33]

Significantly, the one occasion when women did succeed in gaining political influence occurred when Mrs. Roosevelt was an occupant of the White House and the President actively encouraged female participation in party affairs. Just as the Progressive era had provided a vehicle for advancement of the suffrage cause, the New Deal offered an opportunity for female social workers to put their principles to work through government service. As the Depression deepened, women reformers flocked to Washington to help manage the nation's emergency relief and social-welfare programs. Most of the women who came took professional positions in the WPA and other agencies, but some accepted political responsibilities as well. Among the latter was Mary Dewson, a leader of the National Consumers League and a close personal friend of the Roosevelts. Combining impeccable reform credentials with brilliant political instincts, Dewson assumed direction of women's work for the Democratic party in 1932 and succeeded for the first time in bringing women into the center of party councils.[34] Her experience proved that females could work effectively within the party system, even if they still lacked cohesion as a voting bloc.

Like most female reformers, Dewson was convinced that women differed fundamentally from men. Women wanted a better-ordered society and cared primarily about the "security of the home," she believed; men, on the other hand, sought power and individual distinction. In contrast to most reformers, however, Dewson placed her instincts about women's special nature at the service of a specific party. The political organization which first recognized the inherent differences between the sexes, she asserted, would benefit immeasurably. In the past, female politicians had failed to make any impact because they had aped men. The parties in turn had failed to recruit female supporters because they had not appealed to women's sexually distinctive interests. Dewson intended to correct that error by treating women as a special class and directing her attention to issues such as public welfare in which women had a specific interest.[35]

Education constituted the heart of Dewson's political strategy. "In 1932 we did not make the old-fashioned plea that our nominee was charming," she told an interviewer after the election. "Instead, we appealed to the intelligence of the country's women." Relying on what she called the "endless chain principle," Dewson urged women party members to be the "mouth to mouth, house to house interpreters of the New Deal" and its programs. Under her Reporter Plan, female party workers in each community were deputized to become expert on a New Deal program such as social security and to inform the electorate on a door-to-door basis of its importance for their lives. By 1936, 15,000 women Reporters were carrying the information they received from Washington to their local communities, ringing doorbells, explaining federal policies, and converting doubtful voters.[36]

In four years, Dewson transformed the Women's Division from a useless appendage of the Democratic party into a vital element in its continued success. When Jim Farley tried to cut the division's program in an economy move, the President enlarged it instead and gave Dewson added powers.[37] The Chief Executive's vote of confidence paid off in the 1936 election when over 60,000 female precinct workers canvassed the electorate. Local women's committees sponsored Radio Parties focusing on broadcasts by the President, and the Women's Division Rainbow Fliers—one-page pastel fact sheets on major New Deal accomplishments—constituted the principal literature distributed by the national party. Over 83 million fliers were circulated by the end of the campaign, each emphasizing how the New Deal helped the average person to save his home or to keep his family together.[38]

Through her efforts, Molly Dewson contributed significantly to the broadening of the Democratic constituency which occurred in the Roosevelt Administration. She directed her efforts not at solid party followers but at voters without a party affiliation. "There is a big group of people who are interested in issues and these are the ones that I want telling about what the New Deal is doing," she wrote. Despite Jim Farley's objections she dedicated herself to winning over intellectuals and independents. To widen the party's appeal she secured the President's approval of an Advisory Commission of New Dealers to be comprised primarily of independents, and in her own division she established special committees to deal with Negroes, educators, social workers, and writers. At a time when many party leaders still emphasized reliance on the old political machines, she helped to spearhead the New Deal's attempt to reach out beyond the established political structure and build new loyalties based on the issues.[39]

As a result of Dewson's achievement, women gained new recognition in party ranks. The 1936 Democratic convention passed a rule requiring that each delegate to the Platform Committee be accompanied by an alternate of the opposite sex, thereby ensuring fifty-fifty representation on the committee which had excluded

Eleanor Roosevelt twelve years before. A *New York Times* reporter described the new rule as "the biggest coup for women in years," and Emily Newell Blair told a nationwide radio audience that for the first time female delegates were being treated as equals with men. Each day of the convention, the Washington *Times* noted, "the party leaders have recognized in some way the ability of women, and their value to the party." Seven of eight planks desired by the Women's Division were incorporated into the party platform, and Jim Farley named eight females as vice-chairmen of the national committee in an effort to establish parity with men.[40] In addition, women's patronage increased dramatically. Dewson later claimed that she "never cared much about the machinery of politics," but she knew enough to ensure that her own workers were rewarded for their efforts. Female party members were placed in nearly every department of government, and women's share of postmasterships shot up from 17.6 per cent in 1930 to 26 per cent from 1932 to 1938.[41]

The number of females appointed to policy-making posts testified most dramatically to the Roosevelt Administration's appreciation of women's talents. For the first time, women occupied the positions of Cabinet member (Frances Perkins), minister to a foreign country (Ruth Bryan Owen Rohde and Florence Jaffrey Harriman), and judge of the U.S. Circuit Court of Appeals (Florence Allen). Ellen Woodward, Hilda Smith, and Florence Kerr held executive offices in the WPA, and Lorena Hickok acted as Harry Hopkins' eyes and ears in trips across the country to observe the progress of the New Deal's relief program. At times, Washington seemed like a perpetual convention of social workers as women from the Consumers League, the Women's Trade Union League, and other reform groups came to Washington to take on government assignments. Mary Anderson, director of the Women's Bureau, recalled that in earlier years women government officials had dined together in a small university club. "Now," she said, "there are so many of them they would need a hall."[42]

The increased political role of women during the 1930's had a number of causes, but perhaps the most important was the dynamic leadership of Eleanor Roosevelt. As First Lady, Mrs. Roosevelt exercised an influence over public policy unparalleled in the history of the White House. The President relied on her for advice on a variety of issues and trusted her political judgment implicitly. Mrs. Roosevelt was charged with coordination of the women's campaign in 1932 and was asked to supervise the entire re-election effort in 1936. As the Chief Executive's personal representative, she toured the country repeatedly, surveying conditions in the coal mines, visiting relief projects, and speaking out for the human rights of the disadvantaged. Her travels enabled her to provide information on social and political questions which might not otherwise receive the President's attention, and more than one government project owed its existence to her interest and sponsorship.[43]

Not surprisingly, Mrs. Roosevelt played an instrumental part in persuading Mary Dewson and other social welfare workers to become involved in government work. During her years in New York, she had participated actively in the endeavors of the Women's City Club and other civic organizations, and her own ability to combine public service with partisan political activity convinced doubtful female reformers that they could work within the party system without compromising their principles. Women throughout the administration looked upon her as a personal friend and as a "resident lobbyist" for their point of view. Her presence in the White House ensured that the voice of female reformers would not be ignored in government councils and that any grievances they felt would receive prompt and fair consideration at the highest level.[44]

The relevance of New Deal programs to the home and family also contributed to the increase in women's political activity. Throughout the 1920's, with the exception of the Sheppard-Towner bill and the Child Labor Amendment, politics had been dominated by issues essentially unrelated to women's primary sphere of responsibility. With the coming of the Great Depression, however, the actions of government affected every household in the land. Political decisions determined whether children would have new shoes, whether a mortgage would be foreclosed, whether a mother could feed her family. Government ceased to be extraneous to the concerns of the family but instead provided school lunches, aid to dependent children, and relief checks which helped the family to survive. Mary Dewson had devoted her entire life to such welfare measures, and with the encouragement of the President, she sought in every way possible to identify national politics with the "bread and butter" priorities of women in the home.

Nevertheless, it would be a mistake to conclude that under the Roosevelt Administration, the goals of the suffragists were suddenly realized. The women who honeycombed New Deal relief agencies came to Washington primarily because they were reformers, not because they were females. They shared a common commitment with men like Harry Hopkins, Aubrey Williams, and Harold Ickes to an issue-oriented politics and to greater federal involvement in social-welfare programs. For both male and female reformers, the New Deal represented an exciting, humane approach to the problems of government. Its appeal was based not on a distinctively "female" point of view, but on the attitude it brought to the solution of a grave national crisis. The influence which women such as Mary Dewson and Lorena Hickok acquired testified more to their long-standing participation in the social-welfare movement than to a belief that females deserved special recognition by virtue of their sex.[45]

Furthermore, the rise in women's political standing depended to a peculiar extent on their ties to the White House. Mary Dewson was the first to acknowledge the importance of her relationship with the Roosevelts. She had experienced no difficulty in getting started in politics, she recalled, "because FDR backed me." He alone among modern politicians had recognized that women had a contribution to make to politics. Dewson corresponded almost daily with Mrs. Roosevelt, and, when questions of great urgency arose, the First Lady seated her next to the President at dinner so that she could persuade him to her point of view. Women's Division requests for help went in duplicate to the White House, often to be followed up by a personal note of endorsement from the President or his wife to the appropriate government or party official.[46] Dewson succeeded in implementing her educational program because at every critical juncture the President supported her. Significantly, when she retired from active politicking in 1937, her colleagues found it more difficult to see Jim Farley, let alone enlist his support for their demands.[47]

Even with the gains which had been made, therefore, women leaders still lacked the independent power to force equal recognition with men. The critical problem remained the absence of a politically cohesive female constituency. If women voters had formed a separate bloc in the electorate, female leaders could have backed up their claims with convincing threats of reprisal at the polls. Without such a bloc, however, they lacked a base of support and were forced to rely on the help of party leaders for whatever influence they acquired. Although it was likely that the mass of women became more politically conscious during the Depression, there was no evidence that they voted together or shared a distinctive approach to government. Thus the principal assumption of the suffragists still had no basis in reality. Indeed, in some ways the New Deal confirmed the failure of suffragist predictions, because it illustrated the extent to which women's success depended on the favor of those in power.

At least in part, the disappointing results of the suffrage experience could be traced to the inflated rhetoric of female leaders. By treating the Nineteenth Amendment as a panacea, the suffragists had raised hopes which could not be realized. Almost none of the measures adopted during the Progressive era accomplished the goals envisioned by its sponsors, and the suffrage was no exception. As one journalist observed in 1936, the Nineteenth Amendment, "like the secret ballot, the corrupt practices act, the popular election of senators, and the direct primary, promised almost everything and accomplished almost nothing."[48] In effect, the suffragists had demanded too much of the ballot. Political change occurred gradually, and it was unrealistic to expect that extending the vote to women would transform the nation's political and social institutions.

The basic problem, however, was that the suffrage failed to change the special status of women in relation to the wider society. In predicting that women would act together to spearhead a drive for social change, the suffragists had correctly assumed that all females shared a common experience based on their sex. But they failed to realize that, unlike some other minority groups, women were distributed throughout the social structure and had little opportunity to develop a positive sense of collective self-consciousness. More important, they underestimated the barriers obstructing the creation of such consciousness. One of the central experiences which women shared was their relationship with men, yet nothing did more to discourage the growth of an independent female constituency. As long as women were expected to follow the lead of their husbands and fathers in activities outside the home, it was hardly likely that they could act as a separate and autonomous segment within the electorate. Occasionally an issue like the suffrage focused overriding attention on the identity of women as women and generated a heightened sense of sex solidarity. But such issues emerged only rarely, and in the normal course of events women responded to political questions in the manner dictated by the men in their lives. Females did behave alike, but the sameness of their actions represented conformity to the role of helpmate rather than an assertion of their independence as a sex. Indeed, there was something contradictory about the whole notion of a female bloc. If the similarity of women's action was rooted in their subservience to men, once liberated from that "female" role, they would act as individuals, not members of a group.

In the end, therefore, it appeared that Elizabeth Cady Stanton had more correctly assessed the importance of the ballot than her twentieth-century successors. Discrimination against women was deeply rooted in the structure of society—in the roles women played, and in a sexual division of labor which restricted females primarily to the domestic sphere of life. Whatever else it accomplished, the suffrage did not alter that structure. Female leaders understandably believed that they had won a decisive victory with the acquisition of the franchise, but they made the mistake of mislabeling the nature of their accomplishment. The Nineteenth Amendment was a reform, not a revolution.

# 2

# Women and Economic Equality

Although the political role of women attracted primary attention after enactment of the suffrage amendment, many feminists viewed women's economic activities as a more accurate measure of female freedom. The ballot provided an important opportunity to influence public policy, but by itself it did little to eliminate the sexual division of labor or to transform woman's place in the home. If the source of the "woman problem" was the existence of a totally separate sphere for females, real equality could be achieved only when women were able to participate in all areas of life on the same basis as men. Within that context, the economic experience of women in the years after 1920 became a crucial barometer of what had been gained in the fight for the vote.

Not surprisingly, suffrage leaders predicted that passage of the Nineteenth Amendment would help to establish women's emancipation in the economic as well as the political arena. In the years preceding final victory in the battle for the franchise, economic freedom appeared to be a realistic possibility. State legislatures enacted minimum-wage and factory-safety laws to protect women workers. World War I created new job opportunities for females. And Progressive reformers promised to build a world of social and economic justice. In the flush of optimism generated by wartime enthusiasm, leaders of the woman's movement were convinced that a new era of feminine equality was dawning. "Wonderful as this hour is for democracy and labor," Margaret Dreier Robins told the Women's Trade Union League in 1917, "it is the first hour in history for the women of the world. . . . At last, after centuries of disabilities and discrimination, women are coming into the labor and festival of life on equal terms with men."[1]*

The economic ventures of women in the years surrounding passage of the suffrage appeared to lend credibility to Mrs. Robins' observation. The census of 1920 revealed that over 8 million females were employed in 437 different job classifications. Women plastered walls, climbed steeples, preached in churches, trapped furs, managed offices and hauled freight. Before the new decade was a year old, a woman lawyer had defended a man accused of murder, and a group of female entrepreneurs had formed their own bank. News stories told of society matrons starting tea rooms, of universities graduating women engineers, and of female suburbanites volunteering as motorcycle police. "Even the girls who knew that they were going to be married pretended to be considering important business positions," Sinclair Lewis wrote in his 1920 novel *Main Street*.[2]

Social commentators seized on women's economic prowess as one explanation for the "revolution in manners and morals" which was sweeping the country. Although observers differed on the overall significance of the 1920's, almost all agreed that the age was one of unprecedented personal liberation. Magazines and novels portrayed the decade as a non-stop revel featuring jazz bands, risque dances, and uninhibited sex. As much as anyone else, the "new woman" symbolized the era. Cigarette in mouth and cocktail in hand, she appeared to be both shocking and unshockable. In the eyes of many, economic freedom was directly responsible for her liberation. Frederick Lewis Allen noted in 1931 that, after passage of the suffrage amendment, middle-class girls "poured out of

* The purpose of this chapter is to provide an overview of women's economic situation from 1920 to 1940. Chapters 3 and 4 offer a more detailed and analytical examination of women in industry and women in the professions.

schools and colleges into all manner of occupations." Their economic activity, he concluded, provided an indispensable condition
for the "slackening of husbandly and parental authority." Once
girls escaped the tight moral control of the home and found a job
and apartment of their own, the old verities vanished and the celebration began. A job constituted a critical stepping stone in
woman's "headlong pursuit of freedom" and comprised an integral
part of the flapper's life.[3]

With few exceptions, historians have echoed Allen's interpretation of the 1920's. Book after book has described the period as one
of unparalleled economic emancipation for women. George Mowry
has written that the feminine employment revolution "reached
flood tide" in the new decade and was a critical part of the assault
on "traditional institutions, morality and folkways." Arthur Link
has stated that "women found far larger economic opportunities
after 1920 than ever before." And most textbooks have portrayed
the new age as characterized by an unprecedented speed-up of wom-
en's involvement in the labor force. In general, the consensus has
been that women achieved a substantial amount of the economic
equality which the feminists had sought and in the process experienced a new degree of freedom from the restrictions which had formerly bound them.[4]

In part, the popular impression was justified by the statistics. In
absolute numbers, the female labor force grew 26 per cent during
the 1920's—from 8,429,707 to 10,679,048. Over 500,000 of the
new women workers held clerical or kindred positions, and another
450,000 entered the professions. Frederick Lewis Allen's proto-
typical flapper who danced all night and worked all day had a
basis in reality. By 1930 almost 2 million women were employed
as secretaries, typists, and file clerks, and another 700,000 worked
as salesgirls in department stores. Most of these women lived in
sizable cities, the vast majority were single, and some at least enjoyed the freedom and independence which Allen emphasized.
Robert and Helen Lynd noted in 1925 that the much vaunted
"new woman" had made her way to *Middletown*, and that female

employment had become a more accepted part of the city's life.[5]

By and large, however, historians have overstated the amount of economic change which occurred during the 1920's. There is no evidence that a revolution took place in women's economic role after World War I, nor can it be said that the 1920's represented a watershed in the history of women at work. In fact, the period from 1920 to 1940 witnessed very little progress toward the goal of economic equality. If the word "emancipation" is taken to mean the ability of women to function in the world outside the home on the same basis as men, then female workers remained as unemancipated in 1940 as in 1920. Aspiring career women were still limited to positions traditionally set aside for females; the overwhelming majority of American working women continued to toil at menial occupations for inadequate pay; and the drive to abolish economic discrimination enlisted little popular support. Although some changes occurred in the composition of the labor force and the distribution of jobs women performed, most female workers functioned as they always had—second-class citizens powerless to alter their inferior position.

Popular misconceptions about the 1920's can be traced in large part to the belief that World War I dramatically transformed the status of the woman worker. At the height of the fighting in France, thousands of women in Bridgeport, Connecticut, Springfield, Massachusetts, and other cities across the country swarmed into factories to take up the work of men at the front. The number of women employed in iron and steel trebled. Over 100,000 women entered munitions factories. Countless others served as streetcar conductors, elevator operators, furnace stokers, and bricklayer helpers. Female lawyers were appointed to the government's legal advisory committees, and female doctors for the first time gained access to the U.S. Public Health Service. The Women's Bureau—established in large part as a result of the war—required four pages to list all the jobs in which women substituted for men during the fighting.[6]

The wartime experience generated widespread enthusiasm

among female leaders and led many observers to declare that
women had reached a new plateau of economic equality. Alice
Hamilton, a pioneer in industrial medicine and a prominent social
reformer, recalled the "exaltation" of women workers and their
sense of "joyful release" at the chance to serve their country in
time of need. As a result of women's contribution, the writer Mary
Austin asserted, female economic emancipation had moved ahead
a hundred years. The progress made during the war reinforced the
conviction of many women's rights advocates that victory in the
suffrage fight would be accompanied by a lowering of barriers
against women in all spheres of life. "[S]ervice to their country in
this crisis," the militant feminist Harriet Stanton Blatch observed,
"may lead women to that economic freedom which will change a
political possession into a political power."[7]

The facts did not support such an optimistic interpretation, however. Contrary to popular opinion, only 5 per cent of the women
war workers joined the labor force for the first time in the war
years. The rest had transferred from lower paying jobs and were
expected to return to them when the emergency passed. Only 10
of 173 women operators on the Cleveland Street Railway, for example, had never worked before. Despite the critical need for
women in war industries, the Federal Board for Vocational Education provided training only for such traditional female occupations as dressmaking and embroidery, and it actively discouraged
women from registering at its local schools. The Women-In-Industry
Service promulgated strict regulations designed to protect women
doing war work, but the government did little to enforce the new
rules. Less than 20 per cent of the firms sampled by the Women's
Bureau instituted a forty-eight-hour work week and daily rest periods, while only 9 per cent of the women replacing male workers
in New York received the equal pay to which the War Labor
Board said they were entitled.[8]

More important, whatever positive impact the war did have was
short-lived. "The brief interlude . . . which some enthusiasts
heralded as launching a new era for women in industry," Con-

stance Green later observed, "came and went with astonishingly little permanent effect upon women's opportunities." In 1919 the Central Federated Union of New York declared that "the same patriotism which induced women to enter industry during the war should induce them to vacate their positions after the war." Male workers went on strike in Cleveland in order to force women streetcar conductors out of work, and in Detroit female conductors were dismissed despite a National War Labor Board decision in their favor. Twenty women judges in New York were forced to resign immediately after the Armistice on the grounds that their appointments were for the duration of the emergency only.[9]

The federal government itself continued to discriminate against female employees, despite its formal commitment to fair hiring practices and equal pay. A Women's Bureau study in 1919 showed that females were excluded from 60 per cent of all civil service examinations, including 64 per cent of those for scientific and professional positions. Women biologists might analyze potatoes, the government said, but not tobacco. They could study plant diseases, but not animal parasites. (The latter area dealt with breeding). The assumption that females constituted a separate category, inferior to men, pervaded both the assignment of women personnel and the salaries they were paid. Fourteen female lawyers who passed the civil service examinations for law clerk were appointed instead to clerical posts at half the salary. A Treasury official decreed that no woman in his department could earn more than $1,200 yearly; and Congress, when it established the Women's Bureau as a permanent agency, limited the salaries of its professional experts to $1,800 in contrast to the $3,000 received by individuals doing similar work in the Bureau of Labor Statistics.[10]

Contrary to the hopes of female enthusiasts, World War I produced no substantial change in what one observer called women's "nebulous, will-o'-the-wisp" status. In 1920 women's participation in the total labor force had actually declined rather than increased over 1910 (from 20.9 per cent to 20.4 per cent), and their employment in the war-related areas of manufacturing and mechanical industries had dropped from 17.1 to 15.3 per cent. Whatever gains had been made were cut short by the signing of the Armistice. Neither the labor movement nor the government was ready to accept a permanent shift in women's economic role. Called forth in crisis to fill an urgent need, women were relegated to their former position as soon as peace returned. "When the immediate dangers . . . were passed," the reformer Mary Van Kleeck wrote, "the prejudices came to life once more."[11]

In the twenty years after the passage of the Nineteenth Amendment, few changes occurred to alter women's basic economic position. Alice Hamilton noted in 1930 that the public had vastly overestimated the economic advances made by women in the war and afterward, and the evidence supported her judgment. Although slightly more than two million additional women joined the labor force during the 1920's, the proportion of women over fourteen who held jobs increased by only 1 per cent. The latter figure represented a more accurate index of economic change than the former, because it took into account the growth of the population, and measured with greater precision the actual number of women at work relative to those eligible for employment.[12] If the economic role of women had expanded significantly during the 1920's, evidence of the shift should have appeared in the proportion of women employed. The percentage remained almost constant, however, suggesting that the numerical increase in the female labor force reflected the growth rate of the population and economy rather than a radical change in women's economic activity.

In fact, the most important upsurge of female employment had occurred twenty years earlier. At that time, increased urbanization, a large influx of cheap foreign labor, and the development of new mass production industries combined to cause a dramatic increase in the female labor force. Between 1880 and 1920, the country's cities nearly doubled in population, with most of the increase coming from the flood of Eastern and Southern European immigrants who arrived on America's shores at the turn of the century. The tide of immigration coincided with the emergence of consumer industries which took over the production of food, clothing and other goods formerly manufactured in the home. In order to make a profit, the new industries needed a cheap source of labor, and they found it in the swelling ghettoes of the inner city. Most of the immigrants were poor and unskilled, and economic survival frequently hinged on putting the entire family to work, including women and children.[13] As more and more women took jobs in garment factories, canneries, and laundries, the female labor force showed the sharpest upturn of any period prior to 1940. From 1900 to 1910, the proportion of all women who held jobs jumped from 20.4 per cent to 25.2 per cent. Thereafter, it remained almost constant, falling to 23.3 per cent in 1920, rising to 24.3 per cent in 1930, and peaking at 25.7 per cent in 1940.[14] The relative size of the female labor force was thus established at a stable level a full decade before either World War I or woman suffrage, and grew by only five-tenths of 1 per cent in thirty years. If a revolution had taken place in women's work, it occurred at the beginning of the century, not after 1920.

The type of work women performed, however, did undergo substantial restructuring in the years after 1910. At the turn of the century, almost all gainfully employed females worked as domestics, farm laborers, unskilled factory operatives, and teachers. By 1940, white-collar work, and especially clerical jobs, had emerged as an important category of employment. The proportion of female workers engaged in non-manual occupations grew from 28.2 per cent in 1910 to 45 per cent in 1940, and stenography and typing moved from the eighth largest occupational category in 1910 to the third largest in 1930. Once again, however, the critical shift occurred before 1920. Almost one million women joined the clerical force during the decade beginning in 1910, and the proportion of female employees holding clerical and sales jobs jumped from 17 per cent in 1910 to 30 per cent in 1920. The figure grew only one point—to 31 per cent—during the 1920's, and was back to 30 per cent in 1940.[15]

Important changes also took place in the age and marital status

of women workers. In the 1890's the average female employee was
single and under twenty-five. She worked for six or eight years and
then married, leaving her job in the process. From 1900 to 1940,
however, the median age of the woman worker rose to over thirty,
and the proportion of females twenty-five to forty-four who were
employed grew from 18.1 per cent to 30.6 per cent. At the same
time, the number of married women seeking employment increased
substantially. In 1900 only 5.6 per cent of the nation's wives
worked. The figure jumped to 10.7 per cent by 1910 (testifying
anew to the importance of that decade), then climbed dramatically
again from 11.7 per cent in 1930 to 15.2 per cent in 1940. Married
women joined the labor force at a rate five times faster than that
of other females and comprised 35 per cent of all women employed
in 1940, in contrast to 15 per cent in 1900.[16]

Both the upsurge in clerical jobs and the shift in age and marital
status of female workers affected women's long-range economic
situation. White-collar work provided an important employment
outlet for middle- and upper-class girls who previously had been
unable to find positions consistent with their social status. The
teenage girl coming of age in the late 1920's clearly had a larger
number of vocational options than her mother had twenty years
earlier, and, relatively speaking, enjoyed a greater amount of freedom. In addition, the increase in the number of working wives established some precedent for women's employment outside the
home during World War II. In both cases, however, the important
shifts had taken place before the "flood tide" of female employment which allegedly swept the country during the 1920's. Moreover, neither change signified the emancipation of the woman
worker.

The increase in married women workers, for example, had little
if anything to do with female freedom to pursue a life outside the
home on a basis of equality with men. The greatest jump in employment among wives after 1910 occurred during the Depression,
a time when half the nation's families earned less than $1,200 an-
nually. Married women worked, not because they sought liberation

from the burdens of domesticity or enjoyed a new equality with men in the job market but so that their families could survive economically. Moreover, the jobs they filled were of the most menial sort. Thirty-six per cent of married women were employed in domestic and personal service, and another 20 per cent worked in apparel and canning factories. "None of these occupations . . . is notable for its high wages," Mary Anderson wrote Eleanor Roosevelt, "so it is correct to deduce that the married woman must be at work because her husband's wages are not enough." The poorest states—South Carolina, Mississippi, Louisiana, Georgia, and Alabama—had the highest proportion of married women working. All were concentrated in the area of the country least likely to encourage a revolution in women's status. In 1940, only 5.6 per cent of married women held jobs if their husbands earned over $3,000 a year, but 24.2 per cent were employed if their husbands received less than $400. In short, rather than illustrating female emancipation, work by wives more often testified to family poverty.[17]

Assertions of a new era of economic independence also overlooked the makeup of the female labor force and the type of positions held by the majority of women workers. As late as 1930, over 57 per cent of all employed women were either Negroes or foreign-born whites. Both groups worked primarily as domestic servants or operatives in apparel industries. Despite the large number of females who took clerical positions during the 1920's, by far the largest bloc of new workers—almost 700,000—served as domestics in the nation's homes, an increase during the decade of more than 60 per cent. Such women toiled for ten or twelve hours a day at wages which in many cities did not rise above a dollar a day. They enjoyed neither the freedom nor independence associated with the "new woman," yet their story described the economic situation of women in the years after World War I just as much as the emergence of the typist or stenographer.[18]

Significantly, even business and professional women did not benefit that much from enactment of the suffrage amendment. It was the career woman whom economic feminists had in mind during their campaign to eliminate barriers to female employment, yet the status of such women improved only slightly in the period from 1920 to 1940. The absolute number of female professionals increased at approximately the same rate as males during the twenties (approximately 40 per cent), and the proportion of women workers engaged in professional life climbed from 11.9 per cent to 14.2 per cent. But the numerical gains did not signify any expansion of opportunities or represent inroads into fields previously dominated by men. Women's portion of the total college enrollment declined from 47.3 per cent in 1920 to 43.7 per cent in 1930, and female graduates tended to concentrate in careers customarily set aside for women. Three out of four new professional women went into teaching, nursing, or other fields that were "women's" work, and very few entered fields dominated by men, or denoted as the "higher professions." The proportion of architects and lawyers who were women remained almost constant between 1910 and 1930 (less than 3 per cent); female enrollment in professional schools increased by only a small amount; and the number of women doctors declined from 9,015 to 6,825. On the basis of such facts, one economic historian concluded that "the militant feminist approach to careers as the main hope for fulfillment faded into obscurity [during the 1920's]."[19]

The coming of the Depression compounded the already tenuous status of women workers. Although the percentage of females seeking employment reached a new high as a result of the need to supplement meager family incomes, most of the jobs that women took were part-time, seasonal and marginal. The unemployment rate among women fell below that of men in 1931, but by the end of the thirties the percentage of females out of work exceeded that of males. Women experienced special difficulty in finding work which paid a living wage. In Philadelphia there were three times as many applicants as jobs in 1934, and two-thirds of the openings called for domestic servants. Over 175,000 women sought clerical positions in 1937, but only 5,300 were placed. The woman wage-earner, Senator Robert Wagner concluded, was the "first orphan in the storm."[20]

The deepening economic crisis proved especially damaging to college women interested in entering business or the professions. Teaching jobs almost disappeared from the market because of an oversupply of applicants (many of them male), and the number of teachers who were women fell from 85 per cent in 1920 to 78 per cent in 1940. The Barnard placement office reported that only one-third of the class of 1932 desiring jobs secured paid work, most of it part-time, and Smith College officials told students that there were no positions open for women with a bachelor's degree only. A graduate education became essential for a female student desiring a decent position, but even then most fields of advanced study were excluded. The Institute of Women's Professional Relations advised women students to specialize in home economics and interior decoration in order to avoid competition with men. Only by concentrating in "feminine" occupations, the Institute's director declared, could women achieve success. During the Depression, the proportion of all female workers engaged in professional occupations fell from 14.2 to 12.3 per cent, reflecting the extent to which the economic decline had curtailed the opportunities available to prospective career women.[21]

For from stimulating a revolution in women's work, then, the suffrage produced little tangible progress toward the goal of economic equality. Popular articles on the flapper conveyed the impression that women had entered a new era of economic emancipation, but the evidence did not support such an interpretation. The over-all percentage of women at work remained relatively stable, and despite some numerical gains, aspiring career women failed to break down the barriers to professions traditionally dominated by men. The major statistical shifts in the female labor force occurred at the turn of the century, and although the continued growth of clerical positions offered middle-class girls a greater opportunity to work, there was little basis, on balance, for concluding that women had substantially expanded their economic role or risen to a new level of equality with men.

Indeed, what remains most striking in retrospect is the extent to which institutionalized discrimination created a common fate for all female employees, regardless of their job or social status. Despite differences of class, education, and motivation, both career women and female industrial workers were concentrated overwhelmingly in occupations defined as "women's work." Over 40 per cent of all women in manufacturing were employed in textile mills or as apparel operatives, and more than 75 per cent of female professionals were either teachers or nurses. As a general rule, men worked with men and women with women. Furthermore, sexual segregation severely circumscribed the job opportunities open to both groups of female workers. Just as women laborers were discouraged from taking positions as streetcar conductors or steamfitters, potential career women were denied the chance to become doctors or lawyers. The 1920 American Medical Association Directory listed only 40 of 482 general hospitals which accepted women interns, and from 1925 to 1945, American medical schools placed a quota of 5 per cent on female admissions. During the 1920's, both Columbia and Harvard Law schools refused to consider women applicants, and as late as 1937 the New York City Bar Association excluded prospective female members.[22]

For both groups also, discrimination placed a ceiling on possible job advancement. Women industrial workers rarely became supervisors or forewomen, and women in the professions rarely received promotions or executive responsibility. Despite the fact that females constituted over 80 per cent of the nation's teachers, women served as superintendents of schools in only 45 of 2,853 cities. Female teachers were concentrated in the elementary grades, and their numbers declined substantially in the better-paying, more prestigious high school and college positions. Although women received approximately one-third of all graduate degrees, they comprised only 7.9 per cent of the professors in the country's colleges. The disparity prompted widespread despair among female doctoral candidates, and led women students at the University of Chicago to protest against the inequitable number of fellowships and teaching positions they received relative to men.[23]

Inadequate pay constituted the most blatant example of women's inferior economic position, and plagued female workers in every job category. A survey of 9,000 professional women in 1934 revealed that 50 per cent of all teachers, librarians, and social workers had never received a salary of $2,000, and that half the elementary school teachers were paid under $1,500. Women clerical workers in 1931 earned a median wage of $99 a month. The jobs employing the largest number of women, moreover, paid the lowest amounts. Women working in Southern mill towns in 1929 received $9.35 a week, while the average annual income of household workers in 1940 was $312.60. Throughout industry, women earned at best only 50 to 65 per cent of what men were paid, and the Social Security Administration disclosed in 1937 that women workers took home an average of $525 a year in contrast to an annual income of $1,027 for men.[24]

Most disturbing of all, women regularly received less pay than men even when they performed exactly the same work. In 1939 male teachers earned an average salary of $1,953, while females were paid $1,394; men social workers took home $1,718, women $1,442. Eighty per cent of the women college graduates surveyed by the American Association of University Women reported that they received less pay than men for comparable work. The same pattern of discrimination pervaded the lower occupational categories. A male finisher in the paper-box industry in New York earned $35.50 a week, but a female doing exactly the same work was paid only $17.83.[25]

The plight of female workers was further exacerbated by the public's general unwillingness to think of women as equal participants in the labor force. To a large extent, women's economic involvement in the years after 1900 reflected far-reaching social changes which affected the entire nation. Domestic functions such as clothesmaking and baking had been transferred out of the home and into the factory. The rise of the city meant that fewer and fewer women spent their days tending gardens or helping with farm chores. And the inadequate wages paid most industrial workers made it necessary for many wives and daughters to take jobs in order to make ends meet. A few public officials recognized the significance of such developments for women's economic role. During the debate over the creation of the Women's Bureau, one congressional supporter observed that "women, by virtue of the change in the economic conditions of this country are no longer able to remain in the home. They must go out in the field of actual activity and earn a living."[26] Most people, however, rejected the notion that women should depart from their traditional responsibility in the home. In large part, older definitions of family roles persisted, especially the "patriarchal-employer" conception of the husband. "[T]he tradition lingers," Alice Hamilton wrote in 1930, "that woman's place is in the home, and the social philosophy regarding her status has not changed as rapidly as have the various social and economic organizations." If a few public leaders understood the need to recognize women as economic equals, most shared the opinion of Congressman Joe Eagle of Texas who declared that "woman's work should be making one good man a good wife and properly rearing a family of children."[27]

Perhaps the most pernicious example of public misunderstanding was the widely held belief that females joined the labor force solely to earn extra pocket money. Even experts who should have known better gave credence to the impression. Ralph G. Hurlin, writing the authoritative report on employment for President Hoover's Committee on Recent Social Trends, asserted that many women looked for jobs "as only semi-casuals, seeking pin-money, commonly receiving subsidies" from home.[28] The pin-money hypothesis assumed that women workers were already well-supported and sought a paying job only as a means of securing extra cash to indulge frivolous feminine desires. The theory followed women workers wherever they went and, by implication, justified the inequality from which they suffered. If females were subsidized by their families, there was no compelling reason to treat them the same as men. Employers could rationalize paying women low wages on the grounds that they did not need their earnings to live on, and public officials could dismiss women workers as casual members of the labor force who had no serious grievances.

In fact, however, the pin-money argument rested on an almost total misapprehension of the reasons for female employment. Repeated studies by social workers and economists had demonstrated that women sought work primarily to help their families and support themselves. As early as 1907, sociologists investigating industrial conditions in Pittsburgh discovered that many women were forced to take jobs because their husbands in the steel mills and railroad yards received wages which were inadequate for family support. A multi-volume study by the government's Bureau of Labor arrived at essentially the same conclusion. As many as one-half of all industrial workers did not earn enough for a decent standard of living, and the family budget could be maintained only if wives and daughters also took jobs. Employers frequently claimed that women did not need high wages because they had no economic responsibilities, but the facts indicated otherwise.[29]

The most convincing refutation of the pin-money theory came from a series of investigations conducted by the Women's Bureau in the 1920's and 1930's. Approximately 90 per cent of employed females, the Bureau found, went to work because of economic need, and used their income for support of themselves and their dependents. The average family required approximately $1,500 as a minimum for decent living in the late 1920's, yet most families had an annual income of less than that. Hardest hit by poverty were the immigrant and black families from which the majority of female workers came. Far from seeking extra money for luxuries, then, the primary role of women workers was to provide incremental income so that their families could buy the food and clothing necessary for survival. "What [married women] are working at such great cost to obtain," a Women's Bureau official wrote, "is a chance for their children to have health and education, for their families to have a satisfactory home life." One out of every four employed women was the principal wage earner for her family, and as many as 95 per cent of working wives contributed all their earnings to family support. Among single women living at home, two out of three gave all their income to the household. On the basis of such facts, Mary Anderson acidly commented that "a woman's so-called pin money is often the family coupling pin, the only means of holding the family together and making ends meet."[30]

Nevertheless, government spokesmen, employers, and public opinion leaders continued to insist that women belonged in the home and that female employment could be tolerated only as a casual dalliance before marriage. Wives who worked came in for special attack. The employment of married women, Mrs. Samuel Gompers declared, took jobs and bread away from men and obstructed the proper fulfillment of women's natural role. "A home, no matter how small," she observed, "is large enough to occupy [a wife's] mind and time." Echoing the same sentiment, the Secretary of Labor warned in 1923 that the employment of mothers in industry would sooner or later result in the nation's economic system "crashing down about our heads." Women might work for a few years after high school, but they were discouraged from contemplating a full-time career. Female participants at the American Institute of Banking convention in 1923 were told that they were "merely temporary employees" in the nation's banks and businesses and that their ultimate goal should be a return to the home. Even the Women's Bureau—established to protect female workers and educate the public on women's economic role—voiced the opinion that married women's employment represented a dangerous aberration. "The welfare of the home and family is a woman-sized job in itself," the Bureau declared, and wives who worked menaced the health and happiness of the home.[31]

A profound gap thus separated the reality of women's economic situation from public discourse about it. Almost all females who sought employment were motivated by pressing economic need, yet business and political leaders persisted in dismissing them as casual seekers after pin money. Although women had supposedly achieved a new degree of freedom from conventional definitions of their place, most employers continued to treat them as marginal employees and to insist that their real responsibility was in the home. And while popular journals were full of commentary on sexual equality, female job seekers were assigned primarily to segregated positions which provided little challenge and even less possibility of advancement.

Despite the legacy of popular opinion, then, the years after 1920 did not represent a time of economic emancipation for women. Some shifts had taken place, and the woman of 1928 undoubtedly felt more freedom than her counterpart of a generation earlier. But the changes, for the most part, were of degree rather than kind. Most female workers were poorly paid, most were denied the opportunity to participate in occupations not already defined as "women's work," and most were treated as "temporary" employees, even in business and the professions. In the idealistic years surrounding World War I, it had seemed possible that women might substantially enlarge their economic sphere and achieve a new level of equality with men in the labor force. A decade later, such hopes had become illusory. Some might emphasize the changes which had occurred, but more accurate was the observation of Alice Rogers Hagar, a labor expert. "The woman," she wrote in 1929, "is nearly always the cheap or marginal worker, and . . . she is expected by the public and employer to remain one."[32]

# 3

# Women in Industry

On the night of November 23, 1909, thousands of shirtwaist makers gathered at New York's Cooper Union to protest the wages and working conditions in the city's garment industry. Some of the women earned as little as $3.50 a week. Others were forced to buy the needles and thread they used on the job, and to pay for their own electricity. In the preceding months tensions between workers and employers had worsened, and now the women had been called together by the International Ladies Garment Workers Union (ILGWU) to voice their grievances. The meeting progressed in orderly fashion, until suddenly a young Russian girl stood up and announced that she had heard enough speeches. "I am one who thinks and feels from the things they describe," she declared. "I too have worked and suffered. I am tired of talking. I move that we go on general strike." The young woman's plea electrified the crowd, and within minutes, her motion to strike received thunderous endorsement. By the next night, over 25,000 garment workers had walked off their jobs.[1]

The "Uprising of the Twenty Thousand," as the strike came to be called, attracted immediate public sympathy. Most of the strikers were women, and their struggle against sweatshop working conditions had an appeal which crossed class and economic lines. When newspapers headlined stories of police brutality on the picket lines, people from all different backgrounds rushed to the workers' defense. Prominent socialites joined in demonstrations outside garment factories; Mrs. Olive Belmont rented the Hippodrome for a giant rally addressed by leading suffragists; and women's clubs and college girls contributed substantial sums to the strike fund. Most important, the garment workers themselves displayed total dedication to the fight. "Thousands of them have come to worship the union," the *New York Times* reported. "They are not clear about what the union is, what it can do for them, and what they want it to do . . . but the idea of this vague and powerful protector . . . draws them into it."[2]

The garment strike demonstrated the potential of labor organization among women. Although the employers refused to recognize the closed shop, most of them instituted a fifty-two-hour week, limited the use of overtime, and took steps to spread work out over the slack season. The ILGWU grew from a small union of a few hundred before the strike to a mass organization of over 100,000 after. A few years later, the Amalgamated Clothing Workers (ACW) scored a similar success in the men's apparel industry. Like the ILGWU, the ACW championed the principle of organizing workers on an industrial rather than a craft basis, and it quickly gained dominance over its rival, the United Garment Workers, which had consistently ignored the interests of the rank and file. As a result of the success of both unions, almost half the female workers in the clothing trades had been organized by 1920. The ILGWU represented 65,000, the ACW 66,000.[3]

If the precedent set by the garment unions had extended to other industries, much of the poor treatment experienced by female workers might have been alleviated. In many ways, the labor movement held the key to the condition of women in industry. Both male and female workers were underpaid, overworked, and exploited, but, in addition to the problems which beset men, women suffered from the heavy burden of discrimination based on sex. They were assigned to the least skilled jobs, given the fewest possibilities for advancement, and treated as the most expendable members of the work force.

Even more than men, they lacked the strength to combat the methods of unscrupulous employers, and needed a "powerful protector" to guarantee their rights.

As it was, however, almost all women outside the garment industry lacked union representation. In 1924, the Women's Bureau surveyed eighty-two unions with jurisdiction over 3 million women workers and found that barely 140,000 had been organized. Five years later, the Women's Trade Union League (WTUL) upped the estimate to 250,000 out of 4 million, but the change did not signify any radical improvement. Of 471,000 female textile workers, only 20,000 belonged to unions in 1927. Seventy-two thousand women were employed in iron and steel, but only 105 were organized. Overall the labor movement had reached 1 of every 9 male workers, but only 1 of every 34 females. Half of all women union members came from the garment industry, indicating the extent to which females in other industries were unorganized and unprotected.[4]

To some extent, the low degree of female participation in the labor movement reflected the type of work females performed. Most women in industry were clustered in low-paying, unskilled jobs in candy factories, textile mills, apparel centers, and commercial laundries. The seasonal nature of their occupations caused them to change jobs repeatedly, preventing the development of a stable, cohesive work force which a union activist could organize effectively. In addition, the labor movement had historically concentrated its efforts among skilled workers. The majority of its members came from the mining, construction, and transportation industries—areas with few female employees. Since women workers were grouped in occupations which fell outside the mainstream of organized labor's concern, they were largely ignored.[5]

Equally important, many people believed that women were mere transients in the labor force, and that they had no serious commitment to collective organization. Theresa Wolfson observed in 1929 that there was a "mental attitude of impermanency among women workers." Rapid job turnover reinforced the theory that females sought employment for pin money only, and that they had no sense of lasting group consciousness. Women industrial workers could be divided into two categories, Alice Hamilton noted in 1924: the young who were "reckless of health . . . and individualistic," and the old who were tired from carrying a double burden of housework and factory work. Neither group had the interest or the time for union activity.[6]

Fundamentally, however, women failed to join the trade union movement because they were not invited until the late 1930's. Although labor claimed with some justification that women were hard to organize, the example of the garment workers suggested that where an opportunity for collective action presented itself, many women responded with enthusiasm. If unions had tried seriously to organize women workers, their protestations about female indifference might have carried more credibility. With the exception of the garment industry, however, there was little evidence that such an effort had been made. The American Federation of Labor treated women workers with open hostility. And the Women's Trade Union League—the group which others looked to for leadership—proved inadequate to the task.

The WTUL was established in 1903 by a coalition of settlement house workers and labor officials "to assist in the organization of women workers into Trade Unions." Its seriousness of purpose was attested to by the background of its founders. Mary Kenny, a former bindery worker, had organized the women of Boston into a "Ladies Federal Union." Leonora O'Reilly, a shirt-collar worker from New York, had gone back to school to finish her education so that she could devote her life to the labor movement. The women from the settlement houses had an equally distinguished history of affiliation with trade unions. At Hull House, Alice Hamilton recalled, "one got into the labor movement as a matter of course." Mary McDowell of the University of Chicago Settlement helped to form the first women's union in the meatpacking industry, and settlement houses in other cities provided meeting space and moral encouragement for budding labor groups. It was natural, therefore, for social reformers to join trade union women in spearheading a drive to help women "secure conditions necessary for healthful and efficient work and to obtain a just return for such work."[7]

In the first few years of its existence, the League gave some evidence of fulfilling its purpose as a labor organization. Although many of its members were involved with middle-class reform groups such as the Consumers League, the WTUL consciously sought to follow the lead of working women themselves, and explicitly stated in its constitution that trade unionists should compose a majority of the executive board. Mary Dreier of the New York League observed in 1909 that, while passing laws was necessary, organizing women into unions was more important, "for we know that the greatest power to enforce labor laws is trade unions, and a strong trade union can demand better conditions and shorter hours than the law will allow." Pursuing such a philosophy, the League played a major role in the shirtwaist makers' strikes of 1909-10. League leaders recruited women for the union, organized a parade of ten thousand workers to protest the arrest of peaceful picketers, and mobilized hundreds of volunteers to demonstrate outside the garment factories. Almost singlehandedly, Mary Dreier coordinated strike activities, and the WTUL's assistance was as important as any other factor in the ILGWU's victory.[8]

By 1913, however, the League had shifted its emphasis away from organization and toward education and legislation. To some extent, the change in strategy represented a pragmatic response to events. The Triangle Shirtwaist fire of 1910 had demonstrated the need for a radical improvement in factory conditions, and it became increasingly obvious that only statewide legislation could mandate the sweeping reforms which were essential. Consequently, the League devoted more and more of its energies to building public support for stringent new health and safety laws. In addition, local League chapters encountered growing difficulty in their relations with established unions. The New York WTUL expected to exercise a dominant voice in the internal affairs of the labor movement as a result of its contribution to the garment workers' victory, but many unions interpreted the League's intentions as interference, as an attempt to impose direction from outside. The issue came to a head when the White Goods Workers of New York called a strike without consulting the WTUL's leadership. The walk-out caused consternation among League members, and although it ended successfully, League leaders began to reassess the value of working directly with unions, and to place more emphasis on legislative reform instead.[9]

Basically, however, the shift in emphasis reflected a redistribution of power within the WTUL itself. From the very beginning the League had tried to serve two constituencies—reformers and unionists—each of which had had its own conception of how the League should pursue its goals. Reformers viewed the WTUL's primary function as educational, and believed that the interests of the workers could best be served by investigating industrial conditions, securing legislative action, and building public support for the principle of trade unionism. Female unionists, on the other hand, insisted that organizing women and strengthening existing unions represented the League's principal purpose. One group perceived the WTUL as primarily an instrument of social uplift, the other as an agency for labor organization.

The division of opinion was demonstrated most clearly over the issue of who should belong to the League. Reformers encouraged rich "allies" or "sympathizers" to become members, and provide financial support for League activities. The "allies" were urged to exhibit "great patience, lofty faith, and unalterable humility," and to remember that "the girls . . . must ever be the movement," but their participation inevitably created tension. Female unionists looked with distaste on the presence of so many prominent socialites and feared that their influence would compromise the WTUL's integrity. Leonora O'Reilly temporarily resigned in 1905 because she doubted the League's commitment to organize women workers, and four years later, her fellow unionist Josephine Casey left for the same reason. Although the League provided courageous leadership during the garment strikes, its members were not required to subscribe to the principle of a union shop, and many chapters were dominated by "allies" who at times seemed more interested in sponsoring "Union Balls" and teas than in organizing women factory workers.[10]

The conflict between unionists and reformers was held in check in the years before the garment strikes, but in the years afterward the reformers gradually gained the upper hand. Because of their wealth and influence, "allies" exercised considerable control over the League's fate, and many of them preferred the process of legislative change to worker organization. The New York League set the trend for the national WTUL when it established a legislative committee in 1913, and thereafter other chapters as well began to focus primarily on publicity and lobbying activities. The change in emphasis was not without controversy, and a strong minority continued to insist that unionization of women represented the League's primary responsibility. But a shift in philosophical orientation had occurred, and with the passage of time, the WTUL became more and more a social welfare group rather than a labor organization. It retained its basic goal of improving the economic condition of women workers, but its methods increasingly reflected the attitude of reformers rather than trade unionists.[11]

The League's national president, Margaret Dreier Robins, personified the reform approach. Endowed with a warm personality and a considerable fortune, she actively espoused progressive causes. After marrying the popular lecturer, Raymond Robins, she went to live in a Chicago tenement to share the life of those she sought to help. Passionately concerned with social justice, Mrs. Robins protested against the persecution of radicals and anarchists and lent her name and prestige to innumerable reform crusades. During the Chicago garment strikes, she organized a commissary for hungry workers, appointed a platoon of distinguished women to oversee the conduct of city police, and formed a respected citizens committee which condemned sweatshop conditions and urged unionization of the workers. She financed a large share of the League's activities and more than any other person shaped its policies in the years after 1910.[12]

Robin's social philosophy centered on uplift of the individual. The primary value of the trade union movement, she believed, was that it called forth "personality." "The social gains of the union shop are not generally better wages and shorter hours," she declared. "Beyond these is the incentive for initiative and social leadership. . . . The union shop calls up the moral and reasoning faculties, the sense of fellowship." Robins' primary concern was to impart the vision of a better life to the working girl. In that task, education in the arts and humanities played an important part. Poetry reading, concerts, and classes in literature filled the extracurricular programs sponsored by local chapters. "The League believed that the first need of these girls was the awakening of their imagination and sense of beauty," Robins noted in 1920. "The dullness and monotony of factory life had starved them of the very essentials of a young girl's life."[13]

Under Mrs. Robins' leadership, the League often functioned more as a vehicle for redeeming the lives of individual working women than as a force for organizing them into industrial battalions. Robins concentrated on diverting the workers' interests away from the humdrum concerns of industry and toward cultural development. Her approach was maternalistic. She treated the young workers like daughters and sought to improve their minds through education and their social lives through fellowship. Like so many progressives, she placed great faith in spiritual inspiration and voluntarism. During the Depression she opposed Franklin Roosevelt's New Deal because it gave away money and sought to control the economy. What the country really needed in the crisis, she wrote, was a leader like Teddy Roosevelt to call forth the finer spirit of the people and the revival of voluntary self-help projects such as those conducted by the Junior League.[14]

In her own way, Mrs. Robins made a distinct contribution to the League's growth and prestige. Her connections gave the organization access to the highest levels of government and some of the wealthiest individuals in the country. Moreover, her capacity for leadership made the WTUL one of the most influential members of the Progressive coalition. During the garment strikes in Chicago, she brilliantly used her social position to build a broad base of support for the workers, and her contacts with other liberal reformers ensured that the League's voice would be listened to with respect on most social-welfare issues. Nevertheless, her basic approach was that of a missionary, rather than an organizer. She dedicated herself to helping the downtrodden but lacked the background and temperament which would have enabled her to treat the workers as equals and mobilize them into an effective industrial force. Ironically, the very qualities which made her a successful reform leader prevented her from transforming the League into a true labor organization.

The tug of war between union members and reformers persisted throughout the League's history, seriously impeding the group's effectiveness. The WTUL established a trade union school in 1914 to teach a half-dozen workers each year the lessons of English, economics, and parliamentary law, but its principal emphasis was on educational uplift rather than union organization. The remainder of the budget was used up on administrative expenses, legislative activities, and the publication of a journal entitled *Life and Labor* which concentrated on investigating industrial conditions. When financial retrenchment became necessary, field work was the first to suffer. Trade unionists continued to protest the League's sense of priorities, and one troubled member commented with dismay on the absence of a clear commitment to work directly with women in industry. "The purpose of the League as I understand it is to organize workers into trade union groups," she reported in 1921, "and yet at the convention little time was given to this question."[15]

Such observations caused League leaders to engage in frequent self-examination. Their crisis of identity reached a peak in 1925 when the treasurer, concerned with falling revenues, insisted that the League define once and for all its reason for existence. Contributions from friendly unions, she pointed out, had declined from 10 per cent of the total budget in 1920 to 3 per cent in 1925. Over 90 per cent of total revenues came from "allies," many of whom "would not find favor in trade union ranks." Furthermore, the greater the League's dependence on "sympathizers," the less time it spent on organizing unions. Executive Secretary Elizabeth Christman agreed that the time had come for the League to reassess its status. She pointed out to board members that only two chapters out of twelve employed organizers, that only three had budgets, and that League membership had fallen to an appallingly low figure. "It would be illuminating to know," Christman concluded, "how great a contribution to the labor movement is represented in the above summary."[16]

As it had so often in the past, the executive board responded by reaffirming that organization constituted "the heart" of its work. To implement its resolve, the League mounted an ambitious campaign to unionize Southern textile workers, dispatching its only organizer, Matilda Lindsay, to Richmond to set up a regional office. The League had taken on a difficult task, and Lindsay did surprisingly well, especially in the textile uprisings which took place in Marion and Danville, North Carolina, in 1929 and 1930. Once again, however, the League could not escape the inevitable proclivity of its leadership for education. The principal thrust of the Southern drive was devoted to "interpreting . . . the aims of the League," and to securing the "cooperation of understanding people who themselves are not in the tobacco and textile mills." Such efforts were undoubtedly helpful in developing a sympathetic climate of opinion among community leaders, but "finding friends among the thinkers of the South" was not the same thing as organizing workers within the mills.[17]

Despite a divided conscience, therefore, the League remained most concerned with converting the world outside the factory to its point of view. Although it performed yeoman service as an agent of unionism during the garment strikes of 1909 and 1910, its primary focus was on educating the public about the condition of women workers and developing support for legislative reform. In the latter task it was frequently an effective force for social welfare innovations, and it would be a mistake to underestimate the

League's importance as a Progressive organization. By the criterion of its original purpose, however, the WTUL's record was one of disappointment. By the 1930's, the League's budget had fallen below $10,000, and its last full-time field representative had resigned. A skeletal staff remained in Washington until 1950, but in substance the League was dead. The one national group dedicated in theory to unionizing women workers, it expired without having approached its goal. Part of the problem was the obvious difficulty of organizing unskilled workers. But in a deeper sense, the League contributed to its own failure. Torn between two different points of view, it never made the lasting commitment to unionism which was a prerequisite for even the chance of success.[18]

In large part because of the League's ambivalence toward organization, the American Federation of Labor treated it with distrust from the beginning. Samuel Gompers, president of the AF of L, told a 1905 League convention that the unionization of women "is not a work of charity. . . . It is instituted so that the girls and the women may be placed in a position where they may be helped to help themselves."[19] Gompers had little use for intellectual reformers who were primarily concerned with uplifting the poor and examining workers "under the lenses of a microscope." Although he provided verbal support and financial aid to the WTUL, he clearly had reservations about its credentials as a full-fledged labor organization. WTUL representatives were barred from the AF of L's 1905 convention, because Gompers claimed that the fate of the entire working class was involved and that his members would resent the presence of outsiders. Reflecting the same suspicion of the League's motivation, the Carpenter's Union insisted that its 1915 contribution of $500 be spent only on work approved by the AF of L. When League leaders protested, the Carpenter's chief charged them with disloyalty to the labor movement and indifference toward the organization of women workers.[20]

Yet the AF of L itself did almost nothing to unionize women. Despite repeated requests, Gompers failed to hire a full-time woman organizer until 1918. The Federation leadership, in the eyes of one observer, "was guided solely by St. Paul in its policy toward even skilled women." Like the author of the letters to the early church, AF of L leaders seemed to believe that women should be obedient and not compete with men. Both Gompers and his successor William Green attacked the presence of married women in the work force and asserted that females should direct their energies toward getting married and raising a family. The AF of L refused to support a strike by female telephone operators in Boston, and the International Moulders Union resolved at its twenty-fifth convention to restrict the employment of women in all foundries, with the ultimate goal of ending work by women in any job "recognized as men's employment." The problem with most union leaders, Katherine Fisher observed in 1921, was that too many of them believed in "men's right to dictatorship over women."[21]

To some extent, the AF of L's indifference to women workers represented a calculated decision that the benefits to be gained from an organizing campaign did not justify the expense and effort involved. Even during the garment strikes, Gompers had questioned whether "poor undernourished, stunted, weak girls could maintain sufficient cohesiveness and force and determination" to form a permanent union. If females were transients in the labor force, there was little sense in organizing them one day, only to see them replaced by new workers the next. Furthermore, the labor movement had only limited resources, and in many ways the strengthening of existing craft unions constituted the best investment it could make, especially given the conviction of union leaders that women could be helped most if their husbands earned enough to support the entire family. The decade of the 1920's witnessed a concerted campaign by employers to roll back the gains of organized labor. The ILGWU's membership fell from 120,000 to 40,-000, and other unions suffered similar reverses. In a time of peril for labor, there was some basis for fighting to safeguard unions already in existence rather than embarking on an expensive and risky new campaign to organize women.[22]

Too often, however, the AF of L's actions seemed to be motivated by hidebound conservatism rather than intelligent judgment. Even when women workers organized themselves, they were denied recognition. In New York, when female printers who worked side by side with men applied for membership in the International Typographical Union, they were turned down on the ground that they were unskilled. Candy workers in Philadelphia, hairdressers in Seattle, and streetcar conductors in Cleveland all received a similar response. Females could not stay together, the unions said; consequently, they could not be admitted to membership. The result, Philadelphia candy workers charged, was that the AF of L was responsible for "allowing an organization already formed to go to pieces by refusing to give the guidance . . . necessary."[23]

The AF of L's attitude toward women was disclosed most revealingly in 1921 when the WTUL petitioned its executive council to issue federal charters permitting women to organize in sexually segregated unions. The same device had partially mitigated the problem of discrimination against Negroes, and the WTUL proposed it as an acceptable, if not desirable, alternative to membership in the established internationals. Once again, however, the AF of L refused to cooperate, arguing that it could not issue charters unless authorized to do so by its constituent craft unions. Responding to the WTUL's request, the vice-president of the Street Railway Union declared that "the rear end of a street car is [no] place for a woman." On the basis of such reasoning, the AF of L rejected the WTUL's petition. When the women accused the executive council of prejudice, Gompers replied that the AF of L discriminated against "any non-assimilable race," leaving the unmistakable impression that women might never be fully integrated into the labor movement. A vicious circle was thus created. Most of the internationals which asserted jurisdiction over women in male-dominated industries refused to admit females. The AF of L executive council, in turn, rebuffed women's attempt to establish sexually segregated locals. The result was that even in those areas of industry where women had contact with organized labor, they were denied the support necessary to protect themselves through union representation.[24]

In such a situation, cooperation between the AF of L and the WTUL represented the only opportunity for progress. For a brief period after the Supreme Court invalidated minimum wages for women in the 1923 *Adkins* case, the AF of L revived interest in unionizing female workers. The Court's action raised the spectre of women undercutting men in competition for jobs, and the AF of L convention recommended in 1924 that "especial attention be devoted during the coming year to the complete organization of women wage earners . . . not only for their own protection but for the protection of men." Gompers spoke of creating a special women's bureau within the AF of L and corresponded with Mary Anderson and Elizabeth Christman about the possibility of a joint venture.[25]

Organizational jealously doomed the effort before it got started, however. Margaret Dreier Robins viewed the Gompers proposal as a direct threat to the continued existence of the WTUL and refused to contemplate the demise of her own group until the AF of L proved that it was really committed to helping women workers. The AF of L, on the other hand, charged that the WTUL was a largely academic group which had repeatedly shown itself inadequate to the task of unionization. The only course which might have resolved the conflict—choosing a WTUL person to head the new AF of L bureau—was rejected out of hand by leading elements within the AF of L, who alternately protested the employment of a WTUL staff member and claimed that they could not find another woman capable of handling the job. Thus the tentative effort to build a new coalition collapsed. The AF of L campaign to unionize women was so "puny and half-hearted," one observer noted, "that practically nothing was accomplished."[26]

In the absence of labor interest in recruiting women, government action offered the best hope for safeguarding female industrial workers. Many middle-class reformers felt more at home with legislative protection than with trade unionism in any event, and during the years after 1890 they pressed vigorously for state regulation of wages and hours as a solution for women's economic plight. The movement to limit hours received official sanction

when the Supreme Court ruled in 1908 that preservation of a
woman's health fell within the proper police powers of the state.
Using the Court's decision in the *Muller* case as a springboard, reform groups such as the Consumers League embarked on a nationwide crusade to place a floor under women's wages as well as a
ceiling over their hours. A pay scale sufficient for the necessities of
life, the Consumers League argued, was just as essential to a woman's health and morals as reasonable hours of labor. Responding
to the League's appeal, Massachusetts enacted the first minimum-
wage law in 1912, and was followed in the next eleven years by
fourteen other states.[27]

The Supreme Court, however, dashed reform hopes that protective legislation might sweep the nation. In the 1923 *Adkins* case a
conservative majority led by Justice George Sutherland declared
that Washington D.C.'s minimum-wage law was unconstitutional,
because it violated a woman's freedom to bargain directly with her
employer for the value of her services. Although females had previously been exempted from the freedom of contract doctrine on
the grounds that they deserved special protection, Justice Sutherland ruled that the Nineteenth Amendment obviated the need for
such statutes by establishing the equality of the sexes. The judge's
reasoning seemed specious at best, given the de facto inequality
from which women suffered, but it placed an effective constitutional barrier in the way of enacting additional laws which singled
out females for special consideration.[28]

The *Adkins* decision thoroughly demoralized reform groups because it removed the principal grounds on which they had sought
legislative help. In the wake of the judicial action, minimum-wage
statutes were struck down in Arizona, Arkansas, Kansas, and Wisconsin, while in other states similar laws fell into disuse due to fear
of legal challenge by employers. The Court, Florence Kelley declared, had taken "progress backward," and written a "new Dred
Scott decision" which guaranteed the "inalienable right of women
to starve." Without judicial sanction, there seemed little chance
that women could secure the protection they needed through la-

bor laws. "Under the present Constitution, interpreted by the present Court," Kelley concluded, "all effort to improve industrial conditions . . . is purely academic." Only a new philosophy on the Court, and a substantial shift in circumstances could improve the legislative prospects for women workers.[29]

The New Deal and the Depression helped to bring about both conditions. In an effort to mitigate the suffering caused by unemployment and hard times, the government was forced to take ameliorative action, regardless of the Supreme Court's attitude toward social-welfare legislation. Prompted by reports of women receiving starvation wages and sleeping on subways, public officials started a new campaign to safeguard female workers from exploitation. Seven state legislatures enacted minimum-wage laws in the early 1930's; governors throughout the Northeast banded together to regulate women's working conditions; and the Roosevelt Administration established the National Recovery Administration (NRA) with authority to institute industry-wide codes regulating wages and hours. Perhaps the most important step forward was the enactment of the federal Fair Labor Standards Act (FLSA) of 1938. The statute established the unprecedented principle that the federal government had the right to control the wages and hours of both men and women engaged in occupations related to interstate commerce. Although the act contained excessive compromises—permitting a differential in wages between the North and South and setting an initial minimum wage of only twenty-five cents an hour for a forty-four-hour week—it inaugurated a potentially revolutionary course of government intervention in the economy.[30]

For a brief period, the Supreme Court continued to block the implementation of such laws. Within one eighteen-month span in 1935-36, it struck down the NRA, a federal law regulating the pay of miners, and New York's statute setting a minimum wage for women. The Court abruptly reversed itself, however, when public outrage and the decisive re-election of President Roosevelt indicated that popular opinion was running in a different direction. A few weeks after the Chief Executive announced his plan to enlarge the Supreme Court, the judges overruled their own decision in the *Adkins* case and upheld a minimum-wage law which duplicated in almost every respect the New York measure they had invalidated nine months earlier. The Court followed its action in the *West Coast Hotel v. Parrish* case with a series of positive rulings on other New Deal measures, and in 1941 upheld the constitutionality of the Fair Labor Standards Act in the case of *U.S. v. Darby*.[31] Although Florence Kelley did not live to see the day, her hope for a judicial and constitutional revolution had been realized.

The minimum wage laws passed during the 1930's substantially improved the situation of women workers on the lowest rung of the economic ladder. In May 1933, 84 per cent of the female laundry workers in New York City earned less than thirty-one cents an hour. Eighteen months later, after passage of the New York minimum-wage statute, the figure had dropped to 1.4 per cent. The National Industrial Recovery Act had a similar effect. In the textile industry, where women comprised 39 per cent of the work force, average weekly earnings increased from $10.85 in 1932 to $13.06 in 1935. Forty per cent of the women laundry workers in Connecticut were paid less than twenty-five cents an hour in 1932, but two years later the proportion had declined to 1.3 per cent. The Fair Labor Standards Act resulted in an increase of wages for one out of every four workers in the needle trades (166,000) and for 120,000 textile workers. In addition, New Deal legislation helped to eradicate some of the worst abuses of the sweatshop system. The NRA prohibited homework in most industries—employment which paid as little as five to eight cents an hour—and the FLSA decreed that persons who did perform such work must receive the same minimum wage as those employed in the factory.[32]

The most important contribution of the New Deal, however, was its support of legislation protecting the right of unions to organize free of employer interference. Section 7(a) of the NIRA asserted that the workers of any industry had the right to choose their own collective bargaining agent, and when 7(a) was invalidated with the NIRA, the Wagner Act took its place, providing additional administrative machinery to ensure that unionists would not be discriminated against. Both laws offered a much needed incentive to organized labor, and unions which had been on the defensive throughout the 1920's embarked on vigorous organizing campaigns. The ILGWU—down to 40,000 members in 1933—used 7(a) as a basis for reasserting its control over the ladies' garment industry. The union sent out organizers immediately after passage of the NIRA to consolidate its strength before industry codes were adopted, and a timely strike by dressmakers resulted in a growth in membership of the New York Joint Dress Board from 10,000 to 70,000 in two weeks. Under the NIRA, 95 per cent of the workers in the cloak and silk-dress industry were unionized, and the ILGWU's rank and file grew to 200,000 in two years—an increase of 500 per cent.[33]

The formation of the Congress of Industrial Organizations (CIO) marked the most dramatic advance for women in trade unionism. Even under the protective aegis of the New Deal, the AF of L had refused to commit itself to organize unskilled workers on an industrial basis, and had defended the right of craft unions to restrict their memberships. The CIO, however, set out to recruit workers without regard to skill, or sex, and in the years after 1935 engaged in a militant effort to organize the rank and file of the automobile, electrical and textile industries, all of which contained a substantial proportion of female employees. Not all the campaigns met with immediate success, but the CIO's commitment to a policy of industrial unionism meant that for the first time women workers interested in collective representation had a powerful ally within the labor movement.

The history of the textile workers—almost 40 per cent of whom were women—illustrated the transformation accomplished by the creation of the CIO. The United Textile Workers had built a union of 110,000 members by 1920, largely as a result of gains made during World War I. In the next decade, however, the UTW crumbled. A series of disastrous strikes decimated its ranks, and the number of workers in the cotton mills who were organized fell from 80,000 in 1920 to 13,000 in 1930. In part, the collapse reflected the absence of AF of L financial assistance at critical junctures. More important, however, were the union's own reactionary policies. Repeatedly, the UTW used unskilled and foreign-born workers to march on its picket lines, only to refuse them membership in the union lest the skilled craftsmen be outnumbered. Like the garment workers, the women showed themselves willing to risk their jobs for the labor movement, but their devotion was not reciprocated. The UTW's leadership settled disputes without consulting the rank and file, and even went so far as to break strikes called by other labor organizations seeking to help the unskilled workers. Although the UTW enjoyed a brief revival under the NIRA, it suffered a grievous setback in the 1934 textile strike, and by 1935 its membership had fallen from a high of over 200,000 in 1933 to 20,000. Overall, the UTW represented the worst of the AF of L's approach to mass production employees.[34]

The CIO immediately reversed the union's policy of ignoring women and unskilled workers. Through what amounted to a coup d'état, CIO leaders forced the UTW to accept the direction of an ad hoc Textile Workers Organizing Committee, analogous to a similar committee formed to mobilize the steelworkers. The TWOC spearheaded a comprehensive drive to organize unskilled workers in textile mills throughout the country. Led by men like Sidney Hillman of the Amalgamated Clothing Workers, and funded by a substantial war chest, the TWOC developed strong, entrenched locals throughout the South. Women who once walked picket lines only to be ignored by union chieftains now proudly wore the button of the Textile Workers Union of America (TWUA). Because the union demonstrated its staying power and represented the collective commitment of a nationwide organization, the TWUA earned the trust of the workers and succeeded in multiplying the number of union members in the cotton mills from 20,000 in 1936 to 120,000 in 1943.[35]

As a result of the revival of protective legislation and the development of the CIO, prospects for easing the plight of women in industry had clearly been enhanced. Any woman in a job related to interstate commerce could look to the federal government for help in the fight against exploitation, and persons employed in mass-production industries could anticipate the possibility of additional protection through union representation. The courts no longer posed an obstacle to social-welfare measures, and the Roosevelt Administration was more committed than any of its predecessors to providing some help for those least able to help themselves.

Even if some progress had been made, however, women continued to experience a substantial amount of discrimination based on sex. Under the NIRA, for example, one out of every four industry codes permitted women to receive a lower minimum wage than men, and the businesses affected were precisely those which employed the largest percentage of female workers. In the cloak and suit industry, women were assigned a basic wage ten cents an hour lower than men. The same discrepancy appeared in the electrical industry, where 40 per cent of all workers were females. Women who were employed in laundries were permitted to earn as little as fourteen cents an hour, while waitresses in some areas received only twelve cents. Despite the benefits of government protection, female workers gained at a lesser rate than males, and suffered from a persistent pattern of discrimination.[36]

Furthermore, protective legislation by itself did not necessarily ensure an across-the-board improvement in women's economic condition. In both California and New York—the nation's leading industrial states—poor enforcement weakened the positive impact of minimum-wage orders. Observing that the New York law covered only 80,000 of the 1,080,000 women it was designed to affect, Elinore Herrick of the Consumers League suggested that the government might better devote its energies to implementing statutes already on the books rather than enact additional protective laws. Even where minimum-wage laws were enforced, moreover, they frequently mandated pay scales which fell below the level needed to purchase basic necessities. In 1933, New York ruled that a laundry worker must receive $12.41 a week, yet the city's Welfare Council set $16 as the minimum essential for a decent standard of living. The FLSA established a minimum wage of 25 cents an hour for a forty-four-hour week as its original standard, but an $11 weekly pay check was barely enough to survive on in most areas of the country. Thus while wage and hour statutes helped to eliminate the worst instances of industrial exploitation, they did not provide a solution to the problem of low wages, or lead to an end of economic deprivation.[37]

Most important, inequality still pervaded the ranks of organized labor, even in those unions which were most progressive. Although the membership of the Amalgamated Clothing Workers was divided almost equally between men and women, the union sanctioned lower wages for females than for males, and granted women only token recognition in its hierarchy of officers. In the ILGWU, where three out of every four members were women, only one female served on the twenty-four-person executive board as late as 1940.[38] A total of 800,000 women had been organized by the end of the 1930's—a 300 per cent increase over ten years earlier—but in many industries female union members were grouped in sexually segregated locals. Labor contracts frequently included provisions for unequal pay between men and women, and females were assigned to separate seniority lists so that they could not interfere with the accumulated privileges of male workers. Inside as well as outside the union movement, women were still thought of primarily as transients in the labor force. They might be given protection, but they did not receive the same treatment or consideration as men.[39]

The condition of women workers in 1940 thus contained elements which justified both pessimism and optimism. On the one hand, the legislative innovations of the New Deal provided minimum standards of wages and hours for those engaged in interstate commerce. If a cotton garment worker still received only $11 a week under the Fair Labor Standards Act, she at least knew that her wage would not fall below that level and that the federal government was her ally in fighting the abuses of sweatshop labor. Equally important, the philosophy of trade unionism had changed, and for the first time a national labor organization was committed to providing collective protection for people performing unskilled work in mass production industries. The number of women actually enrolled in unions had increased, and the dynamic effectiveness of the CIO had only just begun to make itself felt.

On balance, however, persistent economic deprivation remained the most striking characteristic of women workers. As late as 1939, twenty-one states still had no minimum-wage laws for women, twenty-nine failed to regulate industrial homework, and thirty were without eight-hour statutes. Even where protective legislation did exist, it affected primarily those who were at the bottom of the economic ladder, and did not signify an improvement for all female workers. Despite some inroads, a relatively small percentage of women were unionized, and the CIO registered its greatest impact after 1940, not before. At the close of the decade, women workers, for the most part, remained an oppressed group. The overwhelming majority still earned barely a living wage, and most were concentrated in "marginal" areas of the economy where turnover was frequent. If there were some signs that the future might be better than the past, it was still too early to be optimistic.

To some extent, the absence of greater progress could be attributed to historical conditions which blocked efforts at improvement. The type of work females performed, for example, loomed large as one explanation for the relative paucity of women in the labor movement. With neither skills nor job security, women in industry were difficult to organize, and labor leaders were reluctant to undertake the task. Similarly, attempts to enact protective legislation were frustrated for a long period by the reactionary rulings of the Court. The judicial philosophy which prevailed from 1923 to 1937 had roots not directly related to the issue of women's economic condition, but female workers were among the foremost victims of the Court's laissez-faire policy. At least in part, then, the ill-treatment accorded women in industry was an almost inevitable by-product of circumstances beyond the control of workers or unions.

Such an explanation fails to answer the deeper problems posed by the experience of female industrial workers, however. The garment strikes and repeated walk-outs of textile workers had amply demonstrated that many women wanted to be organized and were willing to do their part. Similarly, the WTUL's success in unionizing activities before 1913 suggested that under different leadership a policy more conducive to the organization of female workers might have been followed. Finally, the AF of L had exhibited an unnecessarily hostile approach toward the unionization of women. Even given the problems facing the labor movement, AF of L leaders frequently displayed an attitude toward women workers which was myopic at best, and prejudiced at worst.

It is at least conceivable, then, that a different set of responses by the trade union movement and others might have substantially altered the fate of women workers. The objective barriers to progress were substantial, and it would be wrong to view discrimination as the only reason for the condition of women in industry. But in assessing the experience of female workers in these years, it is difficult not to conclude that their condition was rooted in an unspoken assumption—that women, as women, were less deserving of good jobs, decent pay, and fair representation than men. Until that reality changed, there was little likelihood that the basic status of women workers would improve.

# 4

# Women in Professions

Although women in industry were important, the feminists centered their hopes for economic equality on the young college women who came of age during the last years of the suffrage fight. The daughters of the poor had always worked outside the home, usually for reasons of economic necessity. Middle- and upper-class women, however, had customarily refrained from taking jobs. Now, women's rights leaders anticipated a reversal of that pattern, with female college graduates seizing the opportunity to assert their equality with men in business and the professions. The number of women receiving higher degrees had skyrocketed in the first two decades of the twentieth century. Female enrollment increased 1,000 per cent in public colleges and 482 per cent in private schools. Many of the students had participated actively in the suffrage movement and other progressive crusades. Since educated women had traditionally formed the vanguard of the feminist struggle, women's rights leaders looked to the new generation to carry forward the fight for equality.[1]

On the surface, developments during the 1920's appeared to fulfill the feminists' expectations. The number of women employed in the professions increased by over 450,000 and in business by over 100,000. The proportion of all women workers who were professionals grew from 11.9 per cent in 1920 to 14.2 per cent in

1930. Women became editors in publishing houses, sold real estate, practiced pharmacology, and took up important positions in banks and department stores. They formed their own business and professional associations, and published national journals focusing on their collective advancement. In no area except domestic service did the female labor force expand so rapidly.[2]

Yet the statistical gains inflated the degree of progress actually achieved. As we have seen, most prospective career women were restricted to "female" occupations and did not enter male-dominated fields. The number of women in medical schools actually diminished from 1,280 in 1902-3 to 992 in 1926. Despite a great deal of talk about new jobs open to women, there were only 60 female Certified Public Accountants and only 151 dentists at the end of the 1920's. Instead of breaking down barriers to positions from which they had previously been excluded, career women of the 1920's clustered in occupations traditionally marked out as women's preserve. Among professional women in New York, there were 63,637 teachers and 21,915 nurses but only 11 engineers and 7 inventors. The distribution accurately reflected the absence of any startling advances by women into new professions.[3]

Significantly, those women who did enter careers rarely received the same treatment accorded men. A woman might sell bonds on Wall Street, but she was listed on company personnel forms as a technician rather than as an account executive. Banks frequently employed women specialists to handle female clients, but those who were hired almost never rose above the position of assistant cashier—an office which quickly became woman's place in the banking community. In addition, businessmen exhibited little confidence in the staying power of potential career women and consciously discouraged them from pursuing their ambitions. Roger Babson, a prominent business spokesman, declared that females represented a poor economic investment because of their brief tenure at work. Another executive wrote that the "highest profession a woman can engage in is that of charming wife and wise mother." And an editorial in the *Commercial and Financial Chron-*

*icle* warned that banking held no future for "bright, capable educated young women" because "propagation among the higher groups" constituted the chief call on the female college graduate's energies.[4]

Even in occupations which they dominated, women were frequently denied top positions. Females constituted 8 out of every 10 teachers but only 1 out of every 63 superintendents of schools. Bryn Mawr had graduated 1,088 Ph.D.'s by 1927, most of whom went into teaching, yet at the end of the 1920's only 21 held full professorships in women's colleges and only 4 in men's colleges. Women chaired less than 1 in 6 of the departments of education in the nation's universities, and headed less than 1 in 3 of the country's women's colleges.[5] While females earned approximately one-third of the graduate degrees awarded in the country, they occupied only 4 per cent of the full professorships. To some extent, the low percentage reflected the preference of females for teaching over publishing, and for small colleges over large universities. Nevertheless, a survey of woman academicians in 1929 found widespread discontent over the apparent lack of correlation between training and rank. No matter how much a woman studied or taught, she was likely to remain an instructor, burdened with the greatest teaching load and recompensed with the smallest salary. "The rank and file [of the women teachers]," the survey concluded, "seem to have developed a defensive attitude bordering on martyrdom."[6]

As the new decade began, prospects for career women grew worse rather than better. When Julia Lathrop died in 1932, the New York *Herald Tribune* described her as one of "the vanishing race of pioneer women," and the obituary had a ring of truth to it. During the 1930's the percentage of women who received doctorates declined relative to men, and those who earned advanced degrees put them to less and less use. Even in women's colleges, the number of female faculty members declined. As the Depression swept the country, it became less and less likely that women would enter male-dominated careers, and the proportion of female work-

ers engaged in the professions fell from 14.2 per cent in 1930 to
12.3 per cent in 1940. The 1940 figure was only .4 per cent more
than the comparable figure for 1920, highlighting the extent to
which women's basic economic status remained unchanged.[7]

At least in part, the absence of greater progress could be attributed to the indifference of the young. Women's rights leaders had
looked to the new generation to fulfill their goals, but as the suffragist Mildred Adams observed, "the first of the future generations seemed little interested" in carrying on the fight for equality.
Ironically, the lack of enthusiasm coincided with, and in some ways
reflected, the burgeoning growth of the female college population.
At an earlier time when higher education was a rarity, female students had been infused with a conscious sense of mission and obligation. The very act of going to college set them apart as a select
group with a special responsibility. Between 1890 and 1910, a
Vassar professor recalled, women students "proudly . . . marched
in militant processions and joyfully . . . accepted arrest and im-
prisonment for the sake of 'Votes for Women,' free speech and to
help a strike." By the 1920's, however, going to college had become an act of conformity rather than deviance, and the atmosphere of special purpose began to evaporate. " 'Feminism' has
become a term of opprobrium [for the young]," Dorothy Dunbar
Bromley noted in 1927. "The word suggests either the old school
. . . who wore flat heels and had very little feminine charm, or
the current species who antagonize men with their constant clamor
about maiden names." Neither type had any appeal for the college girl. She enjoyed the benefits which the feminists had won, but
refused to consider their cause as her own. "We're not out to benefit society . . . or to make industry safe," one student commented.
"We're not going to suffer over how the other half lives." As a
League of Women Voters official lamented, the woman's movement had ceased to hold any attraction for the "juniors."[8]

Youthful apathy to the cause of women's rights inevitably affected the prospects for achieving economic equality. A woman did
not have to be a feminist to pursue a career, but she did have to

display the same kind of dedication to an overriding goal. Females considering a life in business or the professions, a journalist noted in 1921, had to "spurn delight . . . love laborious days," and be prepared to recognize that everything else took second place to her job. Yet it was precisely such a commitment which many young women lacked. The female college student of the twenties, Virginia Gildersleeve of Barnard remarked, was characterized by "blasé indifference, self-indulgence, and irresponsibility." Business and professional women were outraged by the absence of serious-ness among the young and commented that the new generation showed little willingness to "pay the price" of success by careful preparation and discipline.[9]

The story of women in academic life illustrated the impact of the shift in attitude. The founders of women's education, a Wellesley historian observed in 1915, had been motivated by "heady enthu-siasm" and "fiery persistence." On trial before the world, they were dedicated to proving that women had the brains, as well as the endurance, to develop their own institutions of higher learning. Only those who took part in the experience, she wrote, could know "how exciting and romantic it was to be a professor in a woman's college during the last half century." With the passage of time, however, the ardor of the pioneers faded. "By the 1920's," Jessie Bernard has noted, "the éclat of the earlier years had spent itself, and all of a sudden . . . the increase in the percentage of aca-demic personnel who were women slowed down. The excitement which had characterized the first generation of academic women ebbed." Vida Scudder, a prominent reformer and Wellesley profes-sor, described the 1920's as a period of "surging . . . disillusion" and declared that she had never before felt so discouraged. The crusading spirit had disintegrated, and with it the warmth of old comradeships held together by devotion to a transcendent goal. Most observers traced the change in mood to the war, but what-ever the reason, all agreed that the new generation of college women lacked the single-minded purpose which had sustained those who led the battle for female education. During the 1930's the proportion of college teachers who were women fell from 32.5 per cent to 26.5 per cent, and the figure continued to decline until the late 1950's.[10]

If anyone accurately symbolized the new age, it was the carefree flapper rather than the dedicated career woman, and the difference between the two said a great deal about the nature of women's "emancipation." Popularized in the novels of F. Scott Fitzgerald and worried over in magazines as diverse as the *American Mercury* and the *Ladies Home Journal*, the flapper seized the public imagination in the years from 1910 to 1930 and dominated conversation about manners and morals. Checking her corset in the cloakroom, partying without a chaperone, and dancing to hot jazz with skirts hiked above her knees, she personified a life style totally alien to that of the older generation. "I mean to do what I like . . . undeterred by convention," one short-story heroine remarked. "Freedom—that is the modern essential. To live one's life in one's own way." With her bobbed hair and rolled hose, the stereotypical flapper flitted from adventure to adventure, celebrating experience for its own sake. From New York City to Muncie, Indiana, her antics bemused, outraged, and frustrated those who had been raised to believe in an ideal of "dainty femininity." There was no way of knowing how many young women actually behaved in the manner described in magazine articles, and some degree of skepticism was probably warranted. But in Muncie's high school, over half the junior and senior girls agreed that "petting" was nearly universal at teenage parties—a fact which provided at least partial confirmation that a "new woman" had arrived on the national scene.[11]

Indeed, there was a substantial amount of evidence that a revolution in morals and manners had occurred in America. Popular discussion of sex reached an unprecedented level during the years 1910-30. The number of articles on birth control, prostitution, divorce, and sexual morality soared, and an analysis of short stories revealed that "between 1915 and 1925, taboos associated with sex in general and marital infidelity in particular were lifted from the middle class mind in America." More important, it appeared that talk about the new morality was translated into action as well. When Lewis Terman surveyed 777 middle-class females in 1938, he found that among those born between 1890 and 1900, 74 per cent remained virgin until marriage, while among those born after 1910 the figure plummeted to 31.7 per cent. Alfred Kinsey's more elaborate sample corroborated Terman's conclusions. Women born after the turn of the century were twice as likely to have experienced premarital sex as those born before 1900, and the critical change occurred in the generation which came to maturity in the late teens and early 1920's. Extramarital sex increased in the same decades, disproving the notion that the new morality was a youthful fad which would end with the assumption of family responsibilities.[12]

The sexual habits of the flapper generation indicated that many women had been emancipated from conventional patterns of behavior. If the Lynds' survey of Muncie was any measure, a growing number of middle-class women were using artificial contraceptive devices, introducing a new degree of freedom into their personal lives.[13] Family size could be controlled, women could express their sexual desires with less fear of becoming pregnant, and the double standard ceased to exert the same restrictive influence over women's behavior that it once had. There could be little question that the "revolution in manners and morals" had substantially increased the amount of equality which women enjoyed in at least one area of male-female relationships.

If the flapper symbolized a particular kind of "emancipation," however, the nature of her freedom had only the most tenuous connection to the principal concerns of the feminist movement. Most veterans of the women's rights struggle strongly disapproved of the new morality and condemned what appeared to them as an orgy of sexual indulgence. Charlotte Perkins Gilman avowed that sex was intended for procreation, not recreation, and denounced the phallic worship of Freud's disciples. Other suffragists railed against the manners of the young—especially their lack of seriousness—and

attacked the flappers as a disgrace to the sex. Conversely, the most
ardent advocates of sexual liberation had little use for traditional
feminist goals. Ellen Key, an outspoken proponent of free sexual
expression for women, opposed the suffrage for most of her life
and disdained those who emphasized legal equality and the right
of women to work. The primary function of women, she believed,
was to concentrate on love and motherhood, not to compete with
men. Similarly, Margaret Sanger urged women to develop their
own sphere and become as distinctively feminine as they could.
The supporters of the new morality thus advanced a definition of
freedom substantially different from that put forward by more
traditional feminists. One group focused on the right of women to
control their own bodies, the other on the need for achieving equality in the nation's social, political, and economic institutions.[14]

Perhaps most important, the increase in sexual freedom did not
necessarily alter the basic distribution of roles between men and
women. A woman could smoke, drink, swear, and even have extramarital affairs while still remaining a wife and mother. Shifts in
manners and morals did not interfere with the perpetuation of a
sexual division of labor where women assumed responsibility for
the home and men went out into the world to earn a livelihood.
The nuances of a relationship might change, but the structure remained the same. A career, on the other hand, involved a drastic
modification of woman's status and challenged the basic institutions
of society. If women took jobs on the same basis as men, they
would no longer be able to assume sole responsibility for the home.
The family would lose its central personality—the mother who
soothed a distraught child, the wife who provided solace to a discouraged husband, and the housekeeper who performed the chores
of cooking and cleaning. In effect, women could achieve economic
equality only if one of two things happened: the family as presently
constituted ceased to exist, or someone else helped care for the
children, prepare the meals, and preserve the integrity of the home.
In either case, the changes threatened traditional definitions of

woman's place, and required a social revolution which most Americans were unwilling to accept.[15]

The greatest obstacle to economic equality, then, was the existing distribution of sexual roles. Society operated on the assumption that women would carry out certain indispensable functions such as child-rearing and household care, and the entire process of living reinforced the assumption. From earliest childhood, females were trained to assume domestic responsibilities. "One becomes what one plays at," the sociologist Peter Berger has observed, and girls played at keeping house, dressing dolls, and cooking food. Although the Lynds noted that parental authority was declining somewhat in Muncie during the mid-twenties, they also underlined the extent to which children were taught to conform to established group norms. Girls were urged to sew and cook, boys to build club houses and tinker with automobiles.[16] The identity which society bestowed on women was that of wife and mother, not business competitor with men. Marriage and child-bearing constituted the goal of female existence, just as material success in the outside world represented the goal of men.

Within such a system, men and women occupied sharply separate spheres of responsibility. In their study of Muncie, the Lynds discovered that husbands and wives shared little in common and gravitated into separate groups even on social occasions "to talk men's talk and women's talk." Marriage was often characterized by a lack of frankness between mates, and one local minister went so far as to warn prospective bridegrooms against feeling that they "must tell everything they know to their wives." Moreover, members of both sexes readily accepted conventional definitions of each other's place. Men were expected to be providers, women homemakers; husbands made the decisions, women were help-mates. The motto of the local women's club declared that "Men are God's trees; women are his flowers," and the Lynds found little evidence to suggest that wives disagreed with such a sentiment. Indeed, the pattern of male-female relationships constituted one of the most stable features of the community. When the Lynds returned to Muncie in 1935, they found that the worlds of men and women still constituted "something akin to separate subcultures" with each sex emphasizing those attributes most different from the other.[17]

The existence of clearly defined sexual roles provided comfort and security for many, but it also discouraged deviancy and placed a formidable obstacle in the path of those who wished a life of greater independence. The Lynds noted that a woman who consciously endeavored to share more of her husband's world succeeded only at the price of isolation from the rest of the female community. The same point was made with even more cogency in Sinclair Lewis' novel *Main Street*. Carol Kennecott, the doctor's wife, had come to Gopher Prairie inspired by a missionary's impulse to transform the town. College educated, and very much her own person, she aggressively set out to mobilize the support of community leaders for her projects of social and cultural renewal. Instead of being welcomed, however, she was greeted with suspicion and antagonism. The women of the town disliked her because she disparaged traditional patterns of female behavior, and the men viewed her as a meddlesome interloper trying to intervene in matters which were their special domain.

Although Carol invited hostility by her condescension and arrogance, the principal problem was not her personality but her refusal to accept prevailing definitions of the woman's place. "She was a woman with a working brain and no work," Lewis observed. When she tried to engage men in conversation about burning social issues and when she spurred women to take leadership in the community, she violated entrenched social customs and appeared to be a troublemaker. Her husband and others were convinced that the presence of children would ease her discontent, and the antagonism between Carol and the town did diminish after a son was born and she more closely conformed to the ideal of what was expected of women. But motherhood was only a temporary palliative; it quickly gave way to a new round of bitterness and despair. Carol yearned for a "conscious life" of individuality and freedom, not just the housewife's routine of "drudging and sleeping and dying." Yet a woman could not easily find her life's work, or build a "room of [her] own" when all around her was pressure to abandon ideas of independence and settle down. For a brief period, Carol worked in Washington as a government clerk, but in the end, she returned to Gopher Prairie, resigned to accepting the community's values.[18]

The case studies of Muncie and Gopher Prairie illustrated the social barriers to greater female involvement in business and the professions. Beginning at home, most women a girl met reinforced the image of the female as a homemaker. Despite the pioneering achievements of an Elizabeth Blackwell in medicine or an Antoinette Brown in the ministry, there were few successful models in male-dominated professions for the potential career woman to emulate. A young girl met an abundance of female nurses and teachers—one reason for the popularity of these professions among women—but their jobs represented an extension rather than a repudiation of the traditional female role. Magazines generally viewed women's work as a threat to the family, and in novels and short stories the happy ending usually consisted of the single woman rejecting a job for a life of marital bliss. *This Freedom*—one of the most popular novels of 1922—attacked career women as traitors to their sex and announced that "the peace of the home . . . rests ultimately on the kitchen." Other novels of the period adopted the same theme, portraying most flatteringly those women who deviated least from the role of supportive wife.[19]

The woman who did pursue a career in a male-dominated field traveled a largely uncharted course and violated the most deeply held conceptions of her proper role. Instead of serving men at home, she competed against them at work. That fact by itself created difficulty, since it challenged the powerful forces of tradition. Equally important, however, the career woman lacked signposts to direct her in her endeavor. If she acted demurely and accepted a subservient role, she missed opportunities for advancement. On the other hand, if she anticipated prejudice and compensated by being overly aggressive, she alienated those around her and highlighted the extent to which she departed from the female norm. In either case she was bound to experience the ambivalence of being a stranger in foreign territory, confronting repeatedly the conflict between the passivity expected of women and the assertiveness demanded of men.[20]

The greatest dilemma of all involved the choice between marriage and a career. Many college women had been encouraged to compete with men as students and to achieve the best grades possible. On the other hand, as females, they were brought up to act and think of themselves as wives and mothers. If a woman could both marry and have a career, the conflict might have been mitigated. The preponderance of evidence, however, suggested that the two roles were irreconcilable. Only 12.2 per cent of all professional women were married in 1920, and 75 per cent of the women who earned Ph.D.'s between 1877 and 1924 remained spinsters. Many employers refused even to consider hiring married women because of their preoccupation with the home. More important, the traits conducive to winning success in a career were least conducive to winning a husband. A female had two choices, Margaret Mead observed in 1935. Either she proclaimed herself "a woman and therefore less an achieving individual, or an achieving individual and therefore less a woman." If she chose the first option, she enhanced her opportunity of being "a loved object, the kind of girl whom men will woo and boast of, toast and marry." If she selected the second alternative, however, she lost "as a woman, her chance for the kind of love she wants."[21]

For a brief period beginning in 1925, Smith College sought to find ways to combine home and career through its Institute to Coordinate Women's Interests. Headed by Ethel Puffer Howe, a former Wellesley College professor, the Institute tried to end the dichotomy between "the queen bee and the sexless worker" and to make it possible for college-educated wives to enter professional occupations. Experimenting with cooperative nurseries, communal laundries, shopping groups, and central kitchens, it set out to release women from the "inexorable routine of housework." Howe attempted to plan, and then to initiate, a "revolution in the organization of the home," and to establish a pattern of education and professional life geared to the problems of middle-class women. Acting from the same motivation, Virginia Gildersleeve at Barnard College granted maternity leaves with pay to women faculty members. Females had just as much right to a full life as men, she believed, and ought not to be condemned to celibacy in order to pursue a career.[22]

The experiments at Barnard and Smith proved exceptions to the rule, however. Despite its efforts, the Smith Institute expired after only six years. More typical than either Howe or Gildersleeve were the authorities of a Midwestern land grant college who dismissed a woman dean when she married. Upon appealing the ruling, the woman was told that "marriage itself is for a woman an adequate career." The vast majority of Americans agreed. Suzanne La Follette noted in 1924 that, while being a husband represented only one of the many roles assigned to a man, being a wife constituted the only role assigned to a woman. She was expected to devote full time to her family, and if she worked outside the home, her action reflected negatively both on her own womanhood and on the ability of her husband to support her. A married woman of the lower class might seek work for reasons of economic necessity, but employment was fundamentally inconsistent with the status of a middle-class wife. Carol Kennecott repeatedly talked about embarking on a career of her own, yet she knew that a job for herself was impossible in the conservative community of Gopher Prairie and would thoroughly undermine her husband's social standing. "To the village doctor's wife," Sinclair Lewis observed, "[outside employment] was taboo."[23]

In the end, therefore, the real question confronting potential career women was whether they wished to marry and forsake their professional ambitions, or to enter a life-time job and renounce marriage. The distribution of sexual roles made it impossible for them to do both, because, in order to achieve success in a man's world, they had to accept failure in a woman's world. In a different type of family, where "independence [was] equal, dependence mutual, and obligations reciprocal," women might have been able to combine a career with a life in the home.[24] As it was, however, most Americans rejected such a radical change. Even those women who entered careers wondered about their ability to sustain a commitment to work. "We have not the motive to prepare ourselves for a 'life-work' of teaching, of social work," Ruth Benedict confided in her diary. "We know that we would lay it down with hallelujah in the height of our success, to make a home for the right man."[25]

Significantly, during the 1920's an increasing number of female college students expressed a preference for marriage. At the end of the nineteenth century, half of the graduates of the best women's colleges remained single, and they constituted the core of female professional workers. Among Vassar women who graduated prior to 1912, the desire for a career represented one of the most frequently cited reasons for having chosen a Vassar education. Alumnae of the post-World War I period, in contrast, stated over and over again that they had selected Vassar because of its popularity, or because their friends were going there. As the student population broadened and became more representative of middle-class values, it was almost inevitable that a larger percentage of graduates would choose to become wives and mothers rather than career women. A survey of alumnae from Hollins, Bryn Mawr, Barnard, Vassar, and Smith illustrated the change which had occurred since the turn of the century. In one school 80 per cent of those graduating in the years 1919-23 got married, while in another school, the figure was 90 per cent. A newspaper poll of Vassar women in 1923 revealed that 90 per cent wanted to be married, with only 11 of 152 preferring a business or professional position. Most believed that marriage was "the biggest of all careers." Seven years later, almost 70 per cent of the graduates of New Jersey's College for Women agreed that winning a husband and starting a family took precedence over pursuing a career. Thus the female students who attended the schools most likely to produce a new crop of business and professional women chose to marry rather than stay single. Moreover, the critical shift occurred precisely in those years when feminists expected a boom in the number of career women as a result of suffrage and the war.[26]

The curriculum of women's education underwent a striking change at the same time, reflecting a growing concern with preparing women for marriage and the home. The founders of most women's colleges had sought as much as possible to make them carbon copies of Harvard and Yale. Four of the eight original professors at Vassar taught science, and Mount Holyoke, Smith, Barnard, and Bryn Mawr all insisted that they offer the same courses as the best men's colleges. By the early twentieth century, however, the older view of female colleges came under increasing attack. Ethel Puffer Howe, a Radcliffe graduate and later head of the Smith Institute, urged women's colleges in 1913 to develop courses in domestic science, eugenics, hygiene, and the aesthetics of the home in order to train women for the domestic tasks which lay ahead. In a similar vein, an insurgent group at the 1923 convention of the American Collegiate Association condemned women's colleges for not preparing women for the occupation of homemaking and child-rearing.[27]

The leaders of at least one feminist institution heeded the call for reform. In the spring of 1924, the Vassar board of trustees unanimously endorsed the creation of an interdisciplinary School of Euthenics which would focus on the development and care of the family. The purpose of the institute, its first director declared, was to re-route "education for women along the lines of their chief interests and responsibilities, motherhood and the home." Supporters of the program believed that women's colleges had treated females for too long as if they were celibate, while ignoring the chief vocation of the distaff sex—wifehood, maternity, and homemaking. To correct the imbalance, Vassar offered a series of courses: Husband and Wife, Motherhood, and The Family as an Economic Unit, designed to train students to be "gracious and intelligent wives and mothers." As the chief financial backer of the Institute said in 1929, "our purpose . . . is to raise motherhood to a profession worthy of [woman's] finest talents and greatest intellectual gifts."[28]

Although feminists viewed such innovations as a direct threat to the dignity and usefulness of higher education for women, similar endeavors appeared throughout the country. At the University of Chicago, Marion Talbot proposed a graduate program of home economics. Cornell quickly gained prominence as a center for domestic science, and state universities adopted such programs as a mainstay for female students. The field of family care or home economics boomed in the first quarter of the twentieth century, in part as a result of federal financing under the Smith-Lever Act, and in part as a result of a vocational demand for teachers of cooking and hygiene in the public schools. At a time when the sexual division of labor posed the primary obstacle to the advancement of economic equality, it appeared that the nation's colleges and universities were reinforcing the image of woman as wife and mother. Dr. Charles Richmond, head of Union College, articulated the new focus of women's education in his address at the inauguration of Skidmore's president in 1925. "One of the chief ends of a college for women is to fit them to become the makers of homes," he declared; "whatever else a woman may be, the highest purpose of her life always has been . . . to strengthen and beautify and sanctify the home."[29]

With increasing stridency, women's magazines voiced the same theme, insisting that the role of mother and housewife represented the only path to feminine fulfillment. In the years immediately after passage of the Nineteenth Amendment, occasional articles justified female independence and defended the right of women to work. By the late 1920's, however, the attitude of tolerant permissiveness had changed to one of outright condemnation. The switch in tone was announced officially in a 1930 *Ladies Home Journal* editorial. "[A] new keynote is creeping into the lives of American women," the editorial observed. "Yesterday, and for a decade past, the great desideratum was Smartness. Today, and for the years that lie immediately before us, it is Charm."[30] Women's magazines urged their readers to return to femininity and constructed an elaborate ideology in support of the home and marriage to facilitate the process.

As a first step, the magazines defined the role of the housewife as exciting, rewarding, and creative. Homemaking, the *Ladies Home Journal* declared in 1929, "is today an adventure—an education in color, in mechanics, in chemistry." *McCall's* magazine asserted that no other task possessed such universal appeal: "it exercises an even more profound influence on human destiny than the heroism of war or the prosperity of peace." Both magazines urged women to conceive of their job as a profession—home engineering, one called it—and to utilize "current labor saving devices" to ease their burden. The perfection of modern conveniences, the magazine argued, had increased rather than diminished the housewife's role by elevating her position in the world and giving her more time to develop socially and to train her children. With fewer routine chores to perform, a wife could devote herself to the more important job of creating happiness for her family. No task was more important, no profession more demanding. "The creation and fulfillment of a successful home," a *Ladies Home Journal* article declared, "is a bit of craftsmanship that compares favorably with building a beautiful cathedral." Only as a wife and mother, *McCall's* observed, could the American woman "arrive at her true eminence."[31]

The magazines coupled their glorification of domesticity with a bitter attack on feminism. "Liberated women," they claimed, had thrown away the essence of femininity without putting anything better in its place. One article declared that "the office woman, no matter how successful, is a transplanted posey." Another argued that women who pushed for equality had destroyed the "deep-rooted, nourishing, and fruitful man-and-woman relationship." A woman's career was to make a good marriage, to be "deeply, fundamentally, wholly feminine." Laura Cornell, dean of Temple University, told her readers that women who demanded recognition for themselves were violating their own true nature. Women required protection, she wrote, and men needed to give it.[32]

Career women were singled out for special condemnation by the proponents of homemaking. Dorothy Thompson, herself a prime example of a successful professional woman, observed that "men demand and need in marriage the full emotional power of the women they love. . . . If that power is dissipated in demanding intellectual or creative work, or shared with some boss, the husband and children will feel they are being cheated." In Thompson's opinion, society had more need of good mothers than of additional private secretaries or laboratory technicians.[33] Claire Callahan, another veteran of work outside the home, publicly repented her career and declared that, if she had to do it again, she would remain a homemaker. "I know now without any hesitation," she wrote, "that [my husband's job] must come first. . . . I am like the invaluable secretary to a big executive. He produces but I make it possible for him to produce efficiently. And once I had the right slant on my work . . . I would begin to see my job as a real job. . . . I would work toward an executive position in my home."[34] According to women's magazines, a female could achieve a "real" career only by renouncing an outside job and devoting herself to full-time service in the home.

An element of uncertainty occasionally characterized the defense of domesticity. Some writers admitted that housework was monotonous, and others acknowledged that a business career might appear more daring and glamorous. The same writers, however, insisted that, if a woman approached homemaking with the proper attitude, she would find it the most rewarding occupation of all. "Just as a rose comes to its fullest beauty in its own appropriate soil," one article declared, "so does a home woman come to her fairest blooming when her roots are stuck deep in the daily and hourly affairs of her own most dearly beloved." A woman might resent at times "the thoughtlessness and omissions" of her husband, but once she accepted "that big biologic fact that man was intended to be selfish" and woman self-sacrificing, the way to fulfillment was clear. Only if a woman rejected her natural identity would she have cause to experience dissatisfaction and despair.[35]

The editorial policy of women's magazines added one more voice of support to existing beliefs in the value of a sexual division of labor. For the most part, periodicals like *McCall's* and the *Ladies Home Journal* catered to readers who were already housewives; they did not need to be persuaded to renounce careers or devote full time to the home. But the ideology presented in such journals helped to bolster prevailing opinion. Over 7,000 of the 9,200 families in Muncie read either the large women's magazines or *Pictorial Review* and *Delineator,* while fewer than 40 families subscribed to *Harper's* or *Atlantic Monthly*—journals more receptive to a feminist point of view.[36] It may have been coincidental that Muncie's citizens espoused the same values articulated in the periodicals they read, but it seems more likely that the magazines provided reinforcement for existing attitudes and helped to justify their perpetuation.

The advent of the Depression provided the final blow to feminist hopes for economic equality. During a time of massive unemployment, many people believed that women should sacrifice personal ambitions and accept a life of economic inactivity. Congresswoman Florence Kahn spoke for most of her colleagues when she declared that "woman's place is not out in the business world competing with men who have families to support," but in the home. Dean Eugenia Leonard of Syracuse University urged women college graduates to enter volunteer work rather than accept a salary. And George Mullins, acting dean of Barnard, told his students that the greatest service they could render would be to "refuse to work for gain and to prolong [their] study." Liberal women reformers voiced similar sentiments. Francis Perkins denounced the rich "pin-money worker" as a "menace to society, [and] a selfish short-sighted creature, who ought to be ashamed of herself." Any woman capable of supporting herself without a job, the future Secretary of Labor declared, should devote herself to motherhood and the home.[37]

The Depression especially sharpened public disapproval of work by married women. Employed wives were "thieving parasites of the business world," a Kansas woman wrote to President Roosevelt. A Chicago-based civic organization urged that married women workers be forced back to the home because "they are holding jobs that rightfully belong to the God-intended providers of the household," and the executive council of the AF of L resolved that "married women whose husbands have permanent positions . . . should be discriminated against in the hiring of employees." Almost all Americans agreed. When the pollster George Gallup asked in 1936 whether wives should work if their husbands were employed also, a resounding 82 per cent of the respondents said no. Gallup reported that he had "discovered an issue on which voters are about as solidly united as on any subject imaginable— including sin and hay fever."[38]

Consistent with such opinion, employers increasingly denied married women the right to work. A National Education Association study in 1930-31 showed that, of 1500 school systems surveyed, 77 per cent refused to hire wives and 63 per cent dismissed women teachers if they subsequently married. A San Francisco wife was told when applying for a teaching job that she would have to get a divorce first. From 1932 to 1937, federal legislation prohibited more than one member of the same family from working in the civil service. Designed to combat nepotism, the law in fact discriminated almost exclusively against women. In nearly every state, bills were introduced to restrict the employment of married women, and at times whole cities embarked on crusades to fire working wives. The Federation of Labor in Cedar Rapids, Iowa, called on every merchant to dismiss any married woman whose husband could support her, and the City Council of Akron, Ohio, resolved that the school board, the Goodyear Tire Company, and all local department stores should deny employment to wives.[39]

The campaign against women's work in large part reflected the dire circumstances of the Depression. At a time when many fam-

ilies were without any breadwinner, there was understandable re-
sentment against those which had two. Although most working
wives were not taking jobs away from men (women were concentrated in occupations where few men were employed), most Americans believed that in a period of economic distress husbands and
fathers should be given the first opportunity for employment. Implicit in such a belief, however, was the assumption that women
did not deserve the same treatment as men. The Depression did
not create antagonism toward female employment, but it raised it
to a new level of intensity and by so doing placed one more barrier
in the way of economic equality.

From a feminist point of view, the experience of the years after
1920 raised profound questions about the freedom women enjoyed
in America. Many suffragists had been satisfied with gaining the
vote and demanded no more. Militant women's rights leaders,
however, desired more far-reaching change. Until women were
free to maximize their individual talents, the feminists believed,
they could not reach the goal of complete liberation. "No matter
what other equality might be obtained," Charlotte Perkins Gilman
wrote in 1923, "so long as one sex [is] dependent on the other for
its food, clothing and shelter, it [is] not free."[40] For Gilman and
others, sexual equality required economic equality—the right of
women to leave the home and pursue whatever vocation they desired on the same basis as men. By that standard, women in 1940
were still far from being free.

The feminists viewed the results with anger and disillusionment.
"In giving women the vote," one Michigan woman wrote, "men
never had any intention of giving her anything more and never has.
The really interested woman . . . has had to fight for a place, and
in fighting, man has . . . pushed her aside like a sticky fly, and
gone serenely on his way managing the universe." Others were
equally bitter. Woman's influence was "almost totally lacking in
the centers of American national life," Pearl Buck declared in
1940. "Men and children have proceeded with the times, but
woman has not, and today the home is too peculiarly hers." Wom-

en's rights leaders charged that the United States was fundamentally hostile to the cause of female advancement, and unwilling to grant women the basic rights given to men as a matter of course. "Profound as race prejudice is against the Negro American," Buck concluded, "it is not practically as far reaching as the prejudice against women. The truth is that women suffer all the effects of a minority."[41]

The feminists were correct at least in part in their charge that prejudice was responsible for women's status. Professional schools placed strict quotas on the number of female students they would admit. Hospitals, law firms, and business establishments frequently denied women the opportunity to compete for positions held by men. And when females did enter male-dominated fields, unequal pay and inadequate promotion opportunities discouraged them from staying. In general, women were treated as a class apart with separate qualifications which severely restricted the type of jobs they could fill. Even sympathizers perceived career women as a special breed. The Institute of Women's Professional Relations declared that "women must be directed into occupations for which they are [peculiarly] adapted," and Frances Perkins told a conference on women that the greatest need of government was for females "who can be humble . . . and who are willing to begin at the bottom." Character and conscience, she asserted, were more important requirements than brilliance. Such statements reflected a subtle but pervasive attitude that women were less than first-class citizens and had their own place in the world of business and government.[42]

In a deeper sense, however, women's inequality was embedded in the social fabric, part of a process of living which provided its own best defense against change. In most families, boys and girls were trained to assume substantially different responsibilities. Social, political, and economic institutions were all characterized by a sharp division of sexual roles. And the qualities essential to success in a woman's world were directly opposite those necessary to success in a man's world. In a society which functioned on the premise that men and women occupied different spheres and had separate qualities, it was not surprising that most women readily accepted the role of wife and mother. Indeed, woman's place in the home seemed to have been strengthened rather than weakened in the years after 1920. More and more college women married. Over 75 per cent of the female respondents in George Gallup's 1936 poll disapproved of married women working. And no massive outcry greeted the passage of legislation restricting women's right to gainful employment during the 1930's. If females were enslaved, as the feminists claimed, the evidence suggested that theirs was a voluntary servitude, reinforced by the entire socialization process.

The road to economic equality thus proved much longer and more difficult than some women's rights leaders had anticipated. The issue of careers for women challenged nearly every entrenched assumption about the role and responsibilities of the two sexes. For economic equality to become a reality, a fundamental revolution was required in the way men and women thought of each other, and in the distribution of responsibilities within marriage and the family. Yet throughout the 1920's and 1930's, there was little indication that such a revolution was either possible or desired. As the nation entered a new decade, it seemed unlikely that the feminists—by themselves—would be able to foster social change. Only when events made it necessary and desirable for females to assume a new role could there be a realistic chance for modification of woman's status.

# 5

# The Equal Rights Amendment

Although popular indifference constituted the chief reason for the decline in feminism after 1920, factionalism within the woman's movement also played an important part. During the suffrage fight, women of all political persuasions had rallied around a single issue. Despite differences of tactics and ideology, female leaders were committed to the same goal. In the years following enactment of the Nineteenth Amendment, however, feminism lost its unifying focus. Women's rights leaders had never spelled out with precision the ultimate purpose of their movement, and after 1920 the question of how to define equality fragmented women's groups into sharply opposing camps. With neither a common program nor a united leadership, there was little chance that the woman's movement could advance or that it could generate the public support needed for progress in the fight against discrimination.

No issue divided women's organizations more than the Equal Rights Amendment to the Constitution. Proposed in 1923 by the National Women's Party, the amendment read: "Men and women shall have equal rights throughout the United States and every place subject to its jurisdiction." By inscribing the principle of feminine equality in the basic law of the land, the amendment sought to extend the freedom won in the suffrage fight into every area of public policy and to end once and for all the distinction between men and women in laws affecting divorce, possession of property, and employment opportunity. Endorsed by one wing of the suffrage movement and opposed by the other, it immediately became a focal point of controversy. Mary Anderson of the Women's Bureau denounced it as "vicious," "doctrinaire," and "a kind of hysterical feminism with a slogan for a program."[1] Other suffragists viewed it as a direct threat to all the special legislation passed to protect women. For decades, the amendment embroiled the woman's movement in bitter strife and as much as anything else prevented the development of a united feminist appeal.

In some ways, the conflict represented an extension of the split between the Women's Party and NAWSA during the suffrage campaign. The Women's Party (formerly the Congressional Union) constituted the militant wing of the suffrage movement. Its adherents adopted radical tactics, chaining themselves to fences, picketing the White house, and engaging in hunger strikes in prison. NAWSA, on the other hand, sought to cooperate with the government and to work from within to achieve its goals. Alice Paul and the Women's Party burned President Wilson in effigy, while Carrie Chapman Catt invited him to address the NAWSA convention. Although both organizations were seeking the same end, they frequently worked at cross purposes, and many women traced the subsequent conflict within the women's rights movement to the residual distrust of the earlier struggle.[2]

More important, the dispute reflected the different goals sought by various participants in the woman's movement. Female activists could be divided into two groups, W. L. George noted in 1916: the suffragists who wished to remove a specific inequality and the feminists who aimed to transform the attitude of the entire society toward women. Pursuing a similar line of thought, the historian William L. O'Neill has distinguished between "social feminists" who viewed suffrage as a lever for social-welfare reforms and "hard core feminists" who perceived the vote as only an intermediate step on the road to full sexual equality.[3] The basic division seen by both observers—here described as that between reformers and

feminists—emerged explicitly in the period after 1920 and dominated the relationships between the various women's organizations.

The two principal antagonists—the Women's Party and the
League of Women Voters—exemplified the extent of the conflict
between the different points of view. The Women's Party—headed
by Alice Paul—minimized the value of the suffrage victory and
declared in 1921 that "women today . . . are still in every way
subordinate to men before the law, in the professions, in the church,
in industry, and in the home." Rejecting the plea of other women's
groups to build a reform coalition on behalf of disarmament, birth
control, and social-welfare legislation, the WP pledged itself to
work exclusively for the goal of total equality for women. Its members reasoned that any expenditure of energy on issues extraneous
to women's rights would only impede progress toward their primary
end. American women were still enslaved, the feminists believed,
and nothing less than complete dedication could bring about their
emancipation.[4]

The narrowness of the Women's Party approach was manifested
both in its membership and leadership. Although the party boasted
of being able to force through Congress any legislative measure it
sponsored, it suffered from a distinct lack of popular support, and
since its very beginning was dismissed by many as a lunatic fringe.
The NWP consistently refused to broaden its base by recruiting
younger women. At the height of its strength it had only 8,000
members—most of them aging veterans of the suffrage fight and
militant career women. Many party followers were "ingrown to
the point of fanaticism," one member later observed, and seemed
"ignorant of the methods of democracy." Alice Paul ran the organization with a tyrannical hand, setting policy on her own authority,
refusing to call board meetings, and jealously guarding her own
position against encroachment. Although she inspired total dedication from some, she alienated others and her harsh, irascible personality represented at least one cause of the hostility which the
WP provoked among other women leaders.[5]

In contrast to the Women's Party, the League of Women Voters
—NAWSA's successor—attempted to serve a broader constituency.

Although it too was composed primarily of middle- and upper-class women, it forged alliances with other reform groups and addressed itself to a wide spectrum of issues. League members contended that with suffrage women had secured most of their fundamental rights. Marguerite Wells, the League's president during the 1930's, urged that "the well-worn old 'equal rights' slogan [be] reverently and gratefully returned to the suffragists at Seneca Falls. . . . Nearly all discriminations have been removed." While the League continued to work for such measures as equal pay and jury service for women, it concerned itself as much with child labor, wages and working hours, and disarmament as with legislation specifically focused on women's rights. Of the 304 legislative items on the agendas of state leagues in 1931, over half had to do with child welfare and only 25 dealt with women.[6]

In fact, the League went out of its way to avoid being identified as a lobbying agency for one group only. Repeatedly, League representatives sounded the theme that their organization was devoted to the good of the whole nation and not to any special interest. "We of the League are very much for the rights of women," Dorothy Straus, a League leader, wrote, "but . . . we are not feminists primarily; we are citizens." When Congress passed a Depression measure which in effect prevented wives of government employees from working in the federal civil service, the League opposed the bill on the grounds that it infringed on the merit system, not because it discriminated against women. "I do hate to see the League support a position . . . on purely equalitarian grounds when the broad social justification is clear," the League's executive secretary remarked.[7] In contrast to the narrow, authoritarian management of the Women's Party, the League sought the maximum possible consensus of its membership before proceeding with any program. Every measure endorsed by League leaders had to be approved by its biennial convention, and before an item could even be inscribed on the League's legislative calendar, it had to be studied for at least a year by the appropriate standing committee.

The gulf between reformers and feminists was best illustrated by the divergent approaches they adopted in pursuit of their goals. The Women's Party wished to eliminate in one blow all remaining laws which distinguished between men and women. To campaign in each state for piecemeal reform, the feminists reasoned, would take years of effort. Consequently, they relied on a blanket amendment which would outlaw all discriminatory legislation throughout the country. The League of Women Voters, in contrast, endorsed a strategy of gradualism. "The LWV from the beginning has stood for step by step progress," its first president recalled in 1933. "It has been willing to go ahead slowly in order to go ahead steadily. It has not sought to lead a few women a long way quickly, but rather to lead many women a little way at a time." The League rejected the one-shot approach of the Women's Party. "Panaceas work no better for the body politic than they do in the animal body," Dorothy Straus observed. "Radical changes cannot be effected except by gradual steps; sudden and violent advances have invariably been followed by repression."[8]

Despite the hostility of the two groups, it appeared for a time in the early 1920's that compromise might still be possible. Many prominent women shared membership in both camps. Florence Kelley of the National Consumer's League had been a national officer of the Women's Party. Maud Younger, treasurer of the NWP, had served as national vice-president of the Consumers League and was widely known as the "mother" of California's eight hour law for women. Josephine Casey, a former union organizer for the International Ladies Garment Workers, was a prominent force in both the NWP and the Women's Trade Union League. And Alice Paul herself had once served in the WTUL and helped organize a milliner's union. Far from opposing social-welfare reforms, many Women's Party members had been in the forefront of the Progressive movement.[9]

Based on these associations and common participation in the suffrage fight, tentative efforts at cooperation were made in 1921 and 1922. Alice Paul invited a speaker from the League of Women Voters to address the Women's Party convention and requested the League to join the NWP in commemorating pioneers of the suffrage movement at the Capitol. Ethel Smith of the Women's Trade Union League appeared at the NWP convention and reported that the WTUL banner received more applause than any other in the formal procession. People on each side sought to compromise on legislative matters. In Massachusetts supporters of the two groups worked out an agreement whereby they would endorse a common program to end certain discriminatory practices at the same time that they were introducing separate bills on issues where they disagreed. A similar attempt was made in New York. "It is immaterial whether the bills which are passed are those which we have drawn up or those which some other organization has drawn up," Alice Paul wrote a New York official. "The only important thing is to see that they are passed."[10]

On the chief sticking point—protective legislation—the NWP seemed willing to make concessions. The reformers prided themselves on having secured enactment of minimum-wage and maximum-hour laws for women and insisted that the feminists' blanket equal rights bill would abrogate such legislation by eliminating any statute which singled out females for special consideration. Alice Paul proposed that the problem be solved "by raising the standard of protective labor laws for men until they are equal to those now in existence . . . for women," but, failing that, the NWP appeared ready to placate the concern of women reformers. In Massachusetts the NWP agreed to drop its opposition to League of Women Voters bills designed to protect women in industry; Alice Paul wrote her lieutenants in New York that they had leeway to frame a similar compromise; and the New York NWP announced that it was specifically opposed to legislation which discriminated *against* women, the word "against" to distinguish such laws from those which provided protection *for* women.[11]

The Wisconsin Equal Rights Law showed particular promise as a way out of the dispute. The 1921 statute declared in its first clause that "women shall have the same rights, privileges and immunities under the law as men" with respect to jury service, holding office, owning and conveying property, freedom of contract, "and in all other respects." It also provided for the abrogation of the common law disabilities of women. But it specifically declared that nothing in the law should deny women "the special protection and privileges which they now enjoy for the general welfare." In short, the bill met the demands of the feminists for equality while protecting the labor legislation which was of special concern to the reformers. "Its object," a legal expert observed later, "was to place men and women upon an equality in all matters in which sex naturally does not create differences." A study of the statute's effects by the Wisconsin Federation of Women's Clubs several years later concluded that it had served effectively to prevent discrimination against married women and "had worked for a greater degree of justice and greater equality of women with men than they had before."[12]

In the end, however, the accumulated grievances dividing the two groups proved fatal to the effort at compromise. Organizational jealousy, personal hostility, and ideological conflict were stronger than the will to unite. The League of Women Voters rejected the Women's Party's invitation to join in honoring the suffrage pioneers, fearing that the public might get the impression that the two organizations were connected. In Wisconsin the League opposed the Equal Rights Bill and proposed a jury measure instead, arguing that "jury service is already associated with voting citizenship while neither women nor the public generally may be ready for the other provisions." Carrie Chapman Catt complained about the "fake publicity" the Women's Party was receiving, and warned that local League members were being enticed by NWP recruitment efforts. On the other side, Alice Paul adamantly refused to give up her commitment to a national constitutional amendment. At a showdown meeting in December 1921 Florence Kelley and other reformers urged the Women's Party to refrain from introducing the amendment until a solution to the protective legislation dilemma could be found, but Paul rejected the suggestion out of hand. Protective legislation was the concern of reformers, the feminists argued. Consequently, the burden for any legal solution to the conflict rested with Kelley and her friends, not with the Women's Party. The meeting ended with the recognition by all concerned that hope for conciliation on a national level was shattered.[13]

By mid-decade the two opposing camps were engaged in a bitter war. One side fought for the exclusive goal of female equality; the other side for social reform. One side believed that suffrage was only the first step in the campaign for freedom; the other that the Nineteenth Amendment had substantially finished the task of making women equal to men. Protective legislation became the crux of the differences between the two groups, but the issue was as much a symbol as a cause of the antagonism. A solution such as that achieved in the Wisconsin Equal Rights law would have worked had both sides been willing to accept it. Instead, each refused to make the final concession which might have prevented open hostility.

The conflict came to a head in a 1926 confrontation at a Women's Bureau conference on the industrial problems of women. On the second day of the meetings, Gail Laughlin, a lawyer and NWP officer, demanded that one session be devoted to a discussion of equal rights and labor laws for women. A wild floor fight erupted as members of the Women's Party shouted support for their colleague's proposal. "If I had not seen them with my own eyes," one delegate wrote Mary Anderson, "no one could have made me believe there could be such a diabolical group of women."[14] The conference rejected Laughlin's suggestion and voted down a resolution that the Women's Bureau adopt a position of neutrality on protective legislation. But with the consent of Mary Anderson, a debate was agreed upon for the following night, and the delegates voted to have the Women's Bureau conduct an impartial investigation of protective labor laws with the assistance of an advisory committee consisting of three feminists and three reformers.

As might have been expected, the committee exploded in controversy almost immediately. The feminists demanded public hearings with the right to cross-examine witnesses, and urged a special congressional appropriation to finance the investigation. From their point of view the primary function of the committee was to provide a sounding board for feminist agitation. The reformers, on the other hand, insisted that a truly scientific investigation could occur only through quiet research. They opposed open hearings as a publicity gimmick and reasoned that any special appropriation would "virtually make" the Women's Party by conferring on it a status of legitimacy which it did not yet have.[15] When the feminists exerted pressure on congressmen to support their position, the reformers seized the opportunity to resign, and Mary Anderson declared the committee dissolved.

The entire episode revealed the divergent tactical assumptions which guided the two groups. The reformers thought they had won, because theirs was the perspective of insiders who defined victory as control of power. The demise of the committee, the Women's Bureau believed, represented a death blow to the NWP. The feminists had a different perspective, however. They were outsiders who sought to stir up trouble and gain publicity. Disruption of the committee's work, from their point of view, made eminent sense. The Women's Bureau was not neutral. In effect it was investigating a question on which it already held a firm opinion. The Bureau opposed public hearings, Mary Van Kleeck wrote, because it had the data already in hand and needed only to reshape it. Mary Anderson, the director of the Bureau, was an antagonist rather than a referee. Her chief investigator, Mary Winslow, urged Trade Union League people to send petitions supporting labor laws for women and admitted that "we are avoiding going to those people whom we know to be opposed to protective legislation and getting the facts as they see them." Without public hearings, the investigation promised to be a rehash of old data in which the judge was also an advocate. The Women's Party thus had nothing to lose by its tactics. Indeed, for the feminists, the controversy represented a success which focused additional public attention on their grievances.[16]

Although the Women's Bureau believed that the NWP had been silenced by the 1926 confrontation, the public dispute between reformers and feminists increased rather than diminished in intensity as the years passed. Since the Women's Party was already categorized as an extremist minority, it had little reason to curtail its demands. Moreover, it was convinced that compromise, by definition, meant sacrificing the fight for complete sexual equality. The feminists had relatively little strength compared to the reform coalition, but they made up in loudness and dedication what they lacked in numbers, and kept a maximum amount of pressure on congressmen through intensive lobbying, legislative hearings, and imaginative uses of international treaties and conferences which raised the issue of equal rights.[17] Their single-minded persistence guaranteed that the debate within the woman's movement would continue, and although it was unlikely that either side could score a decisive triumph, the controversy served to highlight the depth of disagreement between women leaders over what freedom and equality meant for females.

One point of conflict centered on the propriety of using a constitutional amendment to fight prejudice. The feminists insisted that discrimination against women could be eliminated effectively only by writing the rule of equality into the basic law of the land. Despite the victory achieved in the Nineteenth Amendment, they pointed out, over one thousand state laws continued to discriminate against women. In 1940 eleven states provided that a wife could not hold her own earnings without her husband's consent; sixteen states denied a married woman the right to make contracts; seven gave the father superior guardianship rights; and over twenty prohibited women from serving on juries. Legislation regarding sexual mores was especially egregious. In Virginia a father could not be required to contribute to the maintenance of his illegitimate child. In Maryland a husband could divorce his wife if she had been unchaste before marriage. And in Minnesota a man whose wife was guilty of adultery could collect damages from her lover— a recourse denied the wife in a similar situation.[18]

Common law represented the worst villain of all. According to British precedent, a woman's legal existence merged with that of her husband upon marriage, so that in effect she ceased to be a person in her own right. United States courts ruled that any interpretation of the Constitution had to take common law into account, and on numerous occasions women had been denied legal standing as "persons" before state and federal judges. In 1872 the Supreme Court determined that Myra Bradwell, an aspiring lawyer, could not practice her profession in the state of Illinois because as a married woman she was not covered by the "equal protection" clause of the Fourteenth Amendment. The harmony of the family institution, Justice Joseph Bradley declared, was repugnant to "the idea of a woman adopting a distinct and independent career from that of her husband." Fifty years later the highest court in Massachusetts refused the right of jury service to women on the grounds that they were not "persons in the eyes of the law." And in Georgia the Supreme Court ruled in 1945 that a wife must follow her husband from a five-room house to a log cabin because "the husband is the head of the family and as such has the right to fix the matrimonial residence without the consent of his wife."[19]

In the face of such discrimination, the feminists contended that only a constitutional amendment could establish the principle of equality for the entire nation. "It is strangely unsympathetic," the educator M. Carey Thomas wrote, "for opponents of an Equal Rights Amendment to suggest removing the thousands of inequalities and injustices by slow and piecemeal work . . . while women are being born, living their lives and dying without the justice which they have been waiting for since the time of the cave man." The amendment promised to establish a uniform standard of sexual justice for the entire country and to nullify the pernicious heritage of common law. It was a one-step solution to "the ancestral tradition of sex inferiority and subjection," its supporters claimed, and a noble addition to the Bill of Rights.[20]

The reformers responded by challenging both the content and approach of the feminist program. Most discrimination against women was rooted in custom, not law, they asserted. Consequently, the Equal Rights Amendment was a "quack nostrum" which would have little constructive effect. In addition, they pointed out, the amendment would not even eliminate laws which did discriminate against women since additional legislative action would be required to implement the amendment's principle. "It is not practical," Mary Anderson charged. "It deals with abstract rights, not real rights." The amendment established a standard, but did nothing to make it a reality. "I want equality, yes," wrote Cornelia Bryce Pinchot; "but I want equality that is a fact, not an empty phrase."[21]

What bothered reformers most was the potentially destructive effect of the amendment on protective legislation for women. Equal rights, declared one opponent, was "one of those weasel-like phrases like 'fraternity,' 'equality,' and 'democracy'"; it meant nothing until the Supreme Court interpreted it. On the basis of the Court's decisions on minimum wages for women and on child labor, however, the reformers had good reason to believe that judges would invalidate the protective legislation which the reformers had worked so hard to gain. The Women's Party cavalierly argued that, however the courts decided, "we can rest serene in our reliance on the righteousness of the principle of equal rights for men and women and not worry as to the details of how it will work out"; yet it was the details which perturbed the women reformers.[22] The amendment, they feared, would endanger wage and hour laws for women, undermine support laws for wives and children, and terminate special penalties in the law for rape and sexual offenses against women. "The Equal Rights Amendment would operate like a blind man with a shot gun," one legal expert warned. "No lawyer can confidently predict what it would hit."[23]

As a result of their apprehension, the reformers sought to discredit the entire equal rights drive. "The Constitution is not the place to theorize on the relations between the sexes," one reform lawyer told a congressional hearing. "Law is law. It is not a place for emotions or hopes." Reformers contended that the simplistic formulation of the Women's Party bore no relation to the complexity of women's actual situation. "Only those who are ignorant of the law . . . or indifferent to the exacting aspects of women's life," Felix Frankfurter wrote in 1923, "can have the naïveté, or the recklessness, to sum up women's whole position in a meaningless and mischievous phrase about 'equal rights.' " Legal equality between the sexes could not be achieved, Mary Anderson asserted; indeed, the whole concept of equality was a myth.[24]

More than a question of legal propriety was involved in the dispute, however. At the root of the conflict was the issue of whether protective legislation helped or hindered the quest for equality. From the feminists' point of view, laws which singled out women for special treatment represented a conspiracy to deny them their economic rights. "Whatever the effects on women of sex legislation aimed to protect them," Alma Lutz declared, "it has been a real protection to men by slowing down the competition of women for their jobs." As early as 1836, the New England Association of Farmers, Mechanics and Other Workingmen had advocated special labor legislation for women in order to control the size of the work force, and in 1923 the AF of L offered a similar rationale for its renewed interest in protective statutes. If women were prohibited from lifting certain weights or from working long hours, male workers could feel safe in their jobs. The feminists were convinced that, under the guise of concern for women's health and safety, unions actually sought special wage and hour legislation for females as a way of preventing women from taking work away from men. The only purpose of protective legislation in the age of the new woman, Maud Younger wrote, was "to lower women's economic status, keep them in the ranks with little chance for advancement . . . and perpetuate the psychology that they are cheap labor and inferior to other adult workers."[25]

To support their contention that special labor laws discriminated against women, the feminists marshalled an impressive array of evidence. In New York City over 700 women employees of the Brooklyn Rapid Transit System lost their jobs when a statute prohibiting split shifts for women prevented them from working the morning and evening rush hours. Waitresses, clerks in drug stores, women printers, and reporters all suffered when New York declared that women could not work after 10 p.m. One study concluded that, if it were not for protective legislation, 2 to 5 per cent more women would be gainfully employed, many of them in jobs which represented "frontiers" in women's work. The case of Mollie Maloney, a bookbinder who earned $46.50 working the night shift in 1919, illustrated the feminists' argument. After passage of New York's night work statute, she was forced to move from her former job to the less remunerative day shift. When another law limiting women's hours of overtime prevented her from filling rush orders, she lost her job entirely. From Maloney's point of view, protective legislation was manifestly unfair. "We working women can protect ourselves if we have equality of opportunity under the law," she declared.[26]

The feminists singled out minimum-wage laws for special condemnation. Establishing a set rate for women's services, they argued, placed an unfair value on women's work and invited men to undercut them by accepting lower pay. In Ohio, women's employment declined by over 14 per cent after a minimum-wage law was passed. At Harvard University, twenty scrubwomen were fired when the state ordered their pay to be increased by two cents an hour. And in California, the director of finance reported in 1932 that thousands of women were out of work because men were willing to accept less pay than the legal base set for women. "In not a single state having minimum wage legislation . . . do women receive a living wage," the feminist Jane Norman Smith declared. "On the other hand, whenever this legislation has been enforced . . . women have lost their jobs and been replaced by men."[27]

Ultimately the feminists objected to special labor legislation because it symbolized the evil of a social system which set women apart as a separate class and assigned them a place less equal than that of men. The phrase "protective legislation" carried the distinct connotation that women lacked the ability to care for themselves and were second-class citizens. "Under the common law, women were 'protected' from themselves in being placed under the guardianship of father and husband," a New York equal rights pamphlet declared, "[but] modern women do not wish 'protection' as inferior beings." Special labor laws, the feminists argued, categorized the whole sex as weak and dependent—the equivalent of classifying all men as disabled because a few were wounded veterans.[28] Only when females ceased to be grouped with children as helpless creatures could they enjoy the full status of mature persons that was their birthright.

Within such a context, the real purpose of the Equal Rights Amendment was to obliterate sex as a functional classification within the law. The feminists argued that women could not achieve real freedom until they were treated as individuals, not members of a sexual group. "It is time sex be forgotten and men and women become co-workers in all that concerns the destiny of the human race," Mary Woolley of Mount Holyoke wrote. Not every member of the Women's Party agreed with Alice Paul that equality meant absolute identity with men, but most joined in the conviction that women should be accorded the same legal status as men. "We are not asking for any special rights," Anita Pollitzer told a Senate hearing. "We are not asking for anything but the same opportunity [as men] to be human beings in this land of ours."[29]

As they had on other issues, the reformers rejected both the specific claims and underlying premise of the feminists' argument. Legislation regulating women's hours, wages, and working conditions, they contended, had ameliorated the horrors of sweatshop labor and given workers protection against unprincipled employers. Far from undermining female equality, such laws were responsible for "bringing the women's standard up a little toward the standards of men." Passage of the Equal Rights Amendment might correct a few instances of discrimination, but it would also wipe out years of progress and restore the intolerable factory conditions of the late nineteenth century. For the sake of giving an individual woman the right to drive a taxi in Ohio, the feminists were willing to junk the rights of almost all female industrial workers to decent working conditions. The historian Mary Beard summed up many of the reformers' arguments when she declared that supporters of the Equal Rights Amendment "ran the risk of positively strengthening anachronistic competitive industrial processes; of supporting . . . ruthless laissez-faire; [and] of forsaking humanism in the quest for feminism." In service to an abstract theory, the well-being of millions would be endangered.[30]

Indeed, the reformers believed that the entire feminist drive was motivated by the desire of a few business and professional women to advance their own interests at the expense of the rest of the sex. In a brilliant article analyzing the class bias of feminism, Mary Van Kleeck pointed out that the Women's Party and its allies were concerned primarily with liberating the individual woman. The feminists placed special emphasis on personal freedom and accomplishment—values which appealed to career women who aspired to success in positions which were competitive with men. The nature of industrial labor, on the other hand, barred individualistic competition. The factory was a collective institution, and the women working in it cared more about economic security than personal liberty. The two classes thus had distinctly opposite economic interests, but the feminists refused to acknowledge the difference and instead attempted to impose their own point of view on all women. The result, Van Kleeck declared, was that in the name of freedom a small number of career women were undercutting the only protection which female factory workers had.[31]

Subsequent events seemed to confirm the accuracy of Van Kleeck's analysis. The Women's Party filed a legal brief in the 1923 *Adkins* case urging the Supreme Court to invalidate Washington, D.C.,'s minimum-wage law for women. Thirteen years later, it repeated its performance in the celebrated New York State minimum-wage case. In both instances, the Court appeared to endorse the feminists' contention that placing a floor beneath the wages of women amounted to a denial of their freedom of contract. To the feminists, such decisions represented a bold advance toward equal rights, but to social reformers the opposite was true. Mary Anderson asserted that the Court's ruling in the New York case had about as much to do with freedom for women as the right-wing Liberty League had to do with liberty. The feminist position on equality, the *Nation* commented, "is as always logically sound and theoretically progressive. Humanly, however, it is impractical and reactionary."[32]

Whatever the merits of the specific arguments, however, the conflict ultimately centered on the reformers' assumption that women *did* differ fundamentally from men and *should* be treated as a separate class. Summarizing the reform point of view, the Consumers League declared that, while women had the same rights as men, they were "not identical in economic or social function or in physical capacity" and hence could not be dealt with in the same way. The contention that women possessed distinctive attributes requiring special attention constituted the principal rationale for protective legislation. In his landmark brief before the Supreme Court in 1908 in the case of *Muller* v. *Oregon,* Louis Brandeis stated that the "two sexes differ in structure of body, in the function to be performed by each, in the amount of physical strength [and] in the capacity for long continued labor." The difference, Brandeis asserted, justified special legislation regulating women's hours of work. In its decision, the Court adopted the reformers' position and articulated a theory of women's nature hardly designed to please feminists. "Woman has always been dependent upon man," the Court declared. "Even though . . . she stood as far as statutes are concerned, upon an absolutely equal plane with him, it would still be true that she . . . will rest upon and look to him for protection."[33]

For the most part, reformers accepted such a definition of women's identity as a necessary prerequisite for achieving social-welfare legislation. Rose Schneiderman of the Women's Trade Union League observed that most women could not do the same work as men and needed safeguards to protect their health. In particular, Schneiderman rejected the idea that women should be employed as absolute equals with men. Those who "want to work at the same hours of the day or night and receive the same pay," she declared, "might be putting their own brothers or sweethearts, or husbands out of a job." Full-time work, by implication, remained the exclusive prerogative of men. The Court's interpretation in the *Muller* case coincided with the reformers' own conviction that the two sexes had separate roles to play in life. "Nature made men and women different," Felix Frankfurter asserted; "the law must accommodate itself to the immutable differences of Nature."[34]

Consistent with Frankfurter's reasoning, the reformers placed special emphasis on woman's role within the family in their campaign against the Equal Rights Amendment. "No law . . . can change physical structures that make women the child-bearers of mankind," a group of reformers asserted. Nature had decreed that women should devote their lives to caring for children. A man could not nurse a baby, Al Smith observed. Consequently, the two sexes could not be treated identically. The clear inference of the reformers' argument was that any effort to obliterate sexual differences in the law was a direct assault on God's creation. "To deny that women require care and protection," one writer charged, "is equal to a denial of their physical mission of motherhood."[35]

The reformers and feminists thus held diametrically opposite conceptions of female equality. The Women's Party and its allies were convinced that protective legislation discriminated against females and that women could not be free until they achieved absolute identity with men in all areas of public policy regulated by the law. The reformers, in turn, believed that differences of physical and psychological make-up prevented women from ever competing on a basis of total equality with men and that special labor laws were required if females were to be protected against exploitation and given just treatment in their economic activities. One side was committed to the philosophy that women were exactly the same as men in all their principal attributes, the other to the position that females were a weaker sex whose rights would be destroyed unless safeguarded by special legislation. The division of opinion could hardly have been greater.

Ironically, both sides presented arguments which were legitimate if not carried to an extreme. The number of discriminatory state laws still in existence made the feminists' call for a new constitutional amendment seem a sensible and expedient way of carrying on the fight for equality. Women had a right to determine their own destinies, and the feminists argued convincingly that, when females were grouped together as a dependent sex and treated invidiously, they were denied a full measure of equality with men. On the other hand, the reformers correctly pointed out that women differed from men in some ways and that laws which took such differences into account were not necessarily prejudicial to women's best interests. Minimum-wage and maximum-hour statutes had improved the lot of many female industrial workers, and if career women objected to being covered by the same provisions, there was no reason to eliminate arbitrarily all protective legislation.

By the 1930's, however, the woman's movement had become so embroiled in emotional antagonism over the Equal Rights Amendment that the justice which existed on both sides was ignored. Instead of moving ahead together to attack the practical problems of discrimination, women's groups were polarized over doctrinaire questions of ideology. The conflict had degenerated into a "holy war," with each side resorting to polemics and adopting a position as far from the other as possible. The reformers denounced the Women's Party as a "small but militant group of leisure class women" who resented "not having been born men," and the feminists responded by calling the reformers "Tories" whose hearts bled "for the poor working girl but who would oppose for themselves the restrictions as to pay and hours imposed on these same working girls."[36]

As the amendment fight wore on, the feminists slowly gained ground despite their lesser numbers. A League of Women Voters official noted in 1937 that the Women's Party made such a fuss on Capitol Hill that some congressmen were willing to send the amendment to the floor just to secure peace and quiet. A House Sub-Committee endorsed the amendment in 1936, the Senate

Judiciary Committee reported it to the floor two years later, and the Republican party officially supported it in 1940. When the Fair Labor Standards Act of 1938 established the precedent of wage and hour limitations for both men and women, the protective legislation argument lost much of its force and the reformers became increasingly fearful of defeat. They formed a "Committee of Five Hundred Against the Equal Rights Amendment" and attempted to counter the Women's Party's initiative by proposing an omnibus "Women's Charter" which would establish the principle of equality while recognizing the differences between men and women.[37] Although the feminists lacked the popular backing necessary to win final victory, they had placed the reformers on the defensive and maximized to the fullest their limited political power.

In retrospect, it seems that the leaders of the woman's movement should have been able to devise a compromise which would have advanced the cause of women's rights while still maintaining the recognition of some sexual differences. Once the courts upheld labor legislation for both men and women, a principal obstacle to consensus was removed. If the feminists had reworded their amendment to accommodate the remaining objections of the reformers, or if reformers had been less adamant about opposing blanket legislation, the woman's movement might have secured the broad base of support needed to advance. The Equal Rights Amendment was certainly not a panacea, but its adoption might well have provided an important vehicle for eliminating legal discrimination as well as for establishing the principle that women deserved the same rights as men. As it was, however, antagonism was so congealed on each side that cooperation was impossible. For both reformers and feminists, defeat of the enemy within was more important than joining together in pursuit of a common purpose.

In the end, the principal result of the amendment battle was to highlight the profound divisions within the woman's movement. The suffragists had never clearly explained their goals, and the conflict which developed after 1920 revealed the extent to which different participants in the woman's movement held opposing conceptions of equality. If female leaders themselves could not agree on a goal, there was little likelihood that feminism could retain a popular following. Twenty years after enactment of the suffrage amendment, the women's rights movement had reached a nadir. Beset by controversy, weakened by lack of widespread support, and torn by internecine warfare, it had ceased to exist as a powerful force in American society.

# PART TWO

# World War II and
## Its Impact

# 6

# A Study in Change

At the end of the 1930's, prospects for improving women's economic status appeared bleak. The Depression had fostered a wave of reaction against any change in woman's traditional role. Legislative bodies enacted laws restricting the employment of married women. Labor, government, and the mass media all joined in a campaign urging females to refrain from taking jobs. And the overwhelming majority of average citizens—including women—showed little interest in modifying the existing distribution of sexual roles. Although some important changes had occurred in the two decades after suffrage, the over-all stability of women's economic situation was remarkable. In 1940 the percentage of females at work was almost exactly what it had been in 1910, and there seemed little reason to expect any change in the future.

Within five years, World War II had radically transformed the economic outlook of women. The eruption of hostilities generated an unprecedented demand for new workers, and, in response, over 6 million women took jobs, increasing the size of the female labor force by over 50 per cent. Wages leaped upward, the number of wives holding jobs doubled, and the unionization of women grew fourfold. Most important, public attitudes appeared to change. Instead of frowning on women who worked, government and the mass media embarked on an all-out effort to encourage them to enter the labor force. The war marked a watershed in the history of women at work, and, temporarily at least, caused a greater change in women's economic status than half a century of feminist rhetoric and agitation had been able to achieve.[1]

During the first months of the defense crisis, the attitudes of the 1930's prevailed and employers resisted hiring women to fill jobs historically performed by men. A survey of 12,000 factories in early 1942 showed that war industries were willing to employ women in only one-third of the jobs available. Plant managers feared that use of women would require the construction of expensive new sanitary facilities and would entail a substantial modification of the production process. Equally important, they hesitated to violate traditional ideas of woman's place by enlisting females to do men's jobs. A woman might be permitted to sew fabric for bomber wings in an aircraft factory, but she was not allowed to learn welding or do metal work. Public opinion would not "countenance the use of women as long as men could be found to do the emergency work," a Women's Bureau official remarked, and for the first few months there were enough men available to fill the need.[2]

The reluctance of employers to hire women seriously retarded female participation in government training programs for defense work. After surveying several key war industries in 1940, the Women's Bureau had urged that women be given equal opportunity with men to learn the skills required for production of war materiel. The government's vocational education program, however, was geared to the policies of employers, and public officials were unwilling to enroll women students until industry expressed a desire to use them. When Mary Anderson requested equal training for females, John Studebaker, head of the Office of Education, replied that training would be provided only when employers changed their policy and started to hire women. As a result, women comprised only 1 per cent of the 1,775,000 workers who had received special training as of December 1, 1941. Three hundred thousand persons attended the first series of courses which ended in February 1941, but only 595 were female.[3]

The Japanese attack on Pearl Harbor swiftly erased opposition to hiring women workers and cleared the way for a massive expansion of the female labor force. Within a few months after the United States declared war, millions of men had left their positions in factories and offices to take up arms. Male workers who were ineligible for the draft filled the gap momentarily, but, as their ranks dwindled, women became the only available labor reserve. In quick order, both industry and government abandoned their reluctance to use females in war industries. The government declared that the only answer to the manpower crisis was to "employ women on a scale hitherto unknown," and, after a brief survey of two hundred war jobs, the United States Employment Service concluded that women could fill 80 per cent of the positions with only brief training. Employers experienced a similar change of heart. "Almost overnight," Mary Anderson observed, "women were reclassified by industrialists from a marginal to a basic labor supply for munitions making." A week after Pearl Harbor, the American Management Association asked the Women's Bureau to help it set up new policies on the employment of females. By April 1942, the proportion of women receiving government-sponsored vocational training had leaped from 1 per cent to 13 per cent. And within seven months, the number of jobs for which employers were willing to consider female applicants had climbed from 29 per cent to 55 per cent.[4]

Women responded to the manpower crisis with an unprecedented display of skill and ingenuity. The beautician who overnight became a switchwoman for 600 Long Island Railroad trains represented but one example of women's readiness to assume new responsibilities. Josephine von Miklos, an Austrian aristocrat and designer of perfume bottles, took a job as a precision toolmaker in Hoboken's shipyards. A former cosmetics salesgirl from Philadelphia operated a 1,700 ton keel binder. In Gary, Indiana, women maneuvered giant overhead traveling cranes and cleaned out blast furnaces. Elsewhere, women ran lathes, cut dies, read blueprints, and serviced airplanes. They maintained roadbeds, greased locomotives, and took the place of lumberjacks in toppling giant redwoods. As stevedores, blacksmiths, foundry helpers, and drill-press operators, they demonstrated that they could fill almost any job, no matter how difficult or arduous.[5]

Those who did not go directly into war industry found other ways of helping to meet the manpower shortage. When a scarcity of taxi drivers developed in New York, female hackies took the wheel. A group of grandmothers manned the police radio in Montgomery County, Maryland, and women operated the public buses of Washington, Detroit, and New Orleans. Two thousand girl volunteers saved a million-gallon strawberry crop in Tennessee, while 29,000 others answered the government's plea to "Take a Fruit Furlough" by joining the Women's Land Army. Women's colleges did their part by training girls for wartime work and by encouraging students to enlist in civil defense activities. Barnard offered courses in auto repair, map-reading, and airplane-spotting; Smith set up an Officers Training School for women; and Rockford and Mount Holyoke gave credit to students who devoted part of their week to working in munitions factories.[6]

Volunteer organizations absorbed the energies of those women who did not wish to take full-time jobs but wanted to demonstrate their patriotic fervor. Over 3 million women flocked to local Red Cross headquarters, helping to prepare bandages, run motor pools, and start community centers. The Cleveland Federation of Women's Clubs inaugurated its own Civilian Service Bureau with lists of members who could step in at a moment's notice as teachers, waitresses, and secretaries. Countless civilian defense groups boasted of women airplane spotters and ambulance drivers. Even sports became feminized. Ball fans across the country were entertained by a thirty-four-team women's softball league, called by the *Saturday Evening Post* a "baffling mixture of Dead End Kids and Sweet Alice."[7]

The ease with which women assumed their new responsibilities challenged many of the conventional stereotypes of women's work. Employers resorted to traditional imagery to explain women's success, claiming that an overhead crane operated "just like a gigantic clothes wringer," and that the winding of wire spools in electrical factories was very much like crocheting. But the fact that females were adept at using acetylene torches as well as sewing machines called into question some of the more rigid distinctions which had been established between the type of labor performed by men and women. Females had demonstrated that they could do a man's work and do it well, and, as the war progressed, more and more men in the factory started treating their women co-workers as equals. A Women's Bureau official noted after an extensive tour of a California shipyard that men barked orders at women, refused to pick up their tools when dropped, and withheld the deference associated with traditional male-female relationships. In the midst of the wartime emergency, sex labels lost some of their meaning, both in the type of jobs assigned and in the attitude of workers toward each other. After witnessing the extent to which females had become assimilated into the formerly male-dominated industries of the Connecticut Valley, Constance Green observed that "presenting a tool chest to a little girl need no longer be dubbed absurdly inappropriate."[8]

The greatest changes in female employment occurred in those areas of the country where defense industries were most concentrated. In eight of ten war-impacted cities surveyed by the Women's Bureau, the number of women workers doubled from 1940 to 1945. In Detroit the female labor force soared from 182,000 to 387,000, while in San Francisco it grew from 138,000 to 275,000. Most of the increase came in manufacturing industries. During one fourteen-month period, women comprised 80 per cent of all new workers added to factory payrolls. The number of female industrial workers multiplied five times in Detroit and three times in Baltimore. In many cities, there were more women employed in factories by 1944 than had been in the entire labor force in 1940.[9]

A substantial portion of the new workers had migrated from their former place of residence during the war. As husbands and boy friends left home for duty in distant cities, wives and girl friends followed. Over 7 million women changed their county of residence during the first three and a half years of the war, and a third of them joined the labor force. The migration caused unavoidable social problems. Delinquency increased substantially, especially among young girls, and teenage runaways soared.[10] As newcomers poured into cities like San Diego and Portland, social welfare agencies were frequently unable to cope with the difficulties experienced by people trying to adjust to a new environment. But the women migrants also contributed mightily to the war, comprising approximately 50 per cent of the female labor force in such war centers as Mobile, San Francisco, and Wichita.[11]

Industries directly related to the war attracted the largest bloc of new female workers. Defense plants had the most critical need for additional manpower and the fewest traditions of prejudice to overcome. In addition, the production of airplanes, parachutes, and artillery held a special appeal for women whose primary motivation in working was to help their sons and husbands fighting in the field. Thus while the female manufacturing force as a whole grew 110 per cent during the war, the number of women in war industries shot up 460 per cent. A few months after Germany invaded Poland, a total of 36 women were involved in the construction of ships. By December 1942, over 160,000 were employed welding hatches, riveting gun emplacements, and binding keels. The number of women automobile workers grew from 29,000 to 200,000, electrical workers from 100,000 to 374,000. At the beginning of the conflict, 340,000 women had been engaged as operatives in heavy industry. Four years later, the figure had skyrocketed to over 2 million. In California alone, the increase amounted to 1,697 per cent.[12]

Employment patterns in the aircraft industry highlighted the impact of the war on women workers. When the Women's Bureau visited seven airplane factories in April 1941, it found 143 female employees. Eighteen months later, the same seven plants employed over 65,000 women. Nationwide, women's participation in the air industry soared from 1 per cent, or 4,000 women in December 1941 to 39 per cent, or 310,000 in December 1943. More important, female aircraft workers had graduated from sewing fabric for the wings of planes to assembling navigation systems and welding fuselages. So urgent was the demand for women workers in the air industry that almost 500,000 enrolled in the government's Vocational and College War Training Program to learn about aircraft production alone.[13]

Not all the new female workers entered manufacturing or war industries, of course. A tremendous number—over 2 million—went to work in offices. The war seemed to produce as much tonnage of paper work as of bombs, and women provided almost all the help in reducing it to manageable proportions. As might have been expected, the federal government accounted for the largest increment. The War Department and other agencies in Washington had an endless capacity for absorbing new personnel, and from 1940 to 1945 nearly one million women went to work for Uncle Sam. Female employees multiplied four times faster than male employees (they increased 260.5 per cent from 1941 to 1943 alone), and by the end of the war constituted 38 per cent of all federal workers, more than twice the percentage of the last pre-war year. Nationwide, the clerical force almost doubled, outpaced in the speed of its growth only by the category of craftsmen, foremen, operatives, and laborers.[14]

The war also made a dent in some of the barriers blocking women's employment in business and the professions. Rensselaer Polytechnic Institute enrolled its first female student; the Curtiss-Wright Company sent eight hundred women engineering trainees to college; and giant corporations like Montsanto, Du Pont and Standard Oil began to hire women chemists. In Washington the government sought to fill its depleted legal staffs with women lawyers, and on Wall Street brokerage houses embarked on a concerted campaign to recruit female analysts and statisticians. Even the close-knit Washington press corps opened its ranks. Male reporters still excluded thirty-seven women from the annual White House correspondents dinner—a fact which May Craig protested vigorously—but on Capitol Hill the number of women journalists tripled from thirty to ninety-eight. Mary Anderson declared in 1943 that doors were opening to professional women "in an unprecedented way. Women doctors, dentists, chemists, personnel directors and lawyers are in demand as never before." Although Anderson considerably overstated the case, some progress had been made.[15]

Perhaps the most important unanticipated consequence of the war was that thousands of women already employed received their first experience of occupational mobility. In addition to hiring 1.3 of the 2.5 million women who joined the manufacturing force for the first time, war industries also attracted almost 700,000 women from other industries and occupations. The manpower crisis placed a premium on employing the largest number of women in the shortest period of time, and women who had previously been forced to take menial or low-paying jobs rushed to war plants to take advantage of the opportunity. The assembly line of one airplane factory represented a composite of the female population. Former salesgirls worked alongside filing clerks, stenographers beside seamstresses.[16] A Women's Bureau survey showed that two-thirds of the women who had held jobs in eating and drinking establishments at the beginning of the war had transferred to other work by the end. Over six hundred laundries were forced to shut down in 1942 because they could not find women willing to shake clothes and run hot steam irons. In war-impacted areas like Mobile and San Francisco, nearly half of all women employed before Pearl Harbor shifted from their old jobs into military production.[17]

Negro women benefited more than any other group of female workers from the increased mobility. In the years preceding the war, black women were twice as likely to be employed as whites, but their economic horizons were severely limited. Over 70 per cent worked as domestic servants in private homes, and another 20 per cent toiled in the fields, picking crops and hoeing gardens on small farms. For them, the war represented in some ways a second emancipation. The manpower shortage broke down rigid employment barriers and gave them an unparalleled opportunity to advance. In response to the call for new workers, over 400,000 domestics left their former jobs.[18] The number of black women who held positions as servants fell from 72 per cent to 48 per cent, and the number of farm workers declined from 20 per cent to 7 per cent. At the same time, the proportion of Negro women who were employed as operatives in factories grew from 7.3 per cent to 18.6 per cent. The assimilation of blacks into the manufacturing force came slowly, and with great reluctance on the part of many employers, but it signified a dramatic change for the better in their economic condition.[19]

Many of the women who shifted jobs during the war years were attracted by the better working conditions in war industries. Early in the manpower crisis the Women's Bureau insisted that factories provide rest rooms, adequate toilets, cafeterias, good lighting, and comfortable chairs for their female workers. To a surprising extent, management complied, and conditions in war factories excelled those in other industries. A Women's Bureau study of Bridgeport, Connecticut, for example, reported that women war workers "experienced a marked change in their surroundings. Ventilation, lighting, seating and service facilities . . . usually were much better than on their old jobs." Another survey of upstate New York indicated that half the war plants had established a rest period, and Constance Green's study of the Connecticut Valley showed that twenty-four of twenty-seven factories had instituted improved health and accident facilities. The presence of so many female workers hastened the simplification of jobs and the installation of long-needed safety regulations. Machines were protected; coveralls, slacks, and goggles were made mandatory equipment; and light tools were substituted for heavy ones. One industry official commented, "These are machines we always knew we ought to guard, and now we are guarding them."[20] For the first time in their lives, many women worked in a safe, clean, and pleasant environment.

Higher pay provided the greatest incentive for moving into war industries, however. Wages in munitions plants and aircraft factories averaged 40 per cent higher than in consumer factories. In the

Connecticut Valley, an operative in a war plant earned $34.85 weekly in contrast to $24.65 for an operative in a regular factory. The starting pay for a woman in an aircraft plant was twice that offered by a commercial laundry. The advantages of war work were especially noticeable in low-wage areas like the South. A female shipbuilder in Mobile took home $37 a week, while a sales-girl received $21 and a waitress $14. Not surprisingly, over half the women employed in Mobile in 1940 had changed jobs by 1944.[21]

In addition, the women who entered war plants usually enjoyed the benefits of union representation. Until the late 1930's, with the exception of the garment industry, organized labor had largely neglected the unionization of female employees. The CIO was com-mitted to redressing that imbalance, however, and under the pro-tective aegis of the National War Labor Board, it set out to ensure that all workers in mass-production industries would be organized. During the war years, the CIO became an entrenched power in many of the areas in which a large number of women were em-ployed. The auto, steel, and electrical unions all boasted significant female memberships, and the number of women enrolled in labor organizations jumped from 800,000 in 1939 to over 3,000,000 in 1945. Although women still suffered unequal treatment within indi-vidual unions, they benefited substantially from labor represen-tation.[22]

The most significant change wrought by the war, however, in-volved the age and marital status of the new recruits to the labor force. It was important that Rosie riveted, but far more critical was the fact that she was married and over thirty-five years old. From the time women first joined the ranks of the gainfully employed, the young and single had predominated; now the pendulum swung to the side of the married and middle-aged. By the end of the war it was just as likely that a wife over forty would be employed as a single woman under twenty-five. The proportion of all married women who were employed jumped from 15.2 per cent in 1940 to more than 24 per cent by the end of 1945, and, as the fighting drew to a close, wives for the first time composed almost a majority of women workers.[23]

Margaret Hickey, head of the Women's Advisory Committee to the War Manpower Commission, remarked in 1943 that "employers, like other individuals, are finding it necessary to weigh old values, old institutions, in terms of a world at war." Her observation accurately described the transformation of public and private policy toward the hiring of married women as war workers. In the past, employment of wives had been frowned upon. A woman's place was in the home, and popular convention assumed that if she left its confines, the family and all that was related to it would disintegrate. In the midst of war, however, the services of married women in the labor force became essential to the successful functioning of the economy. Personnel managers attempted to hire single women first, but as *Fortune* magazine observed in 1943, "there are practically no unmarried women left to draw upon." The urban housewife became the principal source of labor supply, her services as assiduously cultivated during the war as they had been shunned in the Depression.[24]

As the manpower crisis intensified, wives of all ages and from all parts of the country flocked to take jobs. Seventy-five per cent of the new women workers were married, and the number of wives in the labor force doubled. To some extent, the dramatic increase reflected a shift in marriage patterns. The outbreak of war prompted a rash of weddings, and by 1944 there were 2.5 million more married women and 830,000 fewer single women in the population than there had been in 1940. Some of the new working wives would have been employed regardless of the war, especially the recently wedded spouses of young soldiers who took jobs near military centers while waiting for their husbands to return from the front.[25] A great many working wives, however, were older women who had been married for a number of years. Over 3.7 million of the 6.5 million female newcomers to the labor force listed themselves as former housewives. Many had children of school and pre-school age, including 60 per cent of those hired by the War Department.

Their employment exemplified a drastic change in policy by business and government. In Connecticut and Ohio, unofficial bans against employment of married women office workers in public positions were discarded. Swift and Company lifted a ninety-year rule against hiring wives. And the large insurance companies, each of which had previously discriminated against married women, began to recruit them actively.[26]

A similar change occurred in the policy of employers toward middle-aged women. In January 1941 many firms refused to consider hiring any female over thirty-five years of age. At the beginning of the war, the majority of women workers were thirty-two or under. Within the next four years, however, 60 per cent of all the women added to the labor force were over thirty-five. Mary Anderson persuaded government arsenals to begin hiring women over forty in early 1942, and private business quickly followed suit. By the end of the war, the proportion of women thirty-five to forty-four in the labor force had jumped from 27 per cent to 38 per cent, and the number over forty-five had grown from 16 to 24 per cent. Almost all the older workers were also married. For the first time in their lives, they played an important part in the economic processes of the country. And four out of five indicated in a Women's Bureau survey that they wished to stay in the labor force after the war.[27]

None of the changes in women's work could have occurred without the active approval and encouragement of the principal instruments of public opinion. While necessity required the employment of millions of new female workers, the mass media cooperated by praising women who joined the labor force. A few years earlier, newspapers and magazines had discouraged women from leaving the home and had supported restrictions on the hiring of married women. Now, radio stations and periodicals glamorized war work and pleaded with women to hurry and enlist at their local employment office. Portland, Oregon, stations sponsored a "Working Women Win Wars Week," and a national network gave time each week to a broadcast by "Commando Mary" on how women could

assist in defeating the enemy. In one radio script, the announcer declared that women possessed "a limitless, ever-flowing source of
moral and physical energy, working for victory." Why do we need
women workers, the broadcast asked? "You know why," came the
answer. "You can't build ships and planes and guns without
[them]."[28]

Newspapers and magazines did their part in the publicity build-
up by depicting Rosie the Riveter as a national heroine and exhort-
ing others to join her. The woman with an acetylene torch became
almost as familiar a figure to magazine readers as the girl with the
Palmolive smile. *Life* featured a pigtailed pilot on its cover and detailed the exploits of Jacqueline Cochran's air ferry service, while
Ruth Sulzberger in the *New York Times* testified to the "Adventures of a [Female] Hackie." Almost every issue of a national
publication contained some laudatory article on women's war
contribution, whether it concerned a female oboeist in a symphony
orchestra, a woman parachute maker in California, or the wives
and mothers who ruled a Cumberland town.[29]

The government provided the impetus for the campaign to
attract women workers. Acknowledging that "getting these women
into industry is a tremendous sales proposition," Paul McNutt, head
of the War Manpower Commission, directed defense agencies to
make an all-out effort to secure female employees. General Her-
shey of Selective Service urged industry and agriculture to hire
women in factories, farms, and offices, and Henry Stimson, Secretary of War, issued a pamphlet entitled "You're Going to Employ
Women," which made recruitment of females into government
service almost a military order. "The War Department," the pamphlet declared, "must fully utilize, immediately and effectively, the
largest and potentially the finest single source of labor available
today—the vast reserve of woman-power." Local United States Employment Service offices sometimes even banned the hiring of men,
insisting that women be employed for every job that did not absolutely require a man.[30]

The War Manpower Commission itself attempted to facilitate

the process by issuing guidelines designed to end sex discrimination. Employers were told to hire and train women "on a basis of equality with men," to "remove all barriers to the employment of women in any occupation for which they are or can be fitted," and to use "every method available" to ensure women's complete acceptance.[31] The Office of War Information conducted a vigorous public relations campaign in support of the WMC's policies, and urged both employers and women to answer the call to national service. Although the government's pronouncements about non-discrimination were not always followed in practice, the war and the effort to legitimize women's work did succeed in changing the average citizen's attitude toward female employment. At the height of the Depression, over 80 per cent of the American people strongly opposed work by married women. By 1942, in contrast, 60 per cent believed that wives should be employed in war industries (only 13 per cent were opposed), and 71 per cent asserted that there was a need for more married women to take jobs.[32]

As a result of the manpower shortage and the aggressive campaign to recruit female workers, women's economic status changed significantly for the first time in thirty years. During the war, the proportion of women who were employed jumped from slightly over 25 per cent to 36 per cent—a rise greater than that of the preceding four decades. By V-E Day, the female labor force had increased by 6.5 million, or 57 per cent. For the first time, more wives were employed than single women, more women over thirty-five than under thirty-five. Manufacturing took the largest number of new workers—2.5 million—but an additional 2 million entered the clerical field, and the only areas of female employment to suffer a relative decline were those of domestic servant and professional. At the close of hostilities, nearly 20 million women were in the labor force—35 per cent of all workers in contrast to 25 per cent in 1940.[33]

In the eyes of many observers, women's experience during the war years amounted to a revolution. The Women's Bureau called the increase in female employment "one of the most fundamental social and economic changes in our time." Erwin Canham of the *Christian Science Monitor* declared that "in the long years ahead, we will remember these short years of ordeal as the period when women rose to full stature." Others commented on the change in woman herself. Instead of being treated as "a social inferior living on the fringe of American life," Rose Schneiderman said, the woman worker had become a first-class citizen whose contribution was recognized by everyone as indispensable to national survival. In a similar vein, Margaret Culkin Banning asserted that women would never again be dependent on men for their bread and butter. Able to earn their own keep, they could even support a husband who was wounded or ill.[34]

To a large extent, the economic activities of women in the war years provided convincing evidence for such conclusions. The exigencies of the crisis had swept away ancient traditions and established ways of doing things. Women substituted for men in many fields of endeavor, and barriers against the employment of the middle-aged and married had been shattered. Millions of women found out for the first time how it felt to receive a pay check, and with growing frequency wives assumed equal responsibility with husbands for earning the family income. Most important, the public's attitude toward women's work changed, at least temporarily, from outright condemnation to tolerant sanction. "[W]e are building up an entirely different social climate," Jennie Matyas, a labor leader, commented in 1943; "what we didn't consider the nice thing to do after the last war will become the regular thing to do after this one."[35]

There were other signs, however, that such optimism might be both premature and exaggerated. Female employment provoked opposition as well as praise, especially as it affected the stability of family life. The war had been accompanied by severe social dislocations, many of them associated directly or indirectly with women's work. The Connecticut Child Welfare Association reported a startling increase in childhood neurosis, and the "latch-key" child who had no supervision during the day while his mother was at work became a subject of national concern. The fact that delinquency and teenage runaways increased in the same period led many observers to view female employment as a principal source of domestic ills. Clare Booth Luce demanded that women return to the home to care for their children, and the Children's Bureau called the growing employment of mothers "a hazard to the security of the child in his family."[36] For some Americans at least, women working represented a threat to the cohesion and sanity of social life. It might be tolerated as a temporary necessity, but not as a permanent reality.

The critical question was how deeply the wartime changes had penetrated, and whether the advances made at a time of crisis would continue into peacetime. The war, by its very nature, had disrupted the established order and forced an adjustment in the patterns of national living. As a result, many of the most overt forms of discrimination against women were eradicated. A permanent change in women's economic status, however, required a continued redistribution of sexual roles, a more profound shift in public attitudes, and a substantial improvement in the treatment and opportunities afforded the female worker. On that score, there was somewhat less reason for optimism. Although the evidence suggested that a dramatic change had occurred in the status of the woman worker, a closer look at the nation's economic institutions indicated that some of the deeper manifestations of female inequality remained and had been only partially mitigated by the impact of the war.

# 7

# The Persistence of Inequality

Female participation in the labor force was essential to victory in the war, but it also raised serious questions about the nation's social values and the future direction of male-female relationships. It was one thing to encourage women to work as a temporary device to meet a manpower shortage and quite another to view females as permanent jobholders with the same rights as men. The achievement of economic equality required more than simply the decision to hire women as replacements for men gone to war. It also entailed the establishment of a uniform standard of pay, equal access for females to the higher ranks of business and government, and, most difficult of all, the development of community services to ease the woman's dual role as worker and homemaker. The American people had to decide, for example, whether it was more important for a mother to care for her children all day long or to contribute her skills to the work force. Not surprisingly, such issues involved substantial controversy, and were not resolved easily. Thus while women's economic role altered dramatically during the war years, inequality persisted in many areas, calling into question the extent to which permanent changes had taken place in attitudes toward women's work.

Discrimination against business and professional women constituted a primary example of enduring prejudice based on sex. The government had urged all women to sign up for jobs, regardless of their occupational background, but for the professional desiring to serve her country few positions existed. Despite the urgent need for medical personnel, the Army refused to commission women doctors until 1943, and it took an act of Congress to correct the injustice. The attitude of private industry was often no better. Businesswomen complained bitterly that they were denied management posts commensurate with their ability, and were expected to serve as trainees rather than executives. Although many women took jobs formerly held by men, in most factories each sex retained its own separate niche. "Women," the National Metal Trades Association explained, "are more patient, industrious, painstaking, and efficient about doing the same thing over and over again." More to the point, a Connecticut Valley industrialist remarked, "They do the monotonous, repetitive work . . . that drives a man nuts."[1]

Women were also excluded from most of the top policy-making bodies concerned with running the war. Mary Van Kleeck, a prominent social welfare worker, charged that the government had totally ignored the experience of women leaders in setting up its production, manpower, and food agencies. The same accusation was made by Minnie Maffett, head of the National Federation of Business and Professional Women. With the exception of Anna Rosenberg, she pointed out, not a single woman had been appointed to an important executive position in the various war agencies. Mary Anderson, director of the Women's Bureau, reported that her experts were never consulted by defense officials on questions involving female employment. Throughout the history of the Office of Defense Production, she observed, "the women had very little chance to be even thought of."[2] When the President finally appointed a Women's Advisory Commission (WAC) as an adjunct to the War Manpower Commission (WMC), it was only after the WMC's chairman had expressed his opposition and the members of at least one all-male committee had threatened to resign if a woman joined them. Mary Anderson concluded that the WAC had been created as a calculated device to put women "off in a corner" while denying them any real power.[3]

To a large extent, the WAC's subsequent history confirmed Anderson's initial judgment. Established to evaluate the problems of women war workers and make recommendations for remedial action, the committee met constant frustration in attempting to carry out its mandate. Despite repeated requests, it had no staff to set up studies and prepare position papers. Frequently, it was not consulted on issues affecting women workers. And more often than not, its recommendations—when made—were ignored. Significantly, the WAC was told only in August 1943 about a government plan to mount a public relations drive in September to attract women to war jobs. By the time the committee was notified, copy had already been written and sent to the printer.[4] The campaign itself testified to the government's commitment to recruit female workers, but the manner in which it was planned indicated that women leaders were not valued to the same degree as women workers.

Under such circumstances, the WAC rapidly developed a sense of its own futility. "If we are an advisory committee," one member declared, "somebody ought to ask us for advice sometimes." The women resented having to travel to Washington each month only to sit around a table and hear each other talk. They had hoped to become a vital force in determining government policy toward the woman worker but found instead that they constituted a "token" body. Complaining that females were tired of being treated as "assistants to assistants," the WAC demanded that the War Manpower Commission appoint women to executive positions where they could exercise some real influence. A woman was finally named as assistant to the deputy chairman, but most members of the committee were not mollified. One member resigned in frustration, complaining that women should be "unwilling to accept such subordinate and ineffective positions," and others contemplated the same course of action.[5]

The WAC's relations with the War Manpower Commission's Labor Management Committee (LMC) illustrated the reason for such discontent. The LMC was established in March 1943 to coordinate all policy regarding the use of manpower in the nation's factories. Mary Anderson, among others, had been assured that the head of the WAC would serve as a full member of the new committee. To her consternation, however, she discovered that, while WAC chairman Margaret Hickey could sit in on committee deliberations, she had neither a vote nor a voice in its decisions. When the WAC protested and asked that its chairman be given a vote, the LMC unanimously rejected the request, claiming that no special representation could be granted to minority groups. In fact, the new committee consistently demeaned Hickey, barring her from one emergency meeting on the forty-eight-hour week and permitting her only fifteen minutes to present her case for the appointment of women to regional Labor Management Committees.[6]

The WAC's experience highlighted the extent to which inequality persisted in the higher ranks of business and government. The WAC was forced to meet as a "woman's" committee because its members were not allowed to participate in other deliberative bodies. Yet all the decisions affecting women were made in a committee composed entirely of men. "The only place you can make yourself felt is if you are where a thing happens," WAC member Elizabeth Christman observed, "[and] they apparently don't happen [here]." Paul McNutt assured the WAC that it enjoyed the same status in the eyes of the War Manpower Commission as the LMC, but committee members learned from bitter experience that separate did not mean equal. "The more I work in government," Margaret Hickey said early in 1943, "the more I know that in the policy there is nothing discriminatory, but in the practice—that is where we have difficulty."[7]

The gap between promise and performance was perhaps best illustrated in those areas where women continued to receive less pay than men. The government could not be faulted on its formal commitment to equal wages. The War Manpower Commission had repeatedly urged a uniform pay scale for men and women, and in a series of decisions handed down in the fall of 1942, the National War Labor Board (NWLB) appeared to give substance to the WMC's policy. In the Brown and Sharp Manufacturing case, the NWLB rejected the company's practice of paying women 20 per cent less than men for the same work and endorsed the principle of equal pay "for female employees who in comparable jobs produce work of the same quantity and quality as that performed by men." The nation had an obligation, the Board declared, "to provide the utmost assurance that women will not be subject to discriminatory treatment in their compensation."[8]

Some industries, at least, conformed to the NWLB's policy, resulting in substantial gains for women workers. Newer businesses, with a shorter history of discrimination against women, offered female employees a better chance for equal treatment than older ones, and most aircraft plants, munitions factories, and shipyards had "pay for the job" policies. In addition, a number of CIO unions wrote equal pay provisions into their contracts and brought suits before the NWLB to correct wage inequities. The electrical workers, with 280,000 female members, succeeded in writing equal pay clauses into contracts covering 460,000 workers in 1944. A Women's Bureau survey of eighty contracts in three Midwestern states showed that half had equal-pay provisions, with the highest percentage in the radio, electrical, aircraft, and machine industries where CIO unions predominated.[9]

In a series of subsequent decisions, however, the NWLB weakened its initial ruling on equal pay and gave employers a series of loopholes through which they could continue to discriminate in their wage scales. One company was allowed to pay women less than men for the same work, because the women were given an extra rest period. In other cases, the Board determined that the equal-pay doctrine did not apply to jobs which were "historically" women's, nor to inequalities which existed between two plants, owned by the same company. Wage rates for jobs to which women alone were assigned, the Board declared, were "presumed to be correct." By the time the NWLB had completed its revisions, employers enjoyed wide latitude in devising ways to avoid the equal-pay principle. General Motors, for example, continued to pay women less than men, simply by substituting the categories "heavy" and "light" for "male" and "female."[10]

The government's concern with controlling inflation further deterred implementation of the equal-pay doctrine. Fearing that an across-the-board wage hike would start an inflationary wage-price spiral, the NWLB *permitted*, but did not require, industry to raise women's wages to the same level as men's. Board Chairman William Davis declared that the order was addressed primarily to employers who wished voluntarily to equalize the pay received by their female employees. The wording of the directive hardly seemed designed to encourage a rash of pay increases for women. More-over, President Roosevelt's Executive Order to "Hold the Line" on spending appeared to countermand even the permissive clause of the NWLB's ruling. Under the President's order, the Board could grant wage increases to correct substandard conditions but not to eliminate inequalities. As a result, the NWLB postponed thirty cases involving wage parity, declaring that it had no more power to grant equal pay for equal work. Subsequently, the NWLB's authority to order pay increases under the equality doctrine was restored, but in the meantime the movement to establish uniform standards of pay had suffered a severe setback.[11]

In the face of government equivocation over the equal-pay question, a great many employers continued to discriminate against women. Only one out of four Bridgeport, Connecticut, manufacturers offered both sexes the same starting rate. In one Eastern war plant, male trainees received a higher wage than the women training them, while in forty-one steel companies surveyed by the Women's Bureau female clerical workers averaged $60 a month less than men doing comparable work. Employers frequently skirted the issue entirely by placing women in separate job categories from men. When the Brooklyn Navy Yard began to use women to replace men, it called them "helper trainees" instead of "mechanic learners" and assigned them a commensurately lower wage. Other companies simply substituted the words "light and repetitive" for "skilled." Under the former category, a female gauge inspector in one plant earned 55 cents an hour, while her male counterpart took home $1.20.[12]

The worst form of discrimination against female workers was the rate paid for "women's" jobs. The NWLB had specifically refused to regulate the wages for such positions, but no class of work exhibited more profound prejudice. A Fort Wayne, Indiana, General Electric plant, for example, had fourteen classifications of male employees and five classifications of females. Many of the jobs required comparable skill and training, yet only the women in the highest female grouping received as much as the men in the lowest male category. At the root of the disparity was the pervasive assumption that any job historically filled by women had less intrinsic value than a comparable position held by men. The premise prevailed even where "objective" evaluations showed a woman's occupation to require more skill than a man's. General Electric assessed the job of janitor at thirty-six points and the job of inspector at sixty-eight points, but, because the first position was held by a man and the second by a woman, it paid twelve cents an hour more. Asked to explain the contradiction, the company asserted that the point totals were not comparable, since men's work and women's work were classified separately. That was precisely the problem, however. Men and women were arbitrarily assigned to separate labor categories on the basis of sex rather than skill, and it was presumed that women deserved less pay than men.[13]

The perpetuation of such categories often represented a tacit alliance between labor and management to keep women in their place. Although industrial unions fought for equal pay when women took jobs left by men, they frequently insisted that females be assigned to separate seniority lists and grouped together in distinct job classifications. A 1944 United Auto Workers contract declared that "men and women shall be divided into separate, non-interchangeable occupational groups unless otherwise negotiated locally." Similar contracts specified that women's membership in a union, and their seniority, should last only for the duration of the war. A legal brief presented by the United Electrical Workers (UEW) to the NWLB in 1945 suggested that many unions supported equal pay less out of a commitment to justice for women workers than out of concern for preserving a high wage for the returning veteran. If females replaced males at a lower rate of pay, the UEW asserted, the soldier coming back from war would find his job reclassified as women's work with a woman's wage.[14]

Despite some important advances, therefore, many women workers continued to suffer from wage discrimination. In 1945 as in 1940, females who were employed in manufacturing earned only 65 per cent of what men received.[15] The NWLB made a brave start toward redressing some of the inequalities which women experienced, but subsequent decisions weakened the impact of the Board's action. In addition, the government's anti-inflationary policies discouraged aggressive implementation of the equal-pay doctrine. Significantly, the NWLB refused to consider the most important source of discrimination against women—the differential in wage rates paid to females doing women's work. Impressive gains had been made in some war industries, especially those with strong unions, but, as long as female employment was judged by a different standard than men's, inequality was inevitable. A wage geared to the job rather than the sex of the worker offered the best solution, but at the end of the war such a goal remained almost as far away as it had been at the beginning.

The only issue more important than wages was the development of community services to ease the woman worker's household burden. From the time of the first women's rights convention at Seneca Falls, feminists had protested against women being saddled with exclusive responsibility for the domestic sphere of life. Charlotte Perkins Gilman pointed out that women could never achieve economic equality until methods were devised for relieving the female of some of her cooking, housekeeping, and child-rearing tasks. Pursuing the same line of thought, Marguerite Zapoleon, a Women's Bureau official, wrote that equal job opportunities for women depended on the creation of public institutions such as child care centers which would "expand rather than contract the possible areas of female usefulness."[16] The arguments of both women had a compelling logic. The wife who worked outside the home and also took care of her family carried two full-time jobs. Her dual responsibility prevented her from functioning on the same basis as a man in the world of business and labor. A strong case could thus be made that substantial modification of the existing domestic pattern was essential if women were to gain economic equality.

The issue of community services, however, involved complicated questions of values and immediately stirred up controversy. The creation of surrogate domestic institutions such as child care centers challenged deeply held convictions about the integrity of the family and the importance of woman's role in the home. Most Americans, female as well as male, believed that the primary responsibility of wives and mothers was to care for the household and to rear children. The development of community services threatened such beliefs by assuming that it was just as valuable and proper for a wife to work outside the home as for her to retain full responsibility for domestic tasks. Furthermore, the establishment of child care centers or central kitchens required a willingness to provide married women with a special form of subsidy to enable them to participate more freely in the job market. In effect, society was asked to give women "unequal" or compensatory treatment so that they could achieve "equality." The issue thus entailed a fundamental clash of values concerning woman's proper place and illustrated better than anything else the difficulty and complexity of achieving full equality between the sexes.

The question of community services first emerged as a result of the high turnover and absenteeism among women in war industries. Female workers changed jobs twice as often as men and stayed home twice as much. For every two women workers hired in warproduction factories in June 1943, one quit. The turnover rate in aircraft plants reached 35,000 a month, and Boeing had to employ 250,000 women over a four-year period to maintain a labor force of 39,000. After surveying the manpower crisis in war industries, Bernard Baruch commented that female turnover and absenteeism in one factory alone caused the loss of forty planes a month. In Elizabeth Hawes' case history of a woman war worker, the fictional foreman asked, "Why is Alma always absent?" The same query echoed in defense plants and government offices throughout the country, posing a critical problem for those in charge of winning the war on the home front.[17]

Although part of the difficulty could be traced to lack of adequate training for wartime jobs, a more important cause was woman's dual role as worker and homemaker.[18] Seventy-five per cent of the new female workers were married, and over 3 million were full-time housewives. Their responsibilities in the home inevitably affected their performance on the job. Some husbands might help with the household work, but the principal burden rested on the wife. A 1943 survey of war plants showed that 40 per cent of all females who left work cited marital, household, and allied difficulties as the reason, while only 9 per cent spoke of poor wages or working conditions. In a parallel study, the National Industrial Conference Board reported that family needs ranked as the cause most often given for female absenteeism after illness. The Sperry Gyroscope Company summarized the problem in a quick acronym. Women, it said, suffered from a bad case of the "d.t.'s"—domestic and transportation difficulties.[19]

Put in the simplest terms, many women workers who were full-time housewives found it impossible to do both jobs without either succumbing to exhaustion or taking time off from work. After toiling eight hours a day on an assembly line, they had to shop for food and buy clothes for themselves and their families. In some areas, merchants accommodated their needs, but, more often, grocery and department stores closed before the woman worker was free. Rationing boards and banks shut down early. Repair shops were dark. And transportation to and from war plants was poor, making it difficult to reach shopping centers quickly. Cooking, cleaning, and laundering added further to the woman worker's burden, and understaffed commercial establishments provided little relief. In some cases at least, the woman worker was forced to take time off to catch up with her household chores. The result was a mounting rate of absenteeism and turnover, and the loss of precious hours needed to produce more ships, planes, and war supplies.[20]

Faced with a similar problem, Britain eased the difficulties of its working wives by creating special community services for their benefit. "Priority certificates" permitted women workers to order food in the morning and pick it up at night, thus avoiding long lines and stale groceries. Industry gave women one afternoon a week to shop, and stores remained open in the evening for the convenience of female employees. Welfare officers were assigned to each war plant to handle any problems which arose, and rest centers in the country were provided for those workers who needed a holiday. Every factory with over 250 employees was required to install a cafeteria, and the Food Ministry set up over 2,000 "Central Kitchens" which each week prepared over 3 million meals—at cost—for women to carry home to their families.[21]

The United States, however, did relatively little to provide special services for female workers. War production centers shot up overnight, many of them without restaurants, laundries, banking facilities, or decent transportation systems. The nearest restaurant to one munitions factory in the Mid-west was a dirty crossroads cafe, and buses to and from the plant were scheduled so that workers had no time to eat at the company cafeteria. Men as well as women suffered from the shortage of decent facilities, but the fact that many females had the major responsibility for care of the home made their burden heavier. The President called for more public help for the woman worker, and the War Manpower Commission urged stores and banks to stay open at night. Yet with the exception of sporadic efforts by individual companies, no programs approaching the British model emerged on a national level. "The essential difference in the way the war effort is organized in Great Britain and the United States," the journalist Agnes Meyer said in a 1943 speech, "lies in the fact that the British are using necessity to conquer their social weaknesses whereas our endeavor to achieve maximum production has gone forward with brutal disregard of the human beings involved, and with a consequent intensification of our social problems."[22]

The question of whether or not to build child-care centers crystallized the conflicts involved in the community services issue. The need for such centers was clear from the beginning of the war. Over half of the new women workers came from the home, many leaving behind their pre-school and young school-age children. In Bridgeport, one-quarter of the students in the elementary and junior high schools reported that both their parents were employed, while in Detroit 35,000 of 138,000 prospective women war workers declared that they had young children who needed care. Surveys of Buffalo, San Diego, Los Angeles, and Baltimore confirmed that approximately 25 per cent of the new members of the female labor force had at least one child who required supervision during the day, and the War Manpower Commission estimated in 1943 that as many as 2 million youngsters needed some form of assistance.[23]

The lack of child-care facilities directly affected war production. In Los Angeles, aircraft manufacturers petitioned the city to reopen schools for the summer of 1943, because women workers departed en masse to supervise vacationing children. Repeated studies by the Women's Bureau and other government agencies showed that the need to care for children represented an important cause of high turnover and absenteeism. A California survey revealed that women were absent most often on Saturday—the day children had no school—and Washington, D.C., officials estimated that 2 million working hours a year were lost in government agencies as a result of women who stayed at home to care for children. Although precise statistics were hard to come by, most studies indicated that approximately 20 per cent of all female absenteeism was due to the need to supervise infant and young school-age youngsters. The West Coast Air Production Council summarized the consequences for the defense industry: "one child care center—adds up to 8,000 man hours a month, in ten weeks equal to one four engine bomber. Lack of twenty-five child care centers can cost ten bombers a month."[24]

In some areas, industry itself made notable strides toward coping with the problem. In Portland, Oregon, for example, the Kaiser company staffed and financed a twenty-four-hour-a-day community school for children from eighteen months to six years. Designed to save time and expense for working families, it was located on the edge of Portland harbor. Structured like a wheel spoke with entrances on every side for easy access by workers, it featured a swimming pool, brightly colored playrooms, and ready-cooked meals which weary employees could carry home for their families. The cost per day was seventy-five cents a family.[25]

On a community basis, Vancouver, Washington, demonstrated how existing facilities could be stretched to accommodate after-school activities for older children. The city's population multiplied five times in the first two years of the war, and its school enrollment soared from 4,000 to 12,000. With working parents unable to supervise the after-school activities of their children, business, industry, and civic leaders developed an extended school program of athletics, dancing, and drama. Using classrooms and recreation halls of housing projects for space, faculty wives and student teachers supervised over 3,000 children a day at a cost of a little over seven cents a child.[26]

Elsewhere, however, the cost of creating adequate facilities far exceeded the financial resources of many local governments. Minneapolis, for example, opened an experimental center in 1942 which offered professional supervision, medical care, and three meals a day for pre-school children. Projected expenses for twenty such centers, however, amounted to $224,000, or $198,000 more than the revenue anticipated from the fees paid by parents. Many communities across the country faced a similar dilemma. With school populations skyrocketing, housing needs increasing, and the cost of municipal services mounting, they were unwilling to commit the financial resources necessary to initiate vast new programs of child care. As a result, most observers agreed that the problem could be handled only through national planning and financing. "The fact is that a war is a national emergency," the head of the Michigan Child Care Committee wrote, "and that its effects on community life are too big and too drastic for [local governments] to handle . . . on their own."[27]

Money represented only one of the obstacles to an effective solution, however. Far more important was the issue of whether the government or community should sanction the employment of mothers by providing public facilities for the care of children. Even if financial resources were available, there was a substantial question whether the benefits of maternal employment outweighed the costs involved. For most Americans, a close relationship between mother and child was essential to family health and stability. A woman might take a job after her children were grown, but employment prior to that time was viewed as violation of a sacred trust and a direct threat to the future of society. As one journalist wrote, "No informed American needs a psychologist to tell him that children separated from home ties and without constant care . . . are the troublemakers, the neurotics and the spiritual and emotional cripples of a generation hence."[28]

Many officials in Washington shared the same concern and emphasized the importance of maintaining women's traditional role in the family. "[A] mother's primary duty is to her home and children," the Children's Bureau declared. "This duty is one she cannot lay aside, no matter what the emergency." Pursuing a similar theme the Women's Bureau observed that "in this time of crisis . . . mothers of young children can make no finer contribution to the strength of the nation than to assure their children the security of the home, individual care and affection." To the extent that child-care centers encouraged the employment of mothers and threatened the perpetuation of such values, many social-welfare workers questioned their efficacy. "We have what amounts to a national policy," one WPA official declared, "that the best service a mother can do is to rear her children in the home."[29]

In addition, many mothers resisted the idea of placing their children in the care of strangers. When George Gallup asked a cross-section of women in 1943 whether they would take a job in a war plant if their children were cared for in a day nursery free of charge, only 29 per cent said yes, while 56 per cent said no. Even mothers who were already employed preferred that their children be cared for by relatives and friends rather than a public nursery.

Charles Taft, a social-welfare official in Washington, noted in 1943 that many mothers whose children needed care distrusted the idea of institutional supervision and associated child-care centers with charity or relief. A survey of women workers in North Charleston, South Carolina, found that most lacked information about day care and confidence in its effectiveness. Citing the same attitude, a West Virginia official wrote that "the whole thing boils down to the fact that West Virginians think nursery schools and kindergartens are frills."[30]

Yet whatever one's opinion on the wisdom of mothers working, the fact remained that millions were employed and that a large number of children were not receiving adequate care. The press was filled with stories of youngsters penned in basement corrals, or exiled to neighborhood movie houses. A social worker in the San Fernando Valley counted forty-five infants locked in cars in a single war-plant parking lot, and the number of child-neglect cases in Norfolk, Virginia, tripled.[31] Although the War Manpower Commission did not encourage mothers to seek employment, it viewed them as an indispensable labor reserve and urged other departments to develop "special provisions" to aid those who were at work. Brigadier General Louis McSherry of the War Production Board wrote Katherine Lenroot of the Children's Bureau that "one of the most important programs before us is the development of adequate facilities for the care of children of working mothers." Similarly, the War Manpower Commission placed primary importance on helping the female worker meet her family responsibilities so that she could remain in the labor market. The Women's Advisory Committee devoted more time to child care than to any other issue, and nine of the largest women's organizations joined in a concerted campaign to force the federal government into action.[32]

Faced with a profound clash of opinion among its own officials, the Roosevelt Administration reacted initially by insisting that responsibility for child care rested with the local community. "We don't want the possibility of federal funds to discourage state and local initiative," Katherine Lenroot of the Children's Bureau declared. Charles Taft wrote a New York official that the government opposed any national movement to set up day-care centers, and the Bureau of the Budget asserted that a bill sponsored by Senator Claude Pepper of Florida to provide federal aid for the establishment of kindergartens and nursery schools did not conform to Administration policy. President Roosevelt, in effect, bridged the gap between his advisers when he allotted $400,000 in August 1942 to help local communities ascertain the need for child-care centers. Although the President's action gave the appearance of a national commitment to day care, it actually postponed such a commitment. No funds were set aside for operating existing facilities, or even for hiring supervisory personnel.[33] The average grant was only $7,000 —a miniscule sum compared to the dimension of the need—and the principal result of the program was to multiply the studies indicating the necessity for day care, while delaying aid for those states which had made their studies and were prepared to move forward. The Administration's approach outraged most day-care advocates and prompted severe criticism from manpower experts. "There are entirely too many agencies studying these problems," Bernard Baruch declared; "What must be done is known. Action alone remains necessary."[34]

As the pressure for federal help mounted, the Administration ruled in 1943 that Lanham Act funds for construction of wartime facilities could be used to build and operate day-care centers as well. The decision was no solution, however. Georgia Congressman Fritz Lanham thoroughly disapproved of the expenditure of money under his act for child-care facilities and made his opinion known by intervening to obstruct the application process. In addition, the grants to the various communities were made on a matching basis, with local governments required to put up 50 per cent of the actual cost. The Lanham Act contained a deficit clause, whereby local authorities had to prove to federal officials that they could not themselves afford to build the centers. If at the end of the fiscal year Washington determined that sufficient local funds were available, it could force the cities and towns to repay the federal contribution. For most local governments, the prospect of having to dip into financial reserves to fund a program which was already controversial seemed a risk too great to take, and relatively few sought help under the Budget Bureau's conditions.[35]

More important, those who did apply encountered a bureaucratic maze which often made the effort hardly worthwhile. Seven separate agencies were involved in the over-all program, each with its own sense of priorities and values. Lanham Act funds were administered by the Federal Works Administration (FWA), but before an application could be approved, it had to be recommended by either the education or welfare department of the local community, the corresponding state agency, the regional FWA office, the Office of Education or Children's Bureau in Washington, and the national FWA office. "What actually happens," one New York representative said, "is that you just don't get the projects under way."[36] The federal program gave the appearance of progress, without the substance. "I'm active," one state official wrote, "but it is pretty much like a horse forever prancing around at his starting place. I am not getting far." Local communities bridled at the delays caused by federal policy and blamed the national government for not being more responsive to their needs. After visiting public nurseries in California, Agnes Meyer reported that "the mere fact that I came from Washington made me a target for violent reproaches." She concluded that the Lanham Act had "delayed more than it had . . . furthered" the development of day-care facilities.[37]

At least in part, the infighting of competing federal agencies reflected a simple contest for control over the federal program. The principal antagonists were the FWA, a construction agency headed by General Philip Fleming, and the Federal Security Agency (FSA), an amalgam of social-welfare departments including the Office of Education and the Children's Bureau. Although the Children's Bureau consistently objected to maternal employment and cautioned against federal involvement in the child-care field in late 1941 and 1942, Katherine Lenroot, the Bureau's chief, had herself proposed a national day-care project in August 1941 to be supervised by her own agency and the Office of Education. Ironically, the reasons she offered at the time were precisely those she opposed a few months later. Small communities, she insisted, would lack the facilities and personnel necessary for a large-scale program. Only a national effort could cope with "the constantly changing nature of the problem, with population shifts as well as military population changes." John Studebaker, head of the Office of Education, made a similar appeal for federal staffing and financing of child care. The fact that both officials reversed position when their own proposals were turned down suggested that considerations of power were not irrelevant in the dispute.[38]

Basically, however, the conflict symbolized a far-reaching difference of opinion between the various departments over how to approach the problem of child care. The FWA viewed public nurseries as an "emergency" device to meet a temporary wartime need. Concerned primarily with problems of physical construction, it paid little attention to education and welfare officials who emphasized the need for high quality centers, and instead sought to build the maximum number of facilities in the shortest possible time. The FSA, on the other hand, focused primarily on developing a program which would serve the best long-term interests of children. As one government official noted, the FSA was more concerned with securing a good location and qualified personnel "than with trying to blast through red tape and get on with the program." It envisioned day-care centers as a permanent addition to the nation's social-welfare institutions, and went out of its way to ensure that each project measured up to the highest professional standards. In particular, it insisted that child-care proposals receive the approval of local education and welfare officials (the people with whom the Children's Bureau and Office of Education had to work on a daily basis) and represent prevailing community sentiment.[39]

Although the Lanham Act placed operational control in the hands of the FWA, the FSA was deeply involved in the application process, and the result was constant bickering. The FSA accused the FWA of bypassing its agencies, belittling its staff, and ignoring its professional expertise. Instead of requiring complete, in-depth investigations of each application, the FSA charged, the FWA wanted canned paragraphs of support for any and every project. Charles Taft accused FWA officials of being engineers who knew nothing about children and demanded that all FWA instructions on child care be cleared with his office. The FWA, in response, refused to share its files on day care, failed to consult local FSA representatives, and dismissed the Office of Education and Children's Bureau as meddling interlopers.[40] Since every application for federal assistance had to be approved by each agency, the internecine conflict caused even further delay in getting day-care centers established. The only answer was to concentrate all control in one department, and it seemed that the FSA was the best qualified for the job. But as long as the Lanham Act remained the principal vehicle for dispensing federal wartime aid, such a solution appeared impossible.

The controversy reached a peak in the debate over legislation setting up permanent authority in the child-care field. The FSA's point of view was embodied in a bill by Senator Elbert D. Thomas of Oklahoma appropriating $20 million to be administered on a grant-in-aid basis under the supervision of the Office of Education and the Children's Bureau. In support of the Thomas Bill, FSA officials argued that the Lanham Act had been completely ineffective, that it was designed to construct buildings, not care for children, and that Congressman Lanham himself had repeatedly interfered to stop the use of federal funds for child-care projects, especially those administered by welfare agencies. The FWA, on the other hand, claimed that it had already solved the problem. Charging that the Thomas bill would "create confusion and overlapping delay," it implied that what the FSA really sought was federal control over the entire educational process.[41] Although the FSA had the better of the argument, the principal effect of the debate was to underline the profound divisions within the Administration over how to proceed with a child-care program.

Finally, the conflict between the two sides became so bitter that the President was forced to intervene. In a July 1943 letter to the FSA, he described the controversy as "unfortunate," and announced that he had asked General Fleming of the FWA to institute revised procedures. The Chief Executive's letter forecast the outcome of the battle, and a month later, in a memo to Roosevelt, the FWA, FSA, and Bureau of the Budget declared a "treaty of peace" which in effect ceded all control over child care to the FWA[42] The power of Congressman Lanham and the fact that the FWA had already established its authority in the field proved too strong a combination to overcome. Although the Thomas bill received the unanimous backing of the Senate in June and was endorsed by most child-care experts, the President's action destroyed any chance for its passage by the House. In the fall of 1943, Congress enacted an amendment offered by Mary Norton which provided that funding for child-care facilities should remain within the Lanham Act and be administered by the FWA.[43]

By the time Congress acted, the problem of child care had reached severe proportions. One journalist estimated that out of 662 war areas needing child-care facilities in the summer of 1943 only sixty-six had operating programs. The FWA told the Senate in June that it had already provided care for 250,000 children and would help an additional 750,000 within six months, but both claims were vastly exaggerated. As of February 2, 1944, some 65,717 children were enrolled in federally supported facilities, and at the height of its effectiveness in the spring of 1945, the Lanham Act offered assistance to only 100,000. From one point of view, the figures represented significant progress, especially given the suspicion with which many Americans viewed child-care centers and the unprecedented nature of the program. On the other hand, the number of children receiving supervision in federal centers represented less than 10 per cent of those needing it, and only one-third of the number cared for in Great Britain, a country with less than half the population of the United States. Despite the government's belated effort, a Women's Bureau survey of ten war areas showed that only one out of ten working mothers with children sent them to a day-care center. "[I]n a substantial proportion of the households," the Bureau concluded, "no real provision was made for [child] care while the woman worker was absent."[44]

The history of the child-care issue dramatized the difficulty of achieving economic equality for women. On the one hand, it seemed clear that women could not compete in the job market on the same basis with men as long as they were expected to bear the principal share of responsibility for the home. Frieda Miller of the Women's Bureau observed in 1947 that "freedom of choice [for married women] to enter or not to enter the labor market is conditioned by the community services available."[45] On the other hand, the decision to build central kitchens or public nurseries entailed a commitment to modify traditional sexual roles and encourage married women to take jobs. The creation of surrogate domestic institutions provoked serious opposition from those who believed that the well-being of society depended on the maintenance of women's role as mother. A strong case could be made that females deserved a position of equality in the work force, but many people questioned whether it was proper for the government to subsidize such equality, especially if the price was the destruction of the family and existing patterns of male-female relationships.

Under more pressing circumstances, Great Britain demonstrated that the problem of child care could be handled, at least in wartime. There, the bombing of London forced public officials to evacuate children and assume direct responsibility for their care. Faced with the prospect of imminent defeat, the government drafted wives and mothers into the labor force and "went out of its way to provide amenities to reorganize social services, and to overcome traditional prejudices."[46] In the United States, however, the crisis was never so urgent. Wives and mothers were recruited as war workers, but they were not drafted. Throughout the period of fighting, most Americans retained a strong belief in the integrity of the family and were reluctant to see women's position in the home taken over by public institutions. In the absence of a pre-

eminent national emergency which required the immediate enlist-
ment of mothers in the work force, it was at least debatable
whether the government should encourage the disruption of family
life by taking over some of the responsibilities of the woman in
the home. If manpower requirements had been the only consideration, the United States might have followed the British example.
But profound social issues were involved as well, and the conflict
between wartime needs and traditional values placed a serious
obstacle in the path of decisive action. As a result, the Roosevelt
Administration at first equivocated on the issue of child care, and
then permitted the rivalry of competing agencies to retard development of an effective program. With strong, determined leadership, a solution might have been found. Without such leadership,
however, a massive child-care program could not be implemented,
and most mothers who worked continued to suffer the disadvan-
tage of being responsible for two full-time jobs.

The absence of greater progress in the areas of equal pay, community services, and recognition of women leaders raised some
doubts about the war's permanent impact on underlying attitudes
toward woman's place. There could be little question that the economic role of women had expanded dramatically during the years
of fighting. The sharp increase in employment of married and
middle-age women provided just one measure of the extent to
which the war had changed women's lives. On the other hand, the
hiring of millions of females did not itself signify that women had
gained the right to be treated exactly the same as men in the job
market. Economic equality could be achieved only through a substantial revision of social values, and a lasting modification in the
nature of male-female relationships. By that criterion, it appeared
that less change had occurred than might have been expected on
the basis of women's participation in the labor force. Female leaders were often denied a voice in policy-making councils; many
women workers were still paid unequal wages; and wives and
mothers who were employed received inadequate public assistance in the area of child-care and community services. The per-

sistence of inequality was understandable given the controversial nature of the issues involved, but the fact remained that many forms of discrimination had not been eliminated.

In the end, the war's ultimate impact on women's status could not be determined until the fighting stopped. Deeply rooted social values were rarely altered overnight, and it seemed likely that any permanent shift in woman's place would depend on whether female workers retained the position in the labor force which they had achieved during the war. Despite the strength of traditional attitudes, change more than continuity had characterized women's experience during the years between 1940 and 1945. The final verdict, however, would have to await the postwar period, when the soldiers came home, the economy returned to a peacetime level of production, and the country attempted to decide where women belonged in a normal social order.

# 8

# The Paradox of Change

When Japan surrendered in August 1945, the American people rejoiced in their victory. Church bells pealed, national leaders praised the dedication of soldiers and war workers, and millions of families looked forward to the luxury of a normal existence. No one knew for sure, however, where women belonged in a world at peace. The nation had experienced fifteen years of turbulence, moving from a decade of depression through nearly half a decade of war. In that time span, attitudes toward women had fluctuated dramatically. In 1938 over 80 per cent of the American people strongly opposed work by married women. Five years later, over 60 per cent approved such employment. In each case, public opinion had been shaped in large part by the exigencies of a crisis situation. Now, with the return of peace, the future social and economic roles of women remained a matter of unresolved controversy. Anxious soldiers wondered whether the war had permanently changed their wives and sweethearts. Parents waited to see if their daughters would come back home and settle down in a nearby community. And social scientists speculated about the war's impact on marriage, the family, and morals. The postwar years became a period of testing, a time of transition, in which women themselves, and the society at large, sought to determine the proper boundaries of women's sphere.

The fate of female workers provided one critical measure of the war's effect on women's status. Despite the persistence of discrimination in some areas, females in the labor force had made significant gains in wages, unionization, and job opportunities during the war years. With enthusiasm and dedication, they had taken the place of men and earned the respect and gratitude of the nation. Now, munitions industries were shutting down. Eleven million soldiers were speeding home. And many experts doubted whether there were enough jobs to give both women and the returning veterans employment. The movement from a wartime to a peacetime economy threatened the advances women had made and raised directly the question of women's future economic role. Would female workers return to the home, or would they stay on the job? More important, would the nation allow wives and mothers to continue working, if to do so posed a threat to employment for men just back from battle?

In anticipation of the postwar employment squeeze, the Women's Advisory Committee (WAC) and other government officials sought to protect the rights of women workers. "Prospects for job security and other new job opportunities after the war are as important to women as to men," the WAC declared. "The American people therefore must demand consideration of the status of women in all postwar plans." The WAC urged government economists to define full employment "to include all women now at work," and lobbied for the establishment of a family assistance program and child-care facilities to help the woman worker. "No society can boast of democratic ideals if it utilizes womanpower in a crisis and neglects it in peace," the Committee asserted. "To take for granted that a woman does not need work and use this assumption as a basis for dismissal is no less unfair than if the same assumption were used as a basis for dismissal of a man."[1]

Other government agencies echoed the WAC's pronouncements. In a democracy, the War Manpower Commission emphasized, every citizen regardless of race or sex enjoyed a "fundamental right to choose whether to work or not." The Department of Labor issued a directive specifically prohibiting employers from discriminating against workers because of race or sex, and the Secretary of Labor warned against any restriction on the hiring of married women. Focusing on the attitudes of returning veterans, the War Department distributed a pamphlet urging soldiers to share housework and support an extension of community services as a way of helping wives who wished to continue on the job. "Family problems are produced by social change," the pamphlet declared, "and often can be solved only by further changes." Administration spokesmen in Congress adopted a similar tone. "Many women who have gone into factories and done such splendid work . . . will want to continue working," Senator Harry Truman said in 1944, "and they are entitled to the chance to earn a good living at jobs they have shown they can do."[2]

A substantial number of Americans, however, believed that the time had come for women to return to the home. Many observers viewed women's work as a primary cause of juvenile delinquency and believed that the continued presence of wives and mothers in the labor force directly threatened the stability of the nation's social institutions. In a widely circulated article reflecting popular concern, the anthropologist Margaret Mead asked, "What's Wrong with the Family?" Mead concluded that, despite troubled times, it was still a flourishing institution, but others were not so sure. Willard Waller, a Barnard sociologist, charged that during the war women had gotten "out of hand," with the result that children were neglected and the very survival of the home was endangered. The only solution, he asserted, was the restoration and strengthening of the patriarchal family. "Women must bear and rear children; husbands must support them." In less blunt terms, others took the same position. Frederick Crawford, head of the National Association of Manufacturers, praised women for their wartime contribution, but declared that "from a humanitarian point of view, too many women should not stay in the labor force. The home is the basic American institution."[3]

In part, the desire to restore old patterns of economic responsibility was motivated by fear of recession. The specter of massive unemployment haunted politicians, economists and working men who remembered all too well the depression which had preceded the outbreak of fighting. If the war had eliminated bread lines and relief rolls, peace threatened to re-establish them. In the eyes of many leaders, a cutback in women's employment offered one guarantee against the possibility of a new economic downturn. A Southern senator, for example, urged Congress to force "wives and mothers back to the kitchen" in order to ensure jobs for the millions of veterans who would be seeking new positions. Labor leaders, with their separate seniority lists and contract clauses providing for an end to women's employment after the war, sought the same end.[4]

Just as important, however, was the persistence of hostility toward the idea of women participating as equals in the economic world. Magazines were full of articles which revived shibboleths about women's inferiority and questioned the ability of females to compete with men. Margaret Pickel, dean of Barnard, declared in the *New York Times Magazine* that women "had less physical strength, a lower fatigue point, and a less stable nervous system" than men. For that reason, she claimed, employers found female workers more demanding, more emotional, and less reliable. "By middle age, when men are at their best, a devoted woman worker is apt to degenerate into fussiness or worse." Union leaders also exhibited a distrust of women workers. R. J. Thomas, president of the United Auto Workers, charged that females accepted the advantages of union membership but not the responsibilities. Many women were reluctant to pay dues, he reported, and few showed any interest in fighting for their own needs. Thomas predicted that at the end of the war, almost all women would lose their jobs—a prospect which seemed more to please than disturb him.[5]

Public opinion surveys, moreover, indicated that most Americans—women as well as men—believed in perpetuating a sharp division of labor between the sexes. Men were expected to earn a living and to make the "big" decisions, while women were expected to take care of the home. Both *Fortune* magazine and the American Institute of Public Opinion found that a sizable majority of the American people were opposed to a wife working if her husband could support her. The people surveyed by *Fortune* asserted that women should be in charge of rearing children and caring for the family, but that men should determine where a family lived and how it spent its money. Less than 2 per cent of the respondents believed that a woman was as qualified as a man was to serve as a mayor.[6]

Despite the changes engendered by war, then, traditional ideas of woman's place retained a strong following. Female workers had been assiduously cultivated in the midst of the military crisis, but now the courtship appeared to be over. "Perhaps intentions were never honorable," Margaret Hickey of the WAC remarked. Frieda Miller, chief of the Women's Bureau, observed that public opinion had shifted from a period of "excessive admiration for women's capacity to do anything, over to the idea . . . that women ought to be delighted to give up any job and return to their proper sphere —the kitchen." Even those women leaders who had been most skeptical of the gains made in wartime were stunned by the "toboggan in public esteem."[7]

If public opinion had turned against female employment, however, women workers themselves gave every indication of desiring to stay on the job. A Women's Bureau survey of ten areas showed that three out of four women who had taken jobs in the midst of the war wanted to continue working. In New York the figure was 80 per cent, in Detroit 75 per cent. If all the women actually worked who wanted to, the numbers employed would far exceed the 1940 totals—by 55 per cent in Detroit and 150 per cent in Mobile. "War jobs have uncovered unsuspected abilities in American women," one worker said in explaining her desire to remain employed. "Why lose all these abilities because of a belief that 'a woman's place is in the home.' For some it is, for others not." A female steelworker agreed. "If [women] are capable," she declared, "I don't see why they should give up their position to men. . . .

The old theory that a woman's place is in the home no longer exists. Those days are gone forever." The testimony of the women workers seemed to vindicate the predictions of those who said that the war had changed the fundamental outlook of women. "Used to money of their own," the *Saturday Evening Post* observed, "millions of the sex are going to sniff at postwar bromides about women's place."[8]

Although some female workers were undoubtedly more committed than others, the desire for employment appeared to characterize women of every age group. Within the labor force the greatest enthusiasm was expressed by women over forty-five, of whom 80 per cent indicated an interest in a permanent job. "These are the women who have been developing new skills during the war," the Women's Bureau observed. With husbands off at work and children grown, they had no pressing tasks in the home to prevent them from remaining in the work force. A job offered both personal satisfaction and financial rewards. The wish for employment extended to the young as well, however. Of 33,000 girl students sampled in a *Senior Scholastic* poll, 88 per cent wanted a career in addition to homemaking, while only 4 per cent chose homemaking exclusively. Even the *Ladies Home Journal,* whose writers preached that "the ideal of every woman is to find the right husband, bear and rear his children, and make . . . for them a cozy, gay, happy home," reported that more women workers wanted to continue on the job than quit and return to the home. As the war hurtled to a climax in the spring of 1945, many women clearly wished to retain an active role in the labor force. The question was, as Mary Anderson phrased it, "[would the nation] meet the days to come in terms of the future, or [would it] try to keep the world bound to an outworn order?"[9]

Demobilization and the return home of servicemen determined part of the answer. Under the Selective Service Act, veterans took priority over wartime workers in the competition for their old jobs. As war plants reconverted to peacetime production, women who were last hired were also first fired. Moreover, many industries

folded overnight as victory approached. The Springfield Arsenal,
where 81 per cent of the women hoped to continue working, dismissed every employee within a week of V-J Day. The changeover
hit women in heavy industry especially hard. In California, where
producers of durable goods employed 144,700 women in October
1944, the number plummeted to 37,000 a year later. The aircraft
industry laid off 800,000 workers in the two months after V-J Day
—most of them women—and the auto industry went through a similar transition. Women fell from 25 per cent of all auto workers in
1944 to 7.5 per cent in April 1946. The last figure was only one
point higher than the percentage employed in October 1939. Over-
all, females comprised 60 per cent of all workers released from employment in the early months after the war and were laid off at a rate
of 75 per cent higher than men. With the manpower crisis over,
some employers revised their age requirements, throwing women
over forty-five out of work, and large companies like Detroit Edi-
son, Thompson Aircraft, and IBM reimposed earlier restrictions
on the hiring of wives.[10]

An appreciable number of women retained positions in the labor
force, however, confounding the expectations of those who believed
that female employment would decline precipitously with the end
of the fighting. The Bureau of Labor Statistics had predicted that
6 million people would lose their jobs in the year after the war,
a substantial proportion of them women. In fact, only a small
percentage of that number remained permanently out of work. A
great many women left their former jobs, creating the impression
of widespread unemployment, but a majority rejoined the labor
force at a later date. Between September 1945 and November
1946, 2.25 million women left work, and another million were
laid off. But in the same period, nearly 2.75 million were hired,
causing a net decline in female employment of only 600,000. Although 100,000 women lost jobs in heavy industry in California,
37,000 continued at work—four times the number that had been
employed in 1941—and in May 1947 there were still 86 per cent
more women working as operatives in California factories than

there had been before the war.[11] Thus while women lost some of their better-paid war positions, they did not disappear from the labor market as some had anticipated.

The experience of women workers in Baltimore represented an important barometer of the direction of postwar female employment. In a Women's Bureau survey conducted in 1944, three out of four Baltimore war workers expressed an interest in staying on the job. Two years later, four out of five were still employed and nearly half of them were in the same position. Fifty per cent of those who planned to quit were also working, and overall one of every two members of the female labor force had joined the working population in the years after Pearl Harbor. The average wage had fallen from $50 to $37, but the Women's Bureau concluded that "for a surprisingly large proportion of women . . . wartime plans [had] materialized."[12]

Two years after the war ended, women had regained many of the losses suffered in the immediate postwar period and started back toward new peaks of employment. The over-all number of women in manufacturing declined by nearly a million, but there were still one million more women in the nation's factories in late 1946 than there had been in 1940. In October 1946, women's hiring rate was greater than men's for the fifth month out of six, and their lay-off rate was down. Aircraft factories in San Diego and Hartford began to call women back to work, and the postwar economic boom resulted in an ongoing demand for female workers in sales and service jobs. Almost all of the wartime clerical employees stayed at work, women still constituted 40 per cent of the operatives in consumer industry, and female participation in heavy industry had grown from 9 to 13 per cent. In addition, severe shortages of stenographers, typists, teachers, and nurses were reported across the nation.[13]

As the decade drew to a close, the imprint of the war years remained strong and clear. Twice as many women were employed in California in 1949 as had been employed in 1940. Nationwide, the female labor force had increased by over 5.25 million—more than twice the increase which might have been expected without the war. The number of female clerical workers had nearly doubled. Women in manufacturing had increased by 50 per cent. And the proportion of women who worked had jumped from 27 per cent to 32 per cent—a change greater than that of the entire three preceding decades. The *Wall Street Journal* declared that "women are taking over," and Frieda Miller, director of the Women's Bureau, speculated that the nation was "approaching a period when for women to work is an act of conformism."[14]

Significantly, the greatest postwar gains occurred among married women who had first joined the labor force in large numbers during the war. By 1952, some 10.4 million wives held jobs—2 million more than at the peak of World War II and almost three times the number employed in 1940. During the 1940's, the proportion of married women at work jumped more than 50 per cent (from 15.2 per cent to 24 per cent), and for the first time wives comprised a majority of the women employed (52.1 per cent in 1950 versus 36.4 per cent in 1940). The number of couples in which both husband and wife worked leaped from 3 million, or 11 per cent, in 1940, to almost 7 million, or 20 per cent, in 1948, and approximately 4.5 million mothers of children under eighteen were employed—nearly 25 per cent of the total female labor force.[15]

The same type of dramatic shift took place in the age distribution of women workers. At the end of the decade, the greatest proportion of new workers were in their early 40s, and women in their 50s entered the labor force in the same numbers as those in their 20s. Two and a half million women over thirty-five went to work from 1940 to 1950, and the median age of female workers rose from thirty-two to thirty-six and one half. While the number of women workers aged eighteen to twenty-four declined 8 per cent, the number from thirty-five to forty-four grew 51 per cent, and those from forty-five to fifty-four gained 77 per cent. By 1950, there were 5.5 million women over forty-five years of age in the labor force, and women between 35 and 54 constituted 40 per cent of the total number of women at work.[16]

Most important, the war enabled women's work to become an increasingly accepted part of middle-class life. In the past, wives from the middle class had been discouraged from taking a job by the fear of social ostracism. If a woman entered an occupation which was competitive with that of her husband, she posed a threat to traditional notions of male superiority and challenged the image of the man as provider. On the other hand, if she took a job which was inappropriate to her class standing, she brought social embarrassment to her family and created a problem of status inconsistency. The war aided in resolving both dilemmas. First, it helped to legitimize work for women of all classes by defining employment as a patriotic necessity. And second, it prompted a boom in white-collar occupations which were "respectable" for women of middle-class status to hold. During the 1940's, the proportion of female workers filling clerical and sales positions jumped from 31 to 37 per cent—a gain matched only in the decade of 1910 to 1920 —and by 1950 over half of all women workers were employed in white-collar jobs, including 66 per cent of native white women. The evidence suggested that as the decade of the 1950's began, work for married women had become an integral element in the lives of many middle-class families. Sociologists observed that more and more wives were seeking jobs even though their husbands earned enough to support them, and the National Manpower Council reported in 1954 that in 40 per cent of all families receiving a total income of $6,000-10,000 a year both the husband and wife worked.[17] Indeed, a plausible argument could be made that female employment was the crucial means by which some families achieved middle-class status.

By almost any criterion, therefore, the war represented a turning point for women workers. It was responsible for millions of women joining the labor market for the first time. It forced the substantial elimination of barriers to the employment of wives. And it opened up the opportunity for a second vocation to thousands of older women whose primary homemaking duties were over. Although female employment was initially conceived of as a temporary measure, the experience of work became an institution in many households as the war continued. Despite the built-in obstacle of demobilization, women succeeded in surprising numbers in retaining their new economic role. Aided by a postwar boom, they solidified their earlier gains and started to move to new records of employment. Many people still opposed the idea of women's work, and it was at least debatable whether the life of a filing clerk was any more rewarding than that of a full-time housewife. But given the strength of the forces opposed to female employment, the statistics told a remarkable story of change, and justified the National Manpower Council's conclusion that the war had prompted a "revolution" in the lives of women in America.[18]

The success of women in holding onto their wartime economic role made all the more inexplicable the relative absence of progress in the fight for equality. One might have expected the expansion of women's sphere to be accompanied by a growing recognition of females as equal participants with males in the job market. Such was not the case, however. While the war produced unprecedented changes in women's numerical representation in the labor force, it failed to bring a parallel improvement in the economic opportunities most women enjoyed. Instead, discrimination persisted in professional employment, wage scales, and community services. Ironically, the areas of traditional concern to the women's rights movement received little attention, even at a time when female involvement in activities outside the home was increasing dramatically.

The area of business and professional employment illustrated the absence of progress on wider issues of equal rights. Despite the shortage of highly trained personnel during the war, the proportion of women entering the professions continued to decline. In a 1948 article in the *Saturday Evening Post,* Susan B. Anthony IV cited the decrease in the number of women lawyers and superintendents of schools as evidence of the "crack-up" of the American woman's movement. Medical schools continued to impose a quota of 5 per cent on female admissions; 70 per cent of all hospitals refused to accept female interns; and medical associations like the New York Obstetrical Society barred women members. Although women comprised 25 per cent of all women workers in government, they represented only 3 per cent of those who held high-level positions, and Margaret Hickey charged that a "campaign of under-cover methods and trumped up excuses" was being used to drive women even further out of upper-bracket public jobs. The same disparity existed in other fields. A survey of Chattanooga banks showed that while women and men served in equal numbers as bank tellers, men were called senior tellers, women junior tellers. Furthermore, business executives professed little confidence in women's ability to hold management positions. In response to a *Fortune* poll, 53 per cent of the executives said that women handled people less well than men, and 65.8 per cent asserted that females were less able to make decisions. (The figures for the average man were 43.6 per cent and 49.7 per cent respectively.) Whether or not discrimination was solely to blame, the evidence clearly indicated that most barriers to women's employment in business and the professions remained intact.[19]

Female workers also continued to receive appreciably lower wages than men. At the end of the war, the National Industrial Conference Board reported that women in manufacturing earned 66 per cent of what men were paid. A female laundry worker in Illinois took home 55 cents an hour, a man $1.10. Five years later, the Bureau of Labor Statistics disclosed that women's median earnings were only 53 per cent of men's. Females in public administration received 74 per cent as much as their male co-workers, but those in retail trade earned only 48 per cent as much. A survey of all industries in 1951 showed that, wherever females constituted more than 50 per cent of the labor force, the industry paid a wage which fell below the national average. In short, there was little reason to believe that any change had occurred in the basic assumption that women's work was worth less than men's.[20]

Senator Wayne Morse of Oregon attempted to eliminate the

worst discrepancies by sponsoring a federal equal pay bill which geared wages to job content, but his legislation failed to gain the support necessary for passage. Although both parties endorsed the measure in principle, the opposition prevented it from coming to a vote. The Chamber of Commerce declared that the problem of equal pay should be handled voluntarily by employers, and George Meany of the AF of L asserted that the issue of wages fell "within the province of collective bargaining, and not of police action by government." A few states had corrective laws on the books, but most of the statutes contained massive loopholes and provided little enforcement power. Industry and labor, meanwhile, failed to deliver on their promise to solve the problem voluntarily. A Women's Bureau survey of 2,044 collective bargaining agreements showed that only 17 per cent had equal-pay clauses.[21]

Advocates of child care met with even more frustration. The Federal Works Administration announced in August 1945 that grants under the Lanham Act would end as soon as the war crisis was over. Most experts agreed that the large number of mothers in the labor force made a continuation of such facilities essential, but since the federal enabling legislation was for the duration of the military conflict only, entreaties for help received little encouragement from Administration officials. When Earl Warren, governor of California, wrote that closing the 530 centers in his state would cause "a great wrench in our community life," the FWA responded that the future of child-care centers rested with the states themselves, not the federal government. Mary Norton and others finally persuaded Congress to extend the Lanham Act for six months, but after March 1, 1946, all federal support for child-care facilities ended.[22]

The history of day care in New York exemplified the difficulties facing those who sought to establish a meaningful permanent program. During the war, the state had been forced to step in to provide funds for hard-pressed local communities which had been unsuccessful in their efforts to get money under the Lanham Act.[23] After the war, however, Governor Thomas Dewey and the state legislature killed legislation designed to fund the centers on a permanent basis. State authorities agreed to temporary appropriations for New York City but insisted that the prime purpose of the limited program was to combat juvenile delinquency in hard-core poverty areas. Mothers who wished to use the centers had to submit to "means" tests to establish their need for public assistance, and the state youth commissioner suggested that working mothers might better go on relief so that they could care for their children in their own homes.

Although a survey showed that seven out of eight families using the centers could not earn a living wage unless the mother worked, state officials continued to discredit the program. The welfare commissioner claimed that many mothers worked "only to satisfy their desire for a career," and others insisted that the Aid to Dependent Children program more faithfully protected the family unit. In 1947, the *New York World Telegram* entered the controversy, charging that child care was conceived by leftists operating out of Communist "social work cells." The campaign for day-care centers, the *Telegram* said, had "all the trappings of a Red drive, including leaflets, letters, telegrams, petitions, protest demonstrations, mass meetings, and hat-passing." Those who benefited from the program, it claimed, were often "furcoated mothers" who arrived with their children in taxicabs. Such charges were absurd on their face, but the disagreement over publicly supported day care testified to the depth of feeling on the issue of wives and mothers working. Throughout the Progressive era and the New Deal, enormous energy had been expended in the effort to secure social-welfare measures which would protect the mother's place in the home, and there was great reluctance to reverse that emphasis. As a result, the child-care program fell into disrepute, and all state aid to child care ended on January 1, 1948.[24]

Finally, hard-core feminists failed in their continuing effort to win adoption of the Equal Rights Amendment. For a brief period during and after the war, the outlook appeared promising. Congressmen talked of approving the amendment as a vote of thanks to women for their "magnificent wartime performance"; both parties endorsed the measure; and luminaries such as Homer Cummings, Henry Wallace, and Harry Truman added their voices in support.[25] The amendment involved a fundamental division of opinion over the meaning of equality, however, and provoked as much opposition as praise. Prominent women like Eleanor Roosevelt and Mary Anderson insisted that protective legislation was more valuable than the establishment of an abstract principle of legal rights, and in the end their viewpoint prevailed despite the increased backing won by the feminists. The Senate first considered the amendment in August 1946 and by a margin of 38 to 35 denied it the two-thirds approval needed for adoption. (The *New York Times* praised the vote, saying "motherhood cannot be amended.") Four years later, the measure passed by a sweeping majority of 63 to 11, but this time it contained a rider introduced by Senator Carl Hayden of Arizona specifying that no protective legislation was to be affected. The Hayden rider in effect voided the operative intent of the feminist bill and rendered it meaningless. "My amendment is a revolving door," Hayden boasted. "We come in one side and go out the other." One Washington reporter observed that Hayden "could put a rider on the Ten Commandments and nullify them completely."[26] Although the Equal Rights Amendment was passed by the Senate one more time in 1953, with the Hayden rider, the Senate's action effectively buried hopes for its adoption until the late 1960's.

The experience of women during the 1940's thus presented a strange paradox. On the one hand, unprecedented numbers of females joined the labor force, substantially altering the existing distribution of economic roles. On the other hand, only minimal progress was made in the areas of greatest concern to women's rights advocates—professional employment, child-care centers, and a uniform wage scale. Women's sphere had been significantly expanded, yet traditional attitudes toward woman's place remained largely unchanged. A job for a wife over thirty-five became normal

—at least by a statistical standard—but most Americans continued to subscribe to the belief that women were (and should remain) primarily homemakers.

Although the paradox seemed inexplicable on the surface, it contained the key to understanding the amount of change which occurred during the decade. The events of the war years suggested that most Americans could accept a significant shift in women's economic activity as long as the shift was viewed as "temporary" and did not entail a conscious commitment to approve the goals of a sexual revolution. On the other hand, when the issue was one of preserving a division of labor between the sexes, they demonstrated their adherence to traditional values. Ironically, then, the less people saw women's work as a threat to woman's place, the greater was the possibility of a permanent alteration in the distribution of sexual roles. In that light, the "lag" between cultural norms and everyday behavior said a great deal about what happened (and did not happen) in the 1940's.

Public opinion surveys provided one clue to the dynamics of the paradox. When the nation's citizens were asked whether a wife should work if jobs were scarce and her husband could support her, 86 per cent said no. The question, in effect, tested the respondents' loyalty to the idea of the man as the principal wage earner in the family, and presumed that, if a wife worked, she would be depriving a man of a job. On the other hand, after the query was rephrased to eliminate the issue of job scarcity, the number of people opposed to the employment of married women fell to 63 per cent. The greatest change, however, occurred when *Fortune* modified the wording a third time and asked whether a wife should hold a job if she had no children under sixteen. In response to the final version of the question, only 46 per cent of the men and 38 per cent of the women still rejected the idea of a wife working.[27] Thus toleration of female employment increased precisely to the extent that traditional definitions of sexual roles were removed or de-emphasized. When the salient issue was man's role as provider, or a mother's responsibility to rear children, opposition to married women working remained high. When neither issue was present, on the other hand, antagonism toward the employment of wives dropped substantially.

Other polls, meanwhile, indicated that women's economic potential, if measured by itself, was viewed as an asset rather than a liability. When *Fortune* asked a group of men whom they would choose to marry among three equally attractive women, only 16.8 per cent selected a woman who had never held a job, while over 55 per cent chose one who had worked and been either moderately or extremely successful. In addition, a majority of those expressing a clear opinion asserted that, if a young couple did not have enough money to get married, the prospective wife should take a job rather than wait until the man could earn more on his own.[28] Thus it appeared that public attitudes toward women working depended in large measure on how the issue was defined. On an economic basis alone, female employment seemed to be acceptable, while when the question became one of social values, opposition grew.

Against such a background, the conditions which prevailed in postwar America assumed a position of decisive importance. In the years immediately following the war, inflation racked the nation. Meat prices rose by 122 per cent between 1945 and 1947, and repeated strikes in major industries sent the cost of basic purchases skyrocketing. The inflationary spiral created a severe economic pinch for almost everyone, but it especially affected those families which had postponed their desire for consumer products during the war. At just the moment when husbands and wives were planning to build new homes, buy new cars, and purchase improved appliances, a series of arbitrary price hikes stood in the way. Many couples found it impossible to fulfill their quest for a higher standard of living on one income alone.[29]

The combination of inflation and rising aspirations cast the issue of women's work in a special light. Husbands who might have opposed married women holding jobs as a matter of principle were nevertheless able to rationalize employment by their own wives as a necessary device to get more money for family needs.

The married woman, it now appeared, was seeking to give her children a better life and a healthier environment, not attempting to strike out on her own in the selfish pursuit of personal ambition. Frieda Miller commented that women's work had become essential to "the quality of family life," and a national conference on work in the lives of married women concluded that the increased economic activity of wives constituted an indispensable element in the improvement of family living standards, the growth of real income, and the rising rate of social mobility.[30]

Significantly, women workers interpreted their role in the same way—at least publicly—thereby reinforcing the sense that female employment was directed primarily to helping the family. When female war workers were asked why they wished to continue on the job, a total of 84 per cent cited "economic need," or the desire to assist with family support. Only 8 per cent, in contrast, gave what could be described as "feminist" explanations such as the need for self-expression or dissatisfaction with the traditional role of women in the home. Thus women workers themselves were not seeking to challenge the existing distribution of sexual roles. Instead, they were fulfilling the sanctioned function of "helpmate" in a new way. As one plant psychologist at Lockheed Aircraft noted, morale among married women employees was high because "they seem to feel they are contributing to home life, not detracting from it."[31]

It would be wrong, of course, to underestimate the changes which were taking place beneath the surface. Frieda Miller pointed out that, although the vast majority of women workers cited "economic need" as a primary motivation, the desire for self-expression was often present also. For many women, the justification of financial need provided a convenient (and acceptable) substitute for more complicated responses. A *Ladies Home Journal* poll, for example, showed that 79 per cent of the workers interviewed enjoyed the experience of being employed, especially the chance to meet new people. More important, it seemed clear that the definition of "economic need" was undergoing a substantial transformation. In the years prior to 1940, married women held jobs only if their husbands received an income below the poverty level. By 1950, on the other hand, a growing number worked in order to purchase new homes or finance the education of their youngsters. As one woman told Gertrude Samuels of the *New York Times,* "the children get more things by my working; it's easier to buy them clothes and pay for school. We get more out of life."[32] Both the census and the National Manpower Council's study of families earning $6,000-10,000 indicated that many middle-class wives were employed. Far from meaning just family survival, therefore, the phrase "economic need" had come to include the quest for a better life. As female employment became a vehicle for upward mobility, a new element of voluntarism entered the equation of women's work.

Nevertheless, what remained most significant was the *impression* that women went to work out of "necessity." If a woman had declared that she sought employment in order to gratify a personal whim or desire, she would immediately have come into conflict with the social norm that a wife should be happy to stay in the home. A large number of such responses, in all likelihood, would have prompted a campaign to discourage married women from working. A wife who sought employment to help the household, on the other hand, complemented rather than challenged conventional perceptions of the female role. The function of inflation, in such a context, was to make the argument of "economic necessity" both convenient and credible. As long as the married woman was working to help pay the bills or move the family ahead, there was little basis for attacking her. A person might question the consequences of her employment, but not the motivation.

Finally, it was important that the women most directly involved in the expansion of the female labor force—wives over thirty-five— had already finished their primary homemaking responsibilities. The 1940 census revealed that the average woman married at twenty-one years of age, had her first child at twenty-three, and her last when she was twenty-seven. All her children attended school by the time she reached her mid-thirties, and all had left home when she was forty-five. With the cares of child-rearing over, and the duties of housekeeping reduced by electrical appliances, she was "ready" to work. Margaret Mead observed that many middle-aged women felt "restless and discontented . . . unwanted and rudderless" after the task of raising a family was over.[33] For such women, a job—even as a file clerk or saleswoman—frequently offered a new focus of activity, a welcome respite from the loneliness of an empty home. The war had made employment for women over thirty-five an increasingly viable possibility, and it was not surprising that the bulk of new female workers during the 1940's came from the middle-aged segment of the population.

From a social point of view, however, the most significant fact about such women was that they had already fulfilled their function as mothers. Their employment did not represent a "feminist" threat to the existing distribution of sexual roles because they had already seen their children through the pre-school years. Nor did their work seem to disturb most people's sense of propriety. A 1946 *Fortune* poll showed that a majority of citizens had no specific objection to married women holding jobs if they had no children under sixteen. Thus the one group best suited to lead the growth of the female labor force actually comprised the largest body of women workers during the 1940's. Such women performed the unique service of setting a precedent for female involvement outside the home, while keeping to a minimum the social conflict which such involvement ultimately entailed.

In a profound sense, then, the expansion of women's economic role depended on circumstances which prevented female employment from being perceived as a feminist threat. During the early 1940's, the war helped to legitimize women's work by making it a question of national necessity. After the war, inflation and rising consumer demands served much the same function. In neither case could female employment be interpreted as part of an overt revolt against traditional values, or a self-conscious movement for equality. Many Americans were deeply concerned about

the future of women—a concern at least partially inspired by
women working—but female participation in the labor force was
defined so as to mitigate the clash of values. Women workers
sought jobs, not careers—an extra pay check for the family rather
than a reputation as a success in business or the professions. Indeed, every aspect of female employment seemed designed to mute
the suggestion that traditional modes of female behavior were under attack.

In such a situation, it was hardly surprising that so little progress
took place on issues involving women's rights. The world of social
ideals existed on one level of reality, the world of economic practice on another. A solution to the problem of child care or community services required some connection between the two—a
conscious commitment to guarantee women the same opportunity
as men in the job market, even at the cost of disrupting traditional
family patterns.[34] Yet there was no evidence that the nation was
prepared to tolerate such a sweeping change in values. The poll
data showed that most citizens preferred to retain traditional definitions of masculine and feminine spheres, even while modifying
the content of those spheres in practice. A married woman might
work after her children were in school, but she was not thought
of as an equal in the labor force, and almost no one believed that
her right to a job was more important than her duty to the home.

If little progress was made toward the goal of equality, however,
the fact remained that women's economic status had shifted more
rapidly than at any other time in the twentieth century. The American people were clearly not ready to dispense with a sexual division
of labor, or to accept the demise of traditional values. But within the
existing set of values, women's economic role had been dramatically
and permanently transformed. Millions of females left the home for
the first time to take an active part in the nation's economic life, and,
while their involvement did not result in a feminist revolution, it did
represent a significant new element in male-female relationships, the
ramifications of which promised to affect substantially the future distribution of sexual roles.

Carl Degler has observed that social change is more likely to occur as a practical response to specific events than as the implementation of a well-developed ideology.[35] The events of the 1940's testify to the validity of his hypothesis. The war made possible what no amount of feminist agitation could achieve: it propelled women into a new and wider sphere of activity. Some women may have been "ready" to assume a new economic role, but the outbreak of the fighting gave them the opportunity and acted as an indispensable catalyst. Moreover, once having entered the job market, most women decided to remain. Their activity outside the home expanded rather than contracted with the passage of time, and by 1950 the wife who worked had become a permanent feature of American life. It could be argued that the growth of the female labor force simply increased the ranks of the victimized. But a shift of such dimensions inevitably affected the whole structure of roles played by men and women, and the greatest impact of women's work was destined to occur indirectly, through "unanticipated consequences" on the home and family.

Despite the persistence of traditional ideas on woman's place, therefore, the decade of the 1940's marked a turning point in the history of American women. There was no question that economic equality remained a distant goal. But the content of women's lives had changed, and an important new area of potential activity had opened up to them, with side effects which could not yet be measured. At the turn of the century, the young, the single, and the poor had dominated the female labor force. Fifty years later, the majority of women workers were married and middle-aged, and a substantial minority came from the middle class. In the story of that dramatic change, World War II represented a watershed event. For that reason, if for no other, the war and its aftermath constituted a milestone for women in America.

# PART THREE

## Since the 1940's

# 9

## The Debate on Woman's Place

In the summer of 1947, *Life* magazine featured a special thirteen-page spread on the "American Woman's Dilemma." The title of the piece summed up its central thesis. A growing number of modern women, the editors claimed, were confused and frustrated by the conflict between traditional ideas on woman's place, and the increasing reality of female involvement in activities outside the home. At an earlier time, the editors asserted, such a conflict had not existed. A woman had been required to make only one big decision—her choice of a husband. Thereafter, her life revolved exclusively around the duties of the household. The woman of 1947, however, faced a more complicated set of options. She still wanted to get married and have children, but she also wished to participate in the world beyond the home, especially after the early years of child-rearing were over. The problem was that cultural norms made little provision for females who were not homemakers. One of the byproducts of the war, therefore, was a deepening sense of bewilderment among many American women over how to define their identity.[1]

Although the editors of *Life* undoubtedly exaggerated the scope of the problem, the evidence indicated that many women were disturbed by the absence of an up-to-date definition of their place. The wife who worked from nine to five and who was still expected to be a full-time homemaker experienced understandable difficulty in resolving the conflicting priorities in her life. She needed guidance to sort out her diverse roles, but the view of femininity handed down by tradition offered little help. The extent to which many women were dissatisfied with their social identity was dramatically revealed in a 1946 *Fortune* poll. When Elmo Roper asked American women whether they would prefer to be born again as women or men, a startling 25 per cent declared that they would prefer to be men (only 3.3 per cent of the men preferred to be women). A few years later, a third of the 1934 graduates of the best women's colleges confessed to a feeling of stagnation and frustration in their lives.[2]

In large part, of course, such overt dissatisfaction was limited to a narrow segment of middle-class, well-educated women. Black and lower-class white women gave less indication of desiring a redistribution of sexual roles. A number of studies suggested that in the Negro family, females had been forced by circumstances to exercise economic and social dominance, and that many longed for the opportunity to devote full-time to their traditional roles as wives and mothers. For such women, a world in which men were able to provide for the family and women had the option of tending the home represented a goal to be sought rather than a fate to be avoided. Similarly, studies of lower-class white families found that most wives neither expected nor desired to be treated as equals. Women exerted a considerable influence over the family, but within a context of a rigid division of labor which both men and women accepted as inevitable. Social and economic activities were segregated into distinct sexual spheres, and there was little overlapping.[3]

Even if discontent was limited to a minority of females, however, the "woman problem" quickly became a subject of nationwide controversy. Hardly a week went by without some new treatise on "the trouble with women," the "manners of women," or the drinking problem of women. A housewife could skim any magazine on the newsstand and find herself "castigated, praised, worried over and analyzed." Every side offered its own interpretation of the female dilemma. Feminists claimed that women were unhappy because they were still tied to the home. Anti-feminists blamed the upsurge of discontent on the fact that females had ventured too far from their traditional role. But persons of all ideological persuasions agreed that a problem existed. "Choose any set of criteria you like," Margaret Mead wrote, "and the answer is the same: women—and men—are confused, uncertain and discontented with the present definition of women's place in America."[4]

The phenomenon of "momism" served as the jumping-off point for the controversy over women's proper role. First articulated by Philip Wylie in 1942, the concept described the fetish of mother-worship in the United States. In no other country, Wylie declared, did veneration of motherhood go to such extremes. Mom was toasted by politicians, feted with a national holiday, and celebrated in song. Marching bands spelled out her name in formation, and young men allegedly used her as the standard by which to choose their own marriage partner. The excess of adoration, in Wylie's opinion, symbolized a pathological emptiness in women's lives. With nothing else to occupy them, women preyed on their children, smothering them with affection so that they would remain tied to the home. The result was a nation criss-crossed with apron strings. Mom's love of her children was in fact "love of herself," the vehicle by which she prevented them from growing up and leaving her. Indeed, the female sex had devolved into a race of parasites—"an idle class, a spending class, a candy-craving class" —devoted to consuming all the money, affection, and virility which men could offer. Mother worship was ostensibly based on the endless self-sacrifice of "mom," but in reality it was rooted in her insatiable appetite for devouring her young and preventing them from developing into independent adults.[5]

Although Wylie clearly bore a substantial grudge against "mom," the experience of military doctors with army recruits during World War II suggested that his analysis constituted something more than an essayist's polemical whim. Psychiatrists administering tests to inductees found a disturbingly high rate of nervous disorders. A total of 3 million men avoided military service for reasons associated with emotional instability, and Dr. Edward Strecker, a psychiatric consultant to the Secretary of War, placed the blame squarely on women who had "failed in the elementary mother function of weaning [their] offspring emotionally as well as physically." Strecker's "mom" was not quite the villain Wylie had depicted, but she exhibited most of the same qualities, overprotecting her sons and creating such emotional dependency that they were unable to grow up and accept the responsibilities of manhood. Strecker's analysis focused renewed attention on the phenomenon described by Wylie a few years earlier and gave it the added credibility of professional endorsement. As one reviewer commented in 1947, " 'Mom' is on the spot." Newspapers and magazines seized on her plight as one more indication that deep trouble was brewing among American women, and feminists and anti-feminists alike used "momism" to support their explanations for the puzzle of female discontent.[6]

The anti-feminist point of view received its most sophisticated presentation in the 1947 publication of *Modern Woman: The Lost Sex* by Ferdinand Lundberg and Marynia Farnham. As Wylie had done, Lundberg and Farnham attributed part of the "woman problem" to the decline of the home as a social institution. After the Copernican Revolution, they argued, men had turned their energies outward, away from the home, in an effort to recoup their sense of importance by conquering the universe through reason and science. The ethos of Calvinism encouraged the drive for material accomplishment and established a convincing rationale for the entrepreneurial thrusts of the Industrial Revolution. In the modern world which resulted, the home had been "reduced to much the same function as a crossroads bus station, wherein people tarried for a brief while until more pressing matters demanded their attention." Men left the home to work in factories and offices, families decreased in size, and children went off to school at the age of six. Man's striving for power had left woman without a valued purpose. Events had passed her by, and she became a peripheral observer rather than a central participant in life. With her primary role reduced to that of caretaker for a family of transients, she had no focal point for her existence, "no certainty of status . . . no security . . . *as a woman, a female being.*"[7]

In Lundberg and Farnham's view, however, the rise of industrialism provided only a necessary pre-condition for women's discontent. The real cause was the feminist response to the Industrial Revolution. The women's rights movement, they argued, represented a neurotic reaction to male dominance, a "deep illness" which encouraged females to reject their natural, sex-based instincts in a futile attempt to become imitation men. Instead of urging women to develop a new way of life based on their true identity, the feminists had attempted to persuade women to seize a share of masculine power, and to beat men at their own game. The result was to obliterate the distinctions between the sexes, to cast women adrift from their biological and psychological moorings, and to generate a collective cultural pathology of which "momism" was but one manifestation.

Lundberg and Farnham based their analysis of feminism on a case history of Mary Wollstonecraft, whose *Vindication of the Rights of Women* had served as a charter of the women's rights movement. Wollstonecraft, they pointed out, had a difficult childhood. Her father frequently beat her mother, and both parents rebuffed the girl's need for affection. The father, in particular, rejected her aspirations to be something more than a self-effacing servant. The one child to receive favorable treatment was an older brother, of whom Mary was deeply jealous. After leaving her parental home, Wollstonecraft devoted her life to publicizing the demands of feminism. At the same time, however, she aggressively pursued a series of love affairs and sought to find a permanent mate.

According to Lundberg and Farnham, Mary's feminism was fundamentally motivated by her neurotic desire to rebel against her family. She hated men, and hence sought to castrate them. By urging that women be made identical to men in education, political power, and economic opportunity, she hoped to topple the tyrannical figure of her father and earn the same kind of fair treatment received by her brother. She believed that the only way to slay the monster was to become like him and she urged women to imitate men in every way. Lundberg and Farnham insisted, however, that underneath her pretensions, Wollstonecraft was a sex-starved female who literally begged to become the servant of any man who would take her in.[8]

With the case history of Mary Wollstonecraft as a reference point, Lundberg and Farnham proceeded to classify all feminists as neurotic. Just as "the shadow of the phallus lay darkly" over Wollstonecraft, they observed, so "it lay over the minds of the latter day feminists." All women with a feminist point of view suffered from difficult childhoods, usually featuring a monster-like father. As with Wollstonecraft, they rebelled in order to injure their families and express their hatred of men. All were masochists, all sought to slay their fathers (at least symbolically), all rejected the idea of motherhood, and all were motivated to some degree by penis-envy. Finally, all were afflicted by the same secret and perverse craving for sexual gratification. Thus, "by professing virtuous indignation about the 'double standard' and all the male lechery it ostensibly permitted, the feminists were able to broach the subject nearest their own hearts: their own deep desires to engage in lecherous and sensual activities."[9]

In contrast to the feminist aberration, the true woman stood forth as an example of self-acceptance and fulfillment. While feminism "bade women commit suicide as women," the normal female exulted in her sexual distinctiveness and found in it her deepest source of happiness. The independent woman was a "contradiction in terms," Lundberg and Farnham declared. Women had been created to be biologically and psychologically dependent on man. The sex act itself constituted a paradigm for female happiness. During intercourse, woman's role was passive, receptive, and accepting, based on the recognition that sexual pleasure could come only from welcoming the male phallus. (The woman could "deliver a masterly performance by doing nothing . . . except being duly appreciative," Lundberg and Farnham said. Her part was easier than rolling off a log. It was as easy as being the log itself.) The only prerequisite for female happiness was that the woman "accept with deep inwardness and readiness . . . the final goal of [intercourse]—impregnation." The desire to be a mother constituted the key to sexual pleasure, and the culmination of the sex act really occurred when the mother nursed the child who had been conceived. The female who wished complete fulfillment had only to extend the attributes displayed during intercourse to the rest of her life. Passivity, dependence, and the desire to raise children comprised the formula for female contentment.[10]

Within such an analysis, the dissatisfaction of modern woman could logically be attributed to the feminists' success in wooing females away from their true instincts. Women had substituted aggressiveness for passivity, rejected motherhood, and dedicated themselves to a masculine norm of behavior. Female employment represented one manifestation of the quest for masculinity. "Momism" represented another. Frustrated by their inability to find security in the role of mother and homemaker, modern women had turned against their sons, and in true feminist fashion had tried to deprive them of their manhood. Both "momism" and female employment demonstrated the extent to which modern woman had been separated from her true identity. The more women turned away from femininity, the more discontented they became and the more the entire society suffered from psychological debilitation.[11]

Since the disaster precipitated by feminism could be ended only by curbing the influence of the "masculine woman," Lundberg and Farnham proposed a concerted program to restore the prestige of the sexually ordained roles of wife and mother. Specifically, they urged a government-sponsored propaganda campaign to bolster the family, subsidized psychotherapy for feminist neurotics, cash subsidies to encourage women to bear more children, and annual awards to mothers who excelled at child-rearing. Lundberg and Farnham insisted that women could achieve mental sanity only if they reclaimed the home as the central focus of their existence. Housewives had to repossess the duties from which they had been displaced and to revive such lost arts as canning, preserving, and interior decorating. If the woman who viewed cooking as a pedestrian task rededicated herself to becoming a gourmet chef (and a food chemist), what had once been a tiresome chore could be transformed into a creative adventure. The key was will power. Government could help by discriminating against feminists, but women themselves had to take the lead in reconstructing their own identity. If they cared enough about achieving happiness, they could move away from an era of discontent into an era of fulfillment in their "higher role" as modern wives and mothers.[12]

Lundberg and Farnham had clearly touched on an issue of great interest, for within a brief period of time the theme they established was echoed by others. As might have been expected, women's magazines led the list of supporters, and the joys of "femininity" and "togetherness" became the staple motifs of periodicals like *McCall's* and the *Ladies Home Journal.* But the cry for women to return to the home was taken up by other authors and journals as well, not all of them with the same vested interest in domesticity as women's magazines. Agnes Meyer, the muckraking critic of government community services during the war, argued in *Atlantic* that, while women "had many careers, they had only one vocation—motherhood." Women served as the "cement of society," Meyer claimed, its preservation against the "competitive, materialistic world" of men. If they followed the example of feminist businesswomen, their natural instincts would be sterilized. "What modern woman has to recapture," she concluded, "is the wisdom that just being a woman is her central task and her greatest honor. . . . Women must boldly announce that no job is more exacting, more necessary, or more rewarding than that of housewife and mother." A few years later, Ashley Montagu expressed the same opinion in the *Saturday Review.* "Being a good wife, a good mother, in short a good homemaker," he wrote, "is the most important of all the occupations in the world. . . . I put it down as an axiom that no woman with a husband and small children can hold a full-time job and be a good homemaker at one and the same time."[13]

The anti-feminist attack also extended to traditional conceptions of women's education. Lynn White, president of Mills College in California, called on women's schools to "shake off their subservience to masculine values" and create a "distinctively feminine curriculum." Citing letters from women graduates complaining of the irrelevance of women's education to the tasks of homemaking and motherhood, White delivered a blistering attack against the feminists for insisting that females receive exactly the same kind of schooling as men. "The great blunder of the old women's rights movement," he told the American Association of University Women, "was its acceptance of the masculine scale of values as the human scale." By declaring that "we are people *too*," the feminists had implied that maleness constituted the norm for women to follow if they desired equality. Women's colleges had fallen into the trap and become obsessed with the idea of duplicating the educational experience of men. In doing so, however, they had guaranteed that women would remain unequal. Men were naturally better suited to achieve success in the sciences, fine arts, mathematics, and areas of learning which placed a premium on the ability to think abstractly. By forcing women to compete in the same disciplines, women's colleges had established the groundwork for women's failure. More important, by "masculinizing" their students, female colleges had cut women off from their true identity as wives and mothers. College women bore fewer children than average, and, according to early returns from the Kinsey survey, they experienced markedly greater difficulty in achieving orgasm. Instead of creating equality and happiness, then, feminist education had produced misery among women and destroyed their opportunity for self-fulfillment.[14]

To solve the dilemma, White and other like-minded educators

suggested that women's colleges emphasize rather than obliterate the sex differences between men and women. "Only by recognizing and insisting on the importance of such differences," White wrote, "can women save themselves, in their own eyes, of conviction as inferiors." Specifically, White proposed that female students take courses oriented to their sexual aptitudes. "Women love beauty as much as men do," he asserted, "but they want a beauty connected with the process of living." Women's instincts were "practical and earthy." Consequently, they should study the "minor" or applied arts such as ceramics, textiles, weaving, leatherwork, and flower arrangement.[15] More important, they should prepare themselves for the tasks of motherhood and homemaker which lay ahead. James Madison Wood, president of Stephens College in Missouri, urged women to specialize in disciplines like home economics, child development, and interior decorating. "If [homemaking] roles are to be played with distinction," he wrote, "the college years must be rehearsal periods for the major performance." In a similar vein, Anne Parnell, head of Sweet Briar College, advocated that "the task of creating a good home and raising good children" be raised to the dignity of a profession and made the primary purpose of women's colleges. Why not study the "theory and preparation of a Basque paella," White asked, instead of a course in post-Kantian philosophy? With such an education, women could learn how to develop to the fullest their sexually distinctive attributes and acquire skill and expertise in their appointed vocation.[16]

The anti-feminist attack on women's education and employment carried substantial appeal. At a time when the nation was experiencing severe social tension, it called forth the image of a simpler era when each person knew his or her own place. The anti-feminists described woman in terms designed to take advantage of traditional cultural stereotypes. She was "soft" rather than "tough," passive rather than aggressive. Devoted to "conserving and cherishing," she offered an attractive counterpoint to the harsh, masculine world of wars and competition. In the home, her inborn proclivity for nurture and love found a creative outlet. Outside the home, her instincts were destroyed by the "masculine" rat race. For the sake of her own fulfillment, and the salvation of the race, she needed to renounce the false god of feminism and revitalize the dormant virtues of femininity.

In addition, many anti-feminist contentions received at least partial confirmation from outside sources. Aptitude tests, for example, showed that the two sexes had somewhat different abilities. Girls rated higher in verbal skills, boys higher in mechanical skills.[17] Surveys of spinster career women disclosed that some females with feminist ambitions were psychologically maladjusted.[18] And a significant minority of women college graduates expressed dissatisfaction with the training offered by an exclusively academic curriculum. "College prepared me for something I am not," one alumnus declared, "and left me woefully lacking in knowledge I now need." Reflecting the same grievance, two out of five Barnard graduates urged greater preparation for the responsibilities of family life.[19]

The greatest advantage of the anti-feminist analysis, however, rested in its simplicity and clarity. All the anti-feminist thinkers presented woman as a static creature, eternal in her attributes and unchanged by events. They assumed that women were polar opposites of men, and that the spheres of the two sexes were ordained to remain permanently separate. Although not all the anti-feminists consciously used Freud to bolster their case, his assertion that "anatomy is destiny" served as the underlying premise of their argument. The anti-feminists believed that woman's psychic life was permanently shaped by her biological status. Whether that status was traced to her lack of a penis or the fact that she bore the children of the race was less important than the conclusion that her options in life were determined by immutable physical characteristics. If a woman followed the path of "normal femininity," the Freudian psychiatrist Helene Deutsch declared, she accepted her distinctive sexuality, repressed her masculine strivings, and related to the outside world through identification with her husband and children. On the other hand, if she rejected her femininity, she

210The American Woman

developed a "masculinity complex," sacrificed the "warm, intuitive knowledge" of womanhood to the "cold, unproductive thinking" of manhood, and betrayed her basic sexual identity. There was no middle ground, no way to combine marriage and a career, a job and motherhood. A woman became either a well-adjusted home-maker or a feminist neurotic.[20]

In light of the popularity of such ideas, it has become customary to view the postwar era as a period of triumph for the anti-feminist position. The 1950's are generally described as a "quiet" time—an age when traditional values gained new energy and influence. There was another side to the debate over woman's place, how-ever. While Lundberg and Farnham were urging a return to the "eternal feminine," a growing number of social scientists rejected the argument of biological determinism, and emphasized the im-pact of environment and society on personality formation. At the core of the sociological approach was the belief that women's lives were molded as much by shifting expectations of their role behav-ior as by immutable characteristics of sex or psychology. "Iden-tity," Peter Berger has written, "is not something 'given,' but is bestowed in acts of social recognition." Since personality develop-ment was a response to cultural norms and social circumstances, there was no reason why individuals and groups should not change over time. Margaret Mead, in her observations of life in the South Sea Islands, found that qualities such as aggressiveness, independ-ence, gentleness, and passivity were not sex-linked at all but rather resulted from social conditioning. "There is no evidence that sug-gests women are naturally better at caring for children [than men]," she said in 1946; "with the fact of childbearing out of the center of attention, there is even more reason for treating girls first as human beings, then as women." If the observations of Mead and others were correct, it made more sense to look for the cause of women's discontent in the changing nature of female roles than in the doc-trines of feminism itself.[21]

In an early postwar article, the sociologist Elizabeth Notting-ham indicated the direction of the social-science approach by attributing the dilemma of modern women to the "precipitating effects of alternating war and depression upon long-term trends that were already making for a recasting of the feminine role in Western culture." Nottingham contrasted woman's family and sexual role with her economic and social role. The former focused on maintaining harmony in interpersonal relationships, while the latter emphasized achievement in a competitive, individualistic society. Through most of history the first role had clearly been dominant, since "unlimited competitiveness [was] inimical to smooth functioning in both the family and sexual roles of women." Under the impact of two world wars, however, women had increasingly added the second, competitive role to the first, conciliatory one. Nottingham noted that World War II in particular had "acted as a stimulus to the . . . flagging aspirations of middle class women in their political, community and vocational roles." Inflation and greater job opportunities facilitated an ever increasing expansion of female employment, and the conflict between woman's two life styles intensified. Fundamentally, then, woman's discontent was rooted in the changing definition of her sphere, and the only solution was to create a new concept of woman's place which would give as much recognition to her economic role as to her family role.[22]

From an anthropological point of view, Florence Kluckhohn arrived at much the same conclusion. Society conferred its greatest rewards, she pointed out, on persons who succeeded as individuals in their own right. Within such a system of values, women suffered from severe "structural strain." On the one hand, they were educated as equals and trained for the same independent, autonomous role as that assumed by men. On the other hand, they were expected after their school years to revert to the "lonely," unstimulating role of homemaker—a role allotted little prestige or value and depicted by advertisers as a bore from which the lucky housewife could escape with the right kind of automatic stove or dishwasher. Confusion was thus built into a woman's life in a modern industrial society. Kluckhohn herself believed that the wife who worked was better off than the one who stayed at home "in a state of frustration," but she recognized the tension involved in making such a decision. In effect, American culture had subjected women to a barrage of conflicting images and expectations, and females could achieve security of status only when an entirely new definition of sexual spheres was developed.[23]

The Barnard sociologist, Mirra Komarovsky, elaborated the theory of role conflict most fully. Addressing herself specifically to the argument of the anti-feminists, she rejected the contention that the discontent among American females could be traced to collective psychological maladjustment, or the predisposition of an entire sex for one set of activities rather than another. Despite differences between the sexes at the extreme ends of the scale in aptitude tests, she pointed out, the vast majority of men and women shared a common ability to master most academic subjects. Furthermore, women who were involved in the culturally approved activities of service clubs displayed the same traits of aggressiveness and assertiveness denounced by anti-feminists as "masculine" in intellectuals and career women. The "woman problem" was thus grounded not in congenital personality differences but in the conflict which resulted from the increased overlapping of masculine and feminine spheres. Woman's status had changed with such lightning speed that her "modern" role contradicted her "feminine" role. "Society confronts the girl with powerful challenges and strong pressure to excel in certain lines of endeavor," Komarovsky noted, "but then, quite suddenly . . . the very success in meeting these challenges begins to cause anxiety." Traits which were defined as "assets" in one role became "liabilities" in the other, generating widespread confusion and conflict.[24]

The tension between the "modern" and "feminine" roles followed a woman through every stage of her life. As a child, she was urged to "select girls toys, and to be more restrained, sedentary, quiet and neat" than her brothers. When she started to school, however, her parents stressed the need for achievement. The contradiction reached a peak in college. On the one hand, she was told to work hard and get good grades. On the other hand, she was warned against being "too smart" and scaring off prospective suitors. Almost a third of the girls at Barnard complained about the inconsistent goals articulated by their parents. "My father expects me to get an 'A' in every subject," one girl said, "[but] my mother says, '. . . don't become so deep that no man will be good enough for you.'" The contradiction especially affected women's behavior in relation to men. Two out of five Barnard girls admitted that they "played dumb" on dates in order to get along with boys. "When a girl asks me what marks I got last semester," a student reported, "I answer, 'Not so good—only one A.' When a boy asks the same question, I say very brightly, with a note of surprise, 'Imagine, I got an A.'" Urged to be competitive on the one hand, and docile on the other, the students faced a bewildering choice of options which inevitably created ambivalence.[25]

The conflict persisted even after college and was heightened by the discontinuity of a woman's life. Just as black college graduates were frustrated when treated like porters or bell boys, female graduates were disturbed by the ordeal of transferring from the life of a scholar to the task of scrubbing floors and washing diapers. "The plunge from the strictly intellectual college life to the 24-hour-a-day domestic one is a terrible shock," one alumna wrote. "We stagger through our first years of child-rearing wondering what our values are and struggling to find some compromise between our intellectual ambition and the reality of everyday living." Even if a woman resolved her conflict temporarily, the cycle of role confusion appeared again when the mother sent her last child off to school. With no full-time task to fill the day, her desire to use her education revived, and she often sought a job. But she was still expected to serve as a full-time homemaker, and the confusion over the priorities in her life remained.[26]

Within Komarovsky's point of view, discontent was clearly not limited to the "morally defective" or "emotionally sick" woman in America, but rather represented an endemic condition of female life, rooted in the contradictions of the social structure. As the so-

ciety changed, woman's place changed also. But the new roles females assumed were added on to the old ones, and the conflict between the two guaranteed that discontent would persist. Women
could not resolve their identity crisis by seeking massive psychotherapy or devoting their energies to canning and preserving fruit.
A solution would come only when "the adult sex roles of women
are redefined in greater harmony with the socioeconomic and ideological character of modern society."[27]

The sociological perspective was adopted by a growing number
of observers as a sensible analysis of women's plight. *Life,* for example, blamed the high rate of divorce in America on the narrowness of the woman's role in the home and the absence of companionship with her husband. Americans divided up their "spheres
of interest too sharply after marriage," the magazine declared, and
the sharp separation between home and work tended "to freeze
women in their subservient social role." As an answer to the problem, *Life* urged that "some means . . . be found to open the door
to a fuller life [for women]." The magazine acknowledged that full-
time employment would be difficult for a wife when her children
were small, but work had the advantage of leaving "her well-
rounded in interests and experience when she reached the free
years after forty." On the other hand, the woman who devoted herself exclusively to the home found it almost impossible to keep up
with the interests of her husband, and "once her children have
grown, a housewife . . . lacking outside interests and training, is
faced with vacant years." In the end, *Life* found the employment
of married women a more attractive alternative than the specter
of 20 million idle women over forty, "bored stiff" with "numbing
rounds of club-meetings and card-playing."[28]

Taking up the same theme, the feminist Della Cyrus attributed
"momism" to the fact that most women were too little involved in
the world outside the home. Philip Wylie had never made clear his
own attitude toward women's rights, but his description of "mom"
in many ways lent itself more to a feminist than an anti-feminist
position. Using Wylie's portrayal of women as a reference, Cyrus

charged that housewives were segregated from reality and denied the opportunity to develop into mature, well-rounded individuals. With no other focal point for their lives, they devoted all their attention to their children and destroyed them with over-affection. The answer to "momism," Cyrus declared, consisted of liberating women from the home, not forcing them further into a domestic routine. If society crippled women psychologically by foreclosing their options, women would continue to cripple their children. Freedom and autonomy represented the answer for both.[29]

Viola Klein, a student of Karl Mannheim's, placed the process of change in an even broader perspective. Tracing the psychological and social treatment of women over the centuries, she found that opinions of woman's place had altered dramatically. Viewed in the seventeenth and eighteenth centuries as underdeveloped creatures with no soul or intelligence, women had come by the mid-twentieth century to be seen by many scholars as complete human beings whose similarities to men outweighed any differences which existed between them. Klein suggested that modern women were actually catching up with history, recapturing the economic and social equality they had enjoyed at an earlier time before the Industrial Revolution. "The more of the formerly masculine functions women fulfill," she wrote, "the more of those traits previously thought 'masculine' they generally develop." Following the lead of Gunnar Myrdal in the *American Dilemma*, she compared women to Jews and Negroes in their relationship to the broader culture. As a minority group, women initially exhibited the traits of the "marginal personality," at one time identifying with the dominant culture, at other times with their own subgroup. Passing in and out of each world daily, they experienced understandable ambivalence and insecurity about their identity. Over the years, however, a process of assimilation had gradually occurred in which differences were downplayed and similarities accentuated. With the rapid change in modern women's status, Klein contended, females were more and more entering the dominant culture and assuming the personality traits of independence and assertiveness.[30]

Both approaches to the dilemma of modern women suffered from shortcomings. The anti-feminist analysis, whatever its appeal, failed to explain the depth and breadth of the "woman problem." The majority of troubled women could not be dismissed as emotionally sick, and some psychiatrists, at least, rejected the idea of a collective neurosis. Bruno Bettelheim, for example, criticized therapists who sought to treat women by asking them to adjust to the status quo. The real problem, he contended, was rooted in the tension of moving from one definition of woman's place to another, and a solution would come only when the transition was completed.[31] The sociological perspective, on the other hand, failed to address some of the nagging issues underlying the controversy. Women might change in response to conditions, but they did bear children, and a great many anthropological studies indicated that the maternal and homemaking roles were a "near-universal" in human societies. Moreover, social scientists offered little in the way of concrete suggestions to solve the problem they perceived. All of them talked about the need for a new concept of woman's place, but the most substantive proposal they made was that men and women share more of each other's worlds.

In the end, the debate over woman's place could be resolved only by the behavior of women themselves. To a large extent, both sides agreed on the symptoms of the problem. Each noted that the rise of modern technology had reduced some of the immediate responsibilities of women in the home, and both commented on the dilemma posed for those females who were in the process of shifting roles. But the intellectual controversy, for the most part, occurred in a vacuum. Many women were unaware of any overt conflict in their own lives, and for those who were troubled, the principal contribution of the debate was to outline—abstractly—a set of opposing alternatives. The important question was how women—especially middle-class, educated women—acted in practice. Did they continue to expand their sphere of activities, or did they find new meaning and significance in their traditional roles?

In some ways, it seemed that the 1950's witnessed precisely the revitalization of family life which people like Lundberg and Farnham had advocated. During the years after World War II, the nation experienced a gigantic "baby boom." The birth rate for third children doubled between 1940 and 1960, and that for fourth children tripled. Advertisements in mass-circulation magazines ceased to show a three-person household and began to feature pictures of five- and six-person families. The editor of *Mademoiselle* declared that women in their teens and twenties had decided to eschew careers and raise as many youngsters as the "good Lord" gave them. As households increased in size, "togetherness" became a watchword. "A family is like a corporation," one writer observed. "We all have to work for it." A plethora of articles celebrated the virtues of families which engaged in "creative" activities together, and the cross-country camping trip and outdoor barbecue became a vogue in family recreation.[32]

The revival of popular concern with the home coincided with a substantial exodus to the suburbs. Between 1950 and 1968, towns and villages within commuting distances of large cities grew more than five times faster than urban areas, and the number of people living in such communities increased from 24 to 35 per cent of the total population. The suburban way of life added a new dimension to woman's traditional role. The nationwide "do-it-yourself" craze infected women as well as men, and wives took pride in redecorating their homes, planting gardens, and making their own clothes. The duties of child-rearing also underwent expansion. Suburban mothers volunteered for library work in the school, took part in P.T.A. activities, and chauffeured their children from music lessons to scout meetings.[33] Perhaps most important, the suburban wife was expected to make the home an oasis of comfort and serenity for her harried husband. "Modern man needs an old-fashioned woman around the house," the novelist Sloan Wilson declared. *Newsweek* stressed the importance of a woman understanding the tensions of her husband's job, and in its "Blueprint for a Wife" emphasized how crucial it was for her to be a "model of efficiency, patience and charm." If popular literature was any index, it appeared that many modern women had found a solution to their "problem" by discovering new meaning in their traditional role in the home and family. The demands of child-rearing, entertaining, and volunteer activities left little time for boredom and provided ample opportunity for fulfillment.[34]

Yet the most striking feature of the 1950's was the degree to which women continued to enter the job market and expand their sphere. The pace of female employment quickened rather than slowed during the postwar years. In 1960 twice as many women were at work as in 1940, and 40 per cent of all women over sixteen held a job. Female employment was increasing at a rate four times faster than that of men. The median age of women workers had risen to forty-one, and the proportion of wives at work had doubled from 15 per cent in 1940 to 30 per cent in 1960. While the number of single women in the labor force declined over a twenty-year span, the number of mothers at work leaped 400 per cent—from 1.5 million to 6.6 million—and 39 per cent of women with children aged six to seventeen had jobs. By 1960, both the husband and wife worked in over 10 million homes (an increase of 333 per cent over 1940), and mothers of children under eighteen comprised almost a third of all women workers.[35]

Significantly, the greatest growth in the female labor force took place among well-educated wives from families with moderate incomes. In households where the husband earned from $7,000-10,000 a year, the rate of female participation in the job market rose from 7 per cent in 1950 to 25 per cent in 1960. Although before World War II married women workers had come almost exclusively from lower-class families, by 1960 it was just as likely for a middle-class wife to be employed. Of the wives twenty to forty-four years old with no children under eighteen, the women whose husbands earned $4,000-10,000 a year worked in almost exactly the same proportion as those whose husbands earned $1,000-4,000. Mothers with children six to seventeen years of age were still employed more frequently at lower income levels, but 37 per cent of those whose husbands received $6,000-7,000 also worked, and the direction of change was clear. By 1964, a larger proportion of wives worked when their husbands received $7,500-10,000 (42 per cent) than when their spouses earned under $3,000 (37 per cent), and by 1970, 60 per cent of all non-farm wives in families with incomes over $10,000 were employed. In addition, a growing number of working women were well educated. Over 53 per cent of female college graduates held jobs in 1962, in contrast to 36.2 per cent of those with only a high school diploma, and among women with more than five years of higher education the employment figure was 70 per cent. Wives with husbands in white-collar occupations sought jobs more frequently than those whose spouses worked in factories, and female workers in clerical positions showed a stronger commitment than women in industry to stay in the labor force. In short, not only was the revolution in female employment continuing; it was also spearheaded by the same middle-class wives and mothers who allegedly had found new contentment in domesticity.[36]

At least in part, the expansion of women's economic role reflected the ongoing impact of inflation and rising expectations. The new connotation of "economic need" which first began to appear in the late 1940's seemed to have spread even further by the 1950's. Clearly, women whose husbands earned between $7,000-10,000 a year were not seeking jobs for bread and rent money alone. Rather, their employment provided a vehicle by which the family could buy a new home, afford luxuries, and send the children to decent colleges. A survey in Illinois showed that families in which both the husband and the wife worked spent 45 per cent more on gifts and recreation, 95 per cent more on restaurant meals for husband and wife, and 23 per cent more on household equipment than did one-earner families. The quest for a better living standard obviously remained one impetus to female employment.[37]

In addition, however, a growing number of women appeared to value a job for its own sake and for the personal rewards it conferred. Almost 90 per cent of working women interviewed in

Greensboro, North Carolina, and Champaign-Urbana, Illinois, stated that they liked their jobs, especially the opportunity to be with other people and receive recognition for their work. In a University of Michigan study in 1955, 48 per cent of working women still gave financial necessity as a reason for seeking employment, but 21 per cent asserted that they worked because of a desire for a sense of accomplishment and even those who cited economic need mentioned the ancillary benefits of social companionship and the sense of independence represented by a pay check. In a culture oriented to the cash nexus, the idea of tangible remuneration for performing a task seemed to carry special meaning.[38]

The same basic syndrome appeared in Mirra Komarovsky's study of blue-collar wives. The women who worked enjoyed the "self-esteem" which an independent income brought, welcomed the opportunity to "get out of the house," and appreciated being able to tell their husbands something interesting about their day. Even those who performed the most menial tasks gained a sense of achievement from their work. "I'm strong and do a good job," one cafeteria worker explained. "They tell me I help digestion because I make cracks and laugh, and they like it." Significantly, a large number of women seemed to derive more gratification from their occupational roles than from more traditional female roles. In one survey, almost two-thirds of married women workers referred to their jobs as a basis for feeling "important" or "useful," while only one-third cited the socially sanctioned activity of housekeeping. In a great many cases, it seemed, gainful employment provided women with a sense of personal and social worth which they did not find elsewhere.[39]

The results of such studies provided at least indirect confirmation for those who traced female employment to deeper social causes. Social scientists in Britain, for example, asserted that the isolation of housewives, the desire for company, and the wish for financial independence all played a part in prompting women to seek jobs. Pursuing a related theme, American sociologists emphasized the particular problems of married women whose children were grown or in school. Describing the plight of one such proto-typical woman, Margaret Mead wrote: "Some day, while she is still . . . young . . . she will have to face a breakfast table with only one face across it, her husband's, and she will be quite alone, in a home of their own. She is out of a job. . . ." In a world where housework was given little prestige, Arnold Rose noted, the mother whose offspring no longer needed constant care felt "partly func-tionless." Volunteer activities remained an option for some, but many charitable endeavors had been professionalized by social workers, leaving energetic women without a constructive outlet. In such a situation, David Reisman observed, many women viewed a "culturally defined job" as a path of liberation, the only alternative to boredom and a sense of uselessness. Although there was no hard evidence to support Riesman's hypothesis, it did seem consistent with the employment statistics. Most of the increase in the female labor force came from married women over thirty-five—precisely the group whose children were reaching maturity—and many of the workers specifically mentioned the rewards of companionship and recognition which came from holding a job.[40]

Perhaps the most important consequence of women's expanded economic role, however, was its impact on the nature of marriage and the distribution of domestic responsibilities. Traditional family life was based on a sharp division both of labor and authority. Men were expected to dominate women and to take charge of activities outside the home. Wives, in turn, were expected to follow their husbands' lead and to tend the house. A number of historical studies, however, suggested that family relationships were influ-enced substantially by economic roles. When Herman Lantz inves-tigated the domestic life of the *People of Coaltown*, he found that in many households husbands had virtually surrendered their posi-tion of authority because they had no sense of control over their economic destiny and were systematically oppressed by their em-ployers. Similarly, Mirra Komarovsky's survey of families during the Depression showed that unemployment sometimes caused men to lose their self-respect and to accept a reversal of roles with their wives. Repeated studies of power in the Negro family arrived at the same conclusion. The structure of authority in the household was frequently determined by who earned the money, and when the man was unable to fulfill his role as provider, a matriarchy often developed. In each case the conditions were abnormal, but the studies indicated that role divisions within the home were significantly shaped by economic considerations.[41]

It was not surprising, then, that the growing employment of married women after 1940 exerted a considerable influence on the distribution of tasks and authority within the family. As more and more wives joined their husbands in the labor force, patterns of sexual separation were gradually replaced by patterns of sharing. Although experts on the family had long noted a trend toward the companionate form of marriage, a series of investigations showed that female employment accelerated the trend. One survey of 200 middle-class families in New Jersey found that, where both spouses worked, husbands more often helped with the children and housekeeping, and role lines tended to be blurred. Other studies disclosed the same pattern. When Lois Hoffman interviewed 178 couples in the Detroit area, she discovered that the husbands of working wives participated more in all aspects of home life, but especially in those activities associated with child care and traditionally female tasks. The redistribution of responsibilities never quite reached a fifty-fifty equality—one study showed that men's share of the housework increased from 15 to 25 per cent of the total—but every investigation revealed some significant change, usually in the direction of husbands taking added responsibility for such "female" chores as cleaning, shopping, preparing meals, and changing diapers. Russell Lyne undoubtedly exaggerated when he called husbands the "new servant class," but there could be little question that the sexual division of labor in the home had broken down, or that women's work had played an important contributing part.[42]

More important, female employment helped to prompt a shift in the distribution of power within the family. David Heer's survey of Irish Catholic couples in Boston showed that in both lower-class and middle-class families women who worked enjoyed considerably more influence over "really important decisions" than did wives who were not employed. The same finding appeared in Deborah Kligler's study of middle-class households in New York, where employed women substantially affected decisions on "major purchases, loans, savings and investments." The new division of power seemed to follow lines of activity. Thus, as a wife left home, she gained authority over decisions involving transactions with the external environment, while losing at least some control over household concerns. The key, Robert Blood hypothesized, was the experience of participating in the world beyond the home. A woman's contribution to the decision-making process, he reasoned, correlated directly with her value as measured by the outside world. Within that system, the working wife possessed far more "resources" than her non-working sister. She had a moral right to help determine how her earnings were spent, she enjoyed the benefit of outside contacts which she might use as a source of ideas and arguments in pressing her position, and she could draw upon the social skills and confidence which came from functioning effectively in an occupational setting. The housewife, in contrast, provided no monetary assistance to the household and performed a job that was accorded little prestige or status. Since she benefited from, but did not add to, the family's resources, she had little basis for demanding a large voice in major economic decisions. One of the consequences of female employment, therefore, was to lessen the dominance of the male by breaking his monopoly on the outside world and giving his spouse some of the authority derived from participating in an "external" environment. "A working wife's husband listens to her more," Robert Blood writes. "She expresses herself and has more opinions. Instead of looking up into her husband's eyes and worshipping him, she levels with him. . . . Thus her power increases, and relatively speaking, the husband's falls."[43]

Whatever else might be said about women working, it seems clear that holding a job significantly affected the distribution of roles within society and the family. The change could not have been predicted when married women first entered the labor market in large numbers, nor did it necessarily occur in an overt manner. But there was a connection between women's new economic role, and the development of a more equalitarian family structure. As the Children's Bureau observed, the family was going through a "quiet revolution," and there was good reason to believe that role divisions in the household would continue to change.[44] In the debate over woman's place, the sociologists had stated that a breakdown of sexual polarity and a greater overlapping of sexual spheres represented one of the solutions to the "woman problem." If social-science surveys were any indication, it seemed that many couples were already in the process of creating such a solution. Husbands, like wives, were adopting new roles. And although female employment was only one of the causes contributing to the change, many experts on the subject believed that it was a decisive factor.

In the end, therefore, the sociological analysis of women's situation at mid-century more closely conformed to reality. Despite the substantial appeal of the anti-feminist argument, women were continuing to add the second role of outside employment to their already existing role of homemaker. The statisticians of the Metropolitan Life Insurance Company observed in 1955 that the average wife in America was employed before her first baby was born, and went back to work shortly after her children started school.[45] The company's assessment did not signify that the family had assumed less importance in American life. Indeed, there was no necessary contradiction between female employment and the new emphasis on the home reflected in popular literature. Most women went to work only after their children no longer required full-time supervision, and the income they earned contributed directly to higher family living standards. But the growth of the female labor force did point to an ongoing modification of woman's place in society—a modification which inevitably affected the traditional polarity between masculine and feminine spheres. Once women were propelled out of their traditional role, they would not go back, and the change produced a series of consequences which promised to alter the basic structure of relationships between the sexes.

The debate over woman's place in the late 1940's and 1950's failed to result in a new definition of women's identity, as some had hoped. But it did provide a framework within which to judge the actions of women themselves. As the nation entered the decade of the 1960's, it seemed clear that any solution to the "woman problem" would entail the creation of new roles for both women and men, rather than the restoration of a rigid division of labor based on sex. The home remained a central focus of female life, but it had ceased to be the only focus. What the sociologists recognized, and the anti-feminists ignored, was that women were already in the process of creating a new sphere for themselves. The process had by no means been completed in the 1950's. But neither had it been halted, as some assumed. And the growing frequency with which women accepted the prospect of entering the world beyond the home created the backdrop against which the drive for equality would revive in the 1960's.

# 10

## The Revival of Feminism

> HELMAN: Before all else, you are a wife
> and mother.
> NORA: That I no longer believe.
> I believe that before all else,
> I am a human being, just as much
> as you are—or at least that
> I should try to become one.
>
> Henrik Ibsen, *A Doll's House* (1879)

In the fall of 1962, the editors of *Harpers* observed a curious phenomenon. An extraordinary number of women seemed "ardently determined to extend their vocation beyond the bedroom, kitchen and nursery," but very few showed any interest in feminism.[1] Both observations were essentially correct. In the years during and after World War II, millions of women had left the home to take jobs, but the expansion of their "sphere" occurred without fanfare and was not accompanied by any organized effort to challenge traditional definitions of woman's place. If many women were dissatisfied with what one housewife called the endless routine of "dishwashing, picking up, ironing, and folding diapers," they kept their frustration to themselves.[2] Women examined their futures privately and with an unmilitant air. They had not yet developed a sense of collective grievance.

Eight years later, feminism competed with the Vietnam war, student revolts, and inflation for headlines in the daily press. Female activists picketed the Miss America contest, stormed meetings of professional associations to demand equal employment opportunities, and forced their way into male bars and restaurants in New

York. They called a national strike, wrote about the oppression of a "sexual politics," and sat in at editorial offices of *Newsweek* and *Ladies Home Journal*. At times, it seemed that the media had been taken over by women's liberation, so often did female activists appear on network television and in national magazines. In an era punctuated by protest, feminism had once again come into its own. If not all women subscribed to the new fight for equality, an energetic minority nevertheless believed that the time had come to finish the task of gaining for women the same rights that men had.

The evolution of any protest movement is a complicated phenomenon. In general, however, at least three preconditions are required: first, a point of view around which to organize; second, a positive response by a portion of the aggrieved group; and third, a social atmosphere which is conducive to reform. To an extent unmatched since the last days of the suffrage fight, all three elements came together in the American woman's movement during the 1960's. Articulate feminists presented a cogent indictment of society's treatment of women. A substantial number of females who had already experienced profound change in their lives were responsive to the call to end discrimination. And the society at large was peculiarly attuned to the need for guaranteeing equality to all its citizens. No one development by itself could have explained the rebirth of the woman's movement, but all three together created a context in which, for the first time in half a century, feminism became a force to be reckoned with in American society.

The ideological keynote of the feminist revival was sounded in 1963 by Betty Friedan. In the years after World War II, she charged, American women had been victimized by a set of ideas—a "feminine mystique"—which permeated society and defined female happiness as total involvement in the roles of wife and mother. Advertisers manipulated women into believing that they could achieve fulfillment by using the latest model vacuum cleaner or bleaching their clothes a purer white. Women's magazines romanticized domesticity and presented an image of woman as "gaily content in a world of bedroom, kitchen, sex, babies and home." And psychiatrists like Marynia Farnham and Helene Deutsch popularized the notion that any woman dissatisfied with a full-time occupation as housewife was somehow emotionally maladjusted. As a result, Friedan declared, a woman's horizons were circumscribed from childhood on by the assumption that her highest function in life was to care for her husband and rear their children. In effect, the home had become a "comfortable concentration camp" which infantilized its female inhabitants and forced them to "give up their adult frame of reference." Just as Victorian culture had repressed the need of women to express themselves sexually, modern culture denied them the opportunity to use their minds.[3]

Despite some exaggerations, Friedan articulated a point of view which struck a responsive chord, and within a year others presented a similar position. Adopting a more academic perspective, Ellen and Kenneth Keniston placed particular emphasis on the fact that young girls had no positive models of career women to emulate. "The most effective forms of oppression are those with which the victim covertly cooperates," they declared, and women provided a case in point. Denied any culturally approved alternative to homemaking, most females internalized society's view of their place and accepted a "voluntary servitude" in the home rather than risk losing their femininity. Alice Rossi made the same point. "There are few Noras in contemporary society," she observed, "because women have deluded themselves that a doll's house is large enough to find complete fulfillment within it."[4]

All the feminists agreed that the limitations placed on women's activities had a profoundly destructive effect. When a woman's sole focus of interest was the home, they claimed, she was forced to overcompensate for her lack of power in other areas by establishing an emotional tyranny over her husband and children. Females who made a full-time occupation of motherhood, Alice Rossi declared, treated their children "like hothouse plants" and tried to live vicariously "in and through them." Consequently, youngsters were stifled and prevented from growing into autonomous personalities. At the same time, the conditions of suburban living made it difficult for a wife to achieve the marital fulfillment which the "mystique" led her to expect. Husbands were away 80 per cent of the time, and it was almost impossible for a wife to derive the same measure of satisfaction from the few hours a couple spent together that a man found in the full variety of his occupational and social experiences. The family thus became a breeding ground of discontent and unhappiness. Female neurosis skyrocketed, divorces multiplied, and a generation of children grew up spoiled and dependent.[5]

Ultimately, however, the feminists traced the "woman problem" to the fact that females were denied the same opportunity as men to develop an identity of their own. The success of any interpersonal relationship depended on the autonomy and strength of each participant. Yet in many cases, cultural conditioning had prevented women from achieving a sense of themselves as persons. While men were encouraged to fashion their own destinies, females were confined to those roles which were rooted in their biological functions. Assigned to a place solely on the basis of sex, women were kept from seeing themselves as unique human beings, distinct from others. All females participated equally in the undifferentiated roles of housewife and mother, but many lacked a more precise image of themselves as individuals. As one young mother wrote:

> I've tried everything women are supposed to do—hobbies, gardening, pickling, canning, and being very social with my neighbors. . . . I can do it all, and I like it, but it doesn't leave you anything to think about—any feeling of who you are. . . . I love the kids and Bob and my home. . . . But I'm desperate. I begin to feel that I have no personality. I'm a server of food and putter-on of pants and a bedmaker, somebody who can be called on when you want something. But who am I?[6]

To the feminists, the question struck at the core of the alienation of modern women and could be answered only if wives and mother rejected cultural stereotypes and developed a life of their own outside the home. A career, the feminists claimed, had two advantages. First, it would allow women to realize their potential as individuals in the wider society. And second, it was the only way by which they could achieve the personal recognition and identity essential to a healthy family life. A study of Vassar students had shown that women with professional aspirations experienced fewer problems of personal adjustment and enjoyed a greater degree of self-fulfillment than those who rejected a career and opted for a life in the home. Another survey by Abraham H. Maslow disclosed that "high dominance" women—those who were aggressive and assertive—had a better sex life and less neurosis than "low dominance" women who more closely conformed to cultural stereotypes. Wives and mothers with careers, Alice Rossi declared, would demand less of their husbands, provide a "living model" of independence and responsibility to their children, and regain a sense of their own worth as persons. With an independent existence outside the home, they would cease to be parasites living off the activities of those around them and instead become full and equal partners in the family community.[7]

To a remarkable extent, the new feminists presented a uniform analysis of women's position in contemporary society. They all believed that the women's rights movement had suffered a grievous setback in the years after 1945, that the "feminine mystique" had forced females to accept a "voluntary servitude" in the home, and that women could break out of their "prison" only if they developed outside interests and rectified the imbalance of social and family relationships. To that end, they urged a radical modification of cultural stereotypes, the creation of new community institutions like child-care centers, and a concerted campaign by women to develop a "lifelong commitment" to the professions or business.

Unfortunately, the feminists also shared in common several misconceptions. To begin with, they assumed that all homemakers secretly resented their position and if given a chance would automatically decide to pursue a career. While such an assumption might describe some women, it certainly did not apply to all. The challenges of a full social life, volunteer work, good cooking, and enlightened child care provided many women with a diverse and rewarding existence—one which they would not choose to sacrifice even if the opportunity presented itself. Such women may have "voluntarily" accepted a life in the home, but their condition was not that of servitude nor could they honestly be described as oppressed. A 1962 Gallup Poll, for example, showed that three out of five women were "fairly satisfied" with their achievements, and believed that they were happier than their mothers.[8]

Second, the feminist analysis betrayed the same middle-class bias which had characterized the women's rights movement from its inception. Even if many housewives were discontented, very few had either the training or motivation to follow a career in business or the professions. Such an option existed only for the best educated and most dedicated segment of the female population; it did not represent a realistic alternative for most women. Furthermore, Friedan and the other feminists concentrated their attention on suburban, college graduates who by definition had been exposed at least briefly to the possibility of a different way of life. Millions of lower-class women, on the other hand, lacked both the sophistication and experience to envision the possibility of an alternative life style. Such women agreed without hesitation that their husbands' sphere of responsibility should remain separate from their own. The wife of the blue-collar worker rarely asked the question "Who am I?", first, because it never occurred to her, and, second, because she already knew the answer. Brought up to be a wife and mother, she accepted her ascribed status as both natural and right.[9]

Finally, contemporary feminists often showed an appalling ignorance of history in their contention that the "feminine mystique" represented a post-World War II phenomenon. The "cult of true womanhood" pervaded nineteenth-century culture, and the ideology of the "mystique" dominated the editorial policy of women's magazines in the twentieth century long before 1945. Indeed, the consistency of anti-feminist arguments constitutes one of the most striking facts of the entire debate in America over woman's place. When Adlai Stevenson told the graduates of Smith in 1955 that their political task was to "influence man and boy" through the "humble role of housewife," he was essentially repeating a point of view which had been expressed for centuries. Similarly, women had been told for over a hundred years that equality would lead to the destruction of the home and the family. There was nothing necessarily new about the feminine mystique, nor could it be said that women in the 1950's were more "victimized" than they had been at other times in history. The feminists had simply given fresh expression to an old problem.[10]

Nevertheless, the fact that the problem was discovered anew represented a development of critical importance. As a result of the feminists' contribution, a cogent if controversial viewpoint emerged around which to build a movement of popular protest. Talk about female discontent had been rife for years, but for the first time in a generation dissatisfied women had a focus for their anger. Friedan, in particular, exerted a significant influence. With eloquence and passion, she dramatized through case studies the boredom and alienation of those afflicted by "the problem that has no name." In addition, she was able to take her readers behind the scenes to editorial offices and advertising firms where they could see first hand the way in which the image of the feminine mystique was formed. It was hard not to be outraged after reading how advertising men —who themselves viewed housework as menial—tried to sell cleaning products as an answer to drudgery and as a means of expressing creativity. If, as Friedan claimed, the women frustrated by such manipulation were legion, her book helped to crystallize a sense of grievance and to provide an ideological position with which the discontented could identify. *The Feminine Mystique* sold more than a million copies, and, if not all its readers agreed with the conclusions, they could not help but re-examine their own lives in light of the questions it raised.

No protest movement occurs in a vacuum, however, and it is unlikely that feminism could have gained the energy it did during the 1960's had not Americans been preoccupied with the demand to eliminate prejudice and discrimination. Historically, women's rights advocates had succeeded in focusing attention on their grievances only at a time of generalized social reform. The feminist movement began when abolitionism provided female activists with an opportunity to organize and exposed them directly to the physical and psychological reality of discrimination based on sex. For nearly forty years after the Civil War, the movement was stagnant and isolated. The advent of Progressivism offered another vehicle for advance, and in a generation dedicated to ending social injustice women's rights leaders succeeded in placing suffrage on the agenda of reform and in building a national coalition sufficient to win enactment of the Nineteenth Amendment. On both occasions, women themselves played an important part in creating the atmosphere of reform, but their own cause benefited most from the climate of opinion which resulted.

It was not surprising, therefore, that the revival of the woman's movement in the 1960's coincided with another national crusade to redress the grievances of oppressed minority groups. The civil rights revolution dramatized the immorality of discriminating against any group of people on the basis of physical characteristics. It provided a model of moral indignation and tactical action which women (as well as Indians and Mexican-Americans) quickly adopted as their own. And it spawned a generation of young female leaders who determined to remove the stumbling block of discrimination from their own path at the same time that they fought for the liberation of their black brothers and sisters. Like their abolitionist ancestors, many latent feminists fully realized the extent of their own oppression only through the "sexism" of their male civil rights colleagues. Forced to do menial women's work, and denied an equal voice in policy-making councils ("the position of women in our movement should be prone," black leader Stokely Carmichael said), they rapidly concluded that their own freedom was also on the line, and set out to win it.[11] Whenever America became sensitive to the issue of human rights, it seemed, the woman's movement acquired new support in one way or another, and the 1960's proved no exception to the rule. The civil rights movement did not cause the revival of feminism, but it did help to create a set of favorable circumstances.

The most important precondition for the resurgence of the woman's movement, however, was the amount of change which had already occurred among American females. If women had been as oppressed as the feminists claimed, no amount of rhetoric could have aroused them from their captivity. Social scientists have pointed out that rebellions almost never occur among people enslaved in a "closed system," especially in a concentration camp. Rather, revolutions begin in response to "rising expectations," after a group has started on the road to improvement and become aware of its relative deprivation. It is reasonable to assume, therefore, that, unless substantial shifts had already taken place in women's lives, the ideology of the feminists would have fallen on barren ground. There was little in the writings of Friedan or Rossi which had not been anticipated in one form or another by Charlotte Perkins Gilman. Yet Gilman never received the enthusiastic reception accorded her latter-day successors. One explanation, it would seem, is that Gilman spoke to an audience which, by virtue of the social structure of the time, was incapable of hearing her message, while Friedan and her colleagues addressed a society which was more prepared to listen. It would be an exaggeration to say that the ideology of the feminists was simply catching up with reality. But if reality had not already altered considerably—if women had not already departed in such great numbers from their traditional sphere—it is doubtful that the feminists' call for further change would have met with the response it did.[12]

In fact, a strong case could be made that the changes which had occurred directly set the stage for the possibility of feminist success. To begin with, over 40 per cent of all women—including wives—held jobs by the end of the 1960's. Included in that number were a substantial number of middle-class women (41 per cent of those whose husbands earned from $8,000-10,000) and approximately 50 per cent of all mothers with children six to eighteen years old. For the first time in the nation's history, almost half the adolescent girls in the country were growing up with examples in their own homes of women who combined outside employment with marriage. To be sure, very few of these women occupied positions which could be described as executive, but they did have interests outside the home and clearly contradicted the image of the captive housewife.[13]

In addition, the evidence suggested that many working mothers already provided a positive model to their children. Repeated surveys of elementary and high school students showed that children of mothers who held jobs approved of maternal employment and that the girls intended to work after they married and had children. Significantly, adolescent females were more likely to name their mother as the person they most admired if she worked than if she did not work. "The [employed] mother," Lois Hoffman has written, "may represent to her daughter a person who has achieved success in areas that are, in some respects, more salient to a growing girl than household skills." Alice Rossi noted that, if a woman had a career, she "might finally provide her children with . . . a healthy dose of inattention, and a chance for adolescence to be a period of fruitful immaturity and growth." But surveys by social scientists indicated that many working mothers were already imparting lessons of self-reliance to their teenage children and that part-time and voluntary employment in particular seemed to foster a healthier child-mother relationship. The family, in the eyes of many experts, was becoming less child-centered and more person-centered, largely as a result of the growing interest of mothers in activities outside the home.[14]

Not surprisingly, maternal employment also exerted considerable influence on the female child's self-image. Most sociologists agree that children learn their future sex roles by observing their parents. Since mothers who worked presented a different role model than most housewives, their children grew up with a substantially revised image of what it meant to be a woman. On a battery of tests administered to female students, daughters of working mothers scored lower on scales of traditional femininity, viewed the female role as less restricted to the home, and believed that both men *and* women participated in and enjoyed a variety of work, household, and recreational experiences. To some extent, the results of maternal employment differed according to the age and sex of the child and the social class of the mother. Women with pre-school children, for example, often felt guilty about not fulfilling their maternal responsibilities and tended to compensate by over-protecting their children. Similarly, in lower-class households where mothers were forced to work because of economic need, maternal employment sometimes reflected negatively on the father's ability as a provider, causing male children to become more dependent, withdrawn, and passive. The evidence indicated, however, that, in most families where both spouses worked, the presence of a working mother had no deleterious affect on the emotional or mental development of children, but instead encouraged young girls in particular to perceive sexual spheres as overlapping. It was likely that, as more and more mothers took jobs, a new generation of daughters would appear, with a commitment to function just as fully in the world outside the home as their brothers.[15]

Finally, female employment seemed to have a salutary effect on the attitudes of both men and women toward equality. Not only did female workers themselves increasingly value their jobs as an opportunity for self-expression and personal recognition, but, in addition, their husbands gave signs of shifting their philosophy on issues involving women's rights. A survey of households in a Western city showed that husbands of working wives were more likely than husbands of non-working wives to favor equal pay (62 per cent versus 49 per cent), to believe that sexual intercourse should occur only when both partners desired it (68 per cent versus 50 per cent), to think that men should help around the house "all the time" (29 per cent versus 13 per cent), and to indicate a willingness to make sacrifices for a wife's career (20 per cent versus 8 per cent). The figures were not overwhelming, and it was possible that a husband's attitudes either preceded or were independent of a wife's working pattern. But together with other data which showed a close relationship between women's work and the companionate family the survey results gave support to the suggestion that female employment, in its own way, was causing a profound modification in relationships between the sexes.[16]

On balance, then, it appeared that the ground was well prepared for a revival of the woman's movement. If the feminists had been correct in their analysis, almost all women might have been expected to cling to their traditional roles, afraid to leave the hearth because of the oppobrium attached to any vocation other than homemaking. The evidence indicated, however, that, despite the popularity of the feminine mystique, a dramatic change in the content of women's sphere had already taken place. Women's rights advocates were correct in claiming that little progress had occurred in areas such as professional opportunities, community services, and fair pay. But they vastly exaggerated the degree of women's servitude.[17] As David Reisman noted in 1964, "there is much less resignation and inhibition among women [today than in my mother's generation]. . . . Instead, there is an effort to lead a multi-dimensional life." If the barriers to equality had not been eliminated, women nevertheless enjoyed more freedom than ever before, and the extent to which ideas and expectations were shifting —especially among the young—created the context in which a renewed drive for equality was possible.[18]

In response to such developments, the woman's movement came to life in the mid-1960's. At first slowly, then with growing confidence and strength, feminist leaders established new organizations to carry on the battle for equal rights. Like most social movements, the new feminism was comprised of different constituencies. On the "right" wing was the National Organization for Women (NOW) formed in 1966 by Betty Friedan. Supported primarily by well-educated professional women, NOW represented a reformist approach to equality and acted on the assumption that the social structure could be changed from within through legislation and persuasion. Women's liberation groups, in contrast, were made up

mostly of younger, more radical women, many of whom had been
involved in the peace, civil rights, and student movements, and who
were convinced that revolutionary change offered the only answer
to sexual inequality. Through such mechanisms as "consciousness-
raising"—a process in which small groups of women share their
common experiences—members of women's liberation sought to
understand the depth of what it means to be female and to explore
ways of overcoming the sources of oppression in their lives.[19]

Although the diffuse structure of the movement encouraged
division and controversy, most feminists subscribed to a core set
of demands which constituted the essence of their program. All insisted on an end to job discrimination, all supported the repeal
of abortion laws, and all urged the creation of twenty-four-hour-a-
day child-care centers. Most important, all wanted an end to class
treatment, to the idea that women, because of their sex, should
automatically be expected to do the housework, act as secretaries
at meetings, or rear children. Women were individuals, they
claimed, not sex objects or servants, and wherever a female was
assigned a place on the basis of sex alone, whether at a news
magazine where women were "researchers" rather than "reporters," or in the home where husbands expected wives to get up with
the baby at night, discrimination existed and had to be rooted out.
Critics of the movement frequently dismissed women's liberation
as a middle-class fad which was irrelevant to the real problems of
society, but, in fact, feminist proposals spoke to all women and, if
implemented, were more likely to benefit the ghetto-dweller than
the affluent resident of the suburb.[20]

Perhaps the most notable characteristic of the movement was
its ability to make news. In an era dominated by the mass media,
the feminists displayed consummate skill in drawing public attention to themselves and "raising" America's consciousness to the
inequalities from which women suffered. Television might spot-
light the more spectacular tactics of the movement such as sit-ins
or boycotts, but it also dealt seriously with more substantive concerns. Every network (and most magazines) devoted special pro-

grams to the reasons for the feminist protest, and enterprising reporters ferreted out impressive documentation to support charges of sex discrimination. Unequal pay, the tragedy of unwanted pregnancies which could not legally be terminated, and the frustration of many women with domesticity—all were given nationwide exposure. The success of the feminists in attracting publicity alerted millions of uninvolved women to the possibility that they too might be victims of discrimination. Many females might have rejected the idea that they were an "oppressed class," but, as they talked about the effort by feminists to "liberate" them, the likelihood increased that they would discern examples of inequality and prejudice in their own lives and develop a heightened sense of sex solidarity.[21]

Significantly, the resurgence of feminism coincided with other signs of independence among American women. The *New York Times* reported that a "new breed of middle class women" was emerging and that suburban housewives who had previously stayed at home all day were seeking jobs, going back to school, and engaging in volunteer work. Both the Protestant and Catholic churches were confronted by an increasing militancy among women who demanded equal recognition. A leader of American Baptist women threatened a floor fight if a female was not included in the top hierarchy of the Baptist convention, and angry nuns insisted on an end to supervision by priests. The feminist message also met with an enthusiastic response among the young women of "middle America." Representatives of the Future Homemakers of America declared that women's liberation had exerted a "definite influence" on their 600,000 members. Teenage girls still wanted to marry and have children, FHA leaders noted, but they now believed that fulfillment as women could come only if they also worked in a gainful occupation. Although such reports were obviously impressionistic, two studies of teenage girls in Georgia and Washington state showed that a sizable majority planned to hold jobs after they married and that less than 25 per cent definitely anticipated *not* being employed.[22]

A 1970 Gallup Poll confirmed that many women—especially the well educated—were developing greater sensitivity to their rights. Although 65 per cent of the respondents believed that women were generally given an even break with men, a majority also declared that females were discriminated against in business and in the professions. Eight years earlier, in a similar poll, less than 30 per cent felt that females suffered from job discrimination, and only 39 per cent said that women were underpaid. More important, the level of discontent in 1970 rose appreciably among women with a college education. Almost half the college respondents (47 per cent) asserted that women did not receive an even break with men, and 75 per cent declared that women were discriminated against in gaining executive positions (significantly, 70 per cent of women with college degrees were in the labor force by the end of the decade).[23] In a parallel finding, Mirra Komarovsky discovered that women who were married to blue-collar workers and who had a high school diploma were far more likely to demand that their husbands share in domestic and child-rearing responsibilities than those with only elementary schooling. Education thus appeared to be another critical variable in fostering self-awareness among females and correlated directly with perceptions of inequality.

Perhaps the greatest evidence that the woman's movement had made an impact was the increased attention it received from politicians. For more than four decades after passage of the suffrage, feminist demands had largely been ignored by government leaders. By the late 1960's, however, a change in attitude began to appear. After having been bottled up in committee for forty-seven years, the Equal Rights Amendment to the Constitution was brought before the House of Representatives where it received enthusiastic support. James Hodgson, Richard Nixon's Secretary of Labor, announced in 1970 that federal contracts would henceforth contain a clause mandating the employment of a certain quota of women. Attorney General John Mitchell initiated federal suits under Title VII of the 1964 Civil Rights Act to end job discrimination against women in such large corporations as Libby-Corning Glass and American Telephone and Telegraph. And under feminist pressure, the Nixon Administration required 2,000 colleges and universities to turn over their personnel files to the federal government so that it could determine whether females were victims of prejudice in hiring and wages.[24]

The same effort to respond to the demands of the woman's movement occurred at other levels of government. Despite the vigorous opposition of the Catholic Church, abortion reform laws were passed in seventeen states. By 1970, over 200,000 women were receiving legal abortions annually—a 1,000 per cent increase over two years earlier. Candidates for public office made support of women's rights a major plank of their platforms. Municipal leaders instructed department chiefs to seek out qualified women for executive posts. And school boards began to change their rules on such things as who could take home economics and shop courses, and who could play on athletic squads. If women's liberationists scorned some of the actions as corrupt tokenism, the fact remained that their movement had become big enough in the eyes of political leaders to merit co-opting.[25]

Nevertheless, there was little reason to be over-optimistic. Although some progress had been made on laws involving job discrimination, resistance to change mounted as the stakes became higher and more deeply entrenched social values were challenged. Once again, the child-care issue symbolized the difficulties faced by women's rights advocates. When Congress enacted a massive day-care program designed to make child-care facilities available to every working mother in the country, President Nixon vetoed the measure, declaring that it would commit "the vast moral authority of the national Government to the side of communal approaches to child-rearing. . . ." The family, Nixon insisted, was "the keystone of our civilization," and enlightened public policy required that it be strengthened rather than weakened. On a second controversial issue, Nixon issued an emotional statement opposing abortion reform and defending the rights of unborn fetuses, thereby lending his support to those in the various states who were striving to overturn liberalized abortion statutes. Thus, while feminists and their sympathizers could draw some encouragement from the progress which had taken place, opposition to change remained both strong and effective.[26]

In most ways, then, the fight had just begun. Radical feminists would not be satisfied with halfway measures or limited legislative reforms. They desired drastic change, the end of a system which assumed that men were powerful and women weak, males aggressive and females passive. American culture, Kate Millett wrote, was permeated by an oppressive ideology in which all that could "be described as distinctly human . . . [was] reserved for the male." If politics meant power, then women were still disenfranchised. Even in "liberal" households, they were expected to do the dirtiest chores, take primary responsibility for rearing the children, and put their aspirations behind those of their husbands. For Millett and her allies, the answer had to be revolution—the abolition of patriarchy, an end to the family as presently constituted, and replacement of the traditional socialization process. Emancipation could be achieved only when every vestige of sexual stereotyping had been eliminated, when "masculine" and "feminine" spheres disappeared, and members of each sex were free to develop as individuals.[27]

In a very real sense, the woman's movement had gone full cycle. The women who started feminism in the nineteenth century had ideas which were similar in substance, if not in tone, to those of their successors. They too wanted an end to the notion that women should occupy a separate sphere, and they too insisted on every person's right to be a human being first and a man or a woman second. "Whatsoever it is morally right for a man to do it is morally right for a woman to do," Sarah Grimké wrote in 1838. And Margaret Fuller added: "What Woman needs . . . is as a nature to grow, as an intellect to discern, as a soul to live freely. . . . We would have every arbitrary barrier thrown down. We would have every path laid open to Woman as well as to Man."

More than a century later, the same plea echoed across the country. Sometimes raucous, often bitter, it nevertheless had the strength of appealing to the basic principle that every human being is unique and sacred and has an inalienable right to determine his or her own destiny.[28]

Whether the new feminism could succeed where its predecessors had failed was an open question. It seemed unlikely that the vast majority of Americans were yet ready to accept the ramifications of complete sexual equality. The nuclear family, the concept of maternal responsibility for child-rearing, the importance of privatism—all were cherished values and all to some extent stood in the way of the revolution envisioned by women's rights advocates. On the other hand, the signs of change were manifold. The number of three and four year olds in nursery schools or kindergartens doubled between 1965 and 1970. Nearly 70 per cent of all women approved in principle the idea of day-care centers. And most young people gave at least verbal allegiance to the values associated with sexual equality. The proportion of women living alone or with roommates rose 50 per cent during the 1960's, and the increase was 109 per cent for those in the crucial marrying range of twenty to thirty-four years old. A Barnard senior, the *New York Times* reported, was introduced to friends "as the only girl at Barnard who's getting married," and applications by women students to professional schools mounted. If such facts were any index, it seemed that fewer women saw marriage and motherhood as their only vocation, and that young mothers were increasingly prepared to utilize day-care facilities so that they could resume careers in the world outside the home.[29]

Whatever the case, there could be little question at the end of the 1960's that feminism had once again become a vital force in American society. Women's liberation groups spread from the city to the suburbs. Groups of welfare mothers, airline stewardesses, and female soldiers all asserted their right to equal treatment with men. And officials in government and business went out of their way to give at least the appearance of meeting feminist demands. America might not be ready for the revolutionary ideas of the more extreme feminists, but more and more women were demonstrating an acute consciousness of the need to end discrimination based on sex. The future was uncertain, but as the nation entered a new decade, feminism exhibited a strength, vitality, and appeal which had not been seen in the United States for half a century.

# CONCLUSION

# Future Prospects

How does social change occur? The question has been implicit throughout the preceding discussion, and the answer to it may hold the key to much that has been said here. There are two fundamental responses to the query. The first is based on the premise that attitudes determine behavior and that ideology is the crucial variable affecting the process of change. According to this argument, people act on the basis of their values or beliefs. Hence a change in society can come about only through persuading the public that a given set of values is wrong and must be modified. The second position—far more skeptical—operates on the assumption that attitudes, especially those involving emotional matters such as race or sex, almost never change except under compulsion and that behavior is a more promising fulcrum for change than attitudes. As Gordon Allport has observed in his study of prejudice, "the masses of people do not become converts [to racial equality] in advance; rather they are converted by the *fait accompli*." Thus social scientists have observed that white workers lose some of their bias against racial minorities when forced to work alongside them, but if the same workers had a choice beforehand, the contact would never occur and the bias would remain intact.[1]

Although the interplay of attitude and behavior is far more complicated than the above paragraph indicates, the distinction provides a useful conceptual device for analyzing the recent history of women. It has seemed to me that attitudes toward woman's place have been so deeply imbedded within the process of living itself that any direct attempt to transform those attitudes through persuasion or ideological confrontation was doomed to failure. The suffragists believed that they had made significant progress toward equality through acquisition of the franchise, but they seriously overestimated the impact of the ballot on the structure of relationships between the sexes. Women might vote, but as long as they followed the lead of their husbands and fathers in the world outside the home, the reform meant relatively little. The real obstacle to equality was the division of spheres between men and women, and the Nineteenth Amendment did not substantially alter that. Males continued to be reared in one way, females in another, and attitude and behavior reinforced each other. In a society with few models of "independent" women to emulate, only a small percentage of college girls were willing to risk failure in the female world of marriage and motherhood in order to prove their worth in the male world of business and the professions. The idea that the two sexes should fulfill different roles and responsibilities was buttressed by institutions such as the family and transmitted from generation to generation through the socialization process. Feminists might protest against discrimination and urge equality, but their agitation had little effect. Only a substantial upheaval could modify the existing division of labor between the sexes.

It was for that reason that World War II assumed so much importance. The event of war, by definition, disrupted traditional patterns of life and propelled men and women into new activities. In the years prior to 1940, employment of married women had been frowned upon as unseemly, and a violation of woman's place. The war made such attitudes irrelevant, and caused women's work to be defined as a national priority. As a result of the crisis, almost 7 million women joined the labor force for the first time, three out of four of them married. Most observers expected that women would go back to the home when the fighting stopped, but once in the labor force, female workers decided to remain on the job. With the passage of time, the number of employed married women grew steadily—partly as a response to inflation and rising family aspirations, but partly also because of a desire by many women to establish an identity beyond the home. Before the war, it had been almost unheard of for a middle-class wife or mother to work. Thirty years later, the labor force contained 60 per cent of all wives from homes with an annual income of more than $10,000, and more than half the mothers of children from six to seventeen years of age.[2] If the nation—including women—had been asked in 1939 whether it desired, or would tolerate such a far-reaching change, the answer would undoubtedly have been an overwhelming no. But events bypassed public opinion, and made the change an accomplished fact. The war, in short, was a catalyst which broke up old modes of behavior and helped to forge new ones. As a result, work for middle-class married women has become the rule rather than the exception, and the content of women's sphere has been permanently altered.

It would be a mistake, of course, to view a job as a panacea for women, or as a solution to the problem of inequality. Today, as fifty years ago, most employed women hold second-echelon jobs which pay low wages and offer little possibility for advancement. Although 70 per cent of all female college graduates are in the work force, nearly 20 per cent are employed in clerical, sales, or factory positions, and the median income of women with degrees is only 51 per cent of that earned by men with a comparable education.[3] Nor can it be said that the woman with a job is necessarily more fulfilled, or happier than the woman who does not work for pay. Many wives enjoy the roles of homemaker and mother, and find a full measure of satisfaction in child-rearing, volunteer activities in the community, and an absorbing family life. Poll data suggest that most Americans—including women—still believe that a woman's *primary* responsibility is in the home, especially during the early years of child-rearing. Thus the dramatic shift in women's economic activities has not immediately transformed the norms governing the appropriate roles of men and women.

Nevertheless, employment has operated as an effective engine of change in the lives of women. To begin with, holding a job has involved women in a role—that of breadwinner—which by all accounts is most salient in defining the differences between the sexes. If, as the feminists claim, one of the principal obstacles to equality is the division of labor between men and women, departing from the home to take a job represents at least a step toward closing the gap between male and female spheres, and creating a new and different kind of life for women. Over and over again during the 1940's and 1950's, female workers spoke of enjoying their jobs, and valuing the social companionship and sense of personal recognition which accompanied employment. In a society where housework is denigrated by men and women alike (despite the efforts of advertisers), the opportunity to take a paying job has represented for many a broadening of experience, a move away from sexual apartheid. Much of women's work might be monotonous and boring, but it is no more so than washing dishes or hanging clothes.

More important, perhaps, the transformation of women's economic role has led to a series of "unanticipated" consequences in relations between the sexes. As more and more women have taken jobs, responsibilities within the home have been redistributed between husbands and wives, women increasingly expect to fill a diversity of roles, and the models available to young children have altered so that daughters of working mothers grow up exhibiting greater assertiveness and less attachment to the values of traditional femininity. To some extent, the changes reflect long-term trends such as the development of the companionate family. Yet every study made by social scientists indicates that female employment acts as an important spur to the greater sharing of domestic tasks. Most married women workers find it difficult to carry a full-time job outside the home and still shoulder the burden of household management. If husbands are to enjoy the benefits of a second income, justice requires that they assume at least some of the responsibilities previously borne by the wife. The process may be resisted at first, but it is not difficult to reconstruct. What begins as a "favor" gradually becomes a routine, then an obligation and duty.

The increased overlapping of sexual spheres could not have been foreseen when married women first entered the labor force in large numbers, but it represents one of the most significant by-products of women's increased economic activity.

Finally, the change in women's economic role has provided a necessary precondition for the revival of the drive for equality. Historians have noted that the ideology of the American Revolution represented in large part the articulation on a level of conscious principle of a set of conditions which already existed in practice. Phrased in another way, ideology requires a base in reality which can be used as a point of departure for raising people's consciousness to the existence of a problem and the presence of a program which applies to it. The woman's movement failed to enlist popular backing for much of the period after 1920, because, as long as most women internalized society's conception of their proper place, they had no experience which would permit them to see the relevance of feminist ideas to their own lives. Once the war dislocated women from conventional patterns of behavior, however, and set in motion a different cycle of behavior, a new set of expectations concerning women's sphere gradually evolved. The altered content of women's lives highlighted the disparity between the myth and reality of woman's place, and provided an important incentive for closing the gap. As more and more women joined the labor force, they gained personal knowledge of discrimination and the need to correct it. In addition, the presence of a working wife in the home appeared to have a liberalizing influence on male attitudes. In sex as in race, direct experience with a feared reality has proved an effective way of dispelling prejudiced or uninformed attitudes.

None of this, of course, means that feminist goals have been reached or that the processs of change has advanced far enough for women to achieve full equality with men. The future of the feminist program depends a great deal on the fate of the family. According to many contemporary women's rights advocates, female "servitude" is rooted in the distinctive roles played by men and women in the nuclear family and can be eliminated only by the creation of alternative institutions and life styles which are more equalitarian in nature. Yet anthropologists have observed that every culture has familial arrangements based on a sexual division of labor. In most cases, women accept responsibility for "expressive" tasks such as child-rearing and men take charge of "instrumental" tasks such as earning a living or providing a defense against attack. Although such distinctions have clearly been muted in modern technological societies, they have not been totally abolished anywhere, and even in the collective kibbutz communities of Israel, sociologists have noted a revival of nuclear family forms.[4] Thus it would seem that any further movement toward equality in America will occur through additional modification of the existing family structure rather than through the establishment of totally new social institutions.

A second and related obstacle to the realization of feminist goals is the degree to which women continue to exhibit behavioral characteristics that differ from those of men. Psychological surveys indicate that girls are more likely to be ingratiating, dependent, sympathetic, and submissive than boys, and to have appreciably less achievement motivation. Such characteristics are as likely to appear in female college students as in those without a higher education. In one test, different groups of college women were given identical sets of articles to read, some bearing the name John McKay, others Joan McKay. The students consistently judged the work associated with the female author as less worthwhile and persuasive than the same work associated with a male author. Reviewing the results, Dr. Philip Goldberg, administrator of the test, concluded that "women are prejudiced against female professionals, and regardless of the actual accomplishments of these professionals, will firmly refuse to recognize them as the equals of their male colleagues." A similar study measuring attitudes toward a female in medical school found that 65 per cent of the women respondents demonstrated a definite "motive to avoid success" in contrast to only 10 per cent of the men.[5] For the most part, such attitudes reflect the fact that women are still brought up to expect that they will not succeed as well as men, and as new socialization patterns take hold, the discrepancy in self-image between the sexes will undoubtedly narrow. But for a time yet, it seems likely that women will be predisposed to take second place in any competition with men and to accept as "normal" the discriminatory treatment of some employers.

Finally, there is the nagging problem of why more women have not pursued careers. At a time when the socio-economic background and marital status of women workers have been transformed, and more than 70 per cent of female college graduates are employed, the proportion of women in business and the professions has changed hardly at all. Much of the reason can be traced to problems we have already discussed—overt discrimination, the expectations transmitted through child-rearing patterns, the lack of professional role models, and the discontinuity in the married woman's career life caused by giving birth to one or more children. Perhaps the most subtle reason, however, is the role stress which develops when a woman seeks to combine a career with marriage and a family. During the last three decades, millions of families have struck "role bargains" which permit wives and mothers to take jobs outside the home while their husbands or others assume responsibility for a share of the domestic tasks. But a job has limits. The time it consumes, the energy it requires, and the rewards it brings can all be fairly well defined in advance, and in most cases the bargain is based on the assumption that the woman is an incidental wage-earner, that her *primary* role is still in the home.

A career, in contrast, requires a commitment of energy and spirit which is inconsistent with such an arrangement. The doctor or lawyer is often faced with a situation in which professional responsibilities must take priority over family responsibilities. If the person is a man, the problem is usually mitigated by the presence of a woman in the home to take up the slack and "carry on" until life returns to normal. If the career person is a woman, however, the man in the home must make the temporary sacrifice. In a strictly equalitarian society, the stress should be similarly tolerable in both cases. But in a society which maintains the assumption that a wife's aspirations come after her husband's, the predicament generates severe tension and makes far more difficult the task of negotiating a satisfactory role settlement. Thus despite some significant changes in relationships between the sexes, most potential professional women still face a profound marriage-career conflict—a conflict which mirrors how far the society still must go to reach equality and which highlights the extent to which even "liberated" individuals remain attached to traditional ideas of male and female roles.[6]

It is precisely in such areas that feminists face their greatest challenge and their greatest opportunity. As we have seen, a great many changes can take place as a matter of course, without conscious intent or direction. But if married women are to sustain a commitment to a career, demand full equality (and mutual sacrifice) in the home, and ensure that their children do not inherit invidious sexual stereotypes, they must be guided by a high degree of ideological energy and awareness. By calling attention to instances of discrimination, and demonstrating that an issue of principle is involved when women are denied certain career opportunities, the woman's movement can help to provide that energy. Enough women have departed from their traditional sphere to create a potential constituency for an effective movement toward equality. Now, the problem is to mobilize the constituency and create a wider consciousness of the meaning of woman's rights.

But whatever the fate of feminism per se, it seems clear that history is on the side of continued change in women's status. Although the nuclear family itself may not be replaced, the distribution of responsibilities within it continues to undergo substantial alteration. And while female children still demonstrate less desire for achievement than male children, social scientists have noted a growing trend to treat youngsters the same regardless of sex and to avoid differentiating between the roles assigned them. "Today we may be on the verge of a new phase in American family history," Robert Blood has observed. "Employment emancipates women from domination by their husbands and secondarily raises daughters from inferiority with their brothers. . . . The classic differences between masculinity and femininity are disappearing as both sexes in the adult generation take on the same roles in the labor market." Such conclusions are perhaps exaggerated, especially the assertion that men and women occupy the *same* roles in the labor market. But the basic thrust of the statement rings true. The doubling of nursery school enrollments from 1965 to 1970, the number of women now foregoing immediate marriage and child-bearing after college, the fact that two out of three new jobs during the 1960's went to women—all provide dramatic reinforcement for the impression of change. At schools like Vassar, the percentage of graduates applying to professional schools skyrocketed at the beginning of the 1970's, and even crime statistics showed a trend toward closing the gap between the sexes. Arrests for prostitution have declined sharply, but the number of women charged with burglary, robbery, and other "major" crimes has soared—an indication to criminologists that women are becoming full partners with men and are no longer merely accomplices in the world of crime.[7]

In the end, of course, conclusions on any subject so complicated and important depend a great deal on the perspective of the observer. It seems quite justifiable, from a feminist point of view, to argue that no meaningful shift in status has occurred among American women during the past fifty years. Very few observers will dispute the fact that women are frequently treated as "sex objects," that they are still expected to place their aspirations behind those of their husbands, and that those who hold jobs are underpaid and exploited. On the other hand, important shifts in behavior have taken place and it seems that the changes bear directly on some of the root causes of sexual inequality: the definition of male and female spheres, the role models we provide our children, the permissible horizons available to men and women. If the thesis presented here is correct—that attitudes toward woman's place run too deep to be changed through direct conversion—then the only alternative means of change is to break into the cycle of behavior which perpetuates the status quo and initiate a new cycle which will undermine the structural basis for traditional views of male and female roles.

It is just such a process which I believe has taken place in the years since 1940. With World War II as a catalyst, a dramatic change has occurred in women's economic role, generating a series of "ripple effects" which ultimately have reached into such crucial areas as home life and child-rearing practices. No one can claim that equality has been achieved as a result of these changes, but it may be that a foundation for seeking equality has been established. As the nation approaches the last quarter of the century, no aspect of contemporary life exhibits greater flux than relations between the sexes. And if the final balance sheet is not yet in, there is good reason to believe that the movement toward greater freedom for women will not soon come to a halt.

# Notes

## PREFACE

1. Undated statement by Carrie Chapman Catt, prior to 1920, in Carrie Chapman Catt Papers, Smith College, Sophia Smith Collection, Box 1.
2. Kate Millett, *Sexual Politics* (New York, 1970), pp. 26, 62.
3. Eleanor Flexner, *Century of Struggle* (New York, 1970), pp. vii, xii, xiii; Aileen Kraditor, ed. *Up from the Pedestal* (Chicago, 1969), pp. 3-7. Two important exceptions are William L. O'Neill, *Everyone Was Brave* (Chicago, 1969) and Anne Firor Scott, *The Southern Lady: From Pedestal to Politics* (Chicago, 1970). Both works deal with developments after 1920, and Anne Scott's book goes beyond the woman's movement into an assessment of changes in the social and economic roles of Southern women.
4. Louis Wirth, "The Problem of Minority Groups," in Ralph Linton, ed., *Man in the World Crisis* (New York, 1945), pp. 347-48; and Alice Rossi, "Equality Between the Sexes: An Immodest Proposal," in Robert J. Lifton, ed., *The Woman in America* (Boston, 1967), p. 101. Wirth points out that a group may constitute a majority of the population and still be treated as a "minority."

## INTRODUCTION

1. President Wilson's statement is quoted in Maud Wood Park, *Front Door Lobby* (Boston, 1960), p. 209.
2. The Worcester and Buffalo newspaper comments are cited in Theodore Stanton, "Seneca Falls and Women's Rights," *Independent,* CXI (August 4, 1923), pp. 42-43; the denunciation of the feminists as "wild enthusiasts" is from the New York *Herald,* September 12, 1852, cited in Aileen Kraditor, ed., *Up from the Pedestal* (Chicago,

1970), p. 189. The abolitionist origins of the women's rights movement are discussed in Eleanor Flexner, *Century of Struggle* (Cambridge, Mass., 1959), pp. 42-51, 82-84.

3. Carl Degler has commented on the suffrage orientation of historians of
   women's rights in his introduction to Charlotte Perkins Gilman,
   *Women and Economics* (New York), p. vii.

4. "The Seneca Falls Declaration of Sentiments and Resolutions," July 19,
   1848, in Henry Steele Commager, ed., *Documents of American History* (New York, 1963). The radical scope of the Declaration is discussed in some depth by William L. O'Neill in his book *Everyone
   Was Brave* (Chicago, 1969).

5. "The Ballot—Bread, Virtue, Power," *Revolution,* January 8, 1868,
   quoted in O'Neill, p. 19. The same theme was articulated by Margaret
   Fuller, a young Transcendentalist teacher and friend of Emerson,
   Channing, and Alcott. Fuller belittled the notion that feminists
   wanted political equality alone. "What Woman needs," she wrote, "is
   not . . . to act or rule, but as a nature to grow, as an intellect to
   discern, as a soul to live freely. . . . We would have every arbitrary barrier thrown down." Her comments were made in her landmark book, *Woman in the Nineteenth Century,* written three years
   before the Seneca Falls conference. For a further discussion, see
   Flexner, p. 67.

6. For a discussion of Gilman's life, see Carl Degler's Introduction to
   *Women and Economics,* pp. viii-xix.

7. Carl Degler, "Charlotte Perkins Gilman on the Theory and Practice of
   Feminism," *American Quarterly,* VIII (spring 1956), pp. 22-24;
   Gilman, *Women and Economics,* p. 71; and William T. Doyle, "Charlotte Perkins Gilman and the Cycle of Feminist Reform," unpublished doctoral dissertation, University of California, 1960, p. 192.
   Gilman used the epigram of Madame de Stael to support her case:
   "love with men is an episode; with women, a history."

8. Charlotte Perkins Gilman, *The Home, Its Work and Influence* (New
   York, 1910), p. 92; Degler, pp. 24-25; Charlotte Perkins Gilman,
   *His Religion and Hers* (New York, 1923), pp. 13-14; and Charlotte
   Perkins Gilman, "Waste of Private Housekeeping," *Annals* of the
   American Academy of Political Science (July 1913), p. 91.

9. Gilman, *Women and Economics,* p. 222; Gilman, *The Home, Its Work
   and Influence;* and *The Forerunner,* October 1910, quoted in Degler,
   p. 24. See also Degler, pp. 32-37.

10. Gilman, *Women and Economics,* p. 313; Degler, pp. 36-38; Doyle, pp.
    175-231; and O'Neill, pp. 38-45.

11. The Emerson quotation is cited in Boyd Guest, "The Position of Women as Considered by Representative American Authors Since 1800," unpublished doctoral dissertation, University of Wisconsin, 1943, p. 72.

12. The Congressional debate is discussed in Flexner, pp. 148-49. The suffrage measure was soundly defeated. Aileen Kraditor has brilliantly analyzed the nation's commitment to the idea that the family constituted the basic unit of society, and has demonstrated the extent to which the feminists' emphasis on individual rights threatened such ideas. See Kraditor, *Ideas*, pp. 25 ff.

13. The Woodhull episode is thoroughly discussed in O'Neill, pp. 25-31.

14. Flexner, pp. 151-53, 216; O'Neill, pp. 18-24, 33-38; and Kraditor, pp. 110-31.

15. At a Rochester convention of the suffrage movement in 1888, a delegate declared that women stood at the top of Mount Sinai, ready to unite the female's spiritual kingdom with the male's material kingdom for the better advancement of both. A New York suffragist presented a similar argument. "The protection of human life has always been woman's great business in life," she asserted. "It is natural that men should give greater care in government to . . . material affairs. To counter-balance this, women's work and votes are needed for the human side." See Mildred Adams, *The Right To Be People* (New York, 1967), p. 167; O'Neill, pp. 50-51; Kraditor, pp. 115-16; and Maud Wood Park, p. 143. Almost all the suffragists agreed that women were morally superior to men. The Kentucky suffragist Laura Clay, for example, stated that women's participation as voters would uplift men, end the double standard, and lower the divorce rate.

16. Jane Addams, "Why Women Should Vote," *Ladies Home Journal*, XXVII (January 1910). See also Kraditor, pp. 68-70. In another publication Addams asked: "May we not say that city housekeeping has failed partly because women, the traditional housekeepers, have not been consulted as to its multiform activities?"

17. Quoted in Maud Wood Park, p. 145.

18. Quoted in Kraditor, p. 125.

19. Kraditor, pp. 131, 172, 213; and Flexner, p. 220. The suffragists continued to exhibit racial prejudice. In 1899 the national convention refused to pass a resolution opposing Jim Crow railroad legislation and in 1913 in a Washington suffragist parade, NAWSA leaders asked Ida Wells-Barnett, head of a suffrage club of black women, not to march with the Chicago delegation. Thus the woman's move-

ment, which began as an offshoot of abolitionism, joined the ranks of those who countenanced segregation half a century later.

20. Mary McDowell, "Woman's City Club," n.d., in Mary McDowell Papers, Chicago Historical Society, folder 19. For an interesting discussion of the inter-relationship of Progressivism, the suffrage, Prohibition, and nativism, see Alan P. Grimes, *The Puritan Ethic and Woman Suffrage* (New York, 1967), especially pp. 99-144.

21. For a discussion of the social-welfare movement and the motivation of those within it, see Christopher Lasch, *The New Radicalism in America, 1889-1963* (New York, 1965), pp. 3-37; Jane Addams, *Twenty Years at Hull House* (New York, 1910); and Josephine Goldmark, *The Impatient Crusader* (Urbana, 1953). Most of the women involved in the movement shared a common background, including a middle-class upbringing, the experience of a higher education, and a feeling of rebellion at the wastefulness of a typical leisure-class woman's life. Unable to adjust readily to the traditional role expected of them, they sought some way to translate their training into purposeful activity and to be of service to the world around them.

22. Robert Wiebe, *The Search for Order* (New York, 1967), p. 127; *Register of Women's Clubs* (New York, 1933), pp. 37-45; Goldmark, pp. 90-91; and O'Neill, p. 150.

23. *History of the Dallas Federation of Women's Clubs, 1898-1936* (Dallas, 1937), pp. 1-14; Mary McDowell, "Women's City Club," *op. cit.*; Doyle, pp. 8-21, 76-77; and James Stanley Lemons, "The New Woman in the New Era: The Woman's Movement from the Great War to the Great Depression," unpublished doctoral dissertation, University of Missouri, pp. 6, 9. For a perceptive treatment of the club movement's impact in the South, see Anne F. Scott, *The Southern Lady: From Pedestal to Politics* (Chicago, 1970).

24. In a 1961 Radcliffe dissertation entitled "Social Change in the Feminine Role: A Comparison of Woman's Suffrage and Woman's Temperance, 1890-1920," Janet Giele found that the percentage of articles advocating social reform doubled from 13 per cent in the period 1875-95 to 26 per cent in the period 1895-1915. Cited in Kraditor, p. 72. See also Goldmark, p. 74; and Flexner, p. 258.

25. Florence Kelley, for example, argued that working women needed the vote to protect themselves with labor legislation. Grace Abbott, Mary McDowell, and Alice Stone Blackwell contended that woman suffrage would eliminate corruption in government. And Margaret Dreier Robins of the Women's Trade Union League felt that the

vote would help working women to organize. See Kraditor, p. 55; O'Neill, pp. 53-55; and "Hull House and New Horizons," Part III of an autobiographical typescript, Grace and Edith Abbott Papers, University of Chicago Library, Addenda II, Box 1.

26. Quoted in Kraditor, p. 252. Kraditor has offered a modified "status revolution" theory to explain the motivation of many middle-class female supporters of suffrage. Such women had already acquired education, leisure time, and the opportunity to participate in activities outside the home. The one area where they had not achieved equal status was politics. The gap between their social and economic standing and their political standing, she says, "bred a sense of grievance and a motive for the struggle to secure redress." Kraditor's insight is particularly pertinent to club women. See Kraditor, pp. x, 121, 260.

27. Kraditor, pp. 4, 11-13; Flexner, pp. 250-53, 262-70; and O'Neill, pp. 166-68. The suffrage movement benefited also from increased support on the nation's campuses. At the 1906 NAWSA convention, such noted educators as Mary Woolley of Mount Holyoke, Lucy Salmon of Vassar, and M. Carey Thomas of Bryn Mawr endorsed woman suffrage, and in 1908 the National College Equal Suffrage League was formed. Until the Progressive period, college women had remained distant from the suffrage cause. Suffrage speakers were not invited on campuses and the Association of Collegiate Alumnae forbade discussion of the question at its conventions. The reason was that college administrators were fearful of endangering the cause of women's education by becoming identified with the disreputable women's rights movement. Incorporation of the suffrage movement within Progressivism, however, solved that problem and college women increasingly became involved on a formal basis with the suffrage effort. See Ethel Puffer Howe, "The National College Equal Suffrage League," *Smith Alumnae Quarterly,* November 1920, in Morgan-Howe Family Papers, Radcliffe Women's Archives, Schlesinger Library, Box 1.

28. Flexner, pp. 273, 279, 367; Park, pp. 17, 19, 32, 38, 41, 43. The Congressional Committee, headed by Maud Wood Park, was made up primarily of non-paid volunteers. The lobbyists were urged to show respect and courtesy to congressmen, to avoid pressure, and to shun controversy. For Southerners and others of traditional outlook, a special corp of women with impeccable family credentials and Southern charm was used.

29. Wilson's endorsement was contained in a letter to Carrie Chapman Catt,

June 7, 1918, quoted in Park, pp. 188-89. See also Lemons, p. 29; Flexner, pp. 290, 292, 311, 313; and Park, pp. 15, 256, 268. Although Catt was a pacifist, she recognized that support of the war was essential if the suffragists were to retain their strength and led NAWSA into a formal endorsement of the war. Suffrage leaders played an important role in the Women's Committee of the Council for National Defense, and suffrage affiliates in states and cities distinguished themselves by organizing Red Cross chapters, selling Liberty Bonds, and canvassing for food conservation pledges. In addition, NAWSA kept silent when Women's Party (formerly the Congressional Union) members were jailed for picketing against the President during the war. See Flexner, pp. 283-86; Lemons, pp. 23-29.

30. Flexner, pp. 311-13. Catt's statement is quoted in Mildred Adams, *The Right To Be People*, p. 162.

31. Carrie Chapman Catt, "Feminism and Suffrage," 1917 NAWSA pamphlet, Carrie Chapman Catt Papers, Sophia Smith Collection, Smith College Library, Box 1.

32. David M. Potter, *The South and Sectional Conflict* (Baton Rouge, 1968), p. 245.

33. Social psychologists have pointed out that people are unable to tolerate contradictory perceptions and ordinarily resolve the conflict by choosing one perception and repressing or distorting the other. The theory of "cognitive dissonance" may illuminate some of the "unconscious" processes at work among the suffragists. Since it would have been difficult for the suffragists to acknowledge that a change had occurred without experiencing tension, they had a vested psychological interest in emphasizing the continuity of the woman's movement. See Leon Festinger, *The Theory of Cognitive Dissonance* (Evanston, 1954).

34. Quoted in Mildred Adams, p. 170.


*CHAPTER 1*

1. Stanton's statement is quoted in William L. O'Neill, *Everyone Was Brave* (Chicago, 1969), p. 19.

2. Part III of an autobiographical typescript, Grace and Edith Abbott Papers, University of Chicago Library, Addenda II, Box 1; Stuart Rice, *Quantitative Methods in Politics* (New York, 1928), p. 177; E. O. Toombs, "Politicians Take Notice," *Good Housekeeping,* LXX (March 1920), pp. 14-15; "Much Surprised City Officials Ousted by

Women," *Literary Digest,* LXVII (December 4, 1920), pp. 52-54; James Stanley Lemons, "The New Woman in the New Era: The Woman's Movement from the Great War to the Great Depression," unpublished doctoral dissertation, University of Missouri, 1967, pp. 142-43.

3. *New York Times,* March 30, 1920; August 14, 1920; February 17, 1920; April 7, 1922; July 24, 1920. See also "Excursion," an account of the early history of the LWV in the Dorothy Kirchwey Brown Papers, the Arthur and Elizabeth Schlesinger Library on the History of Women in America (hereafter SL), Box 1; Olive H. P. Belmont, "Women as Dictators," *Ladies Home Journal,* XXXIX (September 1922); and clipping, n.d., Ethel Dreier Papers, Sophia Smith Collection, Smith College, Box 3.

4. *New York Times,* September 21, 1920; Lemons, pp. 117-18, 136-37; Ida Harper, "The American Woman Gets the Vote," *Review of Reviews,* LXII (October 1920), pp. 380-84; League of Women Voters Press Release, July 2, 1920, in LWV Papers, Library of Congress, Series II, Box 6; and Mrs. Alvin Hirt to Helen M. Rocca, January 23, 1926, LWV Papers Box 43. The LWV platform for 1920 called for passage of maternity and infancy legislation, a federal department of education, federal aid for vocational training, regulation of marketing, a merit system in the civil service, and reform of citizenship qualifications for married women.

5. Lemons, p. 115; Anne F. Scott, "After Suffrage: Southern Women in the Twenties," *Journal of Southern History,* XXX (August 1964), pp. 304-6.

6. Lemons, pp. 232-35; "The Maternity and Infancy Measure," Elizabeth Hewes Tilton Papers, SL, Box 3; April 1956 history of the LWV, Brown Papers, Box 1; Josephine Goldmark, *Impatient Crusader* (Urbana, 1953), p. 9; Charles Selden, "Most Powerful Lobby in Washington," *Ladies Home Journal,* XXXIX (April 1920); and Clarke Chambers, *Seedtime of Reform* (Ann Arbor, 1967), p. 50.

7. See Lemons, p. 249; Chambers, p. 50; and an autobiographical typescript, Madeleine Doty Papers, Sophia Smith Collection, Smith College, Box 1.

8. Edna Kenton, "Four Years of Equal Suffrage," *Forum,* LXXII (July 1924), pp. 37-44; Mrs. H. V. Joslin to the Women's Joint Congressional Committee (WJCC), September 4, 1927, WJCC Papers, Library of Congress, Box 2; and minutes of WJCC Annual Meeting, November 19, 1923, and December 8, 1924, WJCC Papers, Box 6.

9. January 12, 1925, minutes of the WJCC, WJCC Papers, Box 6; Cham-

bers, pp. 40-43; Lemons, p. 339; and "The Maternity and Infancy Measure," Tilton Papers. Another sign of the decline of women's influence as a pressure group was that from 1922 to 1935 only one state passed legislation granting women the right to serve on juries.

10. In the case of *Adkins v. Children's Hospital*, 261 U.S. 525 (1923), Justice George Sutherland declared that women's status had improved to such a point that protective legislation was no longer necessary. Needless to say, female reformers disagreed. The red-baiting attack had the support of many anti-suffragists and emanated from the Office of Chemical Warfare Services in the War Department. Women's organizations were depicted as being part of a "spider web" conspiracy to entrap women into service to the Communist cause. The LWV Papers, Box 31, and the Mary Anderson Papers, SL, Box 1 both contain voluminous information on the smear campaign.

11. Charles E. Russell, "Is Woman's Suffrage a Failure?" *Century*, CVII (March 1924), pp. 724-30; Emily Newell Blair, "Are Women a Failure in Politics?" *Harpers,* CLI (October 1925), pp. 513-22.

12. The estimate of New York's woman vote was made by Mary Garrett Hay in the *New York Times*, January 16, 1922. The Illinois figures are found in Stuart H. Rice and Malcolm Willey, "American Women's Ineffective Use of the Vote," *Current History*, XX (July 1924), pp. 641-47. The Chicago figures come from Charles Merriam and Herbert Gosnell, *Non-Voting* (Chicago, 1924), pp. ix, 7. The *State Journal* quotation is from "Why More Women Voters Don't Vote," *Literary Digest*, LXXXI (May 24, 1924), pp. 5-7.

13. Quoted in O'Neill, p. 264.

14. In 1920, for example, New Jersey women voters were reported to have turned out in large numbers where Prohibition was a significant issue. William Ogburn noted the same phenomenon in Portland, Oregon. But on the basis of extensive poll data, political scientists generally agree that there is no predictable or statistically meaningful connection between sex and voting habits or party affiliation. See William F. Ogburn, "How Women Vote, A Study of Portland, Oregon," *Political Science Quarterly*, XXXIV (September 1919), pp. 413-33; Seymour Martin Lipset, *Political Man* (New York, 1963), pp. 193, 260; Bernard Berelson, Paul Lazarsfeld, and William McPhee, *Voting* (Chicago, 1954), p. 320; Robert E. Lane, *Political Life* (Glencoe, 1959), p. 212; Angus Campbell, Gerald Gurin, and Warren Miller, *The Voter Decides* (Evanston, 1954), pp. 154-55.

15. "Why More Women Voters Don't Vote," *Literary Digest*; and "Recollections and Reflections of a Democratic Campaigner," *Bryn Mawr*

*Alumnae Bulletin*, XIII (May 1933), in Emma Guffey Miller Papers, SL, Box 4.

16. Merriam and Gosnell, pp. 37, 39, 48, 164-67, 181-85, 188-92.

17. *New York Times*, October 17, 1920; Anne Scott, p. 314; Lemons, p. 84; *New York Times*, February 12, 1922, and November 8, 1922; and George Madden Martin, "American Women and Public Affairs," *Atlantic Monthly*, CXXXIII (February 1924), pp. 169-71.

18. Other variables include the relevance of government policies to the prospective voter and ready access to information on politics. See Lipset, pp. 182-229.

19. Political scientists agree that women vote less than men, that they have a lower sense of political efficacy, and that their lack of involvement is directly related to what Lipset calls traditional ideas of woman's place. See Lipset, pp. 209-11; 217, 222-23; Berelson et al., pp. 27, 41, 88-93; Angus Campbell et al., *The American Voter*, pp. 255-61; and Campbell et al., *The Voter Decides*, pp. 154-55, 191.

20. Blair, *op. cit.*

21. Carrie Chapman Catt, "What Have Women Done with the Suffrage," 1923 clipping, Catt Papers, Box 1. The Shaw comments are cited in O'Neill, p. 268. Lipset has noted that "a sharp break with a traditional political allegiance . . . by a group can occur only when some experience is perceived as clearly affecting the group's interests and requiring a new political orientation." The point being made here is that there was no transcendent issue during the 1920's which emphasized the distinctive identity of women as women in the same way that the suffrage had. See Lipset, pp. 203, 293.

22. Quoted in a survey of the first ten years of the LWV presented to the 33rd convention of the Massachusetts chapter on May 15, 1957, by Dorothy Kirchwey Brown, Brown Papers, Box 1; see also Mildred Adams, *The Right To Be People* (New York, 1967), p. 171.

23. See Helen Hill Miller, "Carrie Chapman Catt, The Power of an Idea," a pamphlet in the Catt Papers, Box 3; Lemons, p. 139; and *New York Times*, February 13 and 15, 1920. On February 17, 1921, Catt wrote Edna Gellhorn and Elizabeth Hauser urging the League to eliminate the word "women" from the title and admit independent minded men in order to counter the charge that the League was fostering sex segregation. LWV Papers, Box 3.

24. For a discussion of the second point of view, see the Dreier Papers, Box 1; Marguerite Wells Papers, SL, Box 1 and Volume I. Dorothy Kirchwey Brown recounts the split between Addams and Catt in "The Excursion," Brown Papers.

25. *New York Times*, November 23, 1921; February 10, 1922; January 15, 1922; and Lemons, pp. 86, 152.

26. Helen Hill Miller, "Carrie Chapman Catt . . ." *op. cit.*; and "The Excursion." See Chapter 5 for further discussion of the LWV.

27. Margaret Schonger to Jessie Hooper, December 28, 1920, Jessie Hooper Papers, Wisconsin Historical Society, Box 1; Lemons, pp. 86, 187; O'Neill, pp. 261-62; and the minutes of the Executive Board Meeting, NWTUL, September 11-13, 1925, NWTUL Papers, Box 2.

28. Female involvement in the peace movement is treated in Dorothy Detzer, *Appointment on the Hill* (New York, 1948), and Gertrude Bussey and Margaret Tims, *The Women's International League for Peace and Freedom* (London, 1956). Florence Kelley's life is chronicled in Josephine Goldmark, *Impatient Crusader* (Urbana, 1953).

29. Lemons, p. 86.

30. See O'Neill, p. 267; and Harry Hawes to Emma Guffey Miller, November 9, 1924, Miller Papers, Box 1.

31. New York *Herald Tribune,* April 2 and 3, 1930, clippings, Catt Papers, Box 1; George E. Anderson, "Women in Congress," *Commonweal,* IX (March 13, 1929), pp. 532-34. A memorandum from Lorena Hickok to Mary Norton in October 1945 attributed the failure of women in Congress to their unwillingness to serve for more than a single term and build seniority. Mary Norton Papers, Rutgers University Library, Box 1.

32. Draft of story by May F. Larkin in *Woman's Voice*, March 26, 1931; Mary Norton to Joseph McCaffrey, June 18, 1953, Norton Papers, Box 1; autobiographical typescript, Norton Papers, Box 6. See also Mary Dewson to Jim Farley, February 3, 1938, Mary Dewson Papers, Franklin Delano Roosevelt Library (hereafter FDRL), Box 9.

33. The commentator's statement is quoted in Lemons, p. 164. See also the *New York Times*, October 5 and 8, and November 16, 1922. Mrs. Roosevelt's experience is described in a 1940 issue of the *Democratic Digest,* clipping, Ellen Sullivan Woodward Papers, SL, Box 1.

34. There were two kinds of women, Emily Newell Blair wrote in 1933—those with a social-welfare point of view and those who were selfishly political. "Molly" was the rare exception who combined the best of both. Emily Newell Blair to Mary Dewson, July 28, 1933, Dewson Papers, FDRL, 1933 Volume on Women's Patronage.

35. Notes for a speech before the Kentucky Women's Clubs, April 1933, in Dewson Papers, FDRL, 1932 Campaign Volume; Mary Dewson, "Organizing the Woman Vote," *Women's Democratic News*, December 1932, in 1932 Campaign Volume; and form letter from Mary

Dewson, May 14, 1936, Dewson Papers, FDRL, Box 5. Dewson's feelings about women's distinctiveness bore a remarkable resemblance to those of Marguerite Wells and other LWV officials.

36. Buffalo *Evening News*, January 12, 1933, clipping, Dewson Papers, SL, Box 1; Mary Dewson to Miss Hyde, July 27, 1932, Dewson Papers, FDRL, Box 1; "The Favored State Party Set-Up for Women," n.d., Dewson Papers, FDRL, Box 1; Mrs. James Wolfe to Emma Guffey Miller, April 10, 1936, Dewson Papers, FDRL, Box 2.

37. The President gave the Women's Division authority to increase its budget, enlarge its space at headquarters, and take over the *Democratic Digest.* See Mary Dewson to FDR, December 15, 1934, Dewson Papers, FDRL, Box 1; Mary Dewson to Jim Farley, December 21, 1935, in Democratic National Committee, Women's Division Papers, FDRL, Box 8.

38. "Work of the Women's Division, 1936 Campaign," Dewson Papers, SL, Box 2; "The Favored State Party Set-Up," *op. cit.*; Mary Dewson to Anna C. Struble, July 17, 1936, Dewson Papers, FDRL, Box 5; "Advance of Democratic Women," Dewson Papers, SL, Box 1.

39. Mary Dewson to Joseph McGrath, April 15, 1937, Dewson Papers, FDRL, Box 8; correspondence with Grace and Edith Abbott, Democratic National Committee, Women's Division Papers, FDRL, Boxes 1 and 8; Mary Dewson to FDR, December 1, 1934, Dewson Papers, FDRL, Box 1. Farley was very much opposed to Dewson's ideological approach, but she had the support of the President and other leading figures in the Administration.

40. Mary Dewson to Eleanor Roosevelt, June 19, 1936, Dewson Papers, FDRL, Box 3; the *New York Times* and Washington *Times* stories are cited in Volume II of "An Aid to the End," an autobiographical typescript, Dewson Papers, SL; Mrs. Blair's comments appear in a broadcast transcript in the Democratic National Committee, Women's Division Papers, FDRL, Box 22.

41. Mary Dewson to Lorena Hickok, November 21, 1952, in Dewson Papers, FDRL, Box 16. In letters to Farley throughout 1933 and 1934, Dewson pressed for patronage jobs. In a letter to Mrs. Roosevelt on April 27, 1933 (labeled "about the most important letter I ever wrote you"), she reiterated her plea for jobs. See Dewson Papers, FDRL, 1933 Volume on Patronage. The postal figures are cited in Mary Dewson to Jim Farley, May 18, 1938, Dewson Papers, FDRL, Box 9. The comparative figures come from Sophonisba P. Breckinridge, *Women in the Twentieth Century* (New York, 1933), p. 311.

42. Mary Anderson's comments are quoted in "An Aid to the End," Volume I, *op. cit.* Dewson declared that almost everyone she knew who was doing good work in her own field of regulating labor standards had come to Washington. Mary Dewson to Maud Wood Park, October 16, 1933, Dewson Papers, FDRL, 1932 Campaign Volume.

43. See, for example, Mrs. Roosevelt's letter to Mary Dewson on August 8, 1932, on staff set-up and organizational details for the women's campaign, Dewson Papers, FDRL, Box 1. In 1936 Mrs. Roosevelt instructed Jim Farley, Steve Early, Stanley High, and Mary Dewson to keep her and the President informed on the state of the campaign. Eleanor Roosevelt to Mary Dewson, July 16, 1936, Dewson Papers, FDRL, Box 3. Mrs. Roosevelt championed the cause of Negroes and other oppressed groups and took a direct role in sponsoring the subsistence settlements and Greenbelt communities under the New Deal. For a thorough and perceptive treatment of her activities during these years, see Joseph Lash, *Eleanor and Franklin* (New York, 1971). The Lash volume was published shortly before this book went to press, and for that reason it has not been used extensively here. Lash provides an abundance of additional material documenting Mrs. Roosevelt's role in helping the cause of women in politics and government.

44. See Mary Dewson to Herman Kahn, September 2, 1951, Dewson Papers, FDRL, Box 17; and Eleanor Roosevelt to Mary Dewson, September 1, 1936, Dewson Papers, FDRL, Box 4.

45. Dewson, for example, viewed politics as an extension of social work and declared that she had accomplished most for the objectives of social work "in the six political years under the leadership . . . of FDR." Thus while the women who came to Washington had a keen sense of themselves as women, they came basically because the Administration was pursuing reform objectives which they shared with men. In one sense, of course, their experience represented the ideal of equality. Women, as individuals, were playing an important part in determining national policy. But that was not the same thing as acting on behalf of all women to transform society to a specifically female way of looking at things. Mary Dewson to Jim Farley, August 27, 1937, Dewson Papers, FDRL, Box 9.

46. Mary Dewson to Lorena Hickok, n.d., 1953, Dewson Papers, FDRL, Box 16; Mary Dewson to Stephen Mitchell, May 17, 1953, Box 18; "An Aid to the End," Volume 1. Mrs. Roosevelt wrote Dewson on March 11, 1932, that "the nicest thing about politics is lunching with you on Mondays." For examples of Dewson using her influence with

Mrs. Roosevelt, see her letter of January 18, 1936, urging Mrs. Roosevelt's help in getting good treatment for women at the 1936 Democratic convention, and the correspondence between the two women on patronage. Dewson Papers, FDRL, Box 4; and the 1933 Volume on Patronage.

47. See, for example, letters from Mrs. Earl Kitchen and Florence Whitney protesting the problems placed in the way of seeing Farley and getting his help. Dewson Papers, FDRL, Box 12; and volume labeled, "Letters, 1929-40."

48. John Gordon Ross, "Ladies in Politics," *Forum*, XCV (November 1936), p. 215. See also O'Neill, pp. 270-72.


## CHAPTER 2

1. Quoted in James Stanley Lemons, "The New Woman in the New Era: The Woman's Movement from the Great War to the Great Depression," unpublished doctoral dissertation, University of Missouri, 1967, p. 41.

2. Miriam Simons Leuch, "Women in Odd and Unusual Fields of Work," *Annals* of the American Academy of Political and Social Science, CXLIII (May 1929), p. 166; *New York Times,* September 5, December 26, and July 20, 1920; March 3 and June 12, 1921; and Sinclair Lewis, *Main Street* (New York, 1920), p. 9.

3. Frederick Lewis Allen, *Only Yesterday* (Bantam ed.; New York, 1959), pp. 68, 76; and V. F. Calverton, "Careers for Women—A Survey of Results," *Current History*, XXIX (January 1928), pp. 633-37. For a discussion of the "revolution in manners and morals," see Allen, pp. 61-86, and William E. Leuchtenburg, *The Perils of Prosperity* (Chicago, 1958), pp. 158-77. It should be noted that this chapter is concerned only with the economic question. The issue of manners and morals is taken up in Chapter 5.

4. George Mowry, *The Urban Nation* (New York, 1965), p. 23; Arthur Link, *The American Epoch,* 3rd ed. (New York, 1967), pp. 274-75; John Hicks and George Mowry, *A Short History of American Democracy* (Boston, 1956), p. 658. Other historians have adopted the same view. Citing the fact that 10 million women had jobs by 1930, William E. Leuchtenburg has written that "Nothing did more to emancipate them." In their textbook Henry Steele Commager and Samuel Eliot Morison are somewhat more cautious, but they agree also that women's emancipation "was finally achieved in the years after World War I" and that the winning of economic independence

played an important role. The one exception to the consensus of
opinion is the economic historian, Robert Smuts, who has emphasized the absence of change in women's economic role in the years
prior to 1940. See Leuchtenburg, pp. 159-60; Henry Steele Commager and Samuel Eliot Morison, *The Growth of the American Republic*, 5th ed. (New York, 1952), Vol. II, p. 659; and Robert Smuts,
*Women and Work in America* (New York, 1959).

5. Janet Hooks, "Women's Occupations Through Seven Decades," *Wom-
en's Bureau Bulletin* No. 232 (Washington, 1951), pp. 34, 39; "The
Occupational Progress of Women, 1910 to 1930," *Women's Bureau
Bulletin* No. 104 (Washington, 1933), p. 51; Mary Anderson,
"Women Workers Reflect Social and Economic Change," Women's
Bureau Press Release, August 3, 1932, in League of Women Voters
Papers, Library of Congress, Series II, Box 313; and Robert and
Helen Lynd, *Middletown* (New York, 1929), pp. 25-29.

6. Amy Hewes, *Women as Munition Makers* (New York, 1917), p. 6;
Constance Green, *The Role of Women Production Workers in War
Plants in the Connecticut Valley* (Northampton, 1946), p. vii; Mary
Van Kleeck, "Women and Machines," *Atlantic Monthly*, CXXVII
(February 1921), p. 251; H. B. Wolfe and Helen Olson, "Wartime
Industrial Employment of Women in the United States," *Journal of
Political Economy*, XXVII (October 1919), pp. 639-69; Lemons, p.
39; and "The New Position of Women in American Industry," *Wom-
en's Bureau Bulletin* No. 12 (Washington, 1920).

7. See William L. O'Neill, *Everyone Was Brave* (Chicago, 1969), p. 189;
Mary Austin, "Sex Emancipation Through War," *Forum*, LIX (May
1918), p. 617; and Mary Austin, "Woman and Her War Loot,"
*Sunset*, XLII (February 1919), pp. 13-16.

8. "What Shall Be Done with Women Who Have Replaced Men in Industry?" *Current Opinion*, LXVI (February 1919), pp. 124-25; Wolfe
and Olson, pp. 640, 654-59; Lemons, p. 42; "Women's Work After
the War," *New Republic*, XVII (January 25, 1919), pp. 358-59; and
Van Kleeck, p. 251.

9. Green, p. 3; "Women's Work After the War," pp. 358-59; Lemons,
p. 47; and Valborg Esther Fletty, "Public Services of Women's Organizations," unpublished doctoral dissertation, Syracuse University,
1952, p. 172. The fact that the war lasted only a year and a half, of
course, made it difficult for far-reaching changes to occur.

10. E. E. Lape, "Women in Industry," *New Republic*, XXV (January 26,
1921), pp. 251-53; Lemons, pp. 55, 123-24; Grace Abbott, "Political," typescript in the Grace and Edith Abbott Papers, University of
Chicago Library, Box 25. Government treatment of women during

the war never reached the high standards women's rights leaders had hoped for. The Women's Committee of the Council of National Defense, for example, was assigned innocuous tasks such as securing pledges for food conservation, and was denied any real power to coordinate women's war work. At one point, the committee threatened a collective resignation unless it was given more influence. For a thorough discussion, see O'Neill, pp. 191-94.

11. International Labor Office, *The War and Women's Employment* (Montreal, 1946), pp. 159-60; "Women's Occupations Through Seven Decades," p. 34; Mary Van Kleeck, p. 251. Emily Newell Blair commented on women's nebulous status and claimed that in the war years women were treated as mendicants. See "American Woman's Vast War Work as Revealed by an Official Report," *Literary Digest,* LXCI (August 21, 1920), pp. 54-57.

12. The proportion of women over fourteen who were employed grew from 23.3 to 24.3 per cent. "Women's Occupations Through Seven Decades," p. 34. See also Alice Hamilton, "Women," in Alice Hamilton Papers, SL, Box 1.

13. The urban population increased from 28 per cent in 1880 to 52 per cent in 1920. In 1900, 40 per cent of the people in the nation's twelve largest cities were foreign born, and the biggest wave of immigration was yet to come. Nineteen million immigrants arrived in America between 1900 and 1930, with the greatest concentration in the years before 1910. See Department of Commerce, Bureau of the Census, *Historical Statistics of the United States, Colonial Times to 1957* (Washington, 1960), p. 14; and Samuel Hays, *The Response to Industrialism* (Chicago, 1957), p. 96. For a discussion of the work of immigrant women, see Moses Rischin, *The Promised City* (New York, 1962), pp. 69-70; and Abraham Cahan's novel, *The Rise of David Levinsky* (Harper Torchbook ed., New York, 1960). Both books provide an excellent portrayal of the development of the garment industry.

14. "Women's Occupations Through Seven Decades," pp. 34, 35, 39.

15. "Women's Occupations Through Seven Decades," pp. 5-6, 46; Women's Bureau Press Release, August 3, 1922, *op. cit.*; "The Occupational Progress of Women, 1910-30," p. 4; National Manpower Council, *Womanpower* (New York, 1957), p. 114.

16. "Women's Occupations Through Seven Decades," pp. 37, 39; Smuts, pp. 19, 84; Frieda Miller, "Women in the Labor Force," *Annals* of the American Academy of Political and Social Science, CCLI (May 1947).

17. Women's Trade Union League, *Life and Labor,* No. 9, February 1940;

"An Economic Challenge to American Women," report of the Economic Committee of the Women's Centennial Congress, 1940 in Ethel Dreier Papers, Sophia Smith Collection, Smith College, Box 3; Mary Anderson to Eleanor Roosevelt, January 22, 1938, folder entitled "Eleanor Roosevelt," Women's Bureau Archives (hereafter WBA), Record Group 86, Federal Record Center, Suitland Maryland, Accession No. 55A-556, Container 12.

18. Sophonisba P. Breckinridge, *Women in the Twentieth Century* (New York, 1933), p. 114; Alice Hamilton, "Women," *op. cit.*; Women's Bureau Press Release, August 3, 1932, *op. cit.*; "The Occupational Progress of Women, 1910-1930," p. 4. The exact figure of the increase varies, depending upon whether barbers, hairdressers, and laundresses are included in the category of personal service. Alice Hamilton uses a statistic of 737,878, the Women's Bureau one of slightly more than 600,000.

19. See Sophonisba P. Breckinridge, "The Activities of Women Outside the Home," in President's Committee on Recent Social Trends, *Recent Social Trends in the United States* (New York, 1933), p. 723; Elizabeth K. Nottingham, "Toward an Analysis of the Effects of Two World Wars on the Role and Status of Middle Class Women in the English Speaking World," *American Sociological Review*, XII (December 1947), p. 670; Mabel Newcomer, *A Century of Higher Education* (New York, 1959), p. 46; Willystine Goodsell, "The Educational Opportunities of American Women—Theoretical and Actual," in the May 1929 *Annals*, p. 6; Marguerite Zapoleon, "Education and Employment Opportunities for Women," *ibid.; New York Times*, July 20, 1923; and Smuts, p. 143.

20. In 1931, women's unemployment rate was 18.9 per cent and men's 26.1 per cent. Seven years later, 22.1 per cent of women were totally unemployed and 14.3 per cent of men. See "Unemployment Among Women in the Early Years of the Depression," *Monthly Labor Review*, XXXVIII, pp. 790-95; "Myth of Women Workers as Unemployment Cause Exploded," National Industrial Conference Board press release, November 3, 1938, in WBA, Accession No. 55A-556, container 12; Women's Bureau, "Activities Affecting Gainfully Employed Women," September 1, 1935, in WBA, Accession No. 58A-850, container 4; and speech by Senator Robert Wagner, March 28, 1935, Institute of Women's Professional Relations Papers, SL, Box 1.

21. Zapoleon, *op. cit.*; memoranda from the Vocational Counselor to Dean Virginia Gildersleeve of Barnard College, Box entitled "Speeches,

Barnard Assemblies, Class Days," Virginia C. Gildersleeve Papers, Special Collections, Columbia University; Nottingham, p. 670. The Institute's director was Chase Going Woodhouse.

22. Women's Bureau, "Numbers of Women Employed, Pre-War, War, and Post-War," April 1946, WBA, Accession No. 58A-850, container 2; Florence Lowther and Helen Downes, "Women in Medicine," *Journal of the American Medical Association*, October 13, 1945, reprint in American Association of University Women Papers, SL, folder 59; "Equal Rights for Women Doctors," typescript, Jane Norman Smith Papers, SL, Box 9; Willystine Goodsell, *op. cit.*, p. 6; "Bar Women," *Time*, XXIX (May 24, 1937), p. 44. In 1940, 70 per cent of all males worked in jobs which employed less than 1 per cent of females.

23. Goodsell, pp. 8-9, 12; Chase Going Woodhouse, "The Status of Women," *American Journal of Sociology*, XXXV (May 1930), pp. 1091-96. A copy of the University of Chicago protest is in the Marion Talbot Papers, University of Chicago Library, Box 18. Women comprised 40 per cent of the graduate students at the university but received only 20 per cent of the fellowships. Seven men got full professorships but only two women were appointed instructors. The students urged more female faculty members, more fellowships, and a woman on the University Board of Trustees.

24. Mary Anderson, "The Women's Bureau Looks at Young Women and Their Jobs," typescript of an address delivered in Denver, Colorado, November 20, 1939, in WBA, folder entitled "Anderson, Mary—addresses and statements," Accession No. 58A-850, container 3; Marion Bonner, "Behind the Southern Textile Strikes," *Nation*, October 2, 1929; statement by Mary Anderson before the House Ways and Means Committee, April 9, 1946, in folder of Anderson statements and "Women in the Economy of the United States," *Women's Bureau Bulletin* No. 125 (Washington, 1937), p. 56.

25. Women's Bureau, "Earnings of Professional Workers," WBA, folder entitled "Earnings and Wages, Annual Wages," Accession No. 58A-850, container 3; AAUW Press Release on Equal Pay, February 10, 1938, AAUW Papers, folder 54; Nelle Swartz, "The Trend in Women's Wages," May 1929 *Annals*, op. cit., p. 106.

26. Quoted in Women's Bureau, "Looking Backward and Forward with the Women's Bureau," April 1930, WBA, folder entitled "Women's Bureau—History and Functions," Accession No. 55A-850, container 4.

27. Hamilton, "Review of Findings," *op. cit.; New York Times*, March 18, 1920; July 20, 1923.

28. Quoted in Sophonisba P. Breckinridge, "Comments on Mr. Hurlin's Chapter," for the Committee on Recent Social Trends, Breckinridge Papers, Library of Congress, Box 33.

29. The government report was entitled a *Report on Conditions of Women and Child Wage Earners in the United States* and appeared over the period 1910-13. The volumes were replete with stories of underpaid women—both single and married—who struggled to make enough money for self-support and family subsistence. For a discussion of the government report and the Pittsburgh Survey, see Robert H. Bremner, *From the Depths* (New York, 1956), pp. 152-54, 234-36. See also Mary Van Kleeck, *Artificial Flower Makers* (New York, 1913).

30. "The Share of Wage-Earning Women in Family Support," *Women's Bureau Bulletin* No. 30 (Washington, 1923); Women's Bureau, "Gainful Employment of Married Women," mimeographed statement, n.d. LWV Papers, Box 341A; Mary Winslow, "Married Women in Industry," *Women's Bureau Bulletin* No. 38 (Washington, 1924), pp. 3-4; Women's Bureau statement to the National War Labor Board, 1945 in WBA, folder entitled "Married Women's Employment: II, Employment Policies A. Discrimination," Accession No. 58A-850, container 2; and Mary Anderson statement, September 20, 1929, in LWV Papers, Box 163. The average annual income in 1929 was $1,435.

31. *New York Times*, August 21, 1921; January 11, 1923; July 20, 1923; December 19, 1926.

32. Alice Rogers Hagar, "Occupations and Earnings of Women in Industry," May 1929 *Annals, op. cit.,* p. 73.

*CHAPTER 3*

1. For a description of the Cooper Union meeting and the events leading up to it, see Joel Seidman, *The Needle Trades* (New York, 1942); Benjamin Stolberg, *Tailor's Progress* (New York, 1944); Nancy Schrom, "The Shirtwaist Makers Strike and the Women's Trade Union League," unpublished manuscript, University of Wisconsin, 1970; and Amy McCarthy, "The Women's Trade Union League: 1909-1913," unpublished thesis, Vassar College, 1971.

2. *New York Times*, December 4, 1909; Stolberg, pp. 18, 58-62; Schrom; and McCarthy.

3. Seidman, pp. 126-27; and Theresa Wolfson, "Trade Union Activities of

Women," *Annals* of the American Academy of Political and Social Science, CXLIII (May 1929), p. 121.

4. Mary Anderson to Margaret Dreier Robins, February 16, 1924; Mary Anderson, "Report on American Federation of Labor Conference for the Organization of Women Workers," February 14, 1924 in Mary Anderson Papers, SL, Box 2; National Women's Trade Union League, "How To Organize: A Problem," 1929 mimeographed release, in WBA, folder entitled "WTUL Pamphlets and References," Accession No. 58A-850, Container 3; and Wolfson, pp. 120-21.

5. Leo Wolman, "Are Women Hard To Organize?" *Survey,* LIII (March 15, 1925), pp. 741-42; Wolfson, p. 123. Wolfson listed four variables which were key to successful union activities: "a permanent wage earning group, a skilled craft, strategic economic position within the industry, and a technique of organization based upon an appeal to the masculine psychology of a skilled craftsman."

6. Wolfson, p. 124; and Alice Hamilton, "Protection for Women Workers," *Forum,* LXXII (August 1924), pp. 152-60.

7. See the "Call, Eleventh Convention of the NWTUL, May 6-11, 1929," in Women's Trade Union League Papers, Library of Congress, Box 4; Schrom, *op. cit.*; and Allen F. Davis, "The WTUL, Origins and Organization," *Labor History,* V (winter 1964). The Hamilton statement is quoted in Davis. See Davis for a point of view about the League different from that expressed here.

8. *New York Times,* November 5, 1909; Schrom, pp. 6-8, 13-20; Stolberg, pp. 18, 62; and McCarthy.

9. Amy McCarthy discusses the shift in strategy at some length in her Vassar thesis. During the White Goods Workers strike, Rose Schneiderman, a prominent unionist, temporarily suspended her membership in the WTUL to work with the strikers. Mary Dreier, president of the New York WTUL, dealt with the conflict at the WTUL's national convention in St. Louis.

10. See the "Minutes," March 18, 1909, Executive Board Meeting, WTUL Papers, Box 1; Allen Davis, p. 13; WTUL to Mrs. D. W. Kuefler, May 8, 1908, WTUL Papers, Box 1; "Minutes," WTUL meeting in New York, March 26, 1905, and "Minutes," WTUL meeting in Chicago, October 7, 1904, in WTUL Papers, Box 1. Rose Schneiderman was also skeptical that "men and women who were not wage earners themselves" could understand the problems the workers faced. See Rose Schneiderman, *All for One* (New York, 1967), pp. 77-78, 93.

11. Despite the constitutional provision requiring a majority of trade union-

ists on the executive board, "allies" held the key to the League's future because they controlled the finances. Almost the entire New York chapter—the most important WTUL local—was made up of middle- and upper-class women. See Schrom and McCarthy for an excellent discussion of the New York League.

12. Brooksville, Florida *Journal*, February 22, 1945, clipping of obituary, WTUL Papers, Box 9; "Minutes," May 19, 1910, Board meeting, Box 1; Seidman, p. 118; and Mary E. Dreier, *Margaret Dreier Robins* (New York, 1950), especially pp. 37-43 and 113.

13. See an address by Mrs. Robins to the Third Conference of the International Federation of Working Women Papers, SL, Box 1; the Brooksville *Journal, op. cit.*; and the New York *Tribune*, November 12, 1919, clipping in International Federation of Working Women Papers, Box 1. Poetry was the first class offered by the League.

14. See Margaret Dreier Robins to Mary Anderson, November 12, 1930, November 20, 1931, February 2, 1932, April 7, 1932, April 13, 1933, and June 12, 1936, in Anderson Papers, Box 2; and Margaret Dreier Robins to Agnes Nestor, March 19, 1909, Agnes Nestor Papers, Chicago Historical Society, folder 3. Mrs. Robins had nothing against charity. She warmly endorsed the efforts of the Tampa Garden Club to give people work at $1.50 a day with a hot meal, and she recalled with fondness Al Smith's handling of an unemployment crisis when "all the armories and churches were opened and kept warm and supper and breakfast were served." But she had no use for government giving away money.

15. Elizabeth Christman to Executive Board, April 15, 1925, WTUL Papers, Box 2; Letta Perkins, "Report of the Eighth Annual Convention," WTUL Papers Box 2.

16. See the "Tentative Program for Executive Board Meeting," June 6, 1921; and "Minutes," Executive Board Meeting, September 11-13, 1925, WTUL Papers, Box 2.

17. "Southern Committee Minutes," November 15, 1926, WTUL Papers, Box 2; "Report of the Activities of the NWTUL," November 1927, WTUL Papers, Box 3; and "Minutes," Executive Board Meeting, October 4, 1929, WTUL Papers, Box 4.

18. See Elizabeth Christman to Mary Anderson, March 29, 1924, Anderson Papers, Box 2; Elizabeth Christman to Frances Perkins, June 14, 1937, WTUL Papers, Box 7; "Minutes," Executive Board Meeting, October 1, 1932; April 30, 1932 Audit Report, WTUL Papers, Box 6. In 1946 the Executive Board concluded once again that "we have lost touch with the shop." In 1949 the Chicago League split amidst

charges that it had done nothing for unions or workers for years, and a year later, concluding that it no longer had any function to serve, the WTUL dissolved.

19. Address of Samuel Gompers to the 1905 WTUL Convention, WTUL Papers, Box 1.

20. The Gompers quote is from Allen Davis, p. 5. See also Samuel Gompers to Gertrude Barnum, October 12, 1905, WTUL Papers, Box 1; WTUL to Frank Duffy, June 15, 1915; and Frank Duffy to WTUL, June 18, 1915, WTUL Papers, Box 1.

21. Wolfson, p. 120; "Solidarity," *New Republic*, XIX (June 14, 1919), pp. 202-3; *New York Times*, December 13, 1926; V. F. Calverton, "Careers for Women—A Survey of Results," *Current History*, XXIX (January 1928), pp. 633-37; and Katherine Fisher, "Women Workers and the AF of L," *New Republic*, XXVII (August 3, 1921), pp. 265-67.

22. Samuel Gompers, "The Struggle in the Garment Trades," *American Federationist*, XX (March 1913), p. 189, quoted in Schrom; Stolberg, pp. 136, 148; Seidman, p. 154; Rose Pesotta, *Bread upon the Waters* (New York, 1944), p. 93.

23. "Illustrations of the Need of Federal Charters for Women," n.d., Raymond Robins Papers, Wisconsin Historical Society, Box 17; and Fisher, pp. 65-67. For some labor leaders at least, union membership seemed incompatible with femininity. One AF of L official asked Agnes Nestor whether labor unions did not tend "to unsex [women] and make them masculine." See Frank Carpenter to Agnes Nestor, March 15, 1908, Nestor Papers.

24. "To the Executive Board of the NWTUL from Elizabeth Christman, Jo Coffin and Ethel Smith," August 25, 1921, Robins Papers, Box 17. At the 1921 AF of L convention a resolution to amend the constitution so that women might be admitted to membership on the same terms as men was tabled for a substitute which left the decision up to the internationals. See Fisher, *op. cit.*

25. "Extracts from Executive Councils Report and Convention of the AF of L," January 16, 1923, WTUL Papers, Box 2; Mary Anderson to Margaret Dreier Robins, February 16, 1924, Anderson Papers, Box 1.

26. "Report on American Federation of Labor Conference for the Organization of Women Workers," February 14, 1924; Elizabeth Christman to Mary Anderson, May 2, 1924; Mary Anderson to Samuel Gompers, May 24, 1924, all in Anderson Papers, Box 2; and Wolfson, p. 124. Philip Taft, historian of the AF of L, noted that only four in-

ternationals sent representatives to a conference called to mobilize potential women members and that when the campaign was launched, local unions greeted it with indifference. See Philip Taft, *The AF of L from the Death of Gompers* (New York, 1959), p. 8.

27. Clarke Chambers, *Seedtime of Reform* (Ann Arbor, 1967), pp. 7, 59, 67; and John Chambers, "The Big Switch: Justice Roberts and the Minimum-Wage Cases," *Labor History*, X (winter 1969).

28. *Adkins v. Children's Hospital*, 261 U.S. 525 (1923).

29. Clarke Chambers, pp. 75-76; Florence Kelley, "Progress of Labor Legislation for Women," a reprint from the National Conference of Social Work, May 16-23, 1923, in League of Women Voters Papers, Library of Congress, Box 315; and Florence Kelley to Lucy Randolph Mason, September 5, 1923, Lucy Randolph Mason Papers, William R. Perkins Library, Duke University, Box 1.

30. Elizabeth Brandeis, "Organized Labor and Protective Labor Legislation," in Milton Derber and Edwin Young, eds., *Labor and the New Deal* (Madison, 1957), pp. 198, 217-30.

31. For a discussion of the changes in the Court, see John Chambers, *op. cit.*

32. John M. Peterson, "Employment Effects of State Minimum Wages for Women," *Industrial and Labor Relations Review*, XII (April 1958), p. 414; Herbert J. Lahne, *The Cotton Mill Worker* (New York, 1944), pp. 164-65; Seidman, pp. 65, 218-19; and Women's Bureau, "Activities Affecting Gainfully Employed Women," September 1, 1935, WBA, folder entitled "Industrial Homework—Progress in Control Laws," Accession No. 58A-850, container 4.

33. Stolberg, p. 211; Pesotta, p. 93; Seidman, p. 98.

34. Lahne, pp. 8, 206-9, 232, 235, 247-48.

35. *Ibid.*, pp. 9, 268-72; Mary Heaton Vorse, *Labor's New Millions* (New York, 1938), pp. 176-77.

36. Women composed more than 30 per cent of the employees in ten of the industries which had discriminatory wage provisions. See Mary Anderson to Eleanor Roosevelt, February 19, 1934, Anderson Papers, Box 3; memo from Gwen Geach of the LWV on NRA codes, September 7, 1933; and LWV Press Release, December 5, 1933, in LWV Papers, Box 300.

37. Pesotta, p. 31; the New York *World Telegram*, December 9, 1935, cited in Jane Norman Smith Papers, SL, Box 4; and *Factual Brief for the Appellant, Morehead v. New York ex rel. Tipaldo*, U.S. Briefs 1935, No. 396.

38. Pesotta, p. 395; Stolberg, p. 218; Theresa Wolfson, "Equal Rights in the Unions," *Survey*, LVII (February 15, 1927), pp. 629-30.

39. See, for example, the archives of Local 95 and Local 121, UAW-CIO, Janesville, Wisconsin, Wisconsin Historical Society; and "An Economic Challenge to American Women," report of the Economic Committee of the Women's Centennial Congress, 1940, in Ethel Dreier Papers, Sophia Smith Collection, Smith College, Box 3. Benjamin Stolberg of the ILGWU observed that for men, "the union is a marriage for life [while] to many of the women, it is only an affair of the heart." Stolberg, p. 20.

## CHAPTER 4

1. Robert Smuts, *Women and Work in America* (New York, 1959), p. 143; Willystine Goodsell, "The Educational Opportunities of American Women—Theoretical and Actual," in *Annals* of the American Academy of Political and Social Science, CXLIII (May 1929), p. 2. The percentages are based on a comparison of the years 1902 and 1925.
2. "The Occupational Progress of Women, 1910 to 1930," *Women's Bureau Bulletin* No. 104 (Washington, 1933), p. 51; Elizabeth K. Nottingham, "Toward an Analysis of the Effects of Two World Wars on the Role and Status of Middle Class Women in the English Speaking World," *American Sociological Review*, XII (December 1947), p. 670; and Dorothy Johnson, "Organized Women and National Legislation," unpublished doctoral dissertation, Western Reserve University, 1960.
3. Nottingham, p. 671; Grace Abbott, "Education," typescript, Grace and Edith Abbott Papers, University of Chicago Library, Box 25; Goodsell, p. 6; Institute of Women's Professional Relations Papers, SL, Folder 4; and *Independent Woman*, IV (June 1922).
4. "They Say Women Can Only Spend Money," *Ladies Home Journal*, XXXVI (March 1919), p. 1; *Independent Woman*, V (October 1922), p. 18; Roger Babson, "Why Women Are Underpaid," *Independent Woman*, XI (December 1927), p. 5; *Commercial and Financial Chronicle*, quoted in *Independent Woman*, I (June 1920), pp. 18-19. The Institute of Women's Professional Relations found that 2800 of 3800 women who served as bank officials were assistant cashiers.
5. Goodsell, p. 9; Chase Going Woodhouse, "The Status of Women," *American Journal of Sociology*, XXXV (December 1931), pp. 1091-96; "Report on the Bryn Mawr Graduate School by the Academic Committee of the Alumnae Association of Bryn Mawr College," January 1927, in American Association of University Women Papers, SL, Folder 52; U.S. Office of Education, "Self Help for College

Students," *Bulletin*, 1929, No. 2; and *Educational Directory*, 1931, in AAUW Papers, Folder 52. While women were only 4 per cent of full professors, they were 23.5 per cent of instructors.

6. The quotation is from Marion O. Hawthorne, "Women as College Teachers," *Annals*, p. 151. For a discussion of some of the reasons why women did not fare better, see Jessie Bernard, *Academic Women* (University Park, Pennsylvania, 1964), especially Chapters 5, 6, and 10-13. Bernard argues that women's interest in service rather than standards and in teaching rather than professional objectives played a major part in their low representation among the higher ranks of the profession.

7. Agnes Rogers, *Vassar Women* (Poughkeepsie, 1940), p. 115; Nottingham, p. 670; William L. O'Neill, *Everyone Was Brave* (Chicago, 1969), p. 305; Bernard, pp. 43, 55. At Wellesley, for example, the proportion of men on the faculty increased from 14 per cent in 1930 to 20 per cent in 1940 and 39 per cent in 1960.

8. Mildred Adams, *The Right To Be People* (New York, 1967), pp. 183-90; Agnes Rogers, p. 90; Dorothy Dunbar Bromley, "Feminist—New Style," *Harper's*, CLV (October 1927), pp. 152-60; and Anne O'Hagan, "The Serious-Minded Young—If Any," *The Woman's Journal*, XIII (April 1928), p. 39.

9. *New York Times*, December 26, 1920; Virginia C. Gildersleeve, "The College Girl of the Crisis," address delivered on February 4, 1934, in Virginia C. Gildersleeve Papers, Special Collections, Columbia University, Box entitled, "VCG—Some Speeches and Articles, Complete Texts"; Florence Sands, "Why Many Women Do Not Succeed in Business," *Independent Woman*, IX (October 1925), pp. 12-13; "Why Women Yield the Lash," *Independent Woman*, XI (September 1927), p. 14; and Mary Roberts Rinehart, "Magnet of Success," *Ladies Home Journal*, XXXVIII (July 1921), p. 21. During the Depression, student concern with serious issues revived, but Juliette Thayer, who has analyzed Vassar in this period, found no evidence that female students were drawn to the cause of women's rights. See Juliette P. Thayer, "Schools, Not Battleships: The American Student Movement During the 1930's," Vassar thesis, 1971.

10. Florence Converse, *Wellesley College* (Boston, 1915), p. 128; Bernard, p. 36; Vida Scudder, *On Journey* (New York, 1937), pp. 165, 229-300.

11. Robert W. Chambers, "Gray Iris," *McCall's*, LII (January 1925), p. 12; Robert and Helen Lynd, *Middletown* (New York, 1929), pp. 138-39. Some observers seemed especially concerned with the "siren effects"

and "animal" noises of jazz. The National Dancing Master's Association resolved not to play the new music because its "jerky half-steps invited immoral variations," and Anne Shaw Faulkner suggested in the *Ladies Home Journal* that the musical craze reflected a "bolshevik element of license striving for expression in music." See G. Stanley Hall, "Flapper, Americana Novissima," *Atlantic Monthly*, CXXIX (June 1922); and Anne Shaw Faulkner, "Does Jazz Put the Sin into Syncopation?," *Ladies Home Journal*, XXXVIII (August 1921).

12. See James R. McGovern, "American Woman's Pre-World War I Freedom in Manners and Morals," *Journal of American History*, LV (September 1968), p. 316; Donald R. Makosky, "The Portrayal of Women in Wide Circulation Magazine Short Stories, 1905-55," unpublished doctoral dissertation, University of Pennsylvania, 1966, p. 280; Lewis M. Terman, *Psychological Factors in Marital Happiness* (New York, 1938), p. 321; Alfred C. Kinsey, *Sexual Behavior in the Human Female* (Philadelphia, 1953), pp. 422-23. It is McGovern's hypothesis that the new personal freedom of women began to appear well before the 1920's. The evidence seems to support his theory.

13. Lynds, *Middletown*, pp. 123-26. For a discussion of the birth-control movement, see David Kennedy, *Birth Control in America: The Career of Margaret Sanger* (New Haven, 1970).

14. See Carl Degler's introduction to Charlotte Perkins Gilman, *Women and Economics* (New York, 1966), p. xv; Mildred Adams, pp. 183-90; "Ellen Key and Feminism," *Nation*, CXXII (May 5, 1926), pp. 493-94; *New York Times*, May 2, 1926; and O'Neill, pp. 311-18. The *Nation* observed that Miss Key was "as conservative in her view of woman's functions as Theodore Roosevelt."

15. The sociologist Everett C. Hughes, has observed that "status" is "a defined social position for whose incumbents there are defined rights, limitations of rights, and duties." The contention here is that economic equality involved a fundamental change in women's status, and therefore, could not occur without substantial social upheaval. See Everett C. Hughes, "Dilemma and Contradictions of Status," *American Journal of Sociology*, L (March 1945), pp. 253-59. Chapter 9 elaborates in much greater detail the sociological issues of role conflict and status inconsistency.

16. Peter Berger, "Social Roles: Society in Man," in Dennis H. Wrong and Harry L. Grace, eds., *Readings in Introductory Sociology* (New York, 1967), pp. 107-17; the Lynds, *Middletown*, pp. 132-33, 149. Berger notes that "identity is socially bestowed, socially sustained, and socially transformed." The role "forms, shapes, and patterns both action

and actor," affecting not only external behavior, but internal feelings. "It is very, very difficult to change from Negro to white," Berger says, "and it is almost impossible to change from man to woman." Thus a person's identity is formed by the roles he or she plays and can be altered only if society assigns different roles. Berger's observations provide the theoretical foundation for much of the argument here.

17. Lynds, *Middletown*, pp. 116-21; Robert and Helen Lynd, *Middletown Transition* (New York, 1937), pp. 176-80.

18. Sinclair Lewis, *Main Street* (New York, 1920), especially pp. 50-52; 85, 169, 197, 234, 256, 282-84, 404-5.

19. See Makosky, *op. cit.*; S. M. Hutchinson, *This Freedom* (New York, 1922); *New York Times*, September 22, 1922; and B. June West, "Attitudes Toward American Women as Reflected in American Literature Between the Two World Wars," unpublished doctoral dissertation, University of Denver, 1954.

20. See Jean Frey, "Woman and Her Wage," *Independent Woman*, I (March 1920); Kate M. Tucker, "Are Women Too Aggressive in Business," *Independent Woman*, VIII (January 1924); Elizabeth Frazier, "Miss Graduate Hunts a Job," *Saturday Evening Post*, CCII (October 19, 1929); and Lorine Pruette, "Why Women Fail," *Outlook*, CLVIII (August 1931). All the articles discuss the role conflict experienced by career women.

21. Mabel Lee, "The Dilemma of the Educated Woman," *Atlantic Monthly*, CXLVI (November 1930), pp. 590-95; *New York Times*, October 10, 1925, May 20, 1923; Margaret Mead, "Sex and Achievement," *Forum*, XCIV (November 1935), pp. 301-3.

22. Notes for an address on Continuity for the Educated Woman, 1930, and the *Christian Science Monitor*, October 22, 1925, clipping in Morgan-Howe Family Papers, SL, Box 1; *New York Times*, November 1, 1925; and Sophonisba P. Breckinridge, "University Women in the New Order," address to the AAUW, May 18, 1933, in Sophonisba P. Breckinridge Papers, Library of Congress, Box 5. Commenting on the Smith Institute, Laura Kramer declared that "the modern woman labors under the handicap of not having a wife." The tongue-in-cheek observation in fact described the core of the problem. See Laura Kramer, "Releasing the Energies of Women," *Independent Woman*, IX (May 1920), p. 7.

23. Breckinridge; Suzanne LaFollette, *Concerning Women* (New York, 1926), p. 93; *New York Times*, October 10, 1926; B. June West, p. 49; and Sinclair Lewis, p. 85.

24. The quotation is from Mabel Lee, *op. cit.*

25. Quoted in Bernard, p. 48.

26. Agnes Rogers, pp. 41, 90; William L. O'Neill, *Divorce and the Progressive Era* (New Haven, 1967), pp. 26-27; Mary Anne Nettleton, "A Survey of Hollins Graduates, 1910-34 inclusive," *Hollins Alumnae Quarterly*, X (summer 1935), in AAUW Papers, Folder 52; *New York Times*, June 3, 1923, April 6, 1930.

27. Mabel Newcomer, *A Century of Higher Education for American Women* (New York, 1959), pp. 1, 76, 87; Barbara Cross, ed., *The Educated Woman in America* (New York, 1965); Ethel Puffer Howe, "The Place of Music and Art in the Curriculum of a Cultural College," *Smith Alumnae Quarterly* (November 1913), and mss. by Laura Puffer Morgan narrating the events of the ACA convention, in Morgan-Howe Papers, Box 1.

28. *New York Times*, May 22, 1926, November 9, 1927; Minnie Cumnock Blodgett, Dedication Speech, 1929; and Annie MacLeod, "Euthenics at Vassar," in Vassar College Special Collections. I am indebted to Vicki Metzel, a student at Vassar, for most of the material cited in the above paragraph. Her research paper, an excellent analysis of the Euthenics Institute and its philosophy, is on file in the Vassar College Special Collections.

29. For a hostile feminist reaction to similar programs, see Converse, p. 130. See also Agnes Fay Morgan to Marion Talbot, December 13, 1915, Marion Talbot Papers, University of Chicago Library, Box 4; Newcomer, p. 58; *New York Times*, November 17, 1925.

30. "Editorial," *Ladies Home Journal*, XLVII (May 1930), p. 34.

31. "Editorial," *Ladies Home Journal*, XLVI (February 1929), p. 30; "Editorial," *McCall's*, LVI (October 1928), p. 2; Lita Bane, "What's Next in Homemaking," *Ladies Home Journal*, XLVII (March 1930), p. 29; "Editorial," *McCall's*, LVI (April 1929), p. 2; Elizabeth Cook, "The Kitchen Sink Complex," *Ladies Home Journal*, XLVIII (September 1931), p. 12. Betty Friedan's *The Feminine Mystique* (New York, 1963) popularized the idea that in the years after World War II women's magazines consciously set out to romanticize the home in order to keep women in their traditional place. In fact, the ideology of domesticity began long before 1945.

32. Elizabeth Cook, *op. cit.*; Rose Wilder Lane, "Woman's Place Is in the Home," *Ladies Home Journal*, LIII (October 1936), p. 18; Laura Cornell, "Woman Must Understand Her Job," *Ladies Home Journal*, XLIV (April 1927), p. 39.

33. Dorothy Thompson, "If I Had a Daughter," *Ladies Home Journal*, LVI (September 1939), p. 4. Thompson exemplified the difficulty of re-

solving the career-home conflict. Married to Sinclair Lewis, she suffered bitter personal unhappiness and frequently reflected on the role
of work in her life. At the beginning of her marriage she confided to
her diary that "being a woman has got me at last, too. I saw that if
Hal goes now, I am finished. I cannot live by myself, for myself."
Yet in 1937 she wrote that "work has always been my way out. It
is so quiet, so impersonal. . . . Now when you tell me that my work
has ruined our marriage, *that* statement falls on deaf ears. I *know*
that it saved our marriage for the past six years. It was for me, the
outlet, the escape from something too intense to be borne. . . . I am
grateful to work. Next to you, I love it best of everything. It has
saved me twice in my life from utter shipwreck in emotions." Thompson reversed herself again two years later, however, in a letter to
Lewis. "You say I am brilliant," she wrote. "My dear Hal . . . I am
a woman—something you never took the trouble to realize. My sex
is female. I am not insensitive. I am not stupid. . . . I am a woman.
If you want my friendship you have got to win it. If you care for
anything more, you have to woo it." See Vincent Sheean, *Dorothy
and Red* (New York, 1963), pp. 42, 296, 306.

34. Claire Wallas Callahan, "A Woman with Two Jobs," *Ladies Home Jour-
    nal*, XLVII (October 1930), p. 114. In another article entitled "How
    Not To Get Married," Clarita de Foreauville declared that "working
    for a living and financial independence . . . is a fine deterrent to
    marriage."

35. See Claire Wallas Callahan and Elizabeth Cook, *op. cit.*

36. Elizabeth Bancroft Schlesinger commented that the journals with the
    largest circulation were characterized by "a superabundance of senti-
    mentality" and offered practically no articles on politics or public
    affairs. See "They Say Women Are Emancipated," *New Republic*
    (December 13, 1933), pp. 125-27.

37. The Kahn statement appears in Rita Halle, "Do You Need Your Job?"
    *Good Housekeeping*, XCV (September 1932), pp. 24-25. See also
    Edna C. McKnight, "Jobs—For Men Only?" *Outlook*, CLIX (Septem-
    ber 2, 1931), pp. 12-13; "The Woman Pin-Money Worker," *Literary
    Digest*, CIV (March 1930), p. 12; and Poppy Cannon, "Pin-Money
    Workers," *Forum*, LXXXIV (August 1930), pp. 98-103.

38. Mrs. C. A. Darr to Franklin Delano Roosevelt, October 18, 1933, FDR
    Papers, FDRL, Official File 120; Report of the Executive Council of
    the AF of L to the 51st Annual Convention, LWV Papers, Box 294;
    "America Speaks, the National Weekly Poll of Public Opinion," No-
    vember 15, 1936, in LWV Papers, Box 340; and Lillian Sharpley,

"Married Women at Work," unpublished master's essay, Columbia University, 1945, p. 8.

39. Ruth Shallcross, *Should Married Women Work?* (Washington, 1940), p. 7; San Francisco *Chronicle,* February 3, 1937, clipping, Alma Lutz Papers, SL, Box 1: Alma Lutz, "Why Discharge Women First?" clipping, LWV Papers, Box 340. The federal legislation was Section 213 of the National Economy Act. Mary Dewson and other Democratic leaders were quite defensive about the clause, since it constituted one of the few negative marks on the Roosevelt Administration's record regarding women. On a local level, restrictive legislation was introduced in ten states in 1932 and in twenty-five states in 1939-40. The bills either forbade both spouses from working for the state or asserted that a person could not be employed in public service if her or her spouse earned over a certain amount a month (usually $150-200). Among the states limiting women's employment either under executive order or legislation were Louisiana, Texas, Idaho, Indiana, Pennsylvania, Rhode Island, Alabama, Utah, Oklahoma, Oregon, and Virginia. See folder entitled "Married Women's Employment: II, Employment Policies, A. Discrimination," WBA, Accession No. 58A-850, Container 2.

40. Charlotte Perkins Gilman, "The New Generation of Women," *Current History*, XVIII (August 1923), pp. 731-37.

41. Evelyn Mershon to Sophonisba Breckinridge, n.d., 1932, Breckinridge Papers, Box 33; Pearl Buck, *Of Men and Women* (New York, 1941), pp. 15, 43, 44, 170.

42. Working Paper, Institute of Women's Professional Relations Papers, Folder 6; and Washington *Daily News*, November 11, 1939, clipping in Institute of Women's Professional Relations Papers, Folder 13.

CHAPTER 5

1. Mary Anderson, *Women at Work* (Minneapolis, 1951), p. 168; and Mary Anderson to Congressman Zebulon Weaver, March 20, 1945, WBA, folder entitled "Miscellaneous Subjects and Organizations—Equal Rights," Accession No. 55A-556, Container 10.

2. Mrs. Frank Vanderlip of the League of Women Voters, for example, said: "I have felt that in a number of instances the old suffragists who had been hampered, irritated and distressed for years and years over the members of the Women's Party and their attitude, had been perhaps uncompromising in trying to get on a working basis with

them." See Mrs. Frank Vanderlip to Maud Wood Park, October 11, 1922, LWV Papers, Library of Congress, Series II, Box 43.

3. W. L. George, *The Intelligence of Women* (New York, 1916), pp. 62-63; and William L. O'Neill, *Everyone Was Brave* (Chicago, 1969), pp. 51-52.

4. "Declaration of Principles of the National Women's Party," November 11, 1922, in Jane Norman Smith Papers, SL, Box 9; Freda Kirchwey, "Alice Paul Pulls the Strings," *Nation*, CXII (March 2, 1921), pp. 332-33; and Mabel Reif Putnam to Milwaukee *Journal*, March 3, 1921, clipping, Mabel Reif Putnam Papers, SL, Box 1.

5. *Equal Rights*, XI (February 14, 1925), p. 7; Florence Kitchelt to Margaret Bruton, July 11, 1947, Florence Kitchelt Papers, SL, Box 3; and Florence Kitchelt to NWP, July 21, 1948, Kitchelt Papers, Box 7. For an example of Alice Paul's hold over some people, see Florence Armstrong, "What Alice Paul Has Done for Me," Florence Armstrong Papers, SL, Folder 1. Paul's authoritarian leadership also caused dissension, however, and there was an open membership revolt in the 1940's. See the correspondence between Jane Norman Smith and Laura Berrien in the Smith Papers, Box 4.

6. LWV Press Release, August 22, 1937, LWV Papers, Box 599; Mildred Adams, *The Right To Be People* (New York, 1967), p. 191; "Record of Legislation Supported and Opposed by State Leagues, 1924-5," LWV Papers, Box 54; and statement of the LWV to the Twentieth Century Fund, March 1932, Box 597.

7. Statement by Dorothy Straus, December 21, 1933, on the Equal Nationality Treaty sponsored by the Women's Party, Belle Sherwin Papers, SL, Volume 6; Belle Sherwin to Wesley Jones, May 6, 1932, LWV Papers, Box 295; Miss Frederic to Gwen Geach, April 19, 1933, LWV Papers, Box 294. When an interested citizen inquired about federal legislation of concern to women, the League's Congressional Secretary replied: "The League of Women Voters does not pay particular attention to this subject." Florence Kerlin to Reah Whitehead, January 9, 1940, Box 443.

8. The first president was Maud Wood Park and her statement was quoted in "The League of Women Voters Presents Mrs. Franklin Roosevelt," Illinois Program, January 21, 1933, in Belle Sherwin Papers, Volume 6; Dorothy Straus' statement is from "In Regard to Nationality," a LWV Position Paper, February 4, 1930, LWV Papers, Box 597. See also "Shall Women Be Equal Before the Law?" *Nation*, CXIV (April 12, 1922), pp. 19-21.

9. Alice Paul to Jane Norman Smith, November 29, 1921, Smith Papers,

Box 5; and James Stanley Lemons, "The New Woman in the New Era: The Woman's Movement from the Great War to the Great Depression," p. 277.

10. Alice Paul to Maud Wood Park, January 3, 1921, LWV Papers, Box 6; Report of Emma Steghagen to the Executive Board, February 23, 1921, Women's Trade Union League Papers, Library of Congress, Box 2; Mrs. Frank Vanderlip to Maud Wood Park, October 11, 1922, LWV Papers, Box 43; and Alice Paul to Jane Norman Smith, January 17, 1923, Smith Papers, Box 5.

11. Alice Paul to Jane Norman Smith, November 29, 1921, Smith Papers, Box 5; Esther Mannes to Mrs. Webster, January 18, 1926, LWV Papers, Box 43; report of October 10, 1922 meeting with NWP by Mrs. Frank Vanderlip to Maud Wood Park, LWV Papers, Box 43.

12. Zona Gale, "What Women Won in Wisconsin," *Nation,* CXV (August 23, 1922), pp. 184-85; "Equal Rights for Men and Women in the States," n.d. Armstrong Papers, Box 1; "History and Purpose of the Wisconsin Equal Rights Law," by Edwin Witte, in Putnam Papers, Box 1. The Women's Club quotation is from Lemons, p. 280.

13. See the file on Alice Paul's letter of January 3, 1921, in LWV Papers, Box 6; Milwaukee *Journal,* June 7, 1921, clipping, Putnam Papers, Box 1; Carrie Chapman Catt to Maud Wood Park, December 19, 1921, LWV Papers, Box 3; and a report of the December 1921 conference in the WTUL Papers, Box 2.

14. See Olive Colton to Mary Anderson, February 23, 1926, Anderson Papers, Box 1; and a NWP Press Release, January 20, 1927, Smith Papers, Box 7. Alice Lee, another delegate, observed that "almost everything but hair-pulling took place" at the conference. According to a WTUL account, after an hour of disruption, Anita Pollitzer of the NWP asked the press: "Have we done enough to get into the papers? If we have we'll stop." See Alice Lee, "A Novice Visits Washington," LWV Papers, Box 31; and Lemons, pp. 286-87.

15. Mary Anderson to Mary Van Kleeck, January 26, 1926; May 11, 1926, Anderson Papers, Box 1.

16. Mary Anderson to Margaret Dreier Robins, May 17, 1926, Anderson Papers, Box 1; Mary Van Kleeck to Mary Anderson, January 27, 1926; Mary Anderson to Mary Van Kleeck, May 11, 1926, Anderson Papers, Box 1; Mary Winslow to Mary Anderson, June 19, 1926, and July 12, 1926, Anderson Papers, Box 1. Anderson exulted over the dissolution of the advisory committee and said "the publicity went over beautifully."

17. The Women's Party, for example, succeeded in getting the Inter-Ameri-

can Conference in Montevideo in 1934 to pass an Equal Nationality Treaty which brought the subject of equal rights before Congress in a new form. It also lobbied intensively at the League of Nations for inscription of equal rights for women on the League agenda.

18. "Amendment Ammunition, Notes to be used in the campaign for the Equal Rights Amendment," October 15, 1934, Alma Lutz Papers, SL, Box 2; Julia Carson, "Remaining Legal Discriminations Against Women," December 9, 1940, LWV Papers, Box 598; statement of Burnita Shelton Matthews, *Equal Rights*, Hearing before Senate Judiciary Sub-Committee, 71st Congress, on S. J. Res. 52 (Washington, 1931), cited in Aileen Kraditor, *Up from the Pedestal* (Chicago, 1970).

19. Edna Kenton, "The Ladies Next Step, The Case for the Equal Rights Amendment," *Harper's*, CLII (February, 1926), pp. 366-74; *Smith v. Alabama* (124 U.S. 165), 1873; *Bradwell v. Illinois* (83 U.S. 139), 1872; *Welosky v. Commonwealth of Massachusetts* (284 U.S. 684), 1932; and *New Haven Journal Courier*, June 15, 1945, clipping, Kitchelt Papers, Box 2.

20. Thomas' statement is quoted in a form letter from Alice Morgan Wright to New York state chapters of the American Association of University Women, May 6, 1944, AAUW Papers, SL, Folder 55, See also Florence Kitchelt to Anita Pollitzer, February 21, 1945, in Kitchelt Papers, Box 8.

21. "The Equal Rights Amendment, A Memorandum in Opposition," by Marvin Harrison of the National Committee to Defeat the Unequal Rights Amendment, in the Hattie Smith Papers, SL, Box 2. Anderson's statement is from a transcript of the American Forum of the Air broadcast, July 19, 1942, in the Emma Guffey Miller Papers, SL, Box 5. Mrs. Pinchot's comments appear in "Methods for Improving Women's Status in the United States," March 1939, AAUW Papers, Folder 55.

22. "Equal Rights Amendment," by Charlotte Hankin, a paper given at the AAUW convention, June 1939, in AAUW Papers, Folder 55; and *Equal Rights,* X (March 1924), quoted in O'Neill, p. 283.

23. "The Equal Rights Amendment, A Memorandum in Opposition," *op. cit.*; undated pamphlet by the LWV in the Dorothy Kirchwey Brown Papers, SL, Folder 32; and Dean Fraser to LWV, January 31, 1929, LWV Papers, Box 599. At times during the debate, both sides resorted to demagoguery. An example was a 1944 pamphlet by the respectable Consumers League called "What Is Equality?" which asked: "Should a pregnant wife deserted by her husband have no

recourse to law? Should rape be unpunishable by law? . . . Should widows be deprived of their Social Security benefits?" National Consumers League *Bulletin*, IX (fall 1944).

24. The first statement was made by Dean Acheson and was quoted by Mary Winslow in a January 1, 1945, press release by the WTUL, WTUL Papers, Box 9. The Frankfurter statement was made originally on August 7, 1923, and is reprinted in the AAUW's "Methods for Improving Women's Status in the United States," *op. cit*. Throughout the amendment fight, the reformers relied on male legal experts like Acheson and Frankfurter while the NWP used almost exclusively female attorneys.

25. The Lutz statement is quoted in a paper called "Protection" by Florence Kitchelt, Kitchelt Papers, Box 2. See also Jane Grant, "Confessions of a Feminist," *American Mercury*, LVII (December 1943); and Maud Younger, "The NRA and Protective Laws for Women," *Literary Digest*, CXVII (June 2, 1934), p. 27.

26. *Equal Rights*, October 27, 1928; Elizabeth Faulkner Baker, "At the Crossroads in the Legal Protection of Women in Industry," *Annals* of the American Academy of Political and Social Science, CVLIII (May 1929), pp. 265-79; and a speech by Mollie Maloney on the American Forum of the Air, March 7, 1943, transcript in Caroline Babcock-Olive Hurlburt Papers, SL, Box 1.

27. Olive Hurlburt to NWP, February 5, 1937, Babcock-Hurlburt Papers, Folder 40; Boston *Post*, January 16, 1930, clipping, Lutz Papers, Box 3; Alma Lutz, "Women and Wages," *Nation*, CXXXIX (October 17, 1934), p. 564; *Equal Rights*, February 4, 1933; and Jane Norman Smith to Dorothy Dunbar Bromley, December 17, 1935, in Smith Papers, Box 4.

28. "How New York Laws Discriminate Against Women," a 1923 Women's Party Pamphlet, Smith Papers, Box 9; *Equal Rights*, September 29, 1934; and O'Neill, p. 279.

29. Woolley's statement is quoted in "The Case for the Equal Rights Amendment," a Women's Party pamphlet, n.d. Lutz Papers, Box 2; Florence Kitchelt, "Protection," *op. cit.*; Florence Kitchelt to Alice Paul, July 15, 17, October 11 and 16, 1945, Kitchelt Papers, Box 7; statement of Anita Pollitzer, *Equal Rights*, 1931 Senate hearing; and "Does Equality Mean Identity?" *New Republic*, LX (September 11, 1929), p. 103.

30. Mary Anderson, "Should There Be Labor Laws for Women?" *Good Housekeeping*, LXXXI (September 1925), pp. 52-53; statement of Rose Schneiderman at Senate hearing, *op. cit.*; Alice Hamilton, "Why I Am Against the Equal Rights Amendment," *Ladies Home Journal*,

LXII (July 1945), p. 23; and Mary Beard to Alma Lutz, January 29, 1937, in Lutz Papers, Box 3. It should be noted that Beard also did not approve of the reformers' overemphasis on women's dependence.

31. Mary Van Kleeck, "Women and Machines," *Atlantic Monthly,* CXXVII (February 1921), pp. 250-60. As time passed a great many career women did support the amendment. In Indiana, California, and New York, poorly drafted wage and hour bills proposed that female professional workers and businesswomen be restricted by the same maximum-hour laws as factory women. Local Federations of Business and Professional Women contested such legislation and in the process developed a growing affinity for the principle of equal rights. During the 1930's women lawyers, osteopaths, dentists, doctors, realtors, and accountants flocked to the Equal Rights Banner. See Lemons, pp. 299-302.

32. Washington *Evening Star,* June 4, 1936, clipping, Lutz Papers, Box 3; Mary Anderson to Margaret Dreier Robins, June 10, 1936, Anderson Papers, Box 2; the *Nation,* LXLIV (January 2, 1937).

33. *Muller v. Oregon* (208 U.S. 412), 1908; O'Neill, p. 289. The Consumers League statement is cited in a speech by Emma Guffey Miller, Babcock-Hurlburt Papers, Folder 27.

34. *New York Times,* February 27, 1924; and "Methods for Improving the Status of Women in the United States," *op. cit.*

35. "The Equal Rights Amendment Revised," *Journal of the American Association of University Women* (fall 1943); Al Smith to Jane Norman Smith, October 22, 1930, and Jane Norman Smith to Sue Probst, May 5, 1932, in Smith Papers, Box 3; and May Smith Dean, "Should Women Have Equal Rights?—a Symposium," *Forum,* LXXII (September 1924), p. 421.

36. See "The Women's Bureau Operates as a Major Agency Within the Department of Labor," August 22, 1945, WBA, folder entitled "U.N. Replies to Questionnaire on the Legal Status of Women," Accession No. 58A-550, Container 7; 1938 and 1942 speeches by Emma Guffey Miller, Miller Papers, Box 4 and 5. Although the Equal Rights fight might seem in retrospect to have been a relatively minor concern of many women's organizations, the minutes of reform groups such as the LWV and WTUL suggest that an inordinate amount of time and energy was devoted to it. In 1932, Robert Allen and Drew Pearson declared in their syndicated column that the sole purpose of the LWV's existence seemed to be to combat the NWP.

37. Florence Kerlin to Anna Lord Straus, December 27, 1937, LWV Papers, Box 362; *New York Times,* May 31, 1936; December 20, 27, 28,

1936; February 15, 17 and March 15, 1938; Elizabeth Baker, "About the Women's Charter," *Independent Woman*, XVI (March 1937), pp. 72-74; and "Equal Rights for Women," *New Republic*, XCIV (February 16, 1938), p. 34. Some reformers seemed close to panic in the late 1930's as the NWP made gains among legislators.

## CHAPTER 6

1. The discussion of the war and its impact is divided into three chapters. The present chapter concentrates on the changes in women's economic role which resulted from the war crisis. Chapter 7 explores in more depth some of the areas where females continued to suffer from inequality, and Chapter 8 assesses the developments of the post-1945 period in an attempt to place the experience of the war years in perspective.

2. *Life and Labor*, No. 34, July 1942 in folder entitled "Organizations: WTUL, *Life and Labor*," WBA, Accession No. 58A-850, Container 3; Office of War Information, *Women and the War* (Bureau of Intelligence, 1942), p. 3; Louisa Moore, "Training Women Defense Workers," folder entitled "Training," WBA, Accession No. 54A-78, container 10.

3. Mary Anderson, "Industrial Relations in a Democracy at Work," speech delivered at the Commonwealth Club, May 18, 1942, in folder entitled "Mary Anderson—Addresses and Statements," WBA, Accession No. 58A-850, container 3; "Women's Bureau Conference on Vocational Training of Women," November 7, 1940, folder entitled "Women's Bureau Conferences on Women in War Industries," WBA, Accession No. 54A-78, container 11; "Report of the Conference of the Women's Bureau Advisory Committee, January 21-22, 1942," folder entitled "Conference, Labor Advisory Committee," WBA, Accession No. 58A-850, container 3; Frank Adams, "Women in Democracy's Arsenal," *New York Times*, October 19, 1941.

4. "History of the Women's Advisory Committee," August 15, 1944, in folder entitled "Postwar—General," WBA, Accession No. 58A-850, container 2; Ellen Sullivan Woodward, "Women on the Production Front," speech given June 15, 1942, in Ellen Sullivan Woodward Papers, SL, Box 2; Mary Anderson, "Women on the Labor Front," speech given on May 19, 1942, in folder entitled "Mary Anderson—Addresses and Statements," *op. cit.*; "Vocational Training of Defense Workers," April 30, 1942, in folder entitled "Training," *op. cit.*; and

Margaret Hickey, "Utilization of Women in Wartime Jobs," June 29, 1943, WBA, Accession No. 54A-78, container 9.

5. Katherine Glover, *Women at Work in Wartime* (Washington, 1943), pp. 1, 7; Beatrice Oppenheim, "Anchors Aweigh," *Independent Woman*, XXII (March 1943), p. 20; Office of War Information Press Release, July 4, 1943, WBA, Accession No. 54A-78, container 9; "Women in Steel," *Life*, IV (August 9, 1943), pp. 73-81; Dorothy Rowe, "Womanpower Takes to the Woods," *Independent Woman*, XXII (September 1943), p. 261; *New York Times*, June 27, 1942, and May 28, 1943.

6. Ruth Sulzberger, "Adventures of a Hackie," *New York Times Magazine*, November 28, 1943; *New York Times*, June 27, 1942; *Washington Post*, April 27, 1944; Elizabeth Christman, "Women in War Industries," speech given October 3, 1942, in folder entitled "Speeches," WBA, Accession No. 54A-78, container 10; Florence Hall, "They're Getting in the Crops," *Independent Woman*, XXII (July 1943), pp. 195-96; Rita H. Kleeman, "The College Girl Goes to War," *Independent Woman*, XXII (January 1943), p. 19; Virginia Gildersleeve, *Many a Good Crusade* (New York, 1956), pp. 267-87; Elizabeth Reynard Papers, SL, Box 8.

7. Folder entitled "U.S. Voluntary Organizations," WBA, Accession No. 54A-78, container 10; *Cleveland Press*, September 28, 1943, clipping in folder entitled "Women's Organizations," WBA, Accession No. 54A-78, container 11; *Springfield News*, January 8, 1941; *Kalamazoo Gazette*, February 14, 1941; *Oklahoman*, January 21, 1941, clippings in folder entitled "Defense—Women's Groups," WBA, Accession No. 58A-850, container 3; Robert M. Yoder, "Miss Casey at the Bat," *Saturday Evening Post*, CCXV August 22, 1942), p. 17.

8. NBC Radio Script, "Commando Mary," November 1, 1942, WBA, Accession No. 54A-78, container 9; "Women's Bureau Conference on Vocational Training of Women," *op. cit.*; Augusta Clauson, "What of the Older Woman?" *Altrusan*, XXI (February 1944); Glover, p. 5; and Constance Green, *The Role of Women as Production Workers in War Plants in the Connecticut Valley* (Northampton, 1946), p. 66.

9. "Women Workers in Ten Production Areas and Their Postwar Employment Plans," *Women's Bureau Bulletin* No. 209 (Washington, 1946), pp. 3-4, 7; Eva Lapin, *Mothers in Overalls* (New York, 1943), p. 5. The fourteen-month period was from April 1942 to June 1943.

10. The number of teenage runaways doubled in both Boston and Connecticut between 1941 and 1942. Nationwide, juvenile delinquency increased in 1942 by 8 per cent among boys and 31 per cent among

girls. The problem caused widespread concern and prompted a strong editorial campaign by the Hearst press for greater community services. See a speech by Charles Taft, head of the Office of Community Welfare Services, July 9, 1943; and Helen D. Pidgeon, "Effect of War Conditions on Children and Adolescents in the City of Hartford, Connecticut," both in the Office of Community Welfare Services Archives, Child Care Division, Record Group 215, National Archives, Box 73.

11. "Women Workers in Ten Production Areas," pp. 3-4; "The Wartime Economy of the United States," in folder entitled "Women's Bureau Conferences, 1944-45—Reconversion," WBA, Accession No. 58A-850, container 3.

12. Glover, p. 5; Frieda Miller, "Patterns of Women in Industry," speech given May 24, 1945, in folder entitled "Women's Bureau Conferences, 1944-45," *op. cit.*; Frieda Miller, "The Womenfolk Take Stock," in folder entitled "Statements and Addresses by Frieda S. Miller," WBA, Accession No. 58A-850, container 3; International Labor Office, *The War and Women's Employment: The Experience of the United Kingdom and the United States* (Montreal, 1946), p. 168.

13. "Report of Conference on Women in War Industries," in folder entitled "Conferences, Women's Bureau, General 1943, Women in War Industries," WBA, Accession No. 58A-850, container 3; International Labor Office, pp. 173, 187.

14. "Changes in Women's Employment During the War," *Women's Bureau Bulletin* No. 20 (Washington, 1944), p. 9; "Women in the Federal Service, 1923-1947," *Women's Bureau Bulletin* No. 230 (Washington, 1949), pp. 5, 17, 18, 33; "Employment of Women in the Early Postwar Period," *Women's Bureau Bulletin* No. 211 (Washington, 1946), pp. 4-5. The number of clerical workers grew 84.5 per cent, the number of craftsmen, foremen, operatives, and laborers, 118.7 per cent.

15. International Labor Office, p. 189; Glover, p. 9; Elizabeth Baker, *Technology and Women's Work* (New York, 1964), p. 262; memorandum from Bertha Nienburg to Mary Anderson, February 16, 1943, WBA, Accession No. 54A-78, container 9; "Effect of War on Employment of Women Lawyers," *Monthly Labor Review*, LVII (September 1943), p. 502; Marie C. Chase, "A Closed Door Opens," *Independent Woman*, XXII (October 1943), p. 295; "Skirted," *Time*, XLIII (March 13, 1944), p. 83; and Mary Anderson, "War Demands on the Nation's Woman-Power," speech given on March 24, 1943, folder entitled "Speeches," WBA, Accession No. 54A-78, container 10.

16. "Changes in Women's Employment During the War," p. 12; Mary An-

derson, "Women Work for Victory," speech given on February 14, 1943, folder entitled "Women's Bureau—Functions and History," WBA, Accession No. 58A-850, container 4. Anderson used an example of an actual assembly line in her speech.

17. "Women Workers in Ten Production Areas," p. 8; Office of War Information Press Release, July 30, 1942, folder entitled "U.S. Occupations and Industries—Laundries," WBA, Accession No. 54A-78, container 11; Women's Bureau Press Release, October 8, 1945, folder entitled "Postwar—Employment of Women," WBA, Accession No. 58A-850, container 2.

18. Women's Bureau, "Report on Old Age Insurance for Household Workers," 1945, folder entitled "Health Education and Welfare," WBA, Accession No. 58A-850, container 6. Half of the former domestics entered manufacturing, and an additional 25 per cent went into service industries.

19. "Negro Women Workers," Women's Bureau working paper, n.d., folder entitled "Negro Women," WBA, Accession No. 58A-850, container 4. The Assistant Personnel Manager of the Campbell Soup Company, for example, apologized to a Women's Bureau visitor for the large number of Negro women working in his plant. "We never had them before, and we won't again," he said. "I hope you will discount it." Jennie Mohr to Constance Williams, December 12, 1944, folder entitled "Miller and Williams Memos," WBA, Accession No. 58A-850, container 6.

20. Glover, p. 10; Helen Baker, *Women in War Industries* (Princeton, 1942), pp. 51-58; "Women Workers After VJ Day in One Community," *Women's Bureau Bulletin* No. 216 (Washington, 1947), p. 9; Eva Lapin, p. 16; Constance Green, p. 40; "Mobilization of Manpower and Pressing the Fight for Freedom," *Annals* of the American Academy of Political Science, XX (May 1943), p. 11.

21. "Women Workers in Ten Production Areas," p. 15; Green, n.p. (preface); Women's Bureau Press Release, October 8, 1945, *op. cit.*

22. International Labor Office, p. 237; "Data on Postwar Status of Women Workers," November 15, 1945, Women's Bureau working paper, folder entitled "Postwar—General," *op. cit.* The United Electrical Workers had 280,000 female members, as did the United Automobile Workers. Women constituted 40 per cent of the former, 28 per cent of the latter.

23. "Changes in Women's Employment During the War," p. 17.

24. Margaret Hickey, "Utilization of Women in Wartime Jobs," *op cit.*; *Fortune*, XXVIII (February 1943), p. 99. The Bureau of the Census

reported in March 1942 that 15 million housewives between the ages of eighteen and forty-four represented the principal labor reserve for war jobs.

25. "Changes in Women's Employment During the War," p. 17; Women's Bureau, "Women Workers Today and Tomorrow, a Balance Sheet," mimeographed release, October 9, 1944, p. 4; "Employment of Women in the Early Postwar Period," pp. 7, 10; "Number of Women Employed, Pre-War and Post-War," April 1946, Women's Bureau working paper, folder entitled, "Postwar—Women's Bureau—Labor Force Data," *op. cit.*; Women's Advisory Committee Press Release, January 16, 1945, Women's Advisory Committee Papers, National Archives, Box 138.

26. Frieda Miller, "Patterns of Women in Industry," *op. cit.*; "Womanpower," Civilian Personnel Pamphlet, No. 20, WBA, Accession No. 54A-78, container 12; "Specific Instances as to Wartime Policies Regarding Employment of Married Women," Women's Bureau Working Paper, folder entitled "Married Women's Employment," WBA, Accession No. 58A-850, container 2.

27. Helen Baker, p. 12; "Employment of Women in the Early Postwar Period," p. 7; "Report of Conference on Women in War Industry," *op. cit.*; Frieda Miller, "Statement on Older Women Workers," December 14, 1950, before the New York State Legislature, in folder entitled "Statements and Addresses by Frieda Miller," *op. cit.*

28. Helen Baker, pp. 11-12; War Manpower Commission Reports and Analysis Service, "Recruitment of Women for Wartime Employment," folder entitled "Recruitment for Workers in Industry and Agriculture," WBA, Accession No. 54A-78, container 10; radio script on "Womanpower," CBS, June 7, 1942, in Woodward Papers, Box 2.

29. "Women in Steel," *Life, op. cit.*; "Girl Pilot," *Life*, XV (July 19, 1943); Ruth Sulzberger, *op. cit.*; "Symphony Goes Co-Ed," *Newsweek*, XXII (December 6, 1943); "Manless Industry," *Business Week* (March 10, 1945); and Carrollo Van Ark, "Women Rule a Cumberland Town," *Colliers*, CX (November 7, 1943).

30. *Fortune*, XXVIII (February 1943), p. 101; "Report of the Children's Bureau Committee on Children in Wartime," Office of Community Welfare Services Archives, Box 2; War Department, "You're Going To Employ Women," WBA, folder entitled "Training and Induction," *op. cit.*; *Cleveland Plain Dealer*, October 17, 1943, clipping, WBA, Accession No. 58A-850, container 6.

31. War Manpower Commission statement on "Recruitment, Training and Employment of Women Workers," October 17, 1942, folder entitled

"Defense, Manpower Commission," WBA, Accession No. 56A-284, container 2.

32. War Manpower Commission Reports and Analysis Service, "Recruitment of Women for Wartime Employment," *op. cit.*; Office of War Information Press Release, May 23, 1943, Federal Works Agency Archives, National Archives, Box 82; Hadley Cantril, *Public Opinion, 1935-1946* (Princeton, 1951), p. 1045.

33. International Labor Office, p. 258; John Durand, "The Postwar Employment of Women in the United States," *International Labour Review*, XLVIII (December 1943), pp. 695-713; "Women's Occupations Through Seven Decades," *Women's Bureau Bulletin* No. 232 (Washington, 1951), p. 1; Janet Hooks to Constance Williams, December 5, 1945, WBA, folder entitled "Postwar–Women's Bureau–Labor Force Data," *op. cit.*; "Numbers of Women Employed, Pre-War, War and Post-War," *op. cit.*

34. Women's Bureau, "Progress of Women in the United States, 1947-49," in American Association of University Women Papers, SL, folder 51; *Christian Science Monitor,* January 26, 1943; Rose Schneiderman, "The Challenge to Women's Organizations," speech delivered October 27, 1943, WTUL Papers, Box 9; Margaret Culkin Banning, "Post-War Planning, Will They Go Back Home?" *The Rotarian* (September 1943), reprint in folder entitled, "Postwar–Employment of Women," Accession No. 58A-850, container 2.

35. "Women's Occupations Through Seven Decades," p. 10; Georgene Seward, "Sex Roles in Postwar Planning," *Journal of Social Psychology*, XIX (August 1944), pp. 163-85. The Jennie Matyas quote is from the August 13, 1943, transcript of the Women's Advisory Committee meeting, WAC Papers, Box 135.

36. See Helen D. Pidgeon, "Effect of War Conditions on Children and Adolescents in the City of Hartford Connecticut," *op. cit.*; and Alfred Toombs, "War Babies," *Woman's Home Companion*, LXXI (April 1944), p. 32. Clare Booth Luce's comments were made in *Women's Wear Daily,* October 4, 1943, clipping, folder entitled "Recruitment for Workers in Industry and Agriculture," WBA, Accession No. 54A-78, container 10. See also Children's Bureau, "Understanding Juvenile Delinquency," *Children's Bureau Bulletin* No. 300 (Washington, 1943).

*CHAPTER 7*

1. Florence Cadman, "Womanpower 4 F," *Independent Woman*, xxii (September 1943), p. 261; *Monthly Labor Review*, LVII (July 1943),

p. 33; "A Victory Long Overdue," *Independent Woman*, XXII (May 1943), p. 132; National Metal Trades Association, *Women in Industry* (Chicago, 1943), p. 15. The remarks of the Connecticut Valley Industrialist are quoted in Constance Green, *The Role of Women as Production Workers in the Connecticut Valley* (Northampton, 1946), p. 37.

2. Speech by Mary Van Kleeck to the New York WTUL, December 12, 1943; and Mary Van Kleeck to Mary Anderson, January 14, 1943, both in folder entitled "Russell Sage Foundation—Mary van Kleeck," WBA, Accession No. 55A-556, container 12; and Minnie Maffett, "Under-use of Womanpower Slows the War Effort," *Independent Woman*, XXII (August 1943), p. 230. Anna Rosenberg was Northeast Regional Director of the War Manpower Commission.

3. Mary Anderson to Mary Van Kleeck, January 6, 1943, in Van Kleeck file, *op. cit.*; and Mary Anderson, "War History of the Office of Defense Production," Mary Anderson Papers, SL, folder 3. The members of the WMC's Labor Advisory Committee threatened to resign according to Mary Anderson. In a letter to Mary Van Kleeck, she reported that she had done all she could to block the creation of a WAC and get women appointed to already functioning war committees. She also wrote that when Frances Perkins asked Paul McNutt, head of the WMC, why he had appointed a WAC, McNutt replied that "he didn't want them any more than she did, but there had been so much pressure . . . that he finally had to yield."

4. "History of the WAC," August 15, 1944, folder entitled "Postwar—General," WBA, Accession No. 58A-850, container 2; remarks of Dorothy Bellanca, transcript, WAC meeting, January 13, 1943, WAC Archives, Box 133; remarks of Bess Bloodsworth, WAC meeting May 13, 1943, Box 134; transcript of August 13, 1943, WAC meeting, Box 135.

5. Remarks of Bess Bloodsworth, *op. cit.*; transcript of January 13, 1943, meeting, WAC Archives, Box 133; transcript of March 17, 1943, meeting, Box 133; and Ruth Allen to Margaret Hickey, April 6, 1943, WAC Archives, Box 143.

6. Washington *Star*, March 21, 1943, clipping, folder entitled "WAC—WMC," WBA, Accession No. 56A-284, container 2; Mary Anderson to Mary Van Kleeck, *op. cit.*; transcript of February 10 WAC meeting, WAC Archives, Box 133; and transcripts for the April 15, May 12, and May 13 meetings, WAC Archives, Box 134. The WAC argued that if women really were important to the winning of the war, their representatives should be given equal "status" with men in setting policy.

7. See transcript of the May 12, 1943, WAC meeting, Box 134; the transcript of the August 12, 1943, meeting Box 135; and the transcript of the January 13, 1943, meeting, Box 133. A constant theme of WAC discussions was whether the committee should act as a pressure group for women and emphasize its segregated nature, or present advice in a non-partisan form, hoping thereby to gain respect as an objective body. In the end, the fact that the committee was constituted as a sexually separatist group dictated the answer.

8. Ella J. Polinsky, "National War Labor Board Policy on Equal Pay for Equal Work for Women," September 28, 1945, folder entitled "Miscellaneous Subjects and Organizations—Equal Pay," WBA, Accession No. 55A-556, container 10. In the Brown and Sharp Case (No. 101, September 25, 1942), the Board declared "there is no proof, scientific or otherwise, that women are 20 per cent less capable than men all the time."

9. Mary Anderson, "Women on the Labor Front," speech given May 19, 1942, folder entitled "Mary Anderson—Addresses and Statements," WBA, Accession No. 58A-850, container 3; "Differentials in Pay for Women," Women's Bureau working paper, folder entitled "Equal Pay Set of Documents and Important Data," WBA, Accession No. 58A-850, container 4; "Case Studies of Equal Pay for Women," Women's Bureau working paper, May 25, 1951, folder entitled "Equal Pay Study," WBA, Accession No. 58A-850, container 4.

10. See Ella J. Polinsky, *op. cit.*; "Equal Pay—A Progress Report," May 1944, in folder entitled "Miscellaneous Subjects and Organizations—Equal Pay," *op. cit.*; William Davis to Frances Perkins, June 4, 1943, *ibid.*; and International Labor Organization, *The War and Women's Employment* (Montreal, 1946), p. 221.

11. International Labor Organization, p. 219; Ella Polinsky, *op. cit.*; Katherine Glover, *Women at Work in Wartime* (New York, 1943), p. 13; Louise Stitt to Marjorie Davis, July 15, 1944, and Paul Smith to Mary Anderson, July 1, 1943, both in WBA folder entitled "Miscellaneous Subjects and Organizations—Equal Pay"; Miss Angus to Mary Anderson, April 19, 1943, and Mary Anderson to George Meany, June 18, 1943, also in the WBA equal-pay folder.

12. "Women Workers After V-J Day in One Community," *Women's Bureau Bulletin* No. 216 (Washington, 1947), p. 16; "A Preview as to Women Workers in Transition from War to Peace," *Women's Bureau Special Bulletin* No. 18 (Washington, 1944), p. 9; Women's Bureau testimony before the House Education and Labor Committee, February 10, 1948; Women's Bureau Memorandum, April 15, 1944,

folder entitled "Miller and Williams Memos," WBA, Accession No. 58A-850, container 6; *Life and Labor,* No. 36 (November 1942); and Women's Bureau Memorandum, October 9, 1945, folder entitled "Equal Pay—General," *op. cit.*

13. "Importance of Equal Pay for Women and Men to America's Postwar Objectives," Women's Bureau working paper, folder entitled "Equal Pay—WLB," WBA, *op. cit.*; and Women's Bureau memorandum, October 9, 1945, *op. cit.*

14. John Stewart to Walter Reuther, May 5, 1944, Local 121, Janesville UAW-CIO Papers, Wisconsin Historical Society, Box 2; remarks of Elizabeth Christman at the October 29, 1943, meeting of the WAC, WAC Archives, Box 136; "Excerpts from the United Electrical Workers Brief to the WLB," September 19, 1945, WBA folder entitled "Equal Pay—WLB," *op. cit.* One electrical union official after looking at a page of jobs, said: "Oh, these are all men's jobs on this page. They wouldn't be paying women these rates."

15. International Labor Office, *The War and Women's Employment,* p. 207.

16. Marguerite Zapoleon, "Women and Professional Opportunities," *Annals* of the American Academy of Political and Social Science, CCLI (May 1947), pp. 165-73.

17. "Why Women Quit," *Business Week,* October 16, 1943, p. 94; International Labor Office, p. 226; "Absenteeism," Women's Bureau working paper, folder entitled "Accidents in Industry," WBA, Accession No. 58A-850, container 5; Office of War Information Press Release, October 6, 1943, folder entitled "Turnover," WBA, Accession No. 54A-78, container 10; Eva Lapin, *Mothers in Overalls* (New York, 1943), p. 12; Washington *Daily News,* June 30, 1943, clipping, Federal Works Agency Archives, Box 83; and Elizabeth Hawes, "Woman War Worker: A Case History," *New York Times Magazine,* December 26, 1943.

18. A. C. Dick to Margaret Mettert, May 7, 1943; and Jennie Mohr to Mary Alice Webb, February 18, 1944, in folder entitled "Menstruation," WBA, Accession No. 58A-850, container 5; and August H. Clawson, "Report on Welding Training and Shipyard Employment," folder entitled "Training and Induction," WBA, *op. cit.*

19. Women's Bureau memo on the 1943 study, n.d. in folder entitled "Absenteeism—Study General," WBA, Accession No. 58A-850, container 5; NICB, "Absenteeism Among Married Women Workers," November 23, 1945, folder entitled "Accidents in Industry," WBA, *op. cit.*; and transcript of October 28, 1943, WAC meeting, WAC Archives, Box 136.

20. The above is a paraphrase of a memo sent by Alan Johnstone, General Counsel of the Federal Works Administration to Samuel Rosenberg at the White House, January 20, 1944, in justification of supplemental appropriations for the FWA. Federal Works Agency Archives, Series 6, Box 18. See also Eva Lapin, *Mothers in Overalls,* p. 24; and "Community Services for Women War Workers," *Women's Bureau Special Bulletin* No. 15 (Washington, 1944), p. 2.

21. "Community Services for Women War Workers," p. 4; Lapin, p. 24; Margaret Shoenfield and Alice Whitney, "Wartime Methods of Dealing with Labor in Great Britain and the Dominions," *Law and Contemporary Problems,* IX (summer 1942), pp. 522-43. See also folders entitled "Great Britain, Miscellaneous," and "Great Britain, Mobilization Policies," in WBA, Accession No. 54A-78, container 12.

22. Mary Anderson, "Women's Clubs and Women in Industry," speech given on October 17, 1942, folder entitled "Speeches," WBA, Accession No. 54A-78, container 10; transcript of WAC meeting, October 29, 1943, WAC Archives, Box 136; Mary Heaton Vorse, "Women Don't Quit If—," *Independent Woman,* XXIII (January 1944), p. 9; and Washington *Post,* September 3, 1943. A Georgia plant with a 13 per cent absenteeism rate, for example, installed a grocery shop, a barber shop, and a check-cashing service and cut absenteeism to 3 per cent. A tire plant in Akron provided laundry service for its workers. But these were the exceptions.

23. "Changes in Women's Employment During the War," *Women's Bureau Special Bulletin* No. 20 (Washington, 1944), p. 3; Glover, p. 16; Helen Baker, *Women in War Industries* (Princeton, 1942), p. 68; "Community Factors Contributing to Turnover Among Women in San Diego War Industries," November 1943, folder entitled "Region XII," WBA, Accession No. 58A-850, container 6; War Production Board Press Release October 30, 1943, and FWA Press Release, April 30, 1943, in FWA Archives, Series 38, Box 82.

24. Eva Lapin, p. 17; Margaret Mettert, "Everyday Good Health for Women in War Work," May 1943, in folder entitled "Health of Workers," WBA, Accession No. 58A-850, container 5; transcript of WAC meeting, April 12, 1944, *op. cit.;* "Women Drop Out," *Business Week,* August 21, 1943, p. 88; and "More Child Care," *Business Week,* August 26, 1944, pp. 41-42.

25. "Designed for 24-Hour Child Care," *Architectural Record* XCV (March 1944), pp. 84-88.

26. Margaret M. Romeo, "Shipyards and Playgrounds," *Recreation,* XXXVIII (January 1945), pp. 523-25.

27. "Wartime Care of Working Mothers' Children in Minneapolis," *Monthly Labor Review*, LVII (July 1943), pp. 107-8; and "Employee Counseling, a Report," 1944, folder entitled "Plant and Community Facilities for Working Women," WBA, Accession No. 54A-78, container 9. The writer was Dr. Edna Noble White.

28. G. T. Allen, "Eight Hour Orphans," *Saturday Evening Post*, CCXV (October 10, 1942), p. 20. The Newport News school board, for example, refused to operate a pre-school program because of its opposition to mothers working. In many cities, the Catholic Church was also active in lobbying against child-care centers.

29. Katherine Lenroot, "The Children's Bureau Program for the Care of Children of Working Mothers," folder entitled "III. Married Mothers B. Child Care Problem." WBA, Accession No. 58A-850, container 2; and Mary Anderson, "Women Workers in Wartime," speech, February 8, 1943, in folder entitled "Anderson, Mary—Speeches and Addresses," *op. cit.* A Children's Bureau Conference on the Day Care of Children of Working Mothers in 1941 asserted that "every effort should be made to safeguard home life," and declared that "mothers who remain at home to provide care for children are performing an essential patriotic service in the defense program."

30. Hadley Cantril, *Public Opinion, 1935-1946* (Princeton, 1951), p. 1046; E. Page to F. W. Holmes, June 17, 1943, FWA Archives, Box 86; "Women Workers in Ten Production Areas," *Women's Bureau Bulletin* No. 209 (Washington, 1946), p. 22; *Education for Victory*, II (June 20, 1944), p. 15; and Halling M. Dick to Rose Alschuler, n.d. Office of Community Welfare Services Archives, Box 3.

31. Alfred Toombs, "War Babies," *Woman's Home Companion*, LXXI (April 1944), p. 32; Washington *Post*, April 12, 1943; G. T. Allen, "Eight Hour Orphans," *op. cit.*

32. Katherine Glover, p. 17; Frank McSherry to Katherine Lenroot, March 10, 1942, Office of Community Welfare Services Archives (OCWS), Child Care Division, Box 2; statement by the Office of Defense, Health and Welfare Services, July 27, 1942, "The Day Care Program of the Federal Government," OCWS Archives, Box 1; Washington *Post*, October 10, 1943.

33. Charles Taft to Dr. John Voris, May 17, 1942, OCWS Archives, Box 2; Watson B. Miller to Senator Elbert D. Thomas, October 7, 1942, OCWS Archives, Box 1; transcript for the Northeastern conference on Services for Children of Working Mothers, October 29, 1942, OCWS Archives, Box 3; Glover p. 14; Franklin D. Roosevelt to Paul McNutt, August 28, 1942, OCWS Archives, Box 1. FDR wrote: "I do

not believe that further Federal funds should be provided for actual operation of child care programs at this time."

34. "Plans for Services to Children of Working Mothers Received from State Welfare and Education Departments," OCWS Archives, Box 1; Fred Hoehler, Director of the American Public Welfare Association, to Paul McNutt, n.d., OCWS Archives, Box 2. The Baruch report is quoted in a letter from the United Office and Professional Workers of America to James Byrnes, September 29, 1942, OCWS Archives, Box 2.

35. "Report of Conference on Women in War Industries," folder entitled "Conferences, Women's Bureau, General 1943, Women in War Industries," WBA, Accession No. 58A-850, container 3; Edna Noble White to Mary Norton, Mary Norton Papers, Rutgers University, Box 1; Baird Snyder to Fritz Lanham, March 16, 1942, OCWS Archives, Box 2; January 13, 1943, WAC meeting, *op. cit.*; and Elsie M. Bond, "Day Care of Children of Working Mothers in New York State During the War Emergency," *New York History*, XXVI (January 1945), pp. 51-77.

36. Transcript of conference, no date or title, in folder entitled "Day Care—Conferences, Meetings," OCWS Archives, Box 3. A representative from Elizabeth, New Jersey, had a similar reaction, saying that his people were "not going after Lanham funds; it is too complicated." Federal officials themselves were confused by the plethora of agencies involved. See John Studebaker to Charles Taft, October 26, 1943, OCWS Archives, Box 3.

37. Halling M. Dick to Rose Alschuler, *op. cit.*; and Washington *Post*, April 12, 1943.

38. Katherine Lenroot to the WPA, August 15, 1941, OCWS Archives, Box 3.

39. Florence Kerr to Charles Taft, October 24, 1942, in notebook called "Correspondence Record, FWA, 1941-2," in OCWS Archives; Emma Lundberg to Charles Schottland, January 29, 1942, FWA Archives, Box 3; and a memo from Rose Alschuler, February 8, 1943, FWA Archives, Box 3.

40. The FWA's indifference to welfare and education standards, the FSA charged, "amounted to discarding the entire experience of the field staff of our technical agencies." The FSA was especially concerned about the disruption of its existing good relationships with local communities. See memorandum of conference between Charles Taft and Florence Kerr, September 28, 1942; Robert E. Garrigan to Dean Snyder, September 19, 1942; Paul McNutt to General Philip Fleming,

September 5, 1942; Charles Taft to Harold Smith, May 27, 1943; Dean Snyder to Charles Taft, April 20, 1943; Charles Taft to Harold Smith, April 12, 1943; Florence Kerr to Charles Taft, October 24, 1942, all in FWA correspondence notebook, *op. cit.*

41. Eva Lapin, p. 22; Washington *Post*, October 12, 1943; Harold Schultz memorandum on FSA testimony, June 3, 1943, in FWA correspondence notebook; statement by Florence Kerr to the Thomas Committee, June 8, 1943, FWA Archives, Box 82; and testimony of Philip Fleming, typescript, FWA Archives, Box 86.

42. FDR to Paul McNutt, July 15, 1943; memorandum from the FSA, FWA and Bureau of the Budget to FDR, August 12, 1943, in FWA correspondence notebook, *op. cit.*

43. In an editorial, the Washington *Post* accused Mary Norton of planting a "booby trap in the path of the effective child care program formulated in the Thomas Bill." Noting that the Lanham Act had already proven to be ineffective, the *Post* said that Congresswoman Norton's amendment could be "regarded only as a device to enhance the power of the FWA in the incessant rivalry among Federal agencies for areas of control." Washington *Post*, October 12, 1943.

44. Alfred Toombs, "War Babies," *op. cit.*; statement by women in Congress on behalf of more funds for child care, February 25, 1944, Mary Norton Papers, Box 3; Philip Fleming to Samuel Rosenman, October 2, 1945, FWA Archives, Box 18; Eva Lapin, p. 19; "Women Workers in Ten Production Areas," *op. cit.*, p. 22; International Labor Office, p. 235. At least part of the problem was the failure of the officials involved to provide the information needed to make mothers confident that their children would receive adequate care. The FSA was greatly concerned about the danger of centers sprouting up which did not meet its standards, but it failed to "sell" those centers which it approved. Child-care advocates constantly took the government to task for not giving enough background to mothers on what went on in the centers, or involving them in the activities carried on. See *Education for Victory*, II (June 20, 1944), p. 15; statement by women's organizations, Washington *Post*, October 10, 1943.

45. Frieda Miller, "Women in the Labor Force," *Annals, op. cit.*

46. Alva Myrdal and Viola Klein, *Women's Two Roles* (London, 1956), p. 52.

## CHAPTER 8

1. Women's Advisory Committee, "Work for Women After the War," September 1, 1944, folder entitled "Postwar—Employment of Women,"

WBA, Accession No. 58A-850, container 2; WAC Press Release, October 12, 1944, WAC Papers, Box 138; WAC Press Release, December 2, and December 3, 1943, folder entitled "WAC," WBA, Accession No. 54A-78, container 11; *New York Times*, February 19, 1944.

2. War Manpower Commission, "Women in the Postwar World," April 1945 pamphlet, folder entitled "Postwar Miscellaneous Material," WBA, Accession No. 54A-78, container 11; Labor Department Circular Number 510, November 1, 1945, in folder entitled "Postwar—Women's Bureau—Labor Force Data," WBA, Accession No. 58A-850, container 2; Frieda S. Miller, "What's Become of Rosie the Riveter?" *New York Times Magazine*, May 5, 1946; "Do You Want Your Wife To Work After the War?" War Department Education Manual EM-31, in folder entitled "Postwar Miscellaneous Material," *op. cit.* Senator Truman's statement is cited in Georgina S. Burke, "The Economic Status of Women in 1945—The Postwar Outlook," American Association of University Women Papers, SL, folder 50.

3. Margaret Mead, "What's Wrong with the Family?" *Harpers*, CXC (April 1945), pp. 393-400; Willard Waller, "The Coming War on Women," *This Week*, February 18, 1945; A. G. Mezerik, "Getting Rid of Women," *Atlantic*, CLXXV (June 1945), pp. 79-83. The Crawford statement is quoted in Mezerik. It should be noted that practically all research done on the effects of maternal employment on children has concluded that there is no deleterious result. Delinquency frequently occurs in homes where mothers work, but is more often caused by broken marriages and a culture of poverty than by maternal employment itself. Indeed, some studies have suggested that when a mother works, the child more rapidly develops qualities of independence and self-reliance. For an anthology of research on maternal employment, see F. Ivan Nye and Lois W. Hoffman, eds., *The Employed Mother in America* (Chicago, 1963).

4. The Senator was Charles O. Andrews of Florida. See Lillian Sharpley, "Married Women at Work," unpublished master's essay, Columbia University, 1945, p. 42; "Types of Seniority Rules Relating Especially to Women Found in Trade Union Agreements"; and "Notes on Attitudes of Unions Toward Women," working papers, folder entitled "Postwar—Seniority," WBA, Accession No. 58A-850, container 2.

5. Margaret Pickel, "How Come No Jobs for Women?" *New York Times Magazine*, January 27, 1946; Edith Efron, "Woman Worker Defends Her Kind," *ibid.*, March 31, 1946; A. G. Mezerik, *op. cit.*; and WAC Transcript, October 29, 1943, WAC Archives, Box 136. The fact that women were not allowed to be included in the same job classifications

with men and were placed on separate seniority lists may have had
something to do with their reported indifference to union affairs.

6. The Gallup Poll showed 86 per cent of the American people opposed to
married women's work, the *Fortune* poll 63 per cent. See Hadley
Cantril, *Public Opinion, 1935-46* (Princeton, 1951), p. 1047; and the
*Fortune* survey, *Fortune*, XXXIV (August and September 1946).
For a further discussion of poll data, see below.

7. Margaret Hickey, "What's Ahead for Women Who Earn," March 14,
1946 speech, folder entitled "Conferences, Labor Advisory Committee, Women's Bureau, Postwar, 1945-52," WBA, Accession No. 58A-
850, container 3; and Frieda Miller, "War and Postwar Adjustments
of Women Workers," speech, December 4, 1944, folder entitled
"Postwar—Women's Bureau—Labor Force Data," *op. cit.*

8. International Labor Office, *The War and Women's Employment* (Montreal, 1946), pp. 265-66; "Women Workers in Ten Production Areas
and Their Postwar Employment Plans," *Women's Bureau Bulletin*
No. 209 (Washington, 1946), p. 5; A. G. Mezerik, *op. cit.*; "Can
Women Hold Their Jobs in Peacetime?" *Saturday Evening Post*,
CCXVI (March 4, 1944), pp. 28-29. The first worker's comments
were quoted in "Give Back Their Jobs," *Woman's Home Companion*,
LXX (October 1943), pp. 5-7; the second worker's remarks were
cited in a speech by Emma Guffey Miller, February 10, 1945, in the
Alma Lutz Papers, SL, Box 2.

9. "Employment of Women in the Early Postwar Period," *Women's Bureau
Bulletin* No. 211 (Washington, 1946), pp. 7-8; "High School Girls
Deny the Woman's Place Is in the Home," *Senior Scholastic*, XLVI
(March 5, 1945), p. 26; Mary Anderson, "Sixteen Million Women at
Work," *New York Times Magazine*, July 18, 1943. The *Journal* quo-
tation is from Dorothy Thompson, "Women and the Coming World,"
*Ladies Home Journal*, LX (October 1943), p. 6; the poll results are
in Nell Giles, "What About the Women?" *ibid.*, LXI (June 1944),
p. 23.

10. Elinore M. Herrick, "What About Women After the War?" *New York
Times Magazine*, September 5, 1943; Frieda Miller, "What's Become
of Rosie the Riveter?"; Constance Green, *The Role of Women as
Production Workers in the Connecticut Valley* (Northampton, 1946),
pp. 64, 67; International Labor Office, *The War and Women's Employment*, p. 262; "Data on Postwar Status of Women Workers," November 15, 1945, Women's Bureau working paper, folder entitled
"Postwar—General," WBA, Accession No. 58A-850, container 2; "Recent Trends Affecting the Employment of Women in Automobile

Manufacturing in Detroit," U.S. Department of Labor Statement, July 26, 1946, folder entitled "Postwar—Women's Bureau—Labor Force Data," *op. cit.*

11. Elizabeth Pidgeon to Mary Anderson, August 21, 1943, folder entitled "Postwar—General," WBA; Constance Williams to Jennie Mohr, February 6, 1947, folder entitled "Absenteeism—Study General," WBA, Accession No. 58A-850, container 5; International Labor Office, *The War and Women's Employment*, p. 262; Women's Bureau statement, May 1947, in folder entitled "Region XII—California, Oregon, Washington, Nevada, Arizona," WBA, Accession No. 58A-850, container 6.

12. NWTUL, "Women Workers in 1947," folder entitled "Postwar—Women's Bureau—Labor Force Data," WBA, *op. cit.*; and Women's Bureau survey of ex-war workers in Baltimore, March 26, 1946, folder entitled "Organizations—WTUL—*Life and Labor*," WBA, Accession No. 58A-850, container 3.

13. NWTUL, "Women Workers in 1947," *op. cit.*; Women's Bureau Press Release, January 12, 1947, folder entitled "Women's Bureau—Miscellaneous," WBA, WBA, Accession No. 58A-850, container 4.

14. Women's Bureau statement, May 1949, folder entitled "Region XII . . ." *op. cit.*; Alva Myrdal and Viola Klein, *Women's Two Roles* (London, 1956), p. 58; International Labor Office, *The War and Women's Employment*, p. 259; "Changes in Women's Occupations, 1940-50," *Women's Bureau Bulletin* No. 253 (Washington, 1954), pp. 37, 41; Frieda Miller, "Women in the Labor Force," *Annals* of the American Academy of Political and Social Science, CCLI (May 1947), p. 43. By 1952 there were 5.25 million women in clerical work, 3 million more than in 1940. See also National Manpower Council, *Womanpower* (New York, 1957), p. 112.

15. *New York Times,* September 7, 1953; Myrdal and Klein, *Women's Two Roles*, p. 58; Women's Bureau, "Women in the Labor Force, Including Working Mothers," May 10, 1949, folder entitled "Married Women's Employment III. Employed Mothers," WBA, Accession No. 58A-850, container 2. In April 1949, 4,330,000 mothers of children under eighteen were at work out of the 19,000,000 total employed. Almost 3,000,000 women at work had children under twelve.

16. Women's Bureau, "Labor Day Message, 1953," folder entitled "Statements and Addresses by Frieda S. Miller," WBA, Accession No. 58A-850, container 3; Myrdal and Klein, *Women's Two Roles*, p. 60; "Changes in Women's Occupations, 1940-1950," vii; Chase Going Woodhouse, "Women at Home and in the Community," in Beverly Cassara, ed., *American Women: Their Changing Image* (Boston,

1962). In the decade of the forties, the number of women thirty-five to fifty years old in the work force increased 60 per cent, but women of that age in the population grew only 17 per cent.

17. Talcott Parsons, "Age and Sex in United States Social Structure," *American Sociological Review*, VII (October 1942), pp. 604-17; National Manpower Council, *Womanpower*, pp. 78, 80, 114; Sanford Dornbusch and David Heer, "The Evaluation of Work by Females," *American Journal of Sociology*, LXIII (July 1957), pp. 27-29; and Lawrence J. Sharp, "Employment Status of Mothers and Some Aspects of Mental Illness," *American Sociological Review*, XXV (October 1960), pp. 414-17. Moreover, the employment of middle-class women increased rather than contracted over time. For a discussion of the 1950's, see Chapter 9.

18. National Manpower Council, *Womanpower*, pp. 3, 9.

19. Susan B. Anthony IV, "We Women Throw Our Votes Away," *Saturday Evening Post*, CCXXI (July 17, 1948), p. 23; "Women or Doctors," *Newsweek*, XXVI (November 12, 1945), p. 84; H. Whitman, "M.D. For Men Only?" *Woman's Home Companion*, LXIII (November 1946), pp. 32-33; Marguerite Zapoleon, "Education and Employment Opportunities for Women," *Annals, op. cit.*; Margaret Hickey, "What's Ahead for the Woman Who Earns?" *op. cit.*; "Fortune Survey," *op. cit.*

20. "Importance of Equal Pay for Women and Men to Postwar Objectives," Women's Bureau working paper, folder entitled "Equal Pay—WLB," WBA, Accession No. 58A-850, container 4; Women's Bureau pamphlet on the National Conference on Equal Pay for Equal Work, May 1952; and Women's Bureau, "Equal Pay Indicators," working paper, April 1952, both in folder entitled "Equal Pay No. 9," WBA, Accession No. 58A-850, container 4.

21. "Equal Pay Indicators," *op. cit.*; *Labor News Digest*, December 16, 1953, in folder entitled "Equal Pay Set of Documents and Important Data," WBA, Accession No. 58A-850; container 4; Elizabeth Baker, *Technology and Women's Work* (New York, 1964), p. 414; Alice K. Leopold, "Federal Equal Pay Legislation," *Labor Law Journal* (January 1955), pp. 8, 21, 27; "The American Woman: Her Changing Role," *Women's Bureau Bulletin* No. 224 (Washington, 1948), p. 17. In 1952, twelve states had equal pay laws, but only New York had adequate enforcement provisions.

22. Federal Works Agency Release, August 27, 1945; Earl Warren to FWA, September 12, 1945, and draft reply to same, both in FWA Archives, Series 6, Box 18; Mary Norton to Harry S Truman, September 28,

1945, Mary Norton Papers, Rutgers University, Box 1; Elizabeth
Christman to Helen Gahagan Douglas, September 21, 1945, WTUL
Papers, Library of Congress, Box 10.

23. Elsie M. Bond, "Day Care of Children of Working Mothers in New
York State During the War Emergency," *New York History*, XXVI
(January 1945), pp. 51-77. In addition to New York, Washington,
and Massachusetts passed legislation providing temporary appropriations for day-care centers. Usually, however, the amount of money
allocated was so small that it had little effect. In Massachusetts, for
example, the state promised to reimburse staff salaries by up to 40
per cent, but a limit of $2,500 was placed on the amount of public
assistance which could be given to any one center. Elsewhere, public
opposition blocked an expansion of day-care facilities. In the eyes of
many people, child-care centers suggested the destruction of the institution of motherhood.

24. The above is based on newspaper clippings, public documents, and letters contained in the Child Care Parents Association of New York,
Papers, SL, Box 1. Among the sources used are the following:
*New York Post*, January 12, 1947; *New York Times*, December 8,
1947; *PM*, February 6, 1948; April 7, 1947; New York *Herald Tribune*, January 1, 1948; New York *World-Telegram*, February 24-
March 1, 1948; Welfare Department Press Release, September 22,
1947; statement of the New York City Welfare Commissioner, Benjamin Fielding, to the New York State Youth Commission, January
22, 1948. The Child Care Parents Association favored retention of
child-care facilities, but viewed them as essentially educational rather
than custodial in nature.

25. Harry Truman to Emma Guffey Miller, April 20, 1944; Henry Wallace
to Emma Guffey Miller, January 27, 1944, in Alma Lutz Papers,
SL, Box 2; New York *Herald Tribune*, July 1, 1945, clipping,
Florence Kitchelt Papers, SL, Box 2. The congressman quoted is
Lester Ludlow of Indiana. Other notables to endorse the amendment
were Arthur Schlesinger, Clare Boothe Luce, Carl Sandburg, and
James Farley. Both national parties pledged adoption of the amend-
ment in 1944, and all four parties endorsed it in 1948.

26. *Newsweek*, "Rights for Women," XXVIII (July 29, 1946), p. 17; and
*Newsweek*, "Outsmarting the Ladies," XXXV (February 6, 1950),
p. 20. From a feminist point of view, the nation appeared to be committed, at least in its official actions, to a perpetuation of women's
legal inferiority. In 1948, for example, the United States delegate to
the United Nations Social and Economic Council voted against a
resolution providing for "equal rights with men in employment and

remuneration, leisure, social insurance and professional training," and the United States was the only nation among twenty-two inter-American states to fail to sign a convention guaranteeing women the same civil rights as men.

27. Cantril, *Public Opinion*, p. 1047; "The *Fortune* Survey," *op. cit.*

28. *Ibid.*

29. *Life and Labor*, No. 92, May 1948, WBA, folder entitled "Organizations WTUL—*Life and Labor*"; Mary Anderson, "The Postwar Role of American Women," folder entitled "Addresses and Statements of Mary Anderson," WBA, Accession No. 58A-850, container 3; Frieda Miller, "What's Become of Rosie the Riveter?" The Bureau of Labor Statistics estimated that a family of four required $3,500 to live adequately, yet the highest paid workers in industry received only $4,000 a year.

30. National Manpower Council, *Work in the Lives of Married Women* (New York, 1958), p. 201; and a speech by Frieda Miller, March 1, 1951, folder entitled "Addresses and Statements by Frieda Miller," *op. cit.*

31. Frieda Miller, "Women in the Labor Force," *Annals, op. cit.* The Lockheed psychologist was quoted in Gertrude Samuels, "Why Do Twenty Million Women Work?" *New York Times Magazine,* September 9, 1951.

32. Samuels, *op. cit.*; Miller, "Women in the Labor Force."

33. "The American Woman: Her Changing Role," *op. cit.*, p. 65; Margaret Mead, "Modern Marriage: The Danger Point," *Nation*, CLXXVII (October 31, 1953), pp. 348-50. For other comments similar to those of Mead, see Kingsley Davis, "The American Family," *New York Times Magazine*, September 30, 1951.

34. The sociologist William J. Goode has observed that "when one or more family tasks are entrusted to another agency . . . the change can be made only with the support of much ideological fervor, and sometimes political pressure as well." In the United States, neither element was present. See William J. Goode, *The Family* (Englewood Cliffs, 1964), p. 5.

35. Carl Degler, "Revolution Without Ideology: The Changing Place of Women in America," in Robert J. Lifton, ed., *The Woman in America* (Boston, 1967), pp. 193-210.

*CHAPTER 9*

1. "American Woman's Dilemma," *Life*, XXII (June 16, 1947), pp. 101-12.

2. "Fortune Survey: Women in America," *Fortune*, XXXIV (August

1946), pp. 5-6; John Willig, "Class of '34 (Female) Fifteen Years Later," *New York Times Magazine*, June 12, 1949.

3. For a discussion of the Negro family, see Jessie Bernard, *Marriage and Family Among Negroes* (Englewood Cliffs, New Jersey, 1966), especially pp. 73, 90, 98; E. Franklin Frazier, *The Negro Family in the United States* (New York, 1949); and Daniel Patrick Moynihan, "The Negro Family," in Lee Rainwater and William Yancey, *The Moynihan Report and the Politics of Controversy* (Cambridge, Mass., 1967). On the white family, see Mirra Komarovsky, *Blue-Collar Marriage* (New York, 1962); Herbert Gans, *The Urban Villagers* (Glencoe, 1962), especially Chapter 3; and John P. Spiegel, "The Resolution of Role Conflict Within the Family," in Norman W. Bell and Ezra F. Vogel, eds., *A Modern Introduction to the Family* (Glencoe, 1960), pp. 361-81.

4. Frances Levison, "What the Experts Say," *Life, op. cit.*, p. 112; Margaret Perry Bruton, "Present-Day Thinking on the Woman Question," *Annals* of the American Academy of Political and Social Science, CCLI (May 1947), pp. 10-16; and Margaret Mead, "What Women Want," *Fortune*, XXXIV (December 1946), pp. 172-75.

5. Philip Wylie, *Generation of Vipers* (New York, 1942), Chapters 5 and 11. Wylie wrote in a manner designed to provoke and titillate rather than persuade. For example, he described "mom" as "twenty-five pounds overweight [without] sex appeal enough to budge a hermit ten paces off a rock ledge. . . . She plays bridge with the stupid voracity of a hammerhead shark, which cannot see what it is trying to gobble but never stops snapping its jaws. . . . On Saturday night . . . she loses count of her drinks and is liable to get a little tiddly, which is to say shot or blind. But it is her man who worries about where to acquire the money while she worries only about how to spend it. . . . I have researched the moms to the beady brains behind their beady eyes and to the stones in the center of their fat hearts. . . . Learning the hard way, I have found out that [their devotion] is the same devotion, which, at the altar, splits the lamb from his nave to his chops." Notwithstanding such language, it is difficult to determine where Wylie stood on the issue of women's rights. His analysis lent itself just as readily to a feminist as an anti-feminist point of view.

6. Edward A. Strecker, *Their Mothers' Sons* (Philadelphia, 1946). The review appeared in the *Annals*, May 1947, p. 187, and the author was Ray H. Abrams of the University of Pennsylvania.

7. Ferdinand Lundberg and Marynia Farnham, *Modern Woman: The Lost*

*Sex* (New York, 1947), Chapters 4-6. The quotations are from p. 105 and p. 10. Lundberg was a journalist, Farnham a psychiatrist.

8. Lundberg and Farnham, pp. 144-59.

9. Lundberg and Farnham, pp. 143, 149, 151, 159, 161-63, 165, 169, 178, 196.

10. Lundberg and Farnham, pp. 166, 319, 237, 275, 278, 30, 264-65, 11, 235. "People who voluntarily refrain from having children are deviating from normal behavior," Lundberg and Farnham said.

11. Lundberg and Farnham, pp. 298-321, especially p. 319.

12. Lundberg and Farnham, pp. 355-78.

13. Agnes Meyer, "Women Aren't Men," *Atlantic*, CLXXXVI (August 1950), pp. 32-36; and Ashley Montagu, "The Triumph and Tragedy of the American Woman," *Saturday Review*, XLI (September 27, 1958), pp. 13-15. For a discussion of women's magazines in this period, see Betty Friedan, *The Feminine Mystique* (New York, 1963), pp. 28-61. Not all the reaction to *Modern Woman* was favorable, of course, and some of the negative response was biting. After reading the book, Dorothy Parker said: "there is something curiously flattering in being described by the adjective 'lost.' . . . I find myself digging my toe in the sand and whispering, 'Oh Dr. Farnham and Mr. Lundberg, come on now—you say that to every sex.' " More to the point, Dorothy Sayer, the mystery writer commented: "Probably no man has ever troubled to imagine how strange his life would appear to himself if it were unrelentingly assessed in terms of his maleness. . . . If from school and lecture-room, press and pulpit, he heard the persistent outpouring of a shrill and scolding voice, bidding him remember his biological function." See Frances Levison, "What the Experts Say," *op. cit.*

14. Lynn White, *Educating Our Daughters* (New York, 1950), pp. 18, 32-47, 49, 90-97; Lynn White, "New Yardsticks for Women's Education," *Journal of the American Association of University Women* (fall 1947), copy of address in Women's Bureau Archives.

15. White, *Educating Our Daughters*, pp. 47, 66, 72, 86.

16. James M. Wood, "The Education of Women," *Clubwoman*, XXV (November 1945), p. 6; Anne G. Parnell, "A Nation's Strength Begins in the Home," *Vital Speeches*, XVIII (December 15, 1951), pp. 145-47; White, *Educating Our Daughters*, p. 49. At Stephens, Wood implemented his plan for a new kind of women's education. He boasted of building the finest ballroom in Missouri for his students, imported experts in dress design and grooming, and set up a clinic on facial make-up. Stephens also taught speech to all its students and had an

elaborate program of home economics, interior decoration, and family study. For a further discussion of his viewpoint, see the James Madison Wood Papers, Oral History Project, Special Collections, Columbia University.

17. For a discussion of the aptitude scores, see Mirra Komarovsky, *Women in the Modern World* (New York, 1953), pp. 19-30; White, p. 42; and Viola Klein, *The Feminine Character* (London, 1946), pp. 104-12. Everyone agrees there is some difference on these tests between the sexes. The controversy arises over the interpretation of the differences and what part is played by cultural forces. It seems significant, for example, that the distinctions between sexes become greater as the socialization process continues. The I.Q. scores of girls in high school go down substantially, relative to what they were at an earlier age—a fact which many attribute to the emphasis placed during adolescence on the need for a woman to find a man and settle down to marriage.

18. For one such study, see Evelyn Ellis, "Social Psychological Correlates of Upward Social Mobility Among Unmarried Career Women," *American Sociological Review*, XVII (October 1952), pp. 558-63. Ellis associated the psychological maladjustment with childhood rejection rather than specific sex problems, however.

19. See John Willig, "Class of '34 Fifteen Years Later," *op. cit.*; and Komarovsky, *Women in the Modern World*, p. 13. Once again the evidence is mixed, however. The most comprehensive survey of women college graduates found that only 2 per cent would take a different course if they had a chance. Moreover, even of the Barnard students who were dissatisfied, only 14 per cent proposed courses in homemaking skills, and they desired just a few additions to the liberal arts curriculum. See also Ernest Havemann and Patricia West, *They Went to College* (New York, 1952).

20. The material in this section is based upon Viola Klein, *The Feminine Character*, pp. 125-42; Mirra Komarovsky, *Women in the Modern World*, pp. 31-47; Helen Deutsch, *The Psychology of Women* (New York, 1944), Volume I; and Clara Thompson, *Psychoanalysis: Evolution and Development* (New York, 1950). The quotations are from Deutsch, pp. 290-91. For a critique of Freudian thought on women, see Kate Millett, *Sexual Politics* (New York, 1970), pp. 176-203.

21. Peter Berger, "Social Roles: Society in Man," in Dennis H. Wrong and Harry L. Gracey, eds., *Readings in Introductory Sociology* (New York, 1967), pp. 107-17; Margaret Mead, *Sex and Temperament in Three Primitive Societies* (New York, 1935), p. 280; Margaret Mead, "What Women Want," *op. cit.*

22. Elizabeth K. Nottingham, "Toward an Analysis of the Effects of Two World Wars on the Role and Status of Middle Class Women in the English Speaking World," *American Sociological Review*, XII (December 1947), pp. 666-75.

23. Florence Kluckhohn, "Cultural Factors in Social Work Practice and Education," *Social Service Review*, XXV (March 1951), pp. 38-48.

24. Mirra Komarovsky, *Women in the Modern World*, pp. 19-30, 41; Mirra Komarovsky, "Cultural Contradictions and Sex Roles," *American Journal of Sociology*, LII (November 1946), pp. 184-89. Again, it should be kept in mind that Komarovsky and most of the other persons discussed here are talking about middle-class, educated women. To that extent, the entire debate over the "woman problem" in the postwar period reflected a class bias. Komarovsky herself, of course, has tried to correct for that imbalance by her later work on "blue-collar" wives.

25. Komarovsky, *Women in the Modern World*, pp. 55, 63, 67; and Komarovsky, "Cultural Contradictions. . . ." Paul Wallin replicated the Komarovsky study of dating patterns in a coeducational school, and although he found that the problem seemed less momentous to the girls he sampled, he also found that 46 per cent of the girls admitted to playing dumb while on dates. See Paul Wallin, "Cultural Contradictions and Sex Roles: A Repeat Study," *American Sociological Review*, XV (April 1950), pp. 288-93.

26. Komarovsky, *Women in the Modern World*, pp. 100-165, especially p. 106. See also Margaret Perry Bruton, "Present-Day Thinking on the Woman Problem," *op. cit.*; and Dorothy Barclay, "What's Wrong with the Family?" *New York Times Magazine*, September 16, 1951.

27. Komarovsky, "Cultural Contradictions and Sex Roles."

28. "The American Woman," *Life*, XXI (October 21, 1946), p. 36; and "The Woman Dilemma," *Life, op. cit.*

29. Della Cyrus, "Why Mothers Fail," *Atlantic*, LXXIX (March 1947).

30. Viola Klein, *The Feminine Character*, pp. 6-36, 163-82. For a discussion of the "marginal man" concept, see Everett C. Hughes, "Social Change and Status Protest: An Essay on the Marginal Man," *Phylon*, X (December 1949). See also Gunnar Myrdal, *An American Dilemma* (New York, 1944), Vol. II, pp. 1073-78.

31. Bruno Bettelheim, "Growing Up Female," *Harper's*, CCXV (October 1962), pp. 120-28. For a discussion of the anthropological evidence see Bell and Vogel, *A Modern Introduction to the Family*, especially George Peter Murdock, "The Universality of the Nuclear Family," pp. 37-44, and Clyde Kluckhohn, "Variations in the Human Family," pp. 45-51. See also William N. Stephens, *The Family in Cross-*

*Cultural Perspective* (New York, 1963). For an interesting assessment of research on social conditioning, see Naomi Weisstein, " 'Kinder, Kuche, Kirche' as Scientific Law: Psychology Constructs the Female," in Robin Morgan, ed., *Sisterhood Is Powerful* (New York, 1970), pp. 205-20; and Jo Freeman, Growing Up Girlish," *Transaction*, VIII (November-December 1970), pp. 36-43. It has become somewhat fashionable of late to criticize sociologists—especially functionalists—as arch defenders of the status quo. To some extent, the criticism is justified, particularly insofar as change is defined as "dysfunctional." On the other hand, the sociological perspective on the woman problem represented a substantial advance over previous thinking. Not only do theories of role conflict and conditioning provide an important insight into the roots of the problem. They also give a clue as to how change can occur. On balance, then, it would seem that the social sciences have made a positive contribution, even from the point of view of staunch feminists.

32. "Baby Boom," *Reporter*, XIII (August 11, 1955), p. 4; Jessie Bernard, *Academic Women* (University Park, Pennsylvania, 1964), p. 215; "That Women in a Gray Flannel Suit," *New York Times Magazine*, February 12, 1956; Agnes Johnston, "What Family Teamwork Did For Us," *Parents*, XXIX (November 1954), pp. 44-45; and Dorothy Barclay, "Creative Work Can Unite the Family," *New York Times Magazine*, April 4, 1954.

33. Ben Wattenberg, "The Nonsense Explosion," *New Republic*, April 4 and 11, 1970, pp. 18-23; William Peterson, "New American Family," *Commentary*, XXI (January 1956), pp. 1-6; Dorothy Barclay, "Changing Ideals in Homemaking," *New York Times Magazine*, July 19, 1953; "How To Be Happy and Stay Out of Debt," *Newsweek*, XLVIII (December 17, 1956), p. 83; "Life with Father," *New York Times Magazine*, January 23, 1952.

34. Sloan Wilson, "The Woman in the Gray Flannel Suit," *New York Times Magazine*, January 15, 1952; "Blueprint for a Wife," *Newsweek*, XLIV (October 4, 1954), p. 81. William H. Whyte helped to make the "corporation wife" a popular symbol of business control over American life in his study of *The Organization Man* (New York, 1956). According to Whyte many companies scrutinized the credentials of executive wives as closely as those of their husbands in making personnel decisions. The wife not only provided her husband with comfort and reassurance at home, but also played an important role in his career through entertaining. For a critical point of view see Ethel Ward McLemore, "Manifesto from a Corporation Wife," *Fortune*, XLV (March 1952), p. 83.

35. National Manpower Council, *Work in the Lives of Married Women* (New York, 1957), p. 199; Elizabeth Baker, *Technology and Women's Work* (New York, 1964), vii; National Manpower Council, *Womanpower* (New York, 1957), pp. 17, 72; and F. Ivan Nye and Lois Wladis Hoffman, eds., *The Employed Mother in America* (Chicago, 1963), pp. 7-9.

36. Nye and Hoffman, pp. 9-11; Sanford M. Dornbusch and David M. Heer, "The Evaluation of Work by Females," *American Journal of Sociology*, LXV (July 1957), pp. 27-29; Lawrence J. Sharp, "Employment Status of Mothers and Some Aspects of Mental Illness," *American Sociological Review*, XXV (October 1960), pp. 44-47; Jacob Schiffman, "Marital and Family Characteristics of Workers," *Monthly Labor Review*, LXXXIV (April 1961), p. 263; James N. Morgan, Ismail Sirageldin and Nancy Baerwaldt, *Productive Americans* (Ann Arbor, 1966), p. 48; Alva Myrdal and Viola Klein, *Women's Two Roles* (New York, 1968), p. 64; National Manpower Council, *Womanpower*, p. 21.

37. Jeanne L. Hafstrom and Marilyn M. Dunsing, "A Comparison of Economic Choices of One-Earner and Two-Earner Families," *Journal of Marriage and the Family*, XXVII (August 1965), pp. 403-9.

38. Hafstrom and Dunsing, *op. cit.*; David M. Gover, "Socio-Economic Differentials in the Relationship Between Marital Adjustment and Wife's Employment Status," *Journal of Marriage and the Family*, XXV (November 1963), pp. 452-57; Marion G. Sobol, "Commitment to Work," in Nye and Hoffman, pp. 40-63.

39. Mirra Komarovsky, *Blue-Collar Marriage* (New York, 1962), pp. 62-73; and Robert Weiss and Nancy Samuelson, "Social Roles of American Women: Their Contribution to a Sense of Usefulness and Importance," *Journal of Marriage and the Family*, XX (November 1958), pp. 358-66. Among non-employed women, 55 per cent found housework a basis for feeling important. On the other hand, both workers and non-workers valued their family role in equal proportions.

40. Myrdal and Klein, *Women's Two Roles*, pp. 83-84, 87; Arnold M. Rose, "Social Problems in Mass Society," *Antioch Review* (September 1950); David Riesman, *The Lonely Crowd* (New York, 1953), pp. 300, 322; Margaret Mead, *Male and Female* (New York, 1949), pp. 332-38. In the Weiss and Samuelson survey previously cited, the proportion of women who found their family role important fell from 60 per cent to 40 per cent after the children went to school.

41. Herman R. Lantz, *The People of Coaltown* (New York, 1958), Chapter 8; Mirra Komarovsky, *The Unemployed Man and His Family* (New

York, 1940); Jessie Bernard, *Marriage and the Family Among Negroes, op. cit.*; and Daniel Patrick Moynihan, "The Negro Family," *op. cit.*

42. Mildred Weil, "An Analysis of the Factors Influencing Married Women's Actual or Planned Work Participation," *American Sociological Review*, XVI (January 1951), pp. 91-96; Lois Hoffman, "Parental Power Relations and the Division of Household Tasks," in Nye and Hoffman, pp. 215-30; Robert O. Blood, "The Husband-Wife Relationship," in Nye and Hoffman, pp. 282-305; Robert Hamblin and Robert Blood, "The Effect of the Wife's Employment on the Family Power Structure," *Social Forces*, XXXVI (May 1958), pp. 347-52.

43. David Heer, "Dominance and the Working Wife," *Social Forces*, XXXVI (May 1958), pp. 341-47; Blood, "The Husband-Wife Relationship," *op. cit.*; Lois Hoffman, "Parental Power Relations and the Division of Household Tasks," *op. cit.*; Robert Blood and Donald Wolfe, *Husbands and Wives: The Dynamics of Married Living* (Glencoe, 1960); Robert O. Blood, "The Measurement and Bases of Family Power: A Rejoinder," *Journal of Marriage and the Family*, XXV (November 1963), pp. 475-78; and Robert O. Blood, "Employment of Married Women," *Journal of Marriage and the Family*, XXVII (February 1965), pp. 43-47.

44. Elizabeth Baker, *Technology and Women's Work*, p. 437.

45. *Scientific News Letter*, December 17, 1955, p. 398.

*CHAPTER 10*

1. *Harper's*, XCXXV (October, 1962), pp. 115-19. The *Harper's* editors noted that although modern women shunned the slogans of the old-fashioned feminists, they were troubled by the same questions which had bothered women's rights agitators. A kind of "crypto-feminism" had appeared on the American scene as a result of the mechanized home, the gift of "uncommitted hours," and the reality of facing thirty or more years in the home after the children had grown.

2. The quotation is from a college-educated mother who was interviewed by Mirra Komarovsky. The whole interview, which takes up three pages, is a poignant description of some of the frustrations involved in the task of being a full-time mother and housewife. See Mirra Komarovsky, *Women in the Modern World* (Boston, 1953), pp. 108-10.

3. Betty Friedan, *The Feminine Mystique*, pp. 28-61, 95-141, 197-223.

Friedan based her study of "the sexual sell" on the files of the Institute for Motivational Research, a market research firm. In a 1945 survey, the company found an increased desire for emancipation among women, and advised its client—a women's magazine—to take steps to win these women back by glamorizing the work of the home. The results of such studies seemed to fit Friedan's assertion that women's magazines drastically changed the image of females they presented after 1945. For a contrary view of women's magazines before 1945, see Chapter 5.

4. Ellen and Kenneth Keniston, "An American Anachronism: The Image of Women and Work," *American Scholar*, XXXIII (summer 1964), pp. 355-75; and Alice Rossi, "Equality Between the Sexes: An Immodest Proposal," in Robert J. Lifton, ed., *The Woman in America* (Boston, 1967), pp. 98-143. The Rossi essay was originally published in *Daedalus* in 1964.

5. Rossi, pp. 113-14; Ellen and Kenneth Keniston, p. 362; Friedan, pp. 224-46. Two psychiatrists in the affluent suburbs of Bergen County, New Jersey, reported that "the number of disturbed young wives was more than half again as big as the number of young husbands, and three times as big as any other group." Suicides among women over forty-five also increased, as did psychiatric hospitalization among women whose children had grown and left home. Friedan attributed the increased number of nervous breakdowns among women in the 1950's to the "emptiness" of their lives. See Richard E. Gordon and Katherine Gordon, "Psychiatric Problems of a Rapidly Growing Suburb," *American Medical Association Archives of Neurology and Psychiatry*, 1958, discussed in Friedan, pp. 282, 290.

6. The quotation is from Friedan, pp. 16-17. See also pp. 271-325. Friedan based her discussion of women's identity crisis on the works of Erik Erikson, David Riesman, and Rollo May.

7. Rossi, pp. 114, 125-39; Friedan, pp. 316-63, 165-69. See also Nevitt Sanford, "Personality Development During the College Years," *Journal of Social Issues*, XII (December 1956); A. H. Maslow, "Dominance, Personality and Social Behavior in Women," *Journal of Social Psychology*, X (March 1939), pp. 3-39; and Maslow, "Self Esteem (Dominance Feeling) and Sexuality in Women," *Journal of Social Psychology*, XVI (September 1942), pp. 259-94.

8. Almost 90 per cent of the women polled called childbirth the "most satisfying moment" of their lives. On the other hand, the poll also contained contrary evidence which gave some credence to Friedan's assertion of discontent. Almost 40 per cent of the respondents, for

example, admitted having wondered whether they would be better
off single, 36 per cent were not as happy as their mothers, and only
10 per cent wanted their daughters to live the same kind of lives that
they did. Gallup gave two "typical" quotes of why childbirth was so
valued. One woman said it was "the one time in my life when everything was right," and another asserted, "you've done something that's
recognized as a good thing to do, and you're the center of attention."
Alice Rossi has contended that such quotations "tell us a good deal
about the underlying attitude toward the thousands of days on which
no child is born; things are *not* all right, and there must be some
sense of being on the sidelines, of having a low level of self-esteem, if
childbirth is important because 'society views it as good,' and it is
the only time in her life when she is the important center of attention." Of course the lives of many men were also lacking in "big mo-
ments." See George Gallup and Evan Hill, "The American Woman,"
*Saturday Evening Post* (December 22, 1962); and Alice Rossi, p. 127.

9. For a discussion of the differences between middle-class and lower-class
   women, see Mirra Komarovsky, *Blue-Collar Marriage* (New York,
   1962).

10. Friedan, pp. 53-54. For a discussion of nineteenth-century ideas, see
    Aileen Kraditor, *The Ideas of the Woman Suffrage Movement, 1890-
    1920* (New York, 1965), pp. 14-42, 96-122; and Barbara Welter,
    "The Cult of True Womanhood: 1820-1860," *American Quarterly,*
    XVIII (summer 1966). In a 1933 article which anticipated Friedan,
    Elizabeth Bancroft Schlesinger spoke of the "superabundance of sen-
    timentality" in women's journals in the 1920's and 1930's. She pointed
    out that such magazines contained "virtually no discussion of public
    affairs" and played to all the romantic fantasies of their readers. See
    Elizabeth Bancroft Schlesinger, "They Say Women Are Emancipated,"
    *New Republic* (December 13, 1933), pp. 125-27.

11. Susan Brownmiller, "Sisterhood Is Powerful," *New York Times Maga-
    zine*, March 15, 1970; and Allan Matusow, "From Civil Rights to
    Black Power: The Case of SNCC, 1960-1966," in Barton J. Bern-
    stein and Allan Matusow, eds., *Twentieth Century America* (New
    York, 1969). Just as the civil rights movement gave rise to a more
    militant black nationalist drive, so the "integrationist" woman's move-
    ment of the middle 1960's was gradually replaced by a stronger em-
    phasis on sexual separatism. Many women's groups excluded men
    from their meetings, and the idea of all-female communes gained
    increased currency among some women's rights followers. For a per-
    ceptive treatment of the issue, see Vivian Gornick, "The Light of

Liberation Can Be Blinding," *Village Voice*, December 10, 1970.

12. See Crane Brinton, *Anatomy of a Revolution* (New York, 1938); and Stanley Elkins, *Slavery* (New York, 1963). Elkins points out that in a "closed system" which allows the enslaved person no contact with a wider world, the victim internalizes the image of himself which he is expected to have. Friedan assumes that the home was also a "closed system," and that like the German concentration camps, it infantilized the inmates within by severely limiting their horizons. David Riesman, in contrast, see change as crucial to more change. "The situation of women has improved in all sectors," he said in 1970, "and improvement, as always, leads to heightened expectations." See "Women's Lib: The War on Sexism," *Newsweek* (March 23, 1970).

13. *New York Times*, October 10, 1970; Elizabeth Waldman, "Changes in the Labor Force Activity of Women," *Monthly Labor Review*, XCIII (June 1970), p. 15; "Who Are the Working Mothers?" Women's Bureau, May 1970.

14. Ruth E. Hartley, "Children's Concepts of Male and Female Roles," *Merrill-Palmer Quarterly*, VI (January 1959-60), pp. 83-91; Selma M. Matthews, "The Effects of Mothers' Out-of-Home Employment Upon Children's Ideas and Attitudes," *Journal of Applied Psychology* XVIII (February 1954), pp. 116-36; Elizabeth Douvan, "Employment and the Adolescent," F. Ivan Nye and Lois Wladis Hoffman, eds., *The Employed Mother in America* (Chicago, 1963), pp. 142-64; Lois Hoffman, "Effects on Children: Summary and Discussion," in Nye and Hoffman, pp. 196-202. Hoffman notes that "adolescence is a time when children need a comfortable balance between warmth and guidance on the one hand and autonomy on the other. . . . [Studies] support the present view that the working mother is more likely to encourage independence in the child."

15. Hoffman, Douvan, and Hartley, *op. cit.* Summarizing the evidence, Lois Hoffman writes: "Maternal employment may contribute to a greater admiration of the mother, a concept of the female role which includes less restriction and a wider range of activities, and a self-concept which incorporates these aspects of the female role."

16. Leland J. Axelson, "The Marital Adjustment and Marital Role Definitions of Husbands of Working and Nonworking Wives," *Journal of Marriage and the Family*, XXV (May 1963), pp. 189-95; Robert O. Blood, Jr., "The Measurement and Bases of Family Power: A Rejoinder," *Journal of Marriage and the Family*, XXV (November 1963), pp. 475-78; David M. Heer, "The Measurement and Bases of

Family Power: An Overview," *Journal of Marriage and the Family,* XXV (May 1963), pp. 133-39.

17. Even if most women were grouped in second echelon jobs, moreover, it would be a mistake to underestimate the significance of their participation in the labor market. As Viola Klein has pointed out, most minority groups have started their economic experience by monopolizing marginal areas of the economy. "New crafts, new industries, or new arts," she writes, "afford the opportunities for hitherto excluded social groups to take part in the life of the community and to rise in the social scale." Viola Klein, *The Feminine Character* (London, 1946), p. 19.

18. David Riesman, "Two Generations," in Lifton, ed., *op. cit.,* p. 97. See also Priscilla Robertson, "My Great-Grandmothers Were Happy," *American Scholar,* XXIII (spring 1954), pp. 185-96.

19. See "Women's Lib: The War on Sexism," *op. cit.;* Susan Brownmiller, *op. cit.;* Paul Wilkes, "Betty Friedan: 'Mother Superior' of the Liberation Movement," *New York Times Magazine,* November 29, 1970; and Robin Morgan, ed., *Sisterhood Is Powerful* (New York, 1970).

20. Day-care centers and abortion reform, for example, are far more likely to help welfare mothers and ghetto dwellers than suburban women who have the money to afford nursery schools or private abortions.

21. Almost every national magazine featured stories on the woman's movement and in addition to new specials on feminism, television talk shows frequently spotlighted debates on women's liberation. Although in most cases the movement was being exploited for entertainment purposes, the television audience could not help but be aware of the feminist protest, and that fact alone was the biggest asset the movement had.

22. *New York Times,* March 17, 1969; May 3 and 15, 1970; July 14, 1970. Although the evidence was hardly conclusive, it appeared that some women's magazines were also changing. Under the leadership of journalist Shana Alexander, for example, *McCall's* seemed to be shifting its orientation away from fiction and romance toward material on women's rights, politics, and social protest. In a retrospective editorial, Shana Alexander called 1970 a "seismic year for women" and demanded greater equality for females at every level of professional life. She also blasted the conditioning process whereby women were taught that "any achievement, power, accomplishment, or position outside the home . . . threatens loss of femininity."

23. *The Gallup Opinion Index* (September 1970), Report No. 63; and George Gallup and Evan Hill, "The American Woman," *op. cit.*

24. *New York Times*, August 1, 1970; November 8, 1970; September 22, 1970; November 11, 1970. Ironically, the operative statute under which much of this action took place—Title VII of the 1964 Civil Rights Act—was not initially drafted to include women within its protection. The proposal to broaden the coverage to females was sponsored by Howard Smith of Virginia in an attempt to embarrass Northern liberals and weaken chances of passing the bill. Once enacted, however, the sex clause became a strong weapon for women protestors. See Caroline Bird, *Born Female* (New York, 1968), pp. 1-10.

25. *New York Times*, April 11, 1971; September 22, 1970.

26. *New York Times*, December 10, 1971.

27. Kate Millett, *Sexual Politics* (New York, 1970), especially pp. 26, 62; and Pat Mainardi, "The Politics of Housework," in *Notes from the Second Year* (New York, 1970).

28. Quoted in Eleanor Flexner, *Century of Struggle* (Cambridge, Mass., 1959), pp. 47, 67.

29. *New York Times*, March 9, 1971; June 2, 1971; April 11, 1971; *Gallup Opinion Index, op. cit.*


## CONCLUSION

1. Gordon Allport, *The Nature of Prejudice* (New York, 1958), pp. 438, 140-41, 259-63. For a particularly illuminating discussion of the relation between social values and social change, see William J. Goode, *World Revolution and Family Patterns* (Glencoe, 1960), especially pp. 54-70.

2. *New York Times*, April 11, 1971, May 16, 1971.

3. Joreen, "The 51 Per Cent Minority Group: A Statistical Essay," in Robin Morgan, ed. *Sisterhood Is Powerful* (New York, 1970), p. 40.

4. For a survey of anthropological and sociological findings, see Norman W. Bell and Ezra F. Vogel, eds., *A Modern Introduction to the Family* (Glencoe, 1960), especially pp. 1-100. Bruno Bettelheim's *Children of the Dream* (New York, 1970) is a revealing and provocative study of the Israeli kibbutz and the psychological effects on children of increasing the number of "significant others" in their lives.

5. For a discussion of these and other surveys, see Jo Freeman, "Growing Up Girlish," *Trans-action*, VIII (November-December 1970), pp. 36-43.

6. The conceptual framework for the above paragraphs is based on the

insights contained in William J. Goode, "A Theory of Role Strain," *American Sociological Review*, XXV (August 1960). For an excellent sociological analysis of the problems confronting modern career women, see Cynthia Fuch Epstein, *Women's Place* (Berkeley, 1970).

7. Robert O. Blood, Jr., "Employment of Married Women," *Journal of Marriage and the Family*, XXVIII (February 1965), p. 46; Washington *Post*, September 16, 1971.

# Selective Bibliography

Since historians have written relatively little about the experience of women in modern America, the scholar interested in the period must break new ground and utilize a wide variety of disparate sources. The research for this book consists of manuscript collections, government archives, official publications, popular books and articles, public opinion surveys, and scholarly monographs. Although some sources are used more than others, each presents a different perspective on a complex subject. The primary problem facing the historian is to establish a proper balance among the sources and to ensure that the evidence from one is consistent with the evidence from others.

Although what follows is not meant to be a bibliographical essay, it is perhaps appropriate to single out some of the research material which was most helpful to me. The Mary Anderson Papers at Radcliffe offer an ideal starting place for anyone interested in the broad field of women's economic status and the activities of female reformers toward achieving equality. In the field of politics the Mary Dewson Papers at Hyde Park are equally indispensable, providing rich insights into the character of an outstanding woman and the politics of female participation in the Democratic party. The Jane Norman Smith Papers and the Alma Lutz Collection at Radcliffe present a good introduction into the ideas and politics of the National Women's Party, while the League of Women Voters Papers at the Library of Congress summarize the point of view of female reform groups. The Women's Bureau Archives at the Federal Record Center in Suitland, Maryland, constitute the richest source on female involvement in the labor force. Virtually unused by scholars, the archives contain the raw data on which Women's Bureau publications were based, as well as a myriad of additional studies which bear directly on the experience and attitudes of women who worked. The archives of the Federal Works Administration and the Office of Community Welfare Services provide an inside view of the value conflict within the government over the issues of child care centers and family maintenance during the 1940's.

The material contained in mass-circulation magazines requires that the researcher take a somewhat more skeptical approach. Frequently, popular journals get caught up in a fad and publish a series of self-reinforcing articles which give the impression of widespread social change, but without any hard evidence. Thus while the popular press is very important as an index of what the public is reading, it should be used carefully, with emphasis on the distinction between what is true and what is said to be true. Finally, scholars interested in the study of women in society will find the literature of the social sciences a fertile source of ideas and information. Especially valuable are such journals as the *American Sociological Review, Social Forces,* the *American Journal of Sociology,* the *Journal of Marriage and the Family, Psychology Today,* and the *Journal of Social Psychology.*

For the reader interested in a full bibliography and more extensive footnotes, the dissertation on which the book is based, "From Suffrage to Liberation: The Changing Roles of American Women, 1920 to 1970" (Columbia University, 1971), is available through University Microfilms of Ann Arbor, Michigan. What follows is an abbreviated version of that bibliography, emphasizing those materials which I used the most.

## MANUSCRIPT COLLECTIONS

American Association of University Women Papers, Arthur and Elizabeth Schlesinger Library on the History of Women in America, Radcliffe College, Cambridge, Mass.

Grace and Edith Abbott Papers, University of Chicago Library, Chicago

Mary Anderson Papers, Schlesinger Library, Radcliffe College

Caroline Babcock-Olive Hurlburt Papers, Schlesinger Library, Radcliffe College

Mary Beard Papers, Sophia Smith Collection, Smith College Library, Northampton, Massachusetts

Dorothy Kirchwey Brown Papers, Schlesinger Library, Radcliffe College

Sophonisba P. Breckinridge Papers, Library of Congress, Washington, D.C.

Carrie Chapman Catt Papers, Sophia Smith Collection, Smith College Library

Child Care Parents Association Papers, Schlesinger Library, Radcliffe College

Democratic National Committee, Women's Division Papers, Franklin D. Roosevelt Library, Hyde Park, New York

Mary Dewson Papers, Franklin D. Roosevelt Library

Mary Dewson Papers, Schlesinger Library, Radcliffe College

Ethel Dreier Papers, Sophia Smith Collection, Smith College Library

Federal Works Administration Archives, National Archives, Washington, D.C.

Edna Gellhorn Papers, Schlesinger Library, Radcliffe College

Virginia Gildersleeve Papers, Special Collections, Columbia University Library

Alice Hamilton Papers, Schlesinger Library, Radcliffe College

Elinore Herrick Papers, Schlesinger Library, Radcliffe College

Institute of Women's Professional Relations Papers, Schlesinger Library, Radcliffe College

International Federation of Working Women Papers, Schlesinger Library, Radcliffe College

Florence Kitchelt Papers, Schlesinger Library, Radcliffe College

Alma Lutz Papers, Schlesinger Library, Radcliffe College

Lucy Randolph Mason Papers, William Perkins Library, Duke University, Durham, North Carolina

Mary McDowell Papers, Chicago Historical Society, Chicago, Illinois

Emma Guffey Miller Papers, Schlesinger Library, Radcliffe College

Morgan-Howe Family Papers, Schlesinger Library, Radcliffe College

National League of Women Voters Papers, Library of Congress

National Women's Party Papers, Wisconsin Historical Society

National Women's Trade Union League Papers, Library of Congress

Agnes Nestor Papers, Chicago Historical Society

Katherine Norris Papers, Schlesinger Library, Radcliffe College

Mary T. Norton Papers, Rutgers University Library, New Brunswick, New Jersey

Office of Community Welfare Services Archives, National Archives

Leonora O'Reilly Papers, Schlesinger Library, Radcliffe College

Frances Perkins Papers, Franklin D. Roosevelt Library

Frances Perkins Papers, Schlesinger Library, Radcliffe College

Mabel Reif Putman Papers, Schlesinger Library, Radcliffe College

Raymond Robins Papers, Wisconsin Historical Society

Edith Rockwood Papers, Schlesinger Library, Radcliffe College

Franklin Delano Roosevelt Papers, Franklin D. Roosevelt Library

Josephine Schain Papers, Sophia Smith Collection, Smith College Library

Belle Sherwin Papers, Schlesinger Library, Radcliffe College

Hattie Smith Papers, Schlesinger Library, Radcliffe College

Hilda Smith Papers, Schlesinger Library, Radcliffe College

Hilda Smith Papers, Franklin D. Roosevelt Library

Jane Norman Smith Papers, Schlesinger Library, Radcliffe College

Southern School for Workers Papers, William Perkins Library, Duke University

Doris Stevens Papers, Schlesinger Library, Radcliffe College

Marion Talbot Papers, University of Chicago Library

Elizabeth Hewes Tilton Papers, Schlesinger Library, Radcliffe College

United Auto Workers Papers, Local 95, Wisconsin Historical Society

United Auto Workers Papers, Local 121, Wisconsin Historical Society

Marguerite Wells Papers, Schlesinger Library, Radcliffe College

Mary Winslow Papers, Schlesinger Library, Radcliffe College

Mary Winsor Papers, Schlesinger Library, Radcliffe College

Selective Bibliography

Women's Advisory Committee Archives, National Archives
Women's Bureau Archives, Federal Record Center, Suitland, Maryland
Women's Joint Congressional Committee Papers, Library of Congress
James Madison Wood Papers, Oral History Collection, Columbia University
Ellen Woodward Papers, Schlesinger Library, Radcliffe College
Works Progress Administration Archives, National Archives

## BOOKS

Adams, Mildred. *The Right To Be People*, New York: W. W. Norton, 1967.

Anderson, Mary. *Women at Work*, Minneapolis: University of Minnesota Press, 1951.

Baker, Elizabeth. *Technology and Women's Work*, New York: Columbia University Press, 1964.

Beard, Mary. *Women as a Force in History*, New York: The Macmillan Company, 1946.

Bell, Norman W., and Ezra F. Vogel, eds. *A Modern Introduction to the Family*, Glencoe: The Free Press, 1960.

Bernard, Jessie. *Academic Women*, University Park: University of Pennsylvania Press, 1964.

———. *Marriage and Family Among Negroes*, Englewood Cliffs: Prentice-Hall, 1966.

Bird, Caroline. *Born Female*, New York: David McKay Company, 1968.

Blood, Robert, and Donald Wolfe. *Husbands and Wives: The Dynamic of Married Lives*, Glencoe: The Free Press, 1960.

Bragdon, Elizabeth. *Women Today: Their Conflicts, Frustrations and Fulfillments*, Indianapolis: Bobbs-Merrill Company, 1953.

Breckinridge, Sophonisba. *Marriage and the Civic Rights of Women*, Chicago: University of Chicago Press, 1931.

———. *Women in the Twentieth Century*, New York: McGraw-Hill, 1933.

Buck, Pearl. *Of Men and Women*, New York: John Day Company, 1941.

Campbell, Angus, Philip Converse, and Donald Stokes. *The American Voter*, New York: John Wiley and Sons, 1964.

Cantril, Hadley. *Public Opinion, 1935–1946,* Princeton: Princeton University Press, 1951.

Cassara, Beverly, ed. *American Women: The Changing Image,* Boston: Beacon Press, 1962.

Detzer, Dorothy. *Appointment on the Hill,* New York: H. Holt, 1948.

Deutsch, Helene. *Psychology of Women,* New York: Grune and Stratton, 1944.

Dreier, Mary. *Marguerite Dreier Robins,* New York: Island Press Cooperative, 1950.

Flexner, Eleanor. *Century of Struggle,* Cambridge, Mass.: Harvard University Press, 1959.

Friedan, Betty. *The Feminine Mystique,* New York: W. W. Norton Company, 1963.

George, W. L. *The Intelligence of Women,* Boston: Little, Brown, 1916.

Gilman, Charlotte Perkins. *His Religion and Hers,* New York: Century and Company, 1923.

———. *The Home, Its Work and Influence,* New York: Charlton, 1910.

———. *Women and Economics,* Carl Degler, ed. New York: Harper and Row, 1966.

Goldmark, Josephine. *Impatient Crusader,* Urbana: University of Illinois Press, 1953.

Goode, William J. *The Family,* Englewood Cliffs: Prentice-Hall, 1963.

Green, Constance. *The Role of Women as Production Workers in War Plants in the Connecticut Valley,* Northampton, Mass.: Smith College, 1946.

Groves, Ernest R. *The American Woman,* New York: Emerson Press, 1944.

Hewes, Amy. *Women as Munition Makers in Bridgeport, Connecticut,* New York: Russell Sage Foundation, 1917.

International Labor Office, *The War and Women's Employment,* Montreal: International Labor Office, 1946.

Kennedy, David. *Birth Control in America: The Career of Margaret Sanger,* New Haven: Yale University Press, 1970.

Kinsey, Alfred. *Sexual Behavior in American Females,* Philadelphia: Saunders Press, 1953.

Klein, Viola. *The Feminine Character,* London: Paul, Trench, Trubner and Company, 1946.

Komarovsky, Mirra. *Blue-Collar Marriage*, New York: Random House, 1962.

———. *The Unemployed Man and His Family*, New York: Dryden Press, 1940.

———. *Women in the Modern World*, Boston: Little, Brown, 1953.

Kraditor, Aileen. *The Ideas of the Woman Suffrage Movement, 1890–1920*, New York: Columbia University Press, 1965.

———. *Up from the Pedestal*, Chicago: Quadrangle Press, 1968.

LaFollette, Suzanne. *Concerning Women*, New York: A. and C. Boni, 1926.

Lifton, Robert, ed. *The Woman in America*, Boston: Houghton Mifflin, 1967.

Lundberg, Ferdinand and Farnham, Marynia. *Modern Woman: The Lost Sex*, New York: Harper and Brothers, 1947.

Lynd, Robert and Helen. *Middletown*, New York: Harcourt, Brace, 1929.

———. *Middletown in Transition*, New York: Harcourt, Brace, 1937.

McCall's. *Mother Steps Out*, New York: McCall's, 1927.

Mead, Margaret. *Sex and Temperament in Three Societies*, New York: Morrow, 1935.

———. *Male and Female*, New York: Morrow, 1947.

Mencken, Henry L. *In Defense of Women*, New York: Alfred Knopf, 1926.

Merriam, Charles, and Herbert Gosnell. *Non-Voting*, Chicago: University of Chicago Press, 1924.

Millett, Kate. *Sexual Politics*, New York: Doubleday, 1970.

Myrdal, Alva, and Viola Klen. *Women's Two Roles*, New York: Humanities Press, 1968.

National Manpower Council, *Womanpower*, New York: Columbia University Press, 1957.

———. *Work in the Lives of Married Women*, New York: Columbia University Press, 1958.

Newcomer, Mabel. *A Century of Higher Education*, New York: Harper and Brothers, 1959.

Nye, F. Ivan, and Lois W. Hoffman. *The Employed Mother in America*, Chicago: Rand McNally, 1963.

O'Neill, William L. *Divorce in the Progressive Era*, New Haven: Yale University Press, 1967.

———. *Everyone Was Brave*, Chicago: Quadrangle Press, 1969.

Park, Maud Wood. *Front Door Lobby*, Boston: Beacon Press, 1960.

Pesotta, Rose. *Bread upon the Waters*, New York: Dodd, Mead, 1944.

Rainwater, Lee, and William Yancey. *The Moynihan Report and the Politics of Controversy*, Cambridge, Mass.: MIT Press, 1967.

Rainwater, Lee, Richard Coleman, and Gerald Handel. *Workingman's Wife*, New York: Oceana Publications, 1962.

Roosevelt, Eleanor. *Autobiography*, New York: Harper and Brothers, 1958.

Seidman, Joel. *The Needle Trades*, New York: Farrar and Rinehart, 1942.

Sheean, Vincent. *Dorothy and Red*, Boston: Houghton Mifflin, 1963.

Smuts, Robert. *Women and Work in America*, New York: Columbia University Press, 1959.

Stolberg, Benjamin. *Tailor's Progress,* New York: Doubleday, 1944.

Terman, Lewis. *Psychological Factors in Marital Happiness*, New York: McGraw-Hill, 1938.

White, Lynn. *Educating Our Daughters*, New York: Harper and Brothers, 1950.

Wylie, Philip. *Generation of Vipers*, New York: Farrar and Rinehart, 1942.


## ARTICLES

Adams, Mildred. "Did They Know What They Wanted?" *Outlook*, CXLVII (December 28, 1927).

Anderson, George E. "Women in Congress," *Commonweal*, IX (March 13, 1929).

Anderson, Mary. "Sixteen Million Women at Work: What Will Happen After the War?" *New York Times Magazine*, July 18, 1943.

———. "Should There Be Labor Laws for Women?" *Good Housekeeping*, LXXXI (September 1925).

Anthony, Susan B., IV. "Why We Throw Our Votes Away," *Saturday Evening Post*, July 17, 1948.

Austin, Mary. "Woman and Her War Loot," *Sunset*, XLII (February 1919).

Babson, Roger. "Why Women Are Underpaid," *Independent Woman*, XI (December 1927).

Barclay, Dorothy. "After the Children Leave Home," *New York Times Magazine*, September 19, 1951.

————. "Creative Work Can Unite the Family," *New York Times Magazine*, April 4, 1954.

————. "The Family's Idea of the Ideal Family," *New York Times Magazine*, April 11, 1954.

————. "What's Wrong with the Family?" *New York Times Magazine*, September 16, 1951.

Barnett, James H., and Rhoda Gruen. "Recent American Divorce Novels, 1938–45," *Social Forces*, XXVI (March 1948).

Bennett, Helen M. "Girl Executive," *Woman's Home Companion*, XLIX (July 1922).

Bettelheim, Bruno. "Growing Up Female," *Harper's*, CCXXV (October 1962).

Blair, Emily Newell. "Are Women Failures in Politics?" *Harper's*, CLI (October 1925).

————. "Are Women Really in Politics?" *Independent*, CXIX (December 3, 1927).

————. "Discouraged Feminists," *Outlook*, CLVIII (July 8, 1931).

Bond, Elsie M. "Day Care of Children of Working Mothers in New York State During the War Emergency," *New York History*, XXVI (January 1945).

Bowman, Claude C. "Social Changes as Reflected in the Kinsey Studies," *Social Problems*, II (July 1954).

Bromley, Dorothy. "Are Women a Success in Business?" *Harper's*, CLVI (August 1928).

————. "Feminist—New Style," *Harper's*, CLV (October 1927).

Brossard, James H. S. "War and the Family," *American Sociological Review*, VI (June 1941).

Brownmiller, Susan. "Sisterhood Is Powerful," *New York Times Magazine,* March 15, 1970.

Burgess, Ernest W. "The Effect of War on the American Family," *American Journal of Sociology*, XLVIII (November 1942).

Butler, Sara Schuler. "Women as Citizens," *Review of Reviews*, LXIX (June 1924).

Cadman, Florence. "Woman Power, 4-F," *Independent Woman*, XXII (September 1943).

Calverton, Victor F. "Careers for Women: A Survey of Results," *Current History Magazine*, XXIX (January 1929).

Cannon, Poppy. "Pin-Money Slaves," *Forum*, LXXXIV (April 1930).

Capper, A. "What Will She Do with the Vote?" *Independent*, CI (January 3, 1920).

Catt, Carrie Chapman. "Cave Man Complex vs. Women's Suffrage," *Woman Citizen*, VIII (April 5, 1924).

Cochrane, Doris. "Equal Pay for Comparable Work," *Independent Woman*, XXII (July 1943).

Cyrus, Della. "Why Mothers Fail," *Atlantic*, LXXIX (March 1947).

Davis, Allen F. "The WTUL, Origins and Organization," *Labor History*, V (winter 1964).

Davis, Kingsley. "The American Family," *New York Times Magazine*, September 30, 1951.

Dobyns, Winfred S. "Lady and the Tiger," *Woman Citizen*, XI (January 1927).

Dornbusch, Sanford M., and David Heer. "The Evaluation of Work by Females," *American Journal of Sociology*, LXIII (July 1957).

Dozier, Howard, "Women and Unemployment," *Review of Reviews*, LXXXV (March 1932).

Efron, Edith. "Woman Worker Defends Her Kind," *New York Times Magazine*, March 31, 1946.

Ellis, Evelyn. "Social Psychological Correlates of Upward Social Mobility Among Unmarried Career Women," *American Sociological Review*, XVII (October 1952).

England, R. W., Jr. "Images of Love and Courtship in Family Magazine Fiction," *Journal of Marriage and Family Living*, XXII (November 1957).

Fechter, Joseph. "Decline of Femininity," *Catholic World*, CLXI (April 1945).

Fisher, Katherine. "Women Workers and the AF of L," *New Republic*, August 3, 1921.

Flechter, Grace. "He Wants My Job," *Independent Woman*, XIV (May 1935).

Frazier, Elizabeth. "Adventure in Politics," *Saturday Evening Post*, December 22, 1923.

———. "Woman Graduate Hunts a Job," *Saturday Evening Post*, October 19, 1929.

———. "Mrs. Delegate," *Saturday Evening Post*, August 16, 1924.

Freeman, Jo. "The New Feminists," *Nation*, CCVIII (February 24, 1969).

————. "Growing Up Girlish," *Trans-action*, VIII (November-December 1970).

Frey, Jean. "Woman and Her Wages," *Independent Woman*, I (March 1920).

Gabower, Genevieve. "Look at Ten Communities: Effect of War on Youthful Behavior," *Survey*, LXXX (March 1944).

Gale, Zona. "What Women Won in Wisconsin," *Nation*, CXV (August 23, 1922).

Gallup, George, and Evan Hill. "The American Woman," *Saturday Evening Post*, December 22, 1962.

Gianopulos, Artie, and Howard Mitchell. "Marital Disagreement in Working Wife Marriages as a Function of Husband's Attitude Toward Wife's Employment," *Journal of Marriage and Family Living*, XIX (November 1957).

Giles, Nell. "Do the Women Want To Keep Their Factory Jobs When the War Is Over?" *Ladies Home Journal*, LXI (July 1944).

Gilman, Charlotte Perkins. "The New Generation of Women," *Current History*, XVIII (August 1923).

Goldwater, Ethel. "Women's Place," *Commentary*, IV (December 1947).

Hall, Florence. "They're Getting in the Crops," *Independent Woman*, XXII (July 1943).

Hall, G. Stanley. "Flapper Americana Novissima," *Atlantic*, CCXIX (June 1922).

Halle, Rita. "Do You Need Your Job?" *Good Housekeeping*, LXXXV (September 1932).

Hamilton, Alice. "Protection for Women Workers," *Forum*, LXXII (April 1924).

————. "Why I Am Against the Equal Rights Amendment," *Ladies Home Journal*, LXII (July 1945).

Hansl, Eva Von B. "What About the Children?" *Harper's*, CLIV (January 1927).

Hard, Anthony. "Are Women Making Good in Politics?" *Pictorial Review*, XXIX (July 1928).

Harper, Ida. "The American Woman Gets the Vote," *Review of Reviews*, LXII (October 1920).

Hartley, Ruth. "Children's Concepts of Male and Female Roles," *Merrill-Palmer Quarterly*, V (January 1960).

Hawes, Elizabeth. "Woman War Worker, a Case History," *New York Times Magazine*, May 15, 1944.

Heer, David M. "Dominance and the Working Wife," *Social Forces*, XXXVI (May 1958).

———. "The Measurement and Basis of Family Power: An Overview," *Journal of Marriage and Family Living*, XXV (May 1963).

Herrick, Elinore M. "What About Women After the War?" *New York Times Magazine*, September 5, 1943.

Hill, E., and Florence Kelley. "Shall Women Be Equal Before the Law?" *Nation*, CXIV (April 21, 1922).

Hoffman, Lois W. "Effects of the Employment of Mothers on Parental Power Relations and the Division of Household Tasks," *Journal of Marriage and Family Living*, XXII (March 1960).

Hohman, Leslie B. "Can Women in War Industries Be Good Mothers?" *Ladies Home Journal*, LIX (October 1942).

Hughes, Everett C. "Dilemmas and Contradictions of Status," *American Journal of Sociology*, L (March 1945).

Inglis, Ruth. "An Objective Approach to the Relation Between Fiction and Society," *American Sociological Review*, III (August 1938).

Johnston, Agnes. "What Family Teamwork Did for Us," *Parents*, XXIX (November 1954).

Kelley, Florence. "The New Women's Party," *Survey*, LVII (March 5, 1921).

Keniston, Ellen and Kenneth. "An American Anachronism: The Image of Women and Work," *American Scholar*, XXXIII (summer 1964).

Kenton, Edna. "Four Years of Equal Suffrage," *Forum*, LXXII (July 1924).

———. "The Ladies Next Step, the Case for the Equal Rights Amendment," *Harper's*, CLII (February 1926).

Kirchwey, Freda. "Alice Paul Pulls the Strings," *Nation*, CXII (March 2, 1921).

Kirkpatrick, Clifford. "A Methodological Analysis of Feminism in Relation to Marital Adjustment," *American Sociological Review*, IV (May 1929).

Kleeman, Rita H. "The College Girl Goes to War," *Independent Woman*, XXII (January 1943).

Kluckhohn, Florence. "Cultural Factors in Social Work Practice and Education," *Social Service Review*, XXV (March 1951).

Komarovsky, Mirra. "Cultural Contradictions and Sex Roles," *American Journal of Sociology*, LII (November 1946).

————. "Functional Analysis of Sex Roles," *American Sociological Review*, XV (June 1950).

Lape, E. E. "What Do Women Want with the Vote?" *Ladies Home Journal*, XXXVII (March 1920).

Leach, Ruth M. "Where Women Get a Chance: IBM," *Independent Woman*, XXIII (February 1944).

Lee, Mabel. "Dilemma of the Educated Woman," *Atlantic*, CXLVI (November 1930).

Lester, Israel. "Child Care in Wartime," *American City*, LIX (March 1944).

Levison, Frances. "What the Experts Say," *Life*, XXII (June 16, 1947).

Lewis, Sinclair, and Dorothy Thompson. "Is America a Paradise for Women?" *Pictorial Review*, XXX (June 1929).

Lutz, Alma. "Women and Wages," *Nation*, CXXXIX (October 17, 1934).

McIntosh, Millicent. "New Horizons for Women," *Vital Speeches*, XIX (March 1, 1953).

McLemore, Ethel Ward. "Manifesto from a Corporation Wife," *Fortune*, XLV (March 1952).

Maffett, Minnie L. "Underuse of Women Power Slows War Effort," *Independent Woman*, XXII (April 1943).

Martin, Anne H. "What Women Should Vote For," *Good Housekeeping*, LXIX (November 1919).

Martin, George Madden. "American Women and Paternalism," *Atlantic*, CXXXIII (June 1924).

Maslow, Abraham H. "Dominance, Personality and Social Behavior," *Journal of Social Psychology*, X (1939).

————. "Self-Esteem and Sexuality in Women," *Journal of Social Psychology*, XVI (1942).

Matthews, Selma. "The Effect of Mothers' Out of Home Employment upon Childrens' Ideas and Attitudes," *Journal of Applied Psychology*, XVIII (February 1964).

May, Elizabeth P. "The Occupations of Wellesley Graduates," *School and Society*, XXIX (February 2, 1929).

Mead, Margaret. "Modern Marriage: The Danger Point," *Nation*, CLXXVII (October 31, 1953).

————. "Sex and Achievement," *Forum*, XCIV (November 1935).

————. "What's the Matter with the Family?" *Harper's*, CXC (April 1945).

————. "What Women Want," *Fortune*, XXXIV (December 1946).

Miller, Frieda. "What's Become of Rosie the Riveter?" *New York Times Magazine*, May 5, 1946.

Montagu, Ashley. "The Triumph and Tragedy of the American Woman," *Saturday Review*, XLI (September 27, 1958).

Moore, John W. "Patterns of Women's Participation in Voluntary Associations," *American Journal of Sociology*, LXVI (May 1961).

Nottingham, Elizabeth. "Toward an Analysis of the Effects of Two World Wars on the Role and Status of Middle Class Women in the English Speaking World," *American Sociological Review*, XII (December 1947).

Ogburn, William F. "How Women Vote: A Study of Portland, Oregon," *Political Science Quarterly*, XXXIV (September 1919).

Oppenheim, Beatrice. "Anchors Aweigh: 23,000 Women Work in Shipyards," *Independent Woman*, XXII (May 1943).

Parnell, Anne G. "A Nation's Strength Begins in the Home," *Vital Speeches*, XVIII (December 15, 1951).

Parsons, Talcott. "Age and Sex in the United States Social Structure," *American Sociological Review*, VII (October 1942).

Patrick, Catherine. "Attitudes About Women Executives in Government Positions," *Journal of Social Psychology*, XIX (February 1944).

Patterson, James T. "Mary Dewson and the American Minimum Wage Movement," *Labor History*, V (spring 1964).

Peterson, John M. "Employment Effects of State Minimum Wages for Women," *Industrial and Labor Relations Review*, XII (April 1958).

Peterson, William. "New American Family," *Commentary*, XXI (January 1956).

Potter, David. "American Women and the American Character," in John A. Hague, ed. *American Character and Culture* (Deland, Fla., 1964).

Pruitte, Louise. "Why Women Fail," *Outlook*, CLVIII (August 12, 1931).

Rice, Stuart, and Malcolm Willey. "American Women's Ineffective Use of the Vote," *Current History*, XX (July 1924).

Roche, Mary. "The New Servants: Machines and Husbands," *New York Times Magazine*," June 5, 1955.

Romeo, Margaret. "Shipyards and Playgrounds," *Recreation*, XXXVIII (January 1945).

Ross, John Gordon. "Ladies in Politics," *Forum*, XCV (November 1936).

Russell, Charles E. "Is Woman's Suffrage a Failure?" *Century*, CVII (March 1924).

Samuels, Gertrude. "Why Do 20 Million Women Work?" *New York Times Magazine*, September 9, 1951.

Sands, Florence. "Why Many Women Do Not Succeed in Business," *Independent Woman*, IX (October 1925).

Schlesinger, Elizabeth. "They Say Women Are Emancipated," *New Republic*, December 13, 1933.

Scott, Anne F. "After Suffrage: Southern Women in the Twenties," *Journal of Southern History*, XXX (August 1964).

Selden, Charles A. "Most Powerful Lobby in Washington," *Ladies Home Journal*, XXIX (April 1922).

Sharp, Lawrence J. "Employment Status of Mothers and Some Aspects of Mental Illness," *American Sociological Review*, XXV (October 1960).

Shyrock, Henry and Eldridge, Hope. "Internal Migration in Peace and War," *American Sociological Review*, XII (January 1947).

Smith, Ethel. "What Is Sex Equality?" *Century*, CXVIII (May 1929).

Snedden, David. "Probable Economic Future of the American Woman," *American Journal of Sociology*, XXIV (March 1919).

Solomon, Barbara. "The Most Indifferent Disadvantaged," *Saturday Review*, LI (December 2, 1968).

Stanton, Theodora. "Seneca Falls and Women's Rights," *Independent*, CXI (April 4, 1923).

Toombs, Alfred. "War Babies," *Woman's Home Companion*, LXXI (April 1944).

Toombs, E. O. "Politicians Take Notice! Columbus, Ohio Women Elected a Mayor," *Good Housekeeping*, LXX (March 1920).

Tucker, Kate M. "Are Women Too Aggressive in Business?" *Independent Woman,* VIII (January 1924).

Van Kleeck, Mary. "Women and Machines," *Atlantic,* CXXVII (February 1921).

Von Mering, Faye. "Professional and Non-professional Women as Mothers," *Journal of Social Psychology,* XVII (August 1955).

Vorse, Mary Heaton. "Women Don't Quit, If . . ." *Independent Woman,* XXIII (January 1944).

Wallin, Paul. "Cultural Contradictions and Sex Roles: A Repeat Study," *American Sociological Review,* XV (April 1950).

Weiss, Robert S., and Nancy M. Samuelson. "Social Roles of American Women: Their Contribution to a Sense of Usefulness and Importance," *Journal of Marriage and Family Living,* XX (November 1958).

Wolfe, H. B., and Helen Olson. "Wartime Industrial Employment of Women in the United States," *Journal of Political Economy,* XXVII (October 1919).

Wolfson, Theresa. "Equal Rights in the Union," *Survey,* LVII (February 15, 1927).

Wolman, Leo. "Are Women Hard To Organize?" *Survey,* LIII (March 15, 1925).

Woodhouse, Chase Going. "The Status of Women," *American Journal of Sociology,* XXXV (May 1930).

Younger, Maud. "The NRA and Protective Laws for Women," *Literary Digest,* CXVII (June 2, 1934).


*Annals* of the American Academy of Political and Social Science
    "Women in the Modern World," CXLIII (May 1929).
    "Women's Opportunities and Responsibilities," CCLI (May 1947).
*Architectural Record*
    "Designed for 24 Hour Child Care," XCV (March 1944).
*Business Week*
    "Manless Industry," April 10, 1945.
    "More Older and Married Women Work," March 20, 1948.
    "Why Women Quit," October 16, 1943.
    "Women's Share of Jobs Holds Up," January 3, 1948.
    "Women Drop Out," August 21, 1945.
*Fortune*

"The Fortune Survey: Women in America," XXXIV (August, September 1946).

*Ladies Home Journal*
All issues from 1920-1960.

*Life*
"American Woman's Dilemma," XXII (June 16, 1947).
"Girl Pilots: The Air Force Trains Them," XV (July 19, 1943).
"Women in Steel," XV (August 9, 1943).

*Literary Digest*
"American Women's Vast War Work as Revealed by an Official Report," LXVI (August 21, 1920).
"Awful Danger of Woman's Suffrage," LXVIII (October 23, 1920).
"Can Women Run a Home and a Job Too?" LXXV (November 11, 1922).
"Farewell to the Woman Conductor," LXX (July 2, 1921).
"Limitations of Women Workers," LXII (July 19, 1919).
"Much-Surprised City Officials Ousted by Women," LXVII (October 1920).
"Passing of the Giants in the Woman's Movement," LXXVII (May 5, 1923).
"Shall Women Lose Their Jobs?" LX (January 11, 1919).
"Why More Women Don't Vote," LXXXI (May 24, 1924).
"Women's Suffrage Declared a Failure," LXXXI (April 12, 1924).

*McCall's*
All issues from 1920-1960.

*Monthly Labor Review*
"Commissioned War Jobs for Women Doctors," LVII (July 1943).
"Comparative Stability of Male and Female Wages," XXIV (May 1927).
"Effects of Labor Legislation on Employment Opportunities for Women," XXVII (November 1928).
"Employment in War Work of Women with Young Children," LV (December 1942).
"Equal Pay for Women Workers," LXIII (September 1946).
"Negro Women in Industry," XV (July 1922).

"Position of Women in Government Service," XXIII (October 1926).

"Share of Wage-Earning Women in Family Support," XVII (July 1923).

"Unemployment Among Women in the Early Years of the Depression," XXXVIII (April 1934).

"Wartime Care of Working Mothers' Children in Minneapolis," LVII (July 1943).

"Women in Trade Unions," XIX (April 1924).

*New Republic*

"Breadwinning Women," February 3, 1926.

"Solidarity," June 4, 1919.

"Women's Equality in Industry," November 28, 1928.

"Rosie Is Back: The Riveter," May 10, 1948.

*Newsweek*

"Bringing Up Mother," June 15, 1953.

"Blueprint for a Wife," October 4, 1954.

"Rights for Women," July 29, 1946.

"Women or Doctors," November 12, 1945.

"What Women Want," May 21, 1956.

"Women's Lib and the War on 'Sexism,' " March 23, 1970.

*Senior Scholastic*

"High School Girls Deny That Women's Place Is in the Home," XLVI (March 5, 1945).

*Time*

"Fadeout of the Women," September 4, 1944.

"New Lost Generation?" January 29, 1945.

"New York City Bar Association Decides To Admit Women," May 24, 1937.


## GOVERNMENT PUBLICATIONS

Bureau of Labor Statistics. *Women in Factories, October, 1939-June, 1945* (Washington, 1945).

McMillin, Lucille F. *The First Year: A Study of Women's Participation in Federal Defense Activities* (Washington, D.C., 1941).

————. *The Second Year* (Washington, D.C., 1943).

Office of War Information. *Women and the War* (Washington, D.C., 1942).

————. *War Jobs for Women* (Washington, D.C., 1942).

————. *Women in the War for the Final Push for Victory* (Washington, D.C., 1944).

War Manpower Commission. *America at War Needs Women at Work* (Washington, D.C., 1943).

Women's Bureau. "The New Position of Women in American Industry," *Women's Bureau Bulletin* No. 12 (Washington, D.C., 1920).

————. "Wage Earning Women and the Industrial Conditions of 1930," *Women's Bureau Bulletin* No. 92 (Washington, D.C., 1931).

————. "Women Workers in the Third Year of the Depression," *Women's Bureau Bulletin* No. 103 (Washington, D.C., 1933).

————. "The Occupational Progress of Women, 1910-1930," *Women's Bureau Bulletin* No. 104 (Washington, D.C., 1933).

————. "The Effect of the Depression on Wage-Earners' Families," *Women's Bureau Bulletin* No. 108 (Washington, D.C., 1936).

————. "Women in the Economy of the United States," *Women's Bureau Bulletin* No. 155 (Washington, D.C., 1937).

————. "Trends in the Employment of Women, 1928-1936," *Women's Bureau Bulletin* No. 159 (Washington, D.C., 1937).

————. "Employed Women and Family Support," *Women's Bureau Bulletin* No. 168 (Washington, D.C., 1939).

————. "Economic Status of University Women," *Women's Bureau Bulletin* No. 170 (Washington, D.C., 1939).

————. "The Woman Wage-Earner, Her Situation Today," *Women's Bureau Bulletin* No. 172 (Washington, D.C., 1939).

————. "Women: Work in the War, 1942," *Women's Bureau Bulletin* No. 193 (Washington, D.C., 1943).

————. "Women Workers in Ten War-Production Areas and Their Postwar Employment Plans," *Women's Bureau Bulletin* No. 209 (Washington, D.C., 1946).

————. "Employment of Women in the Early Postwar Period," *Women's Bureau Bulletin* No. 211 (Washington, D.C., 1946).

————. "Women Workers After V-J Day in One Community," *Women's Bureau Bulletin* No. 216 (Washington, D.C., 1947).

————. "The American Woman: Her Changing Role," *Women's Bureau Bulletin* No. 224 (Washington, D.C., 1948).

————. "Women in the Federal Service, 1923-1947," *Women's Bureau Bulletin* No. 230 (Washington, D.C., 1949).

————. "Women's Occupations Through Seven Decades," *Women's Bureau Bulletin* No. 232 (Washington, D.C., 1951).

————. "The Status of Women in the United States," *Women's Bureau Bulletin* No. 249 (Washington, D.C., 1953).

————. "Changes in Women's Occupations, 1940-1950," *Women's Bureau Bulletin* No. 253 (Washington, D.C., 1954).

————. "Community Services for Women War Workers," *Women's Bureau Special Bulletin* No. 15 (Washington, D.C., 1944).

————. "A Preview as to Women Workers in Transition from War to Peace," *Women's Bureau Special Bulletin* No. 18 (Washington, D.C., 1944).

————. "Changes in Women's Employment During the War," *Women's Bureau Special Bulletin* No. 20 (Washington, D.C., 1944).

————. "Women Workers Today and Tomorrow, a Balance Sheet," Miscellaneous Release, October 9, 1944.


## UNPUBLISHED MATERIAL

Doyle, William T. "Charlotte Perkins Gilman and the Cycle of Feminist Reform," unpublished doctoral dissertation, University of California, 1960.

Fletty, Valborg Esther. "Public Services of Women's Organizations," unpublished doctoral dissertation, Syracuse University, 1952.

Guest, Boyd. "The Position of Women as Considered by Representative American Authors Since 1800," unpublished doctoral dissertation, University of Wisconsin, 1943.

Johnson, Dorothy. "Organized Women and National Legislation, 1920-1941," unpublished doctoral dissertation, Western Reserve University, 1960.

Lemons, James Stanley. "The New Woman from the Great War to the Great Depression," unpublished doctoral dissertation, University of Missouri, 1967.

McCarthy, Amy. "The Women's Trade Union League, 1909-13," unpublished thesis, Vassar College, 1971.

Makosky, Donald R. "The Portrayal of Women in Wide-Circulation Magazine Short Stories, 1905-55," unpublished doctoral dissertation, University of Pennsylvania, 1966.

Sharpley, Lillian. "Married Women at Work," unpublished Master's essay, Columbia University, 1945.

Schrom, Nancy. "The Shirtwaist Makers' Strike and the Women's Trade Union League," unpublished manuscript, University of Wisconsin, 1970.

Wiley, Charles G. "A Study of the American Women as Presented in the American Drama of the Nineteen-Twenties," unpublished doctoral dissertation, University of New Mexico, 1957.

# Index